ArtScroll® Series

Rabbi Nosson Scherman / Rabbi Meir Zlotowitz
General Editors

what

MORE fascinating halachic discussions
for the Shabbos table,
arranged according to the weekly
Torah reading

Published by

ArtScroll
Mesorah Publications, ltd

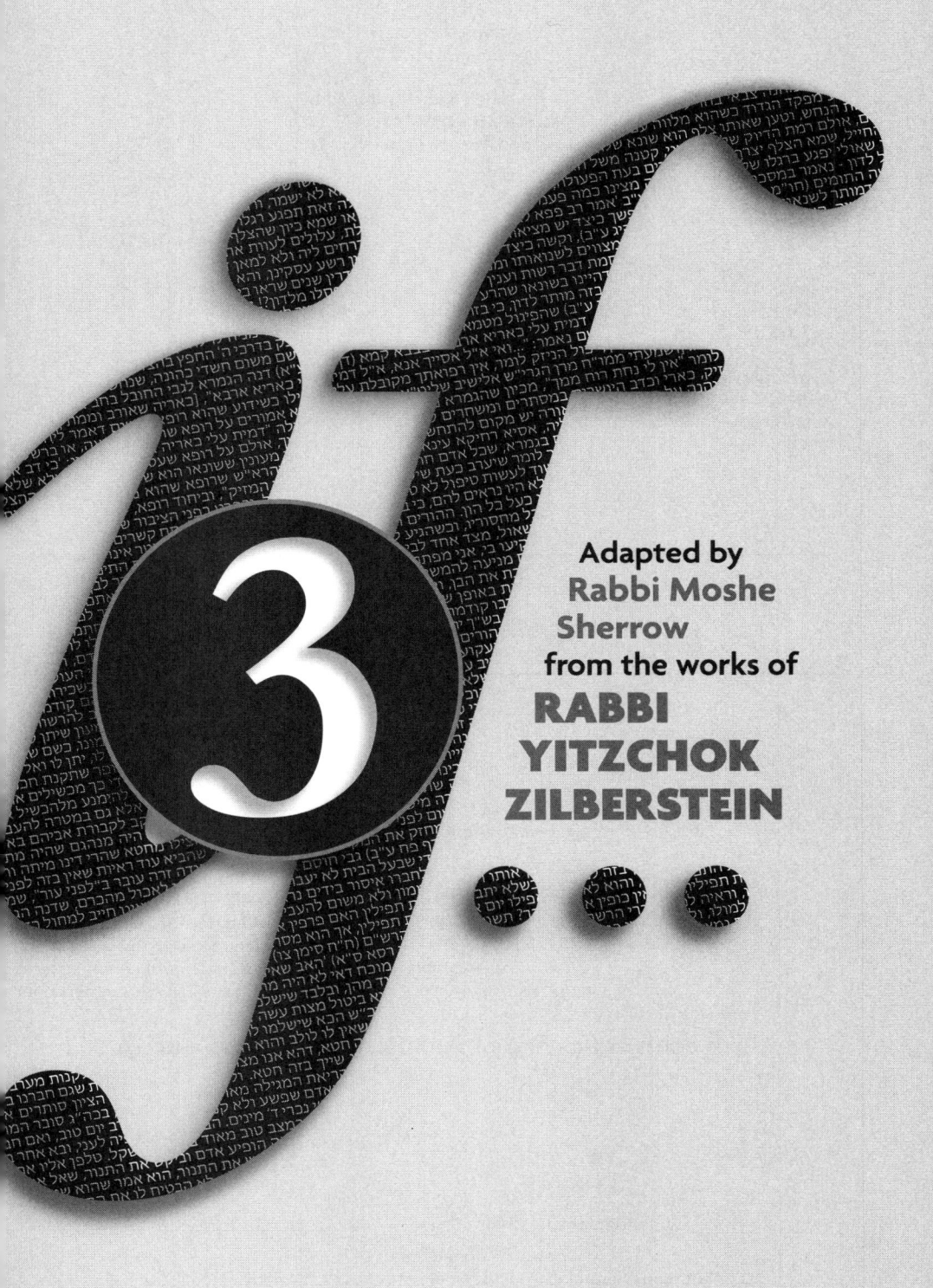

FIRST EDITION
First Impression … June 2016

Published and Distributed by
MESORAH PUBLICATIONS, LTD.
4401 Second Avenue / Brooklyn, N.Y 11232

Distributed in Europe by
LEHMANNS
Unit E, Viking Business Park
Rolling Mill Road
Jarow, Tyne & Wear, NE32 3DP
England

Distributed in Australia and New Zealand
by **GOLDS WORLDS OF JUDAICA**
3-13 William Street
Balaclava, Melbourne 3183
Victoria, Australia

Distributed in Israel by
SIFRIATI / A. GITLER — BOOKS
Moshav Magshimim
Israel

Distributed in South Africa by
KOLLEL BOOKSHOP
Northfield Centre, 17 Northfield Avenue
Glenhazel 2192, Johannesburg, South Africa

ARTSCROLL® SERIES
WHAT IF 3
© Copyright 2016, by MESORAH PUBLICATIONS, Ltd.
4401 Second Avenue / Brooklyn, N.Y. 11232 / (718) 921-9000 / www.artscroll.com

---

ALL RIGHTS RESERVED
The text, prefatory and associated textual contents and introductions
— including the typographic layout, cover artwork and ornamental graphics —
have been designed, edited and revised as to content, form and style.

No part of this book may be reproduced
IN ANY FORM, PHOTOCOPYING, OR COMPUTER RETRIEVAL SYSTEMS
— even for personal use without written permission from
the copyright holder, Mesorah Publications Ltd.
except by a reviewer who wishes to quote brief passages
in connection with a review written for inclusion in magazines or newspapers.

THE RIGHTS OF THE COPYRIGHT HOLDER WILL BE STRICTLY ENFORCED.

ISBN 10: 1-4226-1753-X / ISBN 13: 978-1-4226-1753-3

Typography by CompuScribe at ArtScroll Studios, Ltd.
Printed in United States of America
Bound by Sefercraft, Quality Bookbinders, Ltd., Brooklyn N.Y. 11232

Yitzhak Zilberstein
Rabbi of 'Ramat-Elhanan'
Bnei-Brak
Rosh Kollel 'Beit-David' Holon

יצחק זילברשטיין
רב שכונת רמת-אלחנן
בני ברק
ראש כולל 'בית-דוד' – חולון

בס"ד ל"ג לעומר תשע"ו

הק' זכה זכינו לפרש את התורה לשבעים לשון
מאיר הי"ו. וכעת באתי לברך ולהודות להרה"ג
רבי משה שרן שליט"א על עמלו לתרגם חלקי
מספרינו חשוקי חמד לאנגלית וב"ה כבר תרגם
חלקים מספרינו What if חלק י' בו כבוד השי"ת
יעזרהו להגדיל תורה ולהאדירה מתוך עושר וכבוד
בתורה להשי"ת

יצחק זילברשטיין

Table of Contents

Introduction   17
Acknowledgments   24

Sefer Bereishis

Parashas Bereishis
Hidden Treasure   31
Sleeping In   33
Just the Fax   34
Life Insurance   36

Parashas Noach
Saving It From Their Hands   39
One Lucky Dog   41
Glass Houses   44

Parashas Lech Lecha
House Arrest   46
Obligations   48
Ma'aser!   51

Parashas Vayeira
Same Place, Same Time	54
Location, Location, Location	56
A Lack of Communication	58

Parashas Chayei Sarah
A Bargain	62
A Domestic Match	64
Putting One and One Together	66

Parashas Toldos
The Best Policy	69
Buyer Beware	71
Dealing With the Sly	73

Parashas Vayeitzei
Where There's a Will…	75
How Much Is It Worth?	77

Parashas Vayishlach
Broken Telephone	81
Time Is of the Essence	83

Parashas Vayeishev
Yagati U'matzasi!	87

Parashas Mikeitz
A Day in the Fruit Store	90
Read the Fine Print	92
Magic	95

Parashas Vayigash
Occupational Hazards	99
Whose Wedding Is This, Anyway?	101
A Likely Story	103

Parashas Vayechi
Looks Can Kill	106
Attendance Mandatory	108
Acidic Speech	111

Sefer Shemos

Parashas Shemos
A Timely Gift	117
The Right Name at the Right Time	120
Lasting Impressions	121

Parashas Va'eira
Keep Your Cool	124
Privileged Animals	126
A Sweet Pitch	128

Parashas Bo
A Potentially Dangerous Snack	131
What Motivated You?	133
The Honor of Performing a Mitzvah	135

Parashas Beshalach
(Not) A Time to Sing	138
All for the Boss	141
Keeping the Peace	144

Parashas Yisro
Out of Order	147
Valuable Wine	149
To Understand a Mitzvah	151

Parashas Mishpatim
Sudden Impact	154
Return Policy	156
Mis(ter) Understanding	160
Kosher Loopholes	163
Hidden Costs	164

Parashas Terumah
Almost the Same	167
Dangerously Armed	169
A Bad Shidduch?	172

Parashas Tetzaveh
Presents of Mind	176
Broken Heart	178
The Flood Is Over	181

Parashas Ki Sisa
Precious Time	183
Kiddush Hashem vs. Tznius	185
Publicizing Those Who Do Mitzvos	188

Parashas Vayakheil
Public Relations	190
From Rags to Riches	192

Parashas Pekudei
Something Went Wrong	196
False Representation	199
The Same Pocket	203

Sefer Vayikra

Parashas Vayikra
Part 1: A Gift in the Mouth	207
Part 2: A Gift in the Mouth	209
How Does This Sound to You?	211
Breaking Even	213

Parashas Tzav
Don't Sell Yourself Short	215
Golden Dust	217
Part 1: A Friend Indeed	220
Part 2: A Friend Indeed	222

Parashas Shemini
Expensive Tastes	224
Half a Hechsher	227
No Good Deed…	228

Parashas Tazria
Part 1: Due Honors	230
Part 2: Due Honors	232

Parashas Metzora
Safekeeping	234
Buried Treasure	236
Cannot Part With Art	239

Parashas Acharei Mos
An Expensive Dip	242
The Winning Ticket	244

Parashas Kedoshim
Older Parents	248

An Irregular Story	250
All That Glitters	253
A Waity Decision	256
Soon There Will Be a Beis HaMikdash	258

Parashas Emor
A(n) (Un)Hairy Situation	261
Part 1: To Fix or Not to Fix	263
Part 2: It Was an Acci-Dent	266

Parashas Behar
| Deafening Silence | 268 |

Parashas Bechukosai
Fare Is Fair	270
Davening With Heart	272
Wholesale or Retail	276

Sefer Bamidbar

Parashas Bamidbar
Name Change	281
The Gift of Pidyon Haben	284
Tzedakah, Tzedakah	286

Parashas Nasso
Shamefully Yours	288
Call for Peace	291
The Zechus to Give	293

Parashas Beha'aloscha
A Really Nice Gift	296
A Recipe for Disaster	299
A Loan on Time	302

Parashas Shelach
- Stretching Time — 305
- Hot Buns — 307
- Knot So Simple — 310

Parashas Korach
- Space Management — 313
- Pick It Up! — 315
- Getting Your Priorities Straight — 317

Parashas Chukas
- Part 1: A Man's Real Station in Life — 320
- Part 2: A Man's Real Station in Life — 323
- L'ilui Nishmas — 323
- Zealousness — 327

Parashas Balak
- To Return or Not to Return — 330
- It's Worth the Pain — 332
- A Good Investment — 333

Parashas Pinchas
- The Gift That Keeps on Giving — 335
- Preserving Special Relationships — 337

Parashas Mattos
- Who Should Pay Whom — 340
- Best-Laid Plans — 342

Parashas Mas'ei
- A Time to Rejoice — 346
- An Eye in the Sky — 348
- A Jewish Auction (Not Made in China) — 351
- Vocational Hazard — 353

Sefer Devarim

Parashas Devarim
What Drives the Driver?	357
Work Site or Vacation Site?	359
Good Things Come in Small Packages	361

Parashas Va'eschanan
The Lesser of Two Evils	365
Coming Home Late	367
Return Policy	368

Parashas Eikev
Getting Involved	372
Bad Answer	374
Is First Come Served First?	378

Parashas Re'ei
Free Rebate	381
A Matter of Heart	382
It's Not an Expense — It's an Investment	384
Multiple Answers	386

Parashas Shoftim
Early Bird?	389
One Fine Day …	391
Coming Late for an Appointment	392

Parashas Ki Seitzei
Really Lost	395
So Close	398
Paying on Time	400
Each Person Is Punished for His Own Sin	403

Parashas Ki Savo
An Accessory to the Crime	405
Loyal Support	408
Miss Judged	411

Parashas Nitzavim
Mighty Fine Wine	415
Who Is Fooling Whom?	418
Teshuvah Pays	420

Parashas Vayeilech
Everyone Makes Mistakes	423
Cover-Judging	425
A Lifesaving Sefer Torah	427

Parashas Ha'azinu
On-the-Job Training — Without Telling the Boss	433
A Mooving Story of Two Cows	435
Fasten Your Seatbelt	437

Parashas V'zos HaBerachah
Be Fair to the Wealthy	439
Public Property	442
Together Is Better	445
Glossary	447
Index of Sources	452

Rabbi Zilberstein writes in each volume of *Chashukei Chemed* that the purpose of the *sefer* is to inspire people to learn Torah. ***It is not to be used to issue halachic rulings.*** Each person should present any inquiries to his own Rav and comply with his decision.

If such a statement is made for the original work, how much more so does it apply to this *sefer*, whose author is so much farther from the original sources. Still, it is our hope that many will be enriched and inspired by this presentation.

Some questions conclude with וצ"ע, which means that more research is required to reach a final conclusion.

Unless otherwise indicated, or in the mention of a *gadol* or *posek*, the names of the protagonists in each question are fictitious.

Please avail yourself of the extensive Glossary at the end of this book.

Introduction

Making the Connection

The mishnah in *Pirkei Avos*[1] teaches, "Rabbi Shimon stated: Three who ate together at the same table and did not speak words of Torah are considered as if they ate from the offerings of a foreign god, whereas three who ate together at the same table and spoke words of Torah are considered as if they ate from Hashem's table." This mishnah emphasizes that speaking words of Torah while eating is so imperative that it determines whether one is eating at Hashem's table, or Heaven forfend, from an offering to an *avodah zarah*.

What is the connection between eating and speaking words of Torah? Although the mitzvah of *talmud Torah* is equivalent to all the other 612 mitzvos combined,[2] why is it necessary that it accompany eating? Would it not be sufficient to set aside time for learning during other parts of the day?

---
1. 3:4.
2. *Pe'ah* 1:1.

The Gemara[3] teaches that when one *bentches* after a meal, he must mention the Torah. Hence, Yehoshua bin Nun inserted the words, וְעַל תּוֹרָתְךָ שֶׁלִּמַּדְתָּנוּ, *for Your Torah which You taught us*, into the second *berachah* of *bentching*.[4] This requirement is so fundamental to *bentching* that *Tosafos*[5] suggests that perhaps women, who are not obligated to learn Torah (other than that which is necessary for them to learn in order to keep their mitzvos), are not obligated to *bentch mi'd'Oraisa*, but rather are required to do so only *mi'd'Rabbanan*. What is the connection between learning Torah and *bentching* that makes Torah learning such a fundamental part of *bentching*?

It is very interesting to note that the Mishnah specifies that **three** people who ate together must speak words of Torah. The number three is significant with regard to eating. It is only three men who eat together who are required to *bentch* with a *zimun*. The Gemara learns this from the *pasuk*, כִּי שֵׁם ה' אֶקְרָא הָבוּ גֹדֶל לֵאלֹקֵינוּ, *When I call out the Name of Hashem, you [plural] ascribe greatness to our God*.[6] This very same *pasuk* is the source for *Birchos HaTorah*, as well. Again, the connection between learning Torah and thanking Hashem for the food that one has eaten is emphasized. How can this be explained?

Parashas Emor details all the Yamim Tovim from Pesach to Shavuos, Rosh Hashanah, Yom Kippur, and Succos. Immediately afterward, Hashem tells Moshe Rabbeinu to command the Jews to take pure olive oil for the *Menorah* in the *Mishkan*. The juxtaposition of this mitzvah with those of the Yamim Tovim seems to be an obvious allusion to the Yom Tov of Chanukah. Then, the mitzvah to bake the twelve loaves of bread for the *Lechem HaPanim* is discussed. This can be understood as alluding to the Yom Tov of Purim.

---

3. *Berachos* 45b.
4. Rashi explains that *Eretz Yisrael*, the subject of the second *berachah*, was given in the merit of Torah study.
5. 20b.
6. *Devarim* 32:3. אֶקְרָא, *I call out*, is singular; he is instructing two others to ascribe greatness to Hashem.

Indeed, the *Rokei'ach* draws this parallel and explains that the mitzvah to bake *Lechem HaPanim* is a hint referring to the mitzvah to feast on Purim. The *Chasam Sofer* adds that the Gemara derives a reference to the *Lechem HaPanim* from the name of Memuchan (one of Achashveirosh's seven advisers, who advised the king to replace Vashti after she refused to honor the king's wishes). The *malachim* pleaded with Hashem when Haman sought to destroy *Klal Yisrael*: "Have the other nations **prepared** (מוּכָן) for you a table with *Lechem HaPanim*?" *Chazal* teach that Memuchan was actually Haman. What is the connection between Haman and the *Lechem HaPanim*?

Parashas Emor continues with the incident of the *mekallel* who blasphemed the Name of Hashem. Rashi cites Rabbi Berachya, who opines that the impetus for this man's blasphemy was his ridicule of the mitzvah of *Lechem HaPanim*. The *Lechem HaPanim* was baked on Erev Shabbos and placed on the *Shulchan* in the *Mishkan* on Shabbos day. It would remain there until the following Shabbos, when it would be replaced by new loaves. Then the Kohanim would divide the *Lechem HaPanim* that had been removed, and eat it as their portion from Hashem's table. The blasphemer mocked, "A king eats fresh bread every day. Is it possible that the *Lechem HaPanim,* which is nine days old and cold, should be served from the King's table?"

This comment is very ironic in light of the Gemara in *Menachos*.[7] Reish Lakish taught that the *Shulchan* would be raised from its place in order to show the *Lechem HaPanim* to those who came to the *Beis HaMikdash* on Yom Tov. They would be told by the Kohen, "See how beloved you are to Hashem!" Rabbi Yehoshua ben Levi taught that there was a great miracle that occurred with the *Lechem HaPanim*. It was removed from the *Shulchan* in the same condition in which it had been placed there one week earlier; it was as hot and fresh as if it had just come out of the oven.

It is unthinkable that the very object that miraculously demonstrated Hashem's love for His people could become an object

---

7. 29a.

of scorn and be used as evidence that Hashem lacks a connection with His people!

Haman claimed that Hashem had forsaken the Jews and would no longer protect them from their enemies. He denied Hashem's *hashgachah pratis* (Divine providence) on their behalf, and he sought to destroy a seemingly vulnerable nation.[8] Although from afar one could have mistaken Hashem's hidden Face as apathy and coldness, the truth is that Hashem's attention and Providence on His nation's behalf was just as warm as ever. Just as the blasphemer shamed the *Lechem HaPanim* for being cold, Haman claimed that the Jews were merely "cold leftovers." Upon closer examination, the steaming *Lechem HaPanim* clearly displayed Hashem's interest, just as a review of the *Megillah* shows Hashem's orchestration of every turn of events to draw His nation closer to Him.

Not only did Haman err in his presumptuous premise, as Hashem miraculously saved His people, but Haman's diabolical plan was the catalyst for a *teshuvah* movement that inspired *Klal Yisrael* to mirror the love that Hashem showed them and to reaccept the Torah.

Perhaps this is the connection between Haman and the *Lechem HaPanim*: the object that our enemies seek to scorn only serves as a conduit for Hashem to demonstrate His love for us. True, from a distance the *Lechem HaPanim* may seem cold and neglected, but upon closer inspection one witnesses the *hashgachah pratis* that retains its heat and freshness.

Megillas Esther continues that as a response to the Purim miracle, קִיְּמוּ וְקִבְּלוּ הַיְּהוּדִים, *The Jews confirmed and undertook upon themselves*.[9] The Gemara[10] explains that on Purim, *Klal Yisrael* reaccepted the Torah out of love, whereas at Har Sinai it had been accepted out of fear. On Purim, *Klal Yisrael* realized that although

---

8. Haman inherited this strategy to attack the Jews from his grandfather Amalek: אֲשֶׁר קָרְךָ בַּדֶּרֶךְ. Amalek sought to "cool off the hot water" by denying Hashem's Providence for His people. See *Rashi, Devarim* 25:18.
9. *Esther* 9:27.
10. *Shabbos* 88a.

Hashem had hidden His Face from them, He still loved them and cared for them. The way to reciprocate Hashem's love is to accept upon oneself the Torah, as the *Sifri* teaches on the *pasuk* וְאָהַבְתָּ אֵת ה' אֱלֹקֶיךָ, *You shall love Hashem, Your God*.[11] How does one come to love Hashem? וְהָיוּ הַדְּבָרִים הָאֵלֶּה עַל לְבָבֶךָ: by placing *these words of Torah on one's heart*.[12]

All sustenance comes from Hashem, as the first *berachah* of *bentching* states, הַזָּן אֶת הַכֹּל, *Who nourishes all*. When a person realizes that his food is from Hashem, it is as if he is eating from Hashem's table. If, *chas v'shalom,* a person attributes his sustenance to כֹּחִי וְעֹצֶם יָדִי, *my strength and the might of my hands*,[13] or to foreign sources, it is as if he is eating from an offering to *avodah zarah*.

It is amazing that two people could be eating the very same food and have such different experiences. One person feels Hashem's kindness, while the other person might, *chas v'shalom,* imagine that he is eating by the grace of a foreign god.

According to all opinions, the only *berachah* that a person is required to make *mi'd'Oraisa* is *Bircas HaMazon*. Obviously, it is imperative to make the conscious association that one is eating only by Hashem's grace. When one succeeds in making this connection, it should bring him to feel the *hashgachah pratis* that Hashem has for him, and thus draw him to love Hashem. When a husband provides for his wife, and the wife is grateful for what she receives, it is natural that her love for her husband should be intensified. That is applicable to our relationship with Hashem, as well, as the Gemara[14] teaches that the term *Yom Chasunaso* — Hashem's wedding day — is referring to *Matan Torah*. Hence, it is only appropriate, as part of thanking Hashem for His provision of our needs, to speak words of Torah and strengthen our bond with Hashem.

The *Shulchan* in the *Beis HaMikdash* served as a microcosm upon which Hashem's *berachah* would rest, thereby creating a

---
11. *Devarim* 6:5.
12. Ibid., v. 6.
13. Ibid., 8:17.
14. *Ta'anis* 24a.

conduit for bountiful *parnassah* for all of *Klal Yisrael*.[15] The counterpart to the *Shulchan* was the *Menorah*, as the *pasuk* states,[16] *and the Menorah facing the Shulchan*. The *Menorah* served as a luminary that radiated the power of *Torah Shebe'al Peh* (Oral Law) to *Klal Yisrael*.[17] The influence of Torah emanating from the *Menorah* shone on the *Shulchan* to intensify Hashem's *berachah*.[18] The very same effect takes place when one presents a *d'var Torah* at the table!

This idea is mentioned in the words of the *Zohar*,[19] which states, "A table at which *divrei Torah* were spoken is taken by Hashem and placed in His portion. A *malach* stands by the table and says, 'This is the table of the Holy King that this person set before Him. May this table be set with elevated blessings and oil and may Hashem rest greatness upon it' .... A person's table is a source of merit for him in the World to Come, in addition to bringing sustenance in this world."

Although *HaKadosh Baruch Hu* sustains all life and invites all living beings to eat at His table, when one speaks words of Torah at the table he is reaffirming that it is indeed Hashem's table. Hashem considers this recognition as if the person had set the table before Him! In addition, this affords a person eternal merit, as well as augmenting his *parnassah*. This is much more than a worthwhile investment — it is the way a *Yid* is meant to live.

In the third *berachah* of *Bircas HaMazon*, we begin by asking Hashem to have mercy on *Klal Yisrael*, on Yerushalayim, the Davidic dynasty, and the *Beis HaMikdash*. Indeed, the *berachah* concludes with the proclamation that Hashem is the merciful Builder of Yerushalayim. Seemingly inexplicably, in the middle of the *berachah*, we beseech Him to bestow upon us sustenance and

---

15. *Ramban, Shemos* 25:24.
16. *Shemos* 26:35.
17. *Ha'amek Davar, Shemos* 27:20.
18. Ad loc. 26, 35.
19. *Parashas Terumah* 153b, cited by the *Yesod V'Shoresh Ha'Avodah, Sha'ar* 7, Chapter 6.

to provide all of our needs. What is the connection between this request and Yerushalayim and the *Beis HaMikdash*?

Eliyahu HaNavi taught us[20] that when Hashem hears Jews in shul answering *Kaddish* and praising His Name, He (nods His head in acknowledgement and) says, "Fortunate is the King Who is praised this way in His house! What is there for the Father Who has exiled His sons, and woe to the sons who have been exiled from their Father's table."

When we had a *Beis HaMikdash*, we had a direct relationship with Hashem, like a child at his father's table. Now that there is no *Beis HaMikdash*, our relationship with Hashem is less immediate. When we *bentch*, we ask Hashem to restore the *Beis HaMikdash* and Yerushalayim. Then we will once again merit to sit at Hashem's table, and all of our needs will be fulfilled. It is therefore appropriate to include a request for our livelihood in the *berachah* that relates to the rebuilding of Yerushalayim.

Actually, we still have the opportunity to sit at Hashem's table even today. From the day the *Beis HaMikdash* was destroyed, *HaKadosh Baruch Hu* only has in His world the four cubits of halachah.[21] Hashem rests His Presence in the place where Torah is studied. By infusing our tables with *divrei Torah*, we invite Hashem's Presence, and we can return to Hashem's table by making our table His Own.

Let us all take advantage of the opportunity to bring about our own personal redemption by giving *nachas* to our Father in Heaven and transforming our table into His table. When Hashem sees His children in unity around His table, He will certainly rebuild the *Beis HaMikdash* and bring us back home to Him, speedily and in our days. Amen!

Moshe Sherrow
Yerushalayim
Sivan 5776

---

20. *Berachos* 3a.
21. Ibid., 8a.

Acknowledgments

The Gemara[1] states that there are three partners in a person's creation: *HaKadosh Baruch Hu*, the person's father, and his mother. Although the Gemara is referring the beginning of one's life, as one's life progresses there are others who help to build the person and enable him to reach new heights.

The Mishnah in *Bava Metzia*[2] explains that one is required to return the lost item of one's Rebbi before that of one's father, as one's father is responsible for bringing him into this world, but his Rebbi, who taught him wisdom, is bringing him into the World to Come.

The Gemara in *Makkos*[3] quotes Rabbi Yehudah HaNasi, the author of the Mishnah, as saying, "I have learned much Torah from my Rebbeim, and from my colleagues even more than that, and from my students more than all of them."

---

1. *Kiddushin* 30b.
2. 33a.
3. 10a.

Eliyahu HaNavi told Rabbi Yose[4] that one's wife lights up his eyes and stands him on his feet. If a wife encourages and assists her husband to learn, she can even reach the level of Rabbi Akiva's wife, Rachel, whereupon her husband's learning, as well as that of all who learn from him, is attributed to her.[5]

In *Lashon HaKodesh* the word "to thank" is the same as the word "to admit." The Acknowledgments section is the place where one thanks all those who helped him. Perhaps the deeper meaning behind this is that one acknowledges that he was not capable of accomplishing this by himself.

I am humbled by all the kindness that Hashem bestows upon me constantly. For every breath one takes one has to praise Hashem.[6] For all of the daily miracles and constant wonders that Hashem performs for me and those close to me, and indeed for all of *Klal Yisrael*, I am eternally indebted. I thank Hashem for allowing me to learn His Torah in *Eretz Yisrael* and for helping me to learn, teach, and keep His Torah and mitzvos. I am also appreciative of the very special *zechus* of being able to write this third *sefer*. May Hashem continue to shower His abundant kindness upon us forever.

Rav Yitzchok Zilberstein, *shlita*, has taught me much Torah and afforded me the opportunity to share it with Jews the world over. He is a *gadol baTorah* who is raising and uplifting generations of *b'nei Olam Haba*. I thank him for granting me his permission, with love, to translate his *sefarim* and share them with the

---

4. *Yevamos* 63a.
5. *Kesubos* 63a.
6. *Bereishis Rabbah* 14:11.

English-speaking public. May he merit many more years of Torah dissemination, while enjoying good health and *nachas* from all of his family and *talmidim*.

I thank my wonderful parents for their love and support and for raising me with such devotion. I bless them with health and happiness and *nachas* from all of their offspring.

I thank my other set of parents (originally just my wife's parents) for all of their dedication and caring, as well as for their generosity and shining example. May Hashem bestow His endless kindness upon them, that they should only experience *simchah* and *nachas*.

I am deeply grateful to all of my Rebbeim who have each devotedly invested their energies into molding me into the person that I am today. A special debt of gratitude is due to Rav Doniel Lehrfeld, *shlita*, who helped me on my way to become a *ben Torah*. May Hashem continue to help all of them teach His Torah to His children and amass endless merit amidst good health and success.

I owe a tremendous *hakaras hatov* to HaRav Nosson Tzvi Finkel, *zt"l*, for all of his inspiration and encouragement.

A special thank-you to Rabbi Hillel Dovid Geller, *shlita*, for reviewing the entire *sefer* for accuracy and for interjecting crucial comments that served to improve the work significantly.

It has been an honor and a pleasure to work with the team at ArtScroll/Mesorah. The insightful comments of Mrs. Judi Dick and Mrs. Felice Eisner added immeasurably to this work; Eli Kroen's eye-catching cover design is delightful; I thank Mendy Herzberg for coordinating this project through its many stages; Avrohom Biderman worked closely with me to ensure that every detail was addressed; Mrs. Rivky Kapenstein developed the creative page design and typeset the book; Mrs. Faigie Weinbaum proofread. I am grateful to each of them for their efforts to make this book accurate and beautiful.

I would like to thank Rabbi Yisrael Stilerman, *shlita*, for all of his support (technical and otherwise) and encouragement. Thank you to Mrs. Hannah Hartman for sharing her expertise and talents in putting everything together.

I wish to thank Rabbi Paysach Krohn once again for having been the original inspiration for this book, as explained in the introduction to *What If*, Vol. I.

My wife does not approve of my thanking her in public, and therefore I will honor her wishes and not go on and on about her endless effort and caring for every detail of our lives. Her help in editing this *sefer* is just a very small part of everything she invests. May Hashem grant us true success in raising our children for Torah, *chuppah*, and *ma'asim tovim*, and may we reap the nachas of producing future generations who are all devoted to Hashem and His Torah. Amen.

Moshe Sherrow
Yerushalayim
Sivan 5776

ספר בראשית

Sefer Bereishis

פרשת בראשית
Parashas Bereishis

Hidden Treasure

אֲשֶׁר שָׁם הַזָּהָב
Where the gold is
(2:11)

 Aharon moved from Flatbush to Lakewood, and he hired Meir to transfer some of his furniture to his new home. Meir had recently found a couch in a parking lot; it had apparently been abandoned by its previous owner. Since Meir had no use for it, he presented it to Aharon. As Aharon was cleaning the old couch, he noticed that the wooden armrests were removable. When he pulled out the armrests, he found $6000 that had been hidden in the couch. To whom does the money belong?

 The original owner of the couch was most likely the one who hid the money there, subsequently forgetting about his hiding place. Eventually he disposed of the old piece of furniture together with its valuable contents.

Although he had intended to part with the couch, he did not intentionally part from the money. The money is a classic example of *hefker* by mistake, and thus remains the property of its original owner.[1] In that case, Aharon would have no permission to use the money.

However, since the owner left his couch in a place where it could be taken by anyone who wanted it and it could have wound up anywhere, without any hope of his ever retrieving it, it would seem that the owner can no longer claim any ownership of its contents. This is comparable to the ruling of the *Rema*[2] that if chickens and geese rebel against their owner and run from his property in a way that they cannot be retrieved, whoever grabs them first can acquire them for himself, as the fowl are deemed *hefker*. It is similar to an item washed away by the tide, which is rendered ownerless by virtue of the fact that no one has control over the item.[3] Hence, even if the owner of the couch never intended to relinquish his ownership of the money, it is considered *hefker* due to the fact that he left the couch for anyone to take, and he lost all control over its whereabouts. That is sufficient to deem it ownerless, regardless of the fact that he may have done so unintentionally.

Aharon may keep the money.[4]

---

1. See *Tosafos, Gittin* 47, d"h ada'ta.
2. *Choshen Mishpat.*
3. *Bava Metzia* 22b.
4. Editor's Note: Although Meir acquired the couch when he found it, he never intended to acquire the hidden money, and therefore he has no claim to it. See "Buried Treasure," p. 236.

Sleeping In

וַיִּישָׁן
And he slept
(2:21)

 Yaakov has been suffering from sleep apnea lately, so his doctor referred him to a sleep lab for testing. He will have to spend a few nights at the lab, hooked up to equipment that will monitor his sleep. One of the conditions of the testing is that he is not to be awakened by any stimuli; he is to be allowed to sleep until he awakens on his own. Due to his sleeping problems, if he is left to awaken on his own, he knows he will sleep past the time for *Krias Shema*. Is Yaakov permitted to submit himself for testing if he knows that he will miss reciting the *Shema* on time?

 Sleep is a very important factor in a person's health, as is expressed by the *Rambam*.[5] If Yaakov is suffering from sleep apnea, then it is sure to affect his health. He will not be able to concentrate on his Torah study or his *davening*, and he will be affected in other areas of his service of Hashem. Such a consequence is certainly worth more than one-fifth of Yaakov's assets, and that is beyond the requirement of the obligation to recite the *Shema*, as the *Rema*[6] writes that one does not have to expend more than one-fifth of his assets in order to fulfill a *mitzvas asei* (positive commandment). Surely Yaakov's ability to function would fall into this category. Therefore, he may proceed with the test, even at the expense of missing *Krias Shema*.

---

5. *Hilchos Dei'os* 4:4.
6. *Orach Chaim* 656:1.

Just the Fax

וַיִּקַּח אַחַת מִצַּלְעֹתָיו
And He took one of his sides
(2:21)

Hillel Bilstein is a *kollel yungerman* who is about to publish his first *sefer*. Hillel asked his friend Nachshon if he could send him the *sefer* for his review and critique. Nachshon instructed Hillel to fax him the *sefer* that evening, and he would be happy to accommodate him. Nachshon gave Hillel his fax number and Hillel asked his daughter to fax the *sefer*, which totaled 200 pages. Hillel's daughter accidently misdialed, and instead of sending the *sefer* to Nachshon, she sent it to Zalman, who had absolutely no appreciation for Hillel's work. Hillel was apprised of Zalman's opinion when he angrily called Hillel a few hours later and berated him for wasting 200 pages of his fax paper, as well as his pricey fax toner.

The unfortunate recipient lived quite a distance from Nachshon, so it was not worth his effort or the cost to deliver the printed manuscript to its intended addressee. Zalman demanded that Hillel send him a check to cover his expenses in printing Hillel's pages, for which he has no use. Must Hillel pay Zalman for accidentally sending him a fax?

According to the halachah, Hillel's daughter (assuming she was *bas mitzvah*) must pay for her error, even though she had no intention to do any damage. A person is always liable for his actions.[7]

---

7. *Bava Kamma* 26a.

However, if Zalman loves Hashem and His Torah, he should not demand to be paid for his paper and ink, as his paper and ink have been transformed by precious words of Torah. Imagine that he had received a fax consisting of official documents from an important king. Would he have the nerve to ask the king to pay for his paper and ink? He would save those papers and treasure them, even if he could not sell them to anyone. He would cherish them because they belong to the king.

The Gemara in *Sanhedrin*[8] tells the story of an apostate who challenged Rabban Gamliel, saying that Hashem was a thief! He contended that the Torah says that Hashem put Adam HaRishon to sleep and removed one of his ribs. The apostate's daughter confronted her father with the following rejoinder: She urged her father to call the police, as thieves had broken into their home the previous night. They had stolen a silver goblet and replaced it with a golden one. Her father retorted that such thieves should visit them more often! His daughter pointed out that Adam had also gained immensely from having his rib replaced with a perfect mate!

Since printing or buying *sefarim* is a fulfillment of the mitzvah of writing a *Sefer Torah*,[9] Zalman was quite fortunate to have received such a fax. Therefore, he should not consider his paper and ink "wasted." He should save Hillel's *sefer*. Even if he has no use for it now, he may find it useful in the future, especially when it becomes a best-seller!

---

8. 39a.
9. *Shulchan Aruch, Yoreh De'ah* 270:2.

Life Insurance

וְאֶל עָפָר תָּשׁוּב
And to dust shall you return
(3:19)

Rabbi Newman traveled to Europe in order to solicit funds on behalf of poor families in *Eretz Yisrael*. In the course of his travels, he visited the town of an extremely wealthy man who customarily handed out very paltry sums, even for the most worthy of causes. The man had earned the reputation of being a miser, and most collectors did not even bother visiting him. Rabbi Newman decided that he was going to attempt to open the man's purse strings — and wide.

As soon as the man noticed Rabbi Newman at his door, he flatly declared that he was not interested in donating a penny! Rabbi Newman smiled and thanked the man for his honesty. Then he added that he just wanted to ask the man a simple question: What could he possibly be saving all his money for? The man was not young, and he did not seem to need any of the money that he was holding onto so tightly. What was he planning to do with his wealth?

Surprisingly, the man decided to answer the question. He became very serious, and then confided in Rabbi Newman. Due to the steady advances in the medical field, and the evidence that new cures are frequently being discovered, he strongly felt that one day researchers might discover a medicine that prevents death. He was sure that the medicine would be prohibitively expensive, so he was fiercely guarding his wealth so he would be able to afford it, when the time came.

Rabbi Newman was shocked. He could not believe that the *yetzer hara* could blind a person to such an extent, leading him to believe something as ridiculous as he had just heard. The man's idea bordered on heresy, because the Torah explicitly states that after Adam HaRishon ate from the forbidden fruit, he was punished with inevitable death.[10]

Rabbi Newman realized that he would not be able to convince the man that he was mistaken, so he decided to use a different tactic. He informed the man that although he could not offer him an elixir against death, he could offer him a remedy that extends one's life. The man's face lit up, as he was very interested to acquire this valuable information. Rabbi Newman answered that the tried and true regimen to merit long life is — *tzedakah*. The man asked Rabbi Newman if he would promise that he was telling the truth, and Rabbi Newman readily agreed. The man pulled out his checkbook and wrote Rabbi Newman a very generous check.

Now Rabbi Newman is wondering if he acted correctly. *Tzedakah* truly lengthens one's days, as the *pasuk* says in *Mishlei*:[11] *One who pursues tzedakah and kindness will find life, tzedakah, and honor.* Rabbeinu Bachye[12] writes, "The product of *tzedakah* is length of days, as it is written, '*Tzedakah* saves from death,'[13] and it is written, 'The path of *tzedakah* is life....'[14]

However, it may be that the benefits of *tzedakah* are only merited by those who give for the right reasons, and not for those who are solely interested in their own benefit. Although the Gemara[15] says that one who gives

---
10. *Bereishis* 3:19.
11. 21:21.
12. *Shemos* 22:23.
13. *Mishlei* 10:2.
14. Ad loc. 12:28.
15. *Pesachim* 8a.

a coin to *tzedakah* as a merit for his son's longevity is considered completely righteous, the commentaries explain that the donor certainly had intent to benefit the poor, as well. Rashi writes that he has fulfilled Hashem's mitzvah and *also* intended to merit his son's welfare.

In this case, where the sole purpose of his donation is for selfish reasons, perhaps the benefits of *tzedakah* do not apply. If that is so, would Rabbi Newman be allowed to accept the check in return for a promise that the man will be rewarded with long life?

The *Rambam*[16] teaches us that deep down in every Jew's heart rests the desire to fulfill Hashem's will. Unfortunately, at times that sincerity is obscured by one's evil inclination. If he is coerced by *beis din* to act properly, that merely serves to weaken the *yetzer hara's* grip, in order to bring out the Jew's true desire.

In this case as well, the wealthy man truly wishes to give *tzedakah*, but he is trapped in the clutches of his *yetzer hara*. Therefore, it is proper to coerce him to do what he really wants to do by convincing him that it is for his own benefit.

In addition, Rav Yitzchak Elchanan Spektor[17] writes that if a wicked person does a mitzvah, his mitzvah is rejected (so long as he does not repent). That is not the case with the mitzvah of *tzedakah*. If a wicked person gives *tzedakah*, even if it is with an ulterior motive, it is as if he did the mitzvah with the proper intent, and it is not lost; he will merit eternal reward. The reason *tzedakah* is different from all other mitzvos is because regardless of the intent, the purpose is accomplished, and a Jewish life is sustained with the *tzedakah*.

In this case as well, the wealthy man provided sustenance and life for the poor and downtrodden, and Hashem will pay him in kind by sustaining him. Accordingly, Rabbi Newman could promise that in return for his *tzedakah*, he will merit long life.

---

16. *Hilchos Geirushin* 2:20.
17. Introduction to *Nachal Yitzchak*.

פרשת נח
Parashas Noach

Saving It From Their Hands

וְאַתָּה קַח לְךָ
And as for you, take yourself
(6:21)

Q Yitzchak was being tortured and broken by the inhumane conditions that the Nazis had created in the ghetto. He knew that his neighbor was going to be taken out to be killed within the hour. Yitzchak was aware that his neighbor had some money in his pocket that would either be burned together with him or confiscated by the Nazis. To Yitzchak, who will remain in the ghetto, the money has potential value. Would Yitzchak be allowed to take his neighbor's money without permission, since the money is no longer of benefit to its owner?

A The Torah tells us that Noach was commanded to take *for himself* of each food that would be eaten to sustain himself and the animals during the Flood. The *Kli*

Yakar explains that Hashem did not allow Noach to take food that belonged to others. Noach might have thought that he was allowed to take other people's food, since they would soon die in the Flood. Therefore, Hashem warned him that he had no permission to do so. It would seem to follow that one may not take anything from a person, even if that person is about to lose his life.

However, it could be argued that in Noach's case, it is obvious that he could not take his neighbors' property because Hashem still hoped that they would do *teshuvah* and the Flood would be averted. Even when the rain started to fall, it was originally a beneficial rain.[18] In the case of the Nazis, there was nothing to stop them. There were almost no survivors once they decided to kill their prisoners. Although the decree could always be annulled — indeed, even if a person has a sharp sword lying on his neck he should never despair of Hashem's mercy[19] — still, since there was no natural way for a person to be saved, perhaps his possessions are *hefker*, ownerless. This being the case, *Yitzchak's* situation would not be comparable to the Flood, because the entire Flood was unnatural. It was purely a punishment from Hashem, and Hashem Himself was anticipating that they would do *teshuvah*.

The Gemara in *Bava Kamma*[20] states that if someone realizes that a robber is about to accost him, he is not allowed to use the money in his own pocket to redeem *maaser sheini* fruits that he owns,[21] because his money that is about to be stolen is considered *hefker*. The *Nesivos HaMishpat*[22] explains that the victim has given up hope of retaining his money as surely as if he had lost it already.

---

18. See *Rashi, Bereishis* 7:13.
19. *Berachos* 10a.
20. 115b.
21. In the first, second, fourth, and fifth years of each seven-year *Shemittah* cycle, one is required to separate and designate as *maaser sheini* one-tenth of his crop that grew in *Eretz Yisrael*. In the time of the *Beis HaMikdash* those fruits were taken to Yerushalayim to be eaten, or they were redeemed with money that was taken to buy food in Yerushalayim to be eaten there. Nowadays, *maaser sheini* must be redeemed.
22. 361 §2.

Even if someone else will come and save the victim from the robber, it is as if he has saved the money from a lion or an oncoming river, in which case the Gemara in *Bava Metzia*[23] explains that the rescuer is allowed to keep the money.

The *Chazon Ish*[24] comments on the *Nesivos HaMishpat* that as long as the owner still has hope of retaining his possessions, then the possessions certainly still belong to him. The owner could hope to overcome the robber, escape, or hide his money. The Gemara in *Bava Kamma* is referring to a highway robber, from whom there is no escape; in such a case the owner certainly has no hope of retaining his belongings.

Accordingly, in the Holocaust, when people had no hope of keeping their belongings even before they were imprisoned, it is probable that one could take their money and use it.

One Lucky Dog

וְהָיָה לְךָ וְלָהֶם לְאָכְלָה
And it shall be as food for you and for them
(6:21)

Q Yoav owns a fancy *fleishige* restaurant in an irreligious neighborhood. It is not uncommon for a customer to enter the restaurant with one or more dogs in his company, and order multiple portions: one for himself, and one for the dog!

When Yoav asked one such customer why he felt the need to feed his dog such expensive cuisine, the

---

23. 24a.
24. *Bava Kamma* 16 §5.

customer was taken aback at the thought of eating such delicacies, while his dog is relegated to eating leftovers.

Yoav himself has since become a full-fledged *ba'al teshuvah*, and has raised the standards of kashrus in his establishment. Yoav also attends a *daf yomi shiur*, and one day he learned[25] that food that is fit for human consumption should not be fed to animals. Rashi explains two reasons for this halachah:

1. Serving food to animals is degrading to the food and shows a lack of appreciation to Hashem, Who prepared the food for people to eat.
2. It is a waste of one's money, since the animals could survive with less-expensive fare, and the Torah is particular that a Jew not squander his assets.[26] This halachah is cited in the *Mishnah Berurah*,[27] who adds that the *Elya Rabbah* is unresolved whether this is the accepted ruling.

Yoav wants to know if he is allowed to continue to provide expensive portions of food for the animals that accompany his customers.[28]

Yoav is not serving the dog; rather, he is serving his customer who is ordering the food. Therefore, the only question would be whether Yoav is violating the prohibition of *lifnei iver* by providing food that will be fed to an animal. The answer to that question is that the food that Yoav is providing is not inherently forbidden. The problem lies in the fact that the

---

25. *Ta'anis* 20b.
26. *Rosh Hashanah* 27a.
27. 171 §11.
28. This halachah is also relevant to those who visit the zoo with their children. Some people try to feed the animals various snacks that are still fit for human consumption. Aside from the fact that the zoo may forbid harming the animals by feeding them various foods, doing so is also a disgrace to the food. If anything, the animals should only be fed leftovers that no one was planning to eat.

customer ordering the food may acquire it for a forbidden use. This is not a violation of *lifnei iver* because Yoav is not providing an actual stumbling block; i.e., something that is forbidden in and of itself.

Rav Moshe Feinstein[29] writes that one is allowed to rent out a wedding hall to an irreligious couple even if during the celebration the couple will likely be involved in activities that are not sanctioned by halachah. The hall's owner is not providing any forbidden substance, as the hall could be used for acceptable forms of merriment.

However, Yoav or his waiter should not actually serve the dog. He should place both portions in front of the customer, and explain the halachah to him. If the customer decides to feed his dog the portion of food, that is not Yoav's concern. Similarly, the *poskim* allow restaurant owners to cater to people who will not make a *berachah* or will not wash before eating bread, with the condition that there is a clearly visible sign stating that one should wash before eating bread, and a sign that displays the various *berachos* recited before and after eating.

An exception to the halachah above would be on Erev Pesach. If one has a great deal of usable *chametz* remaining in his possession, there is no degradation to the food by feeding it to an animal, assuming there are no human volunteers available to consume the *chametz*.

---

29. *Igros Moshe, Yoreh De'ah* 1:72.

Glass Houses

וַיִּפְתַּח נֹחַ אֶת חַלּוֹן הַתֵּבָה
And Noah opened the window of the Ark
(8:6)

Q A few children who were guests at a wedding stepped out of the hall to enjoy some fresh air. After a while they started to play rambunctiously and one of the children was pushed against a glass window that smashed on impact. The child was rushed to the hospital and required stitches. The child's father demands that the owner of the hall pay for damages to the child, as well as for medical expenses.

The owner of the hall thinks differently. The window was clearly marked and could not be mistaken for an open window. On the contrary, he asserts, the father of the child should have to pay for a new window. Who is right?

A Even if the child was at fault for smashing the window, a father does not have to pay for damage that his child causes.[30] This is the classic example where the Torah's opinion is the opposite of what the average person would think. A person is responsible for damage committed by his animal, but not for that caused by his child. People think that his child is his responsibility, whereas he has no control over his animal. The Torah's view is that one has responsibility for the damage done by his animal. One does not have that level of liability for his child.[31]

If the window was not properly marked or was located in a dangerous place, the hall owner would have to pay the child's father due to the fact that he maintained a hazard in the public domain. Perhaps the one who installed the window is guilty of

---

30. *Bava Kamma* 87a.
31. Ibid.

installing a potentially dangerous window; although he was hired by the owner, there is no agency to do an *aveirah*,[32] and the one who did the work is responsible. Even though the window was clearly marked, the hall owner is still responsible, as such markings do not prevent children from playing next to them. The hall owner must pay, for he should not have installed a fragile window where children were likely to play during a *simchah*.[33]

---

32. Ibid., 51a.
33. צ״ע מה ישלם נזק לא הי׳ וריפוי הוי מח׳ הפוסקים.

פרשת לך לך
Parashas Lech Lecha

House Arrest

וַתֻּקַּח הָאִשָּׁה בֵּית פַּרְעֹה
And the woman was taken to Pharaoh's house
(12:15)

Q After a prolonged ordeal, a relieved Sara gave birth to a healthy baby girl on Motza'ei Shabbos. When she was released from the hospital on Tuesday morning, her husband brought her directly to a convalescent home for new mothers. Her medical insurance covered a three-day stay, and she informed the administration that she would be leaving on Erev Shabbos. Sara simply could not afford the expense of staying for Shabbos. That Thursday night, there was a raging blizzard, and since the roads remained closed on Friday, Sara had no choice but to stay for Shabbos. Sunday, as well, brought more inclement weather, so Sara stayed on. How much is she required to pay for the extra days that she stayed? Is the fact that she did not choose to stay sufficient reason for them to waive her payment or at least give her a discount?

A Perhaps she should only have to pay two-thirds, as in the case of orphans who slaughtered a cow that they found in their late father's yard, thinking that it was part of their inheritance. After they ate its meat, they were informed that the father had merely been guarding the cow for its owner. The *Shulchan Aruch*[34] rules that they have to pay only two-thirds of the cow's value, since had they known that the cow was not theirs, they would not have eaten the meat. They only ate it because they thought it was theirs. Similarly, in Sara's case, she did not choose to stay in the convalescent home and would not have stayed there had she not been forced to do so. She, like the orphans, would have preferred to buy less-expensive food and sleep at home; she merely stayed and ate the food at the convalescent home because she had no other choice.

In truth, Sara must pay full price. In the case of the orphans, had they known that the cow was not their father's, they would have chosen to eat less-expensive food. In this case, Sara consciously ate food that she knew was not hers, and she intentionally stayed there. Even if she was forced to do so, and doing otherwise would be life-threatening, anyone who saves his own life by consuming someone else's property must still pay for that which he consumed.[35]

Moreover, hotels are operated with the realization that occasionally guests will be stranded and have nowhere else to stay. One cannot suggest that a guest would not have to pay full price for his hotel stay, on the basis that he did not willingly remain in the hotel room.[36]

---

34. *Choshen Mishpat* 341:4.
35. Ibid., 388:2.
36. Editor's Note: Had Sara had numerous children at home, and the only way she could rest would be to stay in the convalescent home, would she also have suggested that she should receive a discount because she had no choice but to stay there?

Obligations

אִם הַשְּׂמֹאל וְאֵימִנָה
If you go left then I will go right
(13:9)

רש"י: וְאֶעֱמוֹד לְךָ לְמָגֵן וּלְעֵזֶר
Rashi: I will stand for you as a protector and a helper

Q Sadly, Yechezkel divorced his wife after a very brief marriage. At first, his wife refused to accept a divorce, but Yechezkel prevailed upon her to come to terms with the realization that their match was just not meant to be. He promised her that even after they divorced, he would not forsake her if she ever needed his assistance. They parted amid many tears.

Yechezkel remarried, and this time succeeded in building a warm Jewish home, while his former wife remained single. Her health deteriorated to the point that she needed a kidney transplant. In light of his promise to her, must Yechezkel pay for her expensive operation when doing so will seriously tax his finances, and his second wife will certainly suffer from the tremendous expense? How far does his pledge to assist his ex-wife extend?

A Avraham Avinu went to war against four powerful kings in order to rescue his nephew Lot, who had been taken captive. The *Midrash* records that Avraham said, "I will go out and fall in battle to sanctify Hashem's Name."[37]

The *Be'er Yosef* questions why Avraham felt obligated to put himself in mortal danger in order to save Lot. Lot had acted

---

37. *Bereishis Rabbah, Parashah* 43.

48 / SEFER BEREISHIS

inappropriately, to the point that Avraham requested that they separate from each other. Lot chose to settle in Sodom, effectively declaring that he did not desire a relationship with Avraham — nor with Hashem.[38] Nevertheless, Avraham laid his life on the line, and survived only due to Hashem's open miracles.[39] Avraham later stated, "and I am dust,"[40] referring to the fact that had it not been for Hashem's abundant mercy, he was certain he would become dust when he battled the four kings.

The *Be'er Yosef* suggests that Avraham was obligated to sacrifice his life in battle in order to avoid a *chillul Hashem*, as he would be accused of not having kept his promise to be there if Lot should ever need him.[41]

Perhaps in this case as well, Yechezkel would have to keep his promise to his ex-wife. His words may even have the status of a vow to do a mitzvah.[42] In addition, his first wife agreed to accept the divorce only because of his promise, and her deteriorating health may even be the result of the fact that they were divorced.

Actually, Yechezkel is not halachically obligated to pay for the kidney transplant, and doing so would only be considered an act of piety. He never intended to undertake such an enormous financial obligation. Therefore, he is not bound to do so, regardless of his promise. Even if it could be considered a vow to do a mitzvah, he never intended to promise or vow to such an extent.

However, he does have a moral obligation to pay for his first wife's operation; such is the trait of Avraham Avinu. Yet the question remains whether Yechezkel's moral obligation to his first wife can be fulfilled at the expense of his second wife. Since Yechezkel's second wife is very happy in her marriage, it would be proper for her to agree to compensate the first wife for having accepted a *get* and allowing Yechezkel to marry again.

---

38. *Bereishis* 13:11, *Rashi*.
39. See *Ta'anis* 21a.
40. *Bereishis* 18:26, *Rashi*.
41. Ibid. 13:9, *Rashi*.
42. See *Yoreh De'ah* 203:6.

Rashi[43] records the story of a young man who gave his word to a young lady that he would marry her. The young lady questioned who would testify to their bond. A well and a weasel were nearby, and the young man declared that the well and the weasel would bear witness. Time passed, and the man did not keep his word. He married another woman, who bore him two children. One child fell into a well and died. The other died from a weasel's bite. His wife asked him if he knew why their children had died in such unusual and tragic circumstances, and the man remembered that long ago he had made a pact to which a well and a weasel had borne witness.

Keeping one's word is a very serious matter, and it is worthwhile to extend oneself to that end. Especially if Yechezkel is a prominent person, and not keeping his word would constitute a *chillul Hashem*, he would certainly be obligated to assist his ex-wife.

The *Yerushalmi*[44] states that the *pasuk* וּמִבְּשָׂרְךָ לֹא תִתְעַלָּם,[45] that enjoins one not to forsake his "flesh," is referring to one's divorced spouse! The *Rema*[46] writes that one has a greater obligation to give *tzedakah* to his ex-wife than to another poor person. The *Midrash*[47] tells of a time of drought when Rabbi Tanchuma declared three days of fasting, after which the skies were still clear and dry. Rabbi Tanchuma declared that the people should act with compassion toward one another in order to be worthy of compassion from Hashem. One man was seen giving a sum of money to his former wife, and he was suspected of improper behavior. When Rabbi Tanchuma asked the man to explain himself, the man defended himself by saying that he had merely fulfilled the Rav's instructions, and had shown mercy to his ex-wife. Rabbi Tanchuma turned toward Heaven and beseeched *HaKadosh Baruch Hu*, saying that if a mere mortal could have compassion

---

43. *Ta'anis* 8a.
44. *Kesubos* 11:3.
45. *Yeshayah* 58:7.
46. *Even HaEzer* 119:8.
47. *Bereishis Rabbah* 33:3.

for a woman that he had divorced, then certainly Hashem should have mercy on His children. Immediately, it began to rain, to everyone's great relief.

For these reasons, it is a great mitzvah for Yechezkel to help his ex-wife even if it will cause him and his second wife financial strain.

Ma'aser!

וַיִּתֶּן לוֹ מַעֲשֵׂר מִכֹּל
And he gave him a tenth of everything
(14:20)

Q Shabsai and Pesach are two brothers who have each been married for 15 years. Shabsai was blessed with 11 children, while his brother Pesach, sadly, had none. Shabsai and his wife decided to do the ultimate *chesed* for his brother, and for a period of time when his wife was expecting their twelfth child, Pesach, Shabsai and their wives traveled to a distant country where Shabsai's wife gave birth to a healthy baby boy. Shabsai and his wife made the enormous sacrifice and graciously gave Pesach and his wife the new baby to raise as their own. When they returned home, everyone was overjoyed to see that Pesach and his wife had finally been blessed with a child. The boy was never told that he was adopted. When he grew up and married, Pesach's name was written in the *kesubah*, as no one ever knew that he was not the child's father. Was this *chesed* as beneficent as it seems, or was it improper for Shabsai and his wife to give up their child and cover up the identity of his true parents?

A Regarding the *kesubah*, there is no problem for Pesach's name to be entered as the father. A *kesubah* is essentially a contract in which the *chassan* accepts financial obligations. If the name of the *chassan* is different from the name in the contract, it is certainly invalid. However, since everyone knows the *chassan* as Pesach's son, the *kesubah* is valid.

However, there is a much greater issue at hand. Rav Chaim Kanievsky ruled that Shabsai and Pesach's behavior was seriously wrong, as there is a halachah of *havchanah*,[48] identifying the child's parents lest he come to marry his sister. That is still a very real concern in this case, as the adopted child may come to marry Shabsai's daughter in the future, thinking that she is his first cousin. In addition, the adopted son may have a son himself, and that son might wish to marry one of Shabsai's daughters, who is really his father's sister!

In addition, the child will never have fulfilled the mitzvah of honoring his father and mother. He will spend his life honoring Pesach, his uncle, thinking that he is his father, when in reality he should be honoring his biological father, whom he thinks is his uncle!

Even though one could argue that the child is honoring his father's will by assuming the role of Pesach's son, Rav Chaim Kanievsky maintained that the adopted son could fulfill the mitzvah so much better if he only knew the truth.

Another problem that this situation creates is that if Pesach dies, his wife will require *chalitzah*,[49] which she will be embar-

---

48. *Even HaEzer* 13:1.
49. If a man dies without leaving children to survive him, his brother has a mitzvah to marry his deceased brother's wife (*yibum*). She is not allowed to marry anyone else unless she is released through the process of *chalitzah*. The *chalitzah* is done at a *beis din* during which she removes her brother-in-law's shoe and spits in front of him. Afterward, she is free to marry another man (*Devarim* 25:5-10).

rassed to perform since everyone thinks that she has borne a child. She may try to excuse herself by saying that one who raises his friend's child is likened to having given birth to that child. If she ever remarries, she will have violated the prohibition of getting married without *chalitzah*, and will have caused her new husband to stumble.

Moreover, if the adopted child dies without having children, his wife will not realize that she must do *chalitzah*, as she will be under the impression that her husband had no brothers, when in truth he has many brothers: Shabsai's sons.

This situation is certainly unacceptable, and due to the many serious implications involved, this child must be informed of his true identity, come what may.

פרשת וירא / Parashas Vayeira

Same Place, Same Time

אֶל הַמָּקוֹם אֲשֶׁר עָמַד שָׁם
To the place where he had stood
(19:27)

Q Mevakshei Hashem is a unique shul comprised of sincere and friendly members. When Ephraim moved into the neighborhood, the shul community welcomed him with open arms. Ephraim became a permanent fixture in the shul and could be found *davening* every morning in one of the three minyanim for Shacharis at 6 a.m., 7 a.m., or 8 a.m. Mordechai, who is also a member of Mevakshei Hashem, asked Ephraim if perhaps it would be better for him to attend a steady minyan instead of alternating between minyanim. The Gemara[50] teaches that one who holds a fixed place for *davening* will be granted assistance

---
50. *Berachos* 6b.

from the God of Avraham Avinu.[51] Ephraim responded that he does have a permanent place for *davening*, as he sits in the same seat every day; he merely does so at different minyanim. Would it be preferable to consistently *daven* in the same minyan, as well as in the same seat?

The Gemara in *Rosh Hashanah*[52] states that those who travel the seas by ship, even if they number ten men, are considered as individuals and do not have the status of a *tzibbur*. The *Parashas Derachim*[53] explains that since each one is in danger, and each one is *davening* for himself and not for his fellow passengers, they cannot be considered a *tzibbur*. The *Shem MiShmuel*[54] adds that since the passengers are not familiar with one another, each one is concerned with his own plight and not with that of his fellow. Therefore, they are considered individuals.

It would seem that one who *davens* in a steady minyan, where he knows his fellow *mispallelim's* problems and cares about them specifically, has given his *davening* the advantage of being offered with a *tzibbur*. Ten strangers who merely gather to *daven* but are not familiar with one another lack that advantage.

Although the strangers on the ship, or in the *shtiebel*, as the case may be, can still *daven* those parts of *davening* that require a minyan (e.g., *Kaddish* and *Krias HaTorah*), they do not have the same optimal power that a *tzibbur* has to have their *tefillos* answered.

Accordingly, it would seem that it is preferable to *daven* consistently in the same minyan, and not just in the same location.[55]

---

51. The source for designating a steady place for *davening* is derived from the actions of Avraham Avinu (*Berachos* 6b).
52. 17b.
53. *Drush* 13.
54. *Shevuos*, p. 89.
55. See "Davening With Heart," p. 272.

Location, Location, Location

אֶל הַמָּקוֹם אֲשֶׁר עָמַד שָׁם
To the place where he had stood
(19:27)

Q There was a shul that held many minyanim and *shiurim* on Shabbos, but had a minyan only for Shacharis during the week. The members decided to rent the shul to a yeshivah to be used as a *beis midrash*, since the building was standing empty for most of the day. However, they stipulated that if the shul needed the premises during the week, the shul's use would take priority over that of the yeshivah.

On Sunday, the members of the shul were off from work, and they were able to arrange a small minyan for Minchah and Maariv, so they politely requested that the yeshivah students leave the main shul to allow the men to *daven* there.

The yeshivah staff asked the members of the shul if they would mind *davening* Minchah and Maariv in a side room, which was certainly large enough to comfortably accommodate the small group. The yeshivah had many more people, and interrupting the boys' learning in order to leave the room would cause *bittul Torah*.

The shul members insisted that according to the contract with the yeshivah, they had the right to ask the boys to leave, since each shul member wanted to *daven* in his own seat. Therefore, they felt that the yeshivah

56 / SEFER BEREISHIS

should crowd into the side room and allow the men to *daven* in their regular places.[56] Who is right?

A Rav Elyashiv answered that, strictly speaking, the shul members are certainly right. Nevertheless, the proper thing would be not to disturb the yeshivah and go to *daven* in the side room.

Perhaps we could explain the Rav's decision based on the words of the *Tz'lach*,[57] who writes that the advantage of *davening* in a set place is because that place has already been infused with the holiness of his previous *tefillos*. If the boys will continue to learn in the shul, it will add even more *kedushah* than the men will with their *davening* (as is explicit in the Gemara in *Berachos*[58]), and this will add holiness that will actually benefit the men when they *daven* there on Shabbos. Rav Chisda explained the *pasuk*, *Hashem loves the gates of Tzion more than all of the dwellings of Yaakov*,[59] to mean that Hashem loves the gates where halachah (which includes Gemara) is studied, more than He loves shuls or *batei midrash*. Abaye said that originally he would learn at home and *daven* in shul, but once he heard that Rabbi Chiya bar Ami quoted Ulla as saying, "From the day the *Beis HaMikdash* was destroyed Hashem has in His world only the four cubits of halachah," he *davened* only in the place where he studied. Even though there were thirteen shuls in Teveria, Rabbi Ami and Rabbi Asi would *daven* only between the pillars where they had learned.[60]

The *Tz'lach* elaborates: The main reason to *daven* consistently in the same place is because once he has *davened* there, the place has become holy. The next time he *davens* there, the location itself will help his *davening* to be accepted. A haughty person feels that he doesn't need the advantage of his location to assist his

---

56. See *Shulchan Aruch, Orach Chaim* 90:19.
57. *Berachos* 6b.
58. 8a.
59. *Tehillim* 87:2.
60. Nevertheless, this does not detract from one's obligation to *daven* with a minyan. See *Orach Chaim* 90:9.

davening, and he will *daven* well regardless of where he *davens*. One who *davens* in a set place realizes that he needs help from his surroundings to assist him in concentrating on his *davening*. That itself testifies to the person's humility.

In our case, where the shul members want to *daven* in their assigned seats, and the only reason they are not doing so is in order to preserve the continuity of the boys' learning and to increase the holiness of their shul, that is certainly an act of humility, and that itself will assist their prayers to be elevated and accepted, wherever they may be offered.

A Lack of Communication

בְּתָם לְבָבִי וּבְנִקְיֹן כַּפַּי עָשִׂיתִי זֹאת
In the innocence of my heart and integrity of my hands have I done this
(20:5)

Q A while back, Shmuel lent $500 to his friend Boruch. On the day the loan was due, Boruch called Shmuel and told him that he was ready to come and repay the loan. Shmuel answered that he was extremely busy at work and would only be home later in the day. Shmuel's wife was also not home, but Shmuel really wanted Boruch to repay the loan on time. He told Boruch to simply put the money into an envelope and slip the envelope into Shmuel's locked mailbox. When Boruch asked if there was reason to suspect that the money would not be safe in the mailbox, Shmuel told Boruch not to worry, as the mailbox was very deep.

Boruch eagerly prepared to follow Shmuel's instructions, as he also wanted to repay his loan on time. The first envelope that came to hand was from a wedding invitation he had received; it was inscribed on the outside, "To Boruch." He placed the money into the envelope, drove over to Shmuel's house, and slipped the envelope into Shmuel's mailbox.

Shmuel's wife arrived home early in the evening and was unaware of her husband's conversation with Boruch. She checked the mailbox and found an invitation addressed "To Boruch." Obviously, there had been some mistake. She remembered that there was someone else in the building named Boruch, and decided to slip the invitation into the neighbor's mailbox.

The neighbor arrived home shortly afterward and found an invitation with a return address that he did not recognize. He grumbled something about junk mail, and tossed the invitation into the trash chute.

When Shmuel arrived home late that evening he headed directly for the mailbox, as Boruch had informed him that he had already delivered the envelope. At first he was concerned when he found the mailbox empty, but then he realized that his wife had most likely emptied it before him. When he asked his wife for the envelope, she told him that there had not been any envelope, with the exception of an invitation for the neighbor. By the time Shmuel was able to ask the neighbor about the mail, the "invitation" was long gone.

Shmuel and his wife, Boruch the borrower, and Boruch the neighbor all came to the Rav to decide who was responsible for the loss of the money. Was it Shmuel who told the borrower to place the loan payment in an envelope in his mailbox, Shmuel's wife who placed the envelope into the neighbor's mailbox, Boruch the borrower who put the money in an envelope that bore his own name, or Boruch the neighbor who tossed the envelope into the garbage?

All four people in this incident acted irresponsibly. Not only did Shmuel foolishly ask his debtor to place $500 into his mailbox, but he did not even notify his wife to expect an envelope containing money. Shmuel's wife was negligent for not questioning her husband regarding the envelope; she hastily disposed of the envelope by inserting it into her neighbor's mailbox. Had she left the envelope for her husband to see, he would have realized that it contained the outstanding loan. The debtor was irresponsible for leaving his own name on the envelope, leading to the misunderstanding that followed. He should have written **Shmuel's** name, so it would be obvious for whom the envelope was intended. Finally, the neighbor acted without thinking by immediately disposing of the envelope before opening it to investigate its contents. By merely feeling the envelope, he should have realized that it was not an invitation.

As far as the halachah, the *Shulchan Aruch*[61] rules that a borrower bears responsibility for the loan until he delivers it to the hands of the lender. If the lender instructed the borrower to throw the payment to him and thereby be absolved, and upon following the lender's instructions the payment was lost, the borrower has no liability, since he acted on the lender's instructions.

In this case, Shmuel asked Boruch to "throw" the payment into his mailbox. Boruch followed his instructions and was thereby released from any liability. Although Boruch was guilty of leaving the money in an envelope that bore his name, the main negligence was Shmuel's, in not having notified his wife about the expected

---

61. *Choshen Mishpat* 120:1.

payment. He thereby caused his own damage. This is coupled by the fact that his wife was negligent as well, for not asking her husband about the envelope. Hence, Boruch is exempt from paying a second time.

As far as the neighbor, he cannot be held accountable for having destroyed the envelope that he found in his own mailbox, because he had no reason to suspect that it held valuable contents.

פרשת חיי שרה
Parashas Chayei Sarah

A Bargain

עֹבֵר לַסֹּחֵר
In negotiable currency
(23:16)

Q David walked into Shimmy's Appliances, intending to purchase a stereo. A salesman helped him choose the one that met his needs, whereupon David approached the cashier, purchase in hand. David noticed a $50 bill lying on the counter in front of him. The cashier had not noticed it because he was busy reciting verses from *Tehillim*. David looked around him and saw that there were no other customers in the store, so he could not ask anyone to whom the money belonged. He decided that he would appropriate the money for himself, as is permitted by the *Shulchan Aruch* [62] in such a case. In all probability, the money on the counter was given as change to a previous customer, who by now had given up hope of retrieving it.

---

62. *Choshen Mishpat* 260:5.

David opened his wallet to add $50 of his own to pay for his purchase, when suddenly the cashier reached out, took the money from the counter, and requested, "Another $50, please." The cashier assumed that the money was David's and placed it into the cash register. David paid the additional $50 and left the store with his purchase. On the way home, David reflected upon the events in the store.

The money on the counter did not really belong to him, since he had not yet picked it up to acquire it. Although the cashier picked up the money, thinking that it was David's, that does not serve to acquire it for David. Perhaps Shimmy's cash register acquired the money for Shimmy. Must David return to the store and pay an additional $50?

A If an ownerless item is found on someone else's property, that person's property can acquire the item on his behalf, even without his knowledge. However, this halachah is limited to property that secures the items that it contains.[63] Accordingly, Shimmy's counter cannot acquire the money on his behalf, as a counter is not a secure place to hold the money, since anyone in the store could easily access it.[64]

Nevertheless, it would seem that David does not have to pay any additional money. The cashier accepted the money on the counter as partial payment, and only asked David to pay $50 for the stereo. Even if the truth were otherwise, the cashier accepted that the money belonged to David. This is similar to a transaction via *O'disa*: One who owns an item can admit that the item belongs to his friend.[65] Even if the facts are otherwise, one's admission is as effective as 100 witnesses, and in fact, his friend will now become the legal owner of the item in question.

---

63. *Bava Metzia* 11a.
64. *Choshen Mishpat* 243:21.
65. *Bava Basra* 149a.

In our case, as well, the cashier "admitted" and accepted that the money on the counter was part of David's payment. This was sufficient for him to release the stereo for David's acquisition. Therefore, David is allowed to keep the stereo for the $50 that he paid.

A Domestic Match

עֶבֶד אַבְרָהָם אָנֹכִי
A servant of Avraham am I
(24:34)

Q Juan was a young non-Jewish immigrant who worked three times a week cleaning the Goldman home. Dr. Goldman was a very successful man, so Juan was surprised to find him in a state of melancholy one day. Juan asked Dr. Goldman why he was so sad, and Dr. Goldman confided that he and his wife were having difficulty finding a match for their eldest daughter. It occurred to the young worker, who was very devoted to his kind employer, that he had recently heard similar sentiments echoed elsewhere. Then he remembered his job at the yeshivah. Juan would mop the floors at the yeshivah every Friday, and he had become acquainted with an older *bachur* who was also having difficulty finding his true match.

Out of the goodness of his heart, Juan decided to try to bring happiness to his employers. However, he realized that if he would speak directly to Dr. Goldman and present the candidate for his daughter, there was no chance that Dr. Goldman would consider it. Juan would have to work behind the scenes. He asked one of the *bachurim* in the yeshivah to write a list of the older *bachur's* particulars, together with all his positive attributes.

Juan left the paper anonymously where Dr. Goldman was sure to find it. Sure enough, Dr. Goldman noticed the paper and read it with great interest. He decided to make inquiries about the boy. Interestingly, the *shidduch* was completed, to everyone's great joy and satisfaction.

Now Juan stepped forward to take credit for the *shidduch*. He explained how he had brought the young people together, and, since he had been working in the Jewish community for a few years, he knew that he deserved to be paid well for having made the match. Dr. Goldman wants to know if he indeed has to pay the young immigrant for being the *shadchan*.

One is obligated to pay a *shadchan* for completing a *shidduch*,[66] regardless of whether one engaged the *shadchan's* services or the *shadchan* offered the suggestion on his own. The *Gra* writes that the source for the obligation is the halachah of one who planted his friend's field without being asked to do so.[67] Since the field had to be planted in any event, the one who did the work deserves to be paid. The same is true for one who initiated a *shidduch* even without being asked to do so. Accordingly, it would seem that Juan deserves payment, except for the fact that these circumstances do not fit the ordinary case that would require a *shadchan* to be paid.

Juan understood that no one would consider a suggestion that he made, and for that reason he chose to remain anonymous. Perhaps originally he never intended to be paid but only to be accorded praise and appreciation. The fact that he did not assume a formal role as a *shadchan* leaves room for doubt that he had originally intended to charge a fee for his efforts. Hence, Dr. Goldman could claim that the burden of proof rests upon Juan to prove that he suggested the *shidduch* with the intent of charging for his participation.

---

66. *Rema, Choshen Mishpat* 87:39.
67. *Bava Metzia* 101a.

In addition, since secular law would not recognize the obligation to pay a *shadchan* in such a context — i.e., an amateur matchmaker who merely suggested a possible match — combined with the fact that Juan is not Jewish, he cannot halachically collect money that he is not entitled to collect according to his own laws.[68]

Nevertheless, it is proper that the *chassan* should buy Juan an impressive gift as an act of appreciation. In this way, the *chassan* will have paid for the aid he was privy to in building his home. Otherwise, he will be forever beholden to Juan for the fact that he assisted him to learn Torah by providing him with a wife.

In a similar vein, we find that Rabbi Tzadok, who was healed by Roman doctors, taught them mathematics in appreciation for their services, in order to be free of an eternal debt of gratitude that would express itself in their having a share in Rabbi Tzadok's future Torah learning.[69]

In summary, halachically, Juan does not deserve payment as a *shadchan*, but they should buy him a nice present in appreciation for his hand in their *shidduch*.

Putting One and One Together

מֵה' יָצָא הַדָּבָר
The matter stemmed from Hashem
(24:50)

Q Zelig had an exceptional daughter who had just returned from seminary in *Eretz Yisrael*, and she was prepared to build a true Jewish home. Zelig knew that he needed

---

68. *Choshen Mishpat* 11:3.
69. *Midrash Eichah* 1:31.

a very special boy for her, and he decided to consult Sruli, who was a relatively new *shadchan*. Sruli listened attentively to Zelig's specifications, opened up his notepad, and began flipping through the pages. Sruli found what he was looking for, and proceeded to describe what seemed to be a perfect match for Zelig's daughter. Zelig was very interested, but suddenly, Sruli let out a long sigh. He admitted that the *shidduch* seemed to be a wonderful match, but the *shadchan* had a confession to make: To date, he had made three *shidduchim*, and all of them had ended in divorce, *rachmana litzlan*!

Zelig wants to know if he should proceed with a *shidduch* suggested by a *shadchan* with such a track record.

The Gemara in *Yevamos*[70] explains that if something happens three times, it is considered a *chazakah*.[71] For example, if three boys from the same family died, *chalilah*, as a result of having a *bris milah*, the next son born into that family is exempt from *bris milah*, as it is assumed that the procedure would be life-threatening for him. The *Kovetz Ha'aros*[72] explains that if something happened less than three times, it is considered a random occurrence. Once it has happened three times, it becomes clear that there is a pattern that is expected to repeat itself.

Accordingly, it would seem that Sruli should look for a new line of work, as he is obviously not meant to be a *shadchan*.

However, the *Mekor Chaim*[73] writes that if a pot was found to contain three wheat kernels on Pesach, that would not be a reason to assume that there were additional kernels in the pot. A *chazakah* is established only when there is a likely cause for all three

---

70. 64b.
71. According to the opinion of *Rebbi*, even twice is enough.
72. *Hosafos* 2.
73. 467 §5.

occurrences. If, however, the three do not share a common catalyst, a recurrence would not be expected.

The *Mekor Chaim* supports his resolution from a halachah in *Even HaEezer*.[74] If a man was widowed three times, he is not forbidden to marry again. Only a woman who was widowed three times is assumed to have a *mazal* (fortune) not to be financially supported, which causes her husbands to die. As women (in the olden days) did not generally support their husbands financially, if a man became widowed three times, his tragedies are looked upon as unrelated events.

The *Beis Shlomo*[75] echoes this idea and writes that if three randomly dug graves were discovered in a field, that would not indicate that there are other people buried there as well, since there is no reason to connect the discoveries to one another.

The fact that three couples shared the same *shadchan* should have no bearing on the fact that their marriages did not last. Therefore, Sruli is not to be faulted, and Zelig may proceed with the suggested *shidduch*.

---

74. 9:2.
75. *Yoreh De'ah* Vol. II, 219.

פרשת תולדות
Parashas Toldos

The Best Policy

וְיַעֲקֹב אִישׁ תָּם
But Jacob was a wholesome man
(25:27)

Q Raphael had been trying to sell his house for many months, but nobody seemed interested in buying it. Raphael decided to visit his Rebbe and ask for a *segulah* to find a buyer quickly. The Rebbe thought for a minute, and then told Raphael that lowering the price of the property from the $450,000 that he was asking to $425,000 would certainly be a *segulah* to sell it quickly.

Raphael accepted his Rebbe's advice and proceeded to call all the real-estate agents whose services he had engaged to inform them of the price change. There was one agent who was out of town and could not be reached. A few days later, Raphael received a call from that agent, notifying Raphael that a buyer had agreed to buy the property for the full amount!

Raphael met with the buyer and they signed a contract for $450,000.

That night, Raphael attended a *shiur* on *Maseches Makkos*. The Gemara[76] extols the virtue of Rav Safra, "who spoke the truth in his heart."[77] Rashi[78] cites the incident relating that Rav Safra had offered an item for sale, but was saying the *Shema* when a customer approached him with a bid on the item. Rav Safra could not respond and continued to say *Shema*. The customer misunderstood Rav Safra's lack of response and interpreted it to mean that his bid had been too low. He offered a higher bid and still did not receive a response. Again he raised his bid, as Rav Safra finished reciting the *Shema*. Rav Safra told his customer that he would sell the item at the original price, because in truth he had already mentally agreed to sell it for that amount. Rav Safra is certainly a role model for integrity!

Raphael thought about his own transaction and realized that since he had already agreed to lower the price, the proper course would be to sell his property for that amount, regardless of the fact that the buyer was willing to pay more. Raphael called the broker and informed him of his decision. The broker was touched by Raphael's strength of character, but since the broker received a two-percent commission, and he had brokered the deal for the original price, he felt that he deserved to collect his full commission. Why should he have to sustain a $500 loss due to Raphael's piety? Must Raphael pay the commission based on the original price, or, since he only received $425,000, must he pay only the commission for the money he received?

---

76. 24a.
77. *Tehillim* 15:2.
78. Ad loc.

A If the buyer and seller agreed to lower the sale price after the deal had already been finalized, without having had any reason to do so, the broker would deserve his full commission, as he had already closed the deal for the full amount.

In this case, there is definitely a firm basis for Raphael to change the price that they had agreed upon, in accordance with Hashem's will that people deal honestly, even if they had merely reached the decision in their minds. Therefore, the original higher price of the property is not binding and is considered to be a mistake. The broker should receive his commission according to the "final" price of $425,000.

Buyer Beware

וַיְבָרְכֵהוּ
And blessed him
(27:27)

Q It was the Shabbos of *Parashas Toldos*, and many people had their eye on the *aliyah* that incorporates the *berachos* that Yitzchak Avinu bestowed upon Yaakov. Many looked at it as a *segulah* for *parnassah* (livelihood) and attributed great value to receiving that *aliyah*. The *gabbai* arose to auction off the *aliyos*. The first *aliyos* went for more modest sums until the *gabbai* announced that he was selling *chamishi* (the fifth *aliyah*), which included the *berachos*! The bidding continued for quite some time as the amounts grew larger and larger. Finally, Moshe Hoffman bought the *aliyah* for $360.

Incredibly, no one realized that the *gabbai* had made a mistake, and that the coveted *berachos* were actually contained in the following *aliyah*. The *gabbai* sold *shishi* for a mere $36 to Shlomie Salem.

After all the honors had been sold, Moshe discovered the mistake. He insisted that he was not going to take the fifth *aliyah*, but rather the sixth *aliyah*, which contained the *berachos*. Shlomie refused to entertain the idea. He had bought *shishi*, fair and square. Why should Moshe take away his *aliyah*?

The shul began to churn with heated discussions over the two positions. Finally, someone offered the following suggestion. "The sixth *aliyah* begins with the word וְיִתֶּן לְךָ הָאֱלֹקִים, "*and* Hashem will give you"; why did Yitzchak Avinu start off the *berachah* with the word "and"? The Ohr HaChaim infers that when the previous *pasuk* ends with the word "and he (Yitzchak) blessed him (Yaakov)," it is not referring to the material *berachah* that is contained in the following *pasuk*, but rather, that Yitzchak blessed Yaakov with spirituality. Hence, the following *pasuk* begins with the word "and," because the material blessing came in addition to the spiritual blessings alluded to in the previous *pasuk*. Hence, *chamishi* contains the spiritual blessings, in which case Moshe actually bought the right *aliyah*! Could this assessment be accurate? Who should get which *aliyah*?

It is clearly understood that when the *gabbai* auctioned off *chamishi* "which contained the *berachos*," everyone intended to buy the *aliyah* with the material *berachos*. Therefore, even if the *gabbai* called it *chamishi*, his words are not binding. The *gabbai* is merely a representative of the congregation; he is only authorized to act for the good of the shul members, not to mislead them. In addition, the price of the *aliyah* is indicative as to which *aliyah* Moshe intended to buy, and therefore he should receive that *aliyah*.

The suggestion that *chamishi* contains the spiritual *berachos*, albeit a charming interpretation, does not seem to be appropriate in this context. It was clear that everyone wanted the *aliyah* that contained the material *berachos*. Since there is a rule that in business matters the buyers' consensus is to be followed,[79] in our case the consensus was obvious that the intention was to buy *shishi*. Therefore, Moshe should be called for *shishi*, and Shloimie should be called up to receive *chamishi*. In that way, Shlomie will also receive tremendous blessings.[80]

Dealing With the Sly

אֲחִי אָבִיהָ הוּא
He was her father's relative
(29:12)

רש"י: אֲנִי אָחִיו בְּרַמָּאוּת
Rashi: I am his brother in deceit

Q Effy sold Mordy a lot of merchandise that he claimed was of superior quality, manufactured in Italy. Afterward, Mordy discovered that without a doubt, Effy had sold him inferior-quality merchandise from China. The difference in the value of the merchandise totaled a few hundred dollars, but Effy would not reimburse Mordy.

---

79. *Choshen Mishpat* 232:6.
80. Editor's Note: An additional option might be to give Moshe *chamishi*, and extend his *aliyah* to include the material blessings as well. Shloimie's *shishi* would then start a few *pesukim* later.

PARASHAS TOLDOS / 73

With no other alternative, Mordy devised a scheme to retrieve his money from Effy.

Mordy waited for some time to pass, and then Mordy called Effy and told him about an investment that could not be passed up. Mordy claimed that he had already transferred his money to the agent involved and advised Effy to do the same. Effy believed Mordy and transferred several hundred dollars to the agent's account. The account actually belonged to Mordy. Was it permissible for Mordy to recover his money from Effy in such an underhanded way?

There are several sources in *Shas*[81] that imply that one may, under certain circumstances, use subterfuge to recover his money, if that is his only recourse.

However, these sources discuss cases of people who are trying to recover their own property or assets borrowed from them. We have yet to see that one is allowed to take different property to replace that which has been stolen from him. The *Mordechai*[82] indeed makes this distinction between recovering one's own property or taking something else instead, and would forbid Mordy's devious attempt to recoup his loss.

When this question was posed to Rav Elyashiv, the Rav refused to countenance such behavior.

---

81. *Gittin* 14a, *Yoma* 83b.
82. *Bava Kamma* 3:30.

פרשת ויצא
Parashas Vayeitzei

Where There's a Will...

כִּי אֲחִי אָבִיהָ הוּא
That he was her father's relative
(29:12)

Aharon Levy was an elderly gentleman who lived with his wife in a two-story home. Their house was in desperate need of painting, so Aharon searched for a painter in the community phone directory and hired him for the job.

Already on the first day, Aharon noticed that items were missing from his house, and when he started monitoring the painter's activities, he noticed him opening drawers and closets in order to see what he could find. Immediately, Aharon and his wife transferred all their remaining valuables to a neighbor for safekeeping, and Aharon racked his brain, trying to think how he could somehow recover his losses from the painter without confronting him. The painter gave the impression of being a strong-armed ruffian, and Aharon knew that there was no point in trying the direct approach.

Suddenly, Aharon had an idea. His front yard had a patio floored with old, broken tiles. For a long time, Aharon had planned to hire workers to rip up the old tiles and replace them with new ones. Now he had a plan that would at least save him the expense of having to remove those tiles.

Aharon wrote a "Last Will" to his dear children. In the will, he informed his children that in addition to the house and the money in a savings account, he was also leaving them a large chest of gold coins buried underneath the old tiles in the yard. Aharon left the document, which was written in large letters, on the desk located in the last room that the painter was supposed to paint.

The day after the painter left, Aharon left his house early in the morning and found that every last tile had been dug up in the middle of the night. "Someone" had decided to look for buried treasure, and had skillfully and silently cleared Aharon's yard to prepare it for new tiling.

Now Aharon's conscience is niggling at him for having acted with such cunning. He feels that he tricked the painter into working hard for nothing, and that he was responsible for the painter's attempt to steal from him. Was Aharon justified in what he did?

A The *Ri'az*[83] writes that if a strong-armed person is taking advantage of his friend, his friend is allowed to act with guile in order to save himself, as it is written, וְעִם עִקֵּשׁ תִּתַּפָּל — *with the corrupt You act perversely*.[84] The *Ri'az* cites the Gemara in *Megillah*[85] on the verse in which Yaakov Avinu informs Rachel that he is her father's brother. The Gemara asks, was Yaakov his brother or his nephew? The Gemara concludes that Yaakov pointed out to Rachel that he was her father's equal in deception,

---
83. *Berachos* 1:2 §6.
84. *II Shmuel* 22:27.
85. 13b.

and Lavan would not be successful in preventing their marriage. Rachel questioned whether a righteous person was allowed to act deceptively, and Yaakov responded that one is allowed to deceive those who seek to deceive him.

In Aharon's case as well, he was allowed to treat the dishonest worker in kind in order to recoup his losses, as he had no other way to do so. He never lied to the painter, who had no business reading the false document in the first place. If the painter had been an honest person, it would be forbidden for Aharon to engage in such behavior, as it would be a violation of the mitzvah to love your brother as you love yourself.[86]

It should be noted that the painter is not even allowed to charge for his services in removing the tiles (even if he had not stolen from Aharon), because one must pay for an improvement to his field only if the worker intended to improve the field for the owner's benefit.[87] If the worker dug up the field driven by his own selfish motives, there is no obligation to pay him for the coincidental benefit.

How Much Is It Worth?

אָסַף אֱלֹקִים אֶת חֶרְפָּתִי
God has taken away my disgrace
(30:23)

Henny was in deep trouble. Her husband had bought her an expensive necklace just a few weeks earlier and she simply could not find it. She felt that she had to tell

---

86. *Vayikra* 19:18.
87. See *Bava Metzia* 101a.

her husband, and when she did so on Erev Shabbos, he overreacted. To his discredit, he did not have anything nice to say to her, as he was too busy saying other things instead. There was a definite possibility that the atmosphere on Shabbos would be miserable.

Ephraim, at 18, was the oldest child. He sized up the situation and took quick action. He hurried to the jewelry store and bought the same necklace that his father had bought for his mother, and he left it where his mother would find it. Fifteen minutes later Henny ecstatically announced that she had found the necklace. Her husband apologized for suspecting her of being irresponsible and other such adjectives, and peace and harmony were restored.

Ephraim borrowed the money to buy the necklace, and he could not afford to pay it back. Is he allowed to take his father's money — without his father's permission — to repay the loan, since he bought it for his father's benefit, or would that be considered stealing?

A Especially on Erev Shabbos, *shalom bayis* is an imperative. The *Mishnah Berurah*[88] writes: The *Zohar* and the Kabbalists warn sternly that there should be no conflict on Shabbos, *chas v'shalom*, especially between husband and wife.[89]

The *Shelah* writes: The *pasuk,* "You shall not kindle fire in any of your dwellings on the Shabbos day," [90] alludes to the fire of *machlokes* and anger. A person always has to be exceedingly careful to avoid discord, all the more so on *Shabbos Kodesh* when the fires of Gehinnom are not burning. One who becomes angry or instigates strife causes the heat of Gehinnom to burn within himself.

---

88. 262 §9.
89. See *Gittin* 52a.
90. *Shemos* 35:3.

The *Chida*[91] warns that Erev Shabbos is a time of danger for confrontation between husband and wife, when the *Satan* works very hard to create a rift between them. One who is careful should control himself and not allow any argument or friction; on the contrary, he should seek harmony. Rabbi Chaim Palagi[92] humbly adds that he himself has seen that any home that saw strife late on Erev Shabbos or on Shabbos night was headed for evil, and they did not get through the coming week without seeing the repercussions of their lapse in harmony. This being so, Ephraim spent the money for his father's benefit, albeit not directly.

Perhaps one could suggest that Ephraim's father must pay for the necklace, since Ephraim spent the money on his father's behalf in order to restore *shalom bayis*.

In addition, the *Shulchan Aruch*[93] states that if Reuven sees Shimon is about to hit Levi, it is permissible for Reuven to hit Shimon to prevent him from sinning. May Ephraim "hit" his father's wallet in order to prevent him from stumbling in the area of strife, hatred, and other associated sins?

That said, it is still far from clear that Ephraim may take his father's money without permission. In *Bava Metzia*[94] it is written that if one deposited fruit with his friend for safekeeping and the fruits began to spoil, the one watching the fruit should allow them to spoil. Rabban Shimon ben Gamliel said that he should sell the fruit with *beis din*'s approval, because doing so is tantamount to returning his friend's lost item.

It is apparent that even though it is a mitzvah to save his friend from losing his fruits, and it is appropriate to sell them, one does not have the authority to do so on his own. In this case, too, Ephraim must receive permission from *beis din*.

Ephraim should go to *beis din*, and *beis din* should investigate the case and decide whether to allow him to take his father's money.

---

91. In his *sefer Moreh Be'etzba* 40.
92. In his *sefer Kaf HaChaim* 26 §35.
93. *Choshen Mishpat* 421:3.
94. 38a.

All the reasons mentioned permitting Ephraim to take his father's money to pay for the necklace are applicable only if there was no other way to save his father's *shalom bayis*. Since in reality there were other ways to restore harmony (e.g., asking someone to explain that his *shalom bayis* is worth much more than the necklace!), he may not steal from his father. The best thing for Ephraim to do now is to "borrow" from his father to repay the loan, and afterward reimburse him.

Parashas Vayishlach

Broken Telephone

וַיִּקֶן אֶת חֶלְקַת הַשָּׂדֶה
And he bought the parcel of land
(33:19)

Q Yosef walked into Avi's real-estate office and apprised Avi that he was interested in buying a four-bedroom house in the area. He was willing to spend up to $400,000. Avi flipped through his card catalog until he located just the right house. It was a beautiful, spacious ranch house with four bedrooms, and it was going for exactly $400,000. Yosef went to see the house and decided that he wanted to buy it. Avi informed Yosef that the seller wanted Avi to handle the finances, so all checks would be made out to the real-estate office. When Yosef met the seller face to face, he discovered that the seller had only asked for $350,000, and that was what Avi had given him. The extra $50,000 had remained in Avi's sticky hands.

Yosef and the seller stormed into Avi's office, claiming that he had stolen their money and that he had no right to profit from someone else's merchandise. Avi maintained his innocence. After all, Yosef had agreed to pay up to $400,000 for the house, and the seller had agreed to sell for $350,000. Isn't Avi entitled to make a living? The three arrived for a *din Torah* to decide who should get the $50,000: Yosef, Avi, or the seller.

The *Tur*[95] records a response from his father, the *Rosh*: Reuven gave an item to a broker to sell for "four" and the broker sold it for "six." Who keeps the extra money? The *Rosh paskened* that the extra money belongs to Reuven, as he never sold the item to the broker. The broker was merely Reuven's agent to sell the item. Therefore, any revenue that the item generated belongs to Reuven, as the buyer intended to pay the purchase price to the owner of the item. Reuven was willing to sell the item for a lower price only because that was how much he thought he could get for it. Even if Reuven knew that he was selling the item for less than its worth and agreed to do so because he was under pressure to raise funds, he never intended to let the broker keep any additional money. The broker is merely to be commended for fulfilling his task faithfully.

Our question is the exact question that was posed to the *Rosh*! This is the ruling of the *Shulchan Aruch*,[96] as well.

Similarly, the Gemara in *Bava Metzia*[97] discusses a case of a homeowner who sent a messenger to hire workers for a wage of four coins. The messenger hired workers, but he told them that the employer was willing to pay only three coins. The Gemara says that the homeowner has to pay only three coins, and such is the ruling in *Shulchan Aruch*.[98] The *Shach* writes that the additional coin does not belong to the messenger, but remains the property of the homeowner. Rabbi Akiva Eiger explains that the workers'

---

95. *Choshen Mishpat* 185.
96. Ibid., 195:2.
97. 76a.
98. 332:3.

agreement to work for three coins is tantamount to giving the employer a gift.

The question remains why the workers should lose out. If the employer was willing to pay four coins, why shouldn't the workers benefit from the original offer? In the case of the *Rosh* as well, since the seller was willing to sell the product for four, why shouldn't the buyer benefit from the lower price, and get a rebate of two?

A broker works on behalf of the seller; i.e., the homeowner. Therefore, any profit that the agent generates is produced on behalf of the one who sent him. Hence, the homeowner who secured the successful agent deserves all the profit.

Accordingly, in this case, where the broker was the agent who was working for both the buyer and the seller, the profit should be divided between them, and the price of the house should be set at $375,000.

Time Is of the Essence

וַיִּקֶן אֶת חֶלְקַת הַשָּׂדֶה
And he bought the parcel of land
(33:19)

Q Five businessmen decided to pool their assets to place a bid on a tract of land that was being auctioned. The bids were to be accompanied by a bank check that was to be delivered to the Davidson law firm by 12 p.m. on Wednesday afternoon. The check would be made out for a certain percentage of the bid, and whoever submitted the highest bid would win the right to buy the land.

The five partners worked very hard to raise the $1.3 million, and finally reached that sum by 10 a.m. on Wednesday. One of the partners, Tzvi Fischer, who had a background in law, was chosen to deposit their checks in the bank and procure a bank check in their stead. At that point, he would go to the law firm to submit the bid.

Tzvi carried out his job with diligence. He had the bank check in his pocket and was in transit to the law firm, when his cell phone rang. It was the bank. They apologized, and explained that the check had been written for the wrong amount. Instead of $1.3 million, they had written it for $1,300,200, and therefore the check could not be cashed. They promised to prepare a new check for him that would be ready by the time he returned to the bank. Tzvi had no choice but to return to the bank. He collected the new check within seconds, and rushed off to the law office, but by the time he arrived it was already 12:10 p.m. He had missed the deadline.

Now the four partners are asking him to pay damages. They think that he was negligent for not ascertaining that the check was written properly before leaving the bank. The only reason he was chosen to be their agent was because he had experience with such dealings. A million-dollar check is a serious matter, and he should have scrutinized it before putting it into his pocket. The mistake was so glaring that he could not possibly have missed it.

They are demanding compensation for all the losses involved in raising such a large sum of money in such a short period of time. In addition, since their bid would have been the highest, they could have anticipated a profit of $750,000, and they feel that he should pay them a portion of the expected revenue that they lost because he did not submit their bid on time. Do they have the right to demand this of him?

A The Gemara in *Bava Metzia*[99] states that if someone gave his friend money to buy wine on sale, and the messenger was negligent in fulfilling his task and the wine is no longer available at that price, the messenger must compensate the sender for the price difference he now has to pay.

The *Shitah Mekubetzes* quotes the *Ritva*, who points out that the messenger's negligence did not cause any direct damage. Why should he have to pay, as the halachah is that one is not liable for indirect damage (*grama*)? The *Ritva* cites that his rebbi ruled that since the messenger was entrusted with the money, and the one who sent him relied on the messenger's promise to buy the wine, the messenger must pay for any losses that resulted from the promise. The fact that someone placed his trust in him gives the messenger pleasure, in return for which he is willing to accept financial liability, similar to one who is guarantor on a loan. In return for the trust that the lender expresses in the guarantor, the guarantor in kind obligates himself to insure against any losses that may be incurred in the course of the loan.

The *Nesivos HaMishpat*[100] rules like the *Ritva* and applies it to a case of partners as well, such that each bears responsibility for lost profits because each one trusted the other to act responsibly. In this case as well, it would seem that Tzvi should have to pay for his error.

However, in reality, they were *all* negligent for not having had the money in on time. One does not make a million-dollar deal at the last minute. Had the money been ready even one day earlier, there would not have been as much pressure on the messenger, and he would have had the peace of mind to catch the error on

---

99. 73b.
100. 7176 §31.

the check. Although Tzvi was negligent at the end, they were negligent from the outset; therefore, he cannot be blamed, as they are all guilty.

Most importantly, they did not have Divine assistance to close the deal, because in Heaven, the property was not listed under their name.

פרשת וישב
Parashas Vayeishev

Yagati U'matzasi!

בֶּן זְקֻנִים
A child of his old age
(37:3)

תרגום: בַּר חַכּוּם
Targum: Wise son

Q In honor of Chanukah, the *cheder* scheduled an early dismissal. Rabbi Framer wanted the boys in his class to make good use of their free time, so he would pose riddles to the boys to figure out at home, and he promised a prize to whoever produced the correct answer.

One day, Rabbi Framer told his class that he had a very hard riddle for them, and therefore the prize would be a valuable one. The question was: What do *Parashas Vayeishev* and *Megillas Rus* have in common? Rabbi Framer added that he was not referring to the fact that both of them discuss the ancestry of Mashiach (Peretz from Yehudah, and David HaMelech from Boaz), because that answer would be too simple.

The next day, David Schramm ran to *cheder*, grinning from ear to ear. He had found the answer to the riddle! In both *Parashas Vayeishev* and *Megillas Rus*, all of the *pesukim* begin with the letter *vav*, with the exception of eight *pesukim* each. (This is explicitly stated in the *Midrash Lekach Tov* in the end of *Parashas Vayeishev*, as well as in the *Midrash Zuta* on *Rus*.)

Rabbi Framer congratulated David on his clever answer. David proudly told the class that he had gotten the answer from his father. Just then, Yitzi Sharp burst out crying. The rebbi asked Yitzi why he was crying. Yitzi replied between sobs that he also knew the answer to the riddle. However, he had looked through the *parashah* and had found that there were actually **nine** *pesukim* that did not start with a *vav*! (There is actually an opinion that one of the *pesukim* starts with a *vav*, but it does not appear in our *Chumashim*.)

Now the question is, does Yitzi also deserve the prize, since he actually knew the answer, and only remained silent because he had every reason to believe that it was not correct, or, since he didn't give the answer, does he not deserve a prize?

A The point of the riddle was to encourage the boys to work hard to find the answer. Therefore, if anyone deserves the prize, it is Yitzi. All David did was ask his father and repeat his father's answer in class. Although David surely deserves a prize, it should be commensurate with his effort. Yitzi, on the other hand, who actually tried to verify the accuracy of the answer, deserves a bigger prize.

Responsa Rav Pe'alim[101] records the following incident: Reuven posed a riddle to Shimon and promised him a gold coin if he could solve it. Shimon realized that he could not figure out the answer,

---

101. Vol. 4, *Choshen Mishpat siman* 5.

so he secretly visited a very wise *Chacham* and told him the entire story. The *Chacham* provided Shimon with the answer, and he gleefully went off to collect the prize. The question is, did the *Chacham* do anything wrong by providing the answer and causing Reuven to pay the gold coin, since Reuven thought that Shimon had produced the answer by himself?

The *Rav Pe'alim* responded that initially, he thought that this story was comparable to that which is related in the *Midrash*.[102] A visitor once entered a classroom full of children, only to find that the rebbi was not present. The man posed riddles to the children, and the children answered him. The children challenged the man that whoever would ask a riddle that the other could not answer would receive the other's clothing as a prize, and the man agreed. The children asked him a perplexing riddle that the man could not answer. He had no choice but to forfeit his clothes! The man stomped off to find their rebbi, Rabbi Yochanan, and complained that the children wished to appropriate his clothes. Rabbi Yochanan inquired whether the children had posed him a question that he could not answer. The man affirmed that they had. Rabbi Yochanan supplied the man with the answer, and the man went to reclaim his garments. The children understood that their rebbi had provided the man with the answer, and they cited the words of Shimshon: "Had you not 'plowed with my calf,' you would not have solved my riddle."[103]

The *Rav Pe'alim* inferred from this story that the *Chacham* did nothing wrong by supplying the answer.[104]

However, it is certainly clear from his question that one who toils to find the answer himself is more deserving of the prize than someone who merely heard the answer from someone else.[105]

---

102. *Eichah Rabbah* 1:14.
103. *Shoftim* 14:18.
104. See *Rav Pe'alim* for further discussion and his final decision.
105. See *What If*, Vol. 1, "Easy as Pi." p. 79.

פרשת מקץ
Parashas Mikeitz

A Day in the Fruit Store

וְיוֹסֵף הוּא הַשַּׁלִּיט ... הוּא הַמַּשְׁבִּיר
Now Yosef — he was the viceroy ... he was the provider
(42:6)

Q Yanky walked into a small vegetable store to buy some produce. The shelves were well stocked, but the owner was nowhere to be seen in the vicinity. It became apparent that he had to rush to the hospital and did not have time to lock the store. Is Yanky allowed to stand behind the counter and sell the man's produce for him until he returns?

A If Yanky would like to do the man a favor, it would certainly seem that the man would want someone to sell his produce before it spoils. Even though the Gemara in *Bava Metzia*[106] says that when one gives his friend fruit for safekeeping, the friend may not sell the fruit even if it has started

---
106. 38a.

rotting, this case is different. When someone gives his friend fruit, he has no one to blame but himself if the fruit spoils. In our case, the owner wants to sell his produce, but cannot because he was forced to go to the hospital. In such circumstances, it makes sense that one may sell the fruit on his behalf.

Another reason to permit selling the man's fruit is based on the Gemara in *Mo'ed Kattan*.[107] Reish Lakish was guarding a grove when a man came along and started eating from the trees. Reish Lakish raised his voice at the man, but the latter simply ignored him. Reish Lakish put the man in *cherem*. The man responded by placing Reish Lakish in *cherem*, because he felt that Reish Lakish had wrongly ostracized him. All he owed for the fruit was money, and he did not deserve to be ostracized. When Reish Lakish related the story in the *beis midrash*, they agreed that the *cherem* Reish Lakish had imposed was not valid, while the other man's *cherem* was. They told Reish Lakish to find the man so the *cherem* could be removed.

The *Nimukei Yosef* asks why Reish Lakish was wrong in imposing a *cherem* on a man who had stolen. One could impose a *cherem* for a Rabbinic prohibition; is stealing any less than that? The *Nimukei Yosef* quoted the *Ra'avad*, who answers that Reish Lakish had erred by not warning the man not to eat. Perhaps the man thought that the fruits were for sale and intended to pay. In such a case there is no prohibition against eating, and a *cherem* would be undeserved.

Thus, when something is offered for sale, one is allowed to eat first and pay later. The *Shulchan Aruch*[108] rules that one may not steal even if he intends to pay back superior items. There is an opinion that if the payment is available, the one eating may ask someone to acquire the payment now for the owner, and he would then be allowed to switch items with him, since he is offering something superior. The *Shach* stipulates that it has to be clear

---

107. 9a.
108. *Choshen Mishpat* 359:2.

that this is for the owner's benefit; i.e., items that were offered for sale as opposed to personal items.[109]

In conclusion, items that are meant to be sold may be taken on condition that one pay for them, and certainly one could sell them on behalf of the owner, in order to save the produce before it spoils.

Read the Fine Print

אָנֹכִי אֶעֶרְבֶנּוּ
I will personally guarantee him
(43:9)

Q Yaakov had to marry off his eldest daughter, but he did not have a penny to his name. He approached his friend Binyamin, a well-to-do businessman, and poured out his troubled heart. Yaakov had calculated that he needed $20,000 just to cover the most basic expenses, and beseeched Binyamin to lend him this sum. Binyamin had known Yaakov for years and truly believed that Yaakov meant well. He also knew that if he lent Yaakov the money, the loan would never be repaid, despite his good intentions. On the other hand, he could not ignore Yaakov's pleas in his hour of need and ruin their friendship. Binyamin gently told Yaakov that he was willing to lend him the entire sum if Yaakov would provide a guarantor who had the means to repay the outstanding

---

109. See *What If*, Vol. 1, "Pure Profit," page 31.

loan. In addition, it had to be someone Binyamin knew — someone who would agree to be an *arev kablan*.[110]

Yaakov joyfully went directly to speak to Yehudah and asked him to sign a contract to guarantee the loan. Yehudah was also familiar with Yaakov's financial capability and did not want to sign the document, but Yaakov persisted to the point that Yehudah could not refuse, and Yehudah wrote out a contract to guarantee the loan.

As expected, Yaakov did not repay the loan. Binyamin approached Yehudah and asked him to honor his obligation. Yehudah asked Binyamin if he had the contract of guarantee, and when he answered in the affirmative, Yehudah requested that they read the contract together, carefully. They read the contract until the words, "… and I accept upon myself to be an *arev kabtzan*"! (A *kabtzan* is a poor man who collects donations. In Hebrew the words are almost identical, with the exception of a single letter.) An irate Binyamin shouted that it was obviously a spelling mistake! Yehudah insisted that there was no mistake. He had intentionally written a meaningless contract, as he couldn't refuse Yaakov, and he had been sure that Binyamin would read through the meaningless document, notice the relevant word, and withhold the loan. Now that Binyamin had not done so, he has no one to blame but himself. Is Yehudah justified in his claim?

A One could argue that Yehudah must pay, because the principle that obligates a guarantor to pay is the fact that the loan was given based on the lender trusting the guarantor. That factor was certainly present in this loan, as well. If Yehudah did not intend to guarantee the loan, he should have said

---

110. This means that Binyamin could collect the loan directly from the guarantor if he wished to, without having to approach Yaakov first.

so explicitly, instead of misleading Binyamin to believe that he was actually backing the loan. Since Yehudah caused Binyamin to lose money, he should have to pay, if for no other reason than *garmi*.[111]

On the other hand, Yehudah was being pressured by Yaakov and had no other way to release himself from Yaakov's pleadings than to resort to the tactic of the meaningless contract. The Gemara in *Bava Basra*[112] records the incident of landowners who were trying to protect their land by writing contracts against the halachah. Abaye refused to write such contracts for them. The landowners continued to pressure Abaye, until Abaye instructed his scribe to write the contract they wanted on parchment that had already been erased, effectively rendering the contract invalid.

In that case as well, Abaye misled the landowners into thinking that their interests were protected, which might have caused them losses. Nevertheless, Abaye acted in such a way because they were pressuring him to contradict halachah, and therefore they were responsible for their own losses.

This case is different, since Binyamin was not the one pressuring Yehudah; Yaakov was. Yehudah had no right to fool Binyamin and cause him to lose his money, just because he wanted Yaakov to leave him be.

Even so, it seems that Yehudah should not have to pay, as Binyamin should have read the contract carefully and noticed the intentional misspelling. Then he would have at least consulted with Yehudah and verified his true intent. Binyamin has no one to blame but himself. When one lends out large sums he must read the contract not once, but twice and three times, and examine every word. Alternatively, he could have shown the contract to a *dayan* to ask if the would-be contract was binding. As Binyamin did not do so, he is responsible for his own loss.

---

111. "*Garmi*" is damage directly caused by someone's actions, even if they did not actually inflict the damage.
112. 68b.

Magic

כִּי נַחֵשׁ יְנַחֵשׁ
Practices divination
(44:15)

Q Rabbi Avi Dressler was an energetic young Rav who had recently assumed the position of rabbi in an out-of-town community. Right at the outset, he received a visit from a couple who were seeking advice on how to improve their *shalom bayis*. The couple would begin to quarrel over seemingly trivial matters, but their voices inevitably grew louder until they found themselves mired in monumental disputes. They begged Rabbi Dressler to help them find peace with each other.

The rabbi had an inspiration. He told the couple that he would let them in on a secret. He possessed a small quantity of "holy water" that was known to work wonders for *shalom bayis*. He would happily give them a free bottle, but more importantly, he would instruct them on how to use the water to improve their marriage. The instructions were simple: Each time one of them wanted to raise his or her voice to criticize the other, he or she had to drink one cup of the water first — but only after the water had been boiled.

The rabbi had no intention of presenting himself as a kabbalist or a miracle worker. He merely discerned that the husband and wife were a little too impatient with each other, and if they would allow themselves the time to calm down, they could avoid unleashing their tempers, which until now, had not been reined in.

This idea has a source in *Chazal*,[113] who enacted the "*get mekushar*" for Kohanim who wished to divorce their wives. *Chazal* understood that Kohanim are naturally quick tempered, and since a Kohen is not allowed to marry a divorcee, he would not be able to remarry his wife after his temper subsided. Therefore, *Chazal* instituted a halachah that a Kohen may only give a *get mekushar*, which requires lengthy preparations, within which time the Kohen could reconsider a hasty and unsound decision.

Similarly, the Alter from Kelm had a special suit made for occasions when he felt he would become angry. He took upon himself that he would not allow himself to get angry until he had changed into that suit. The time it would take for him to change his clothing would allow his anger to dissipate and he would avoid getting angry in the first place.

Rabbi Dressler's "magical" potion actually worked! A month later, the couple returned and joyfully reported that their marriage had remarkably improved; they argued much less frequently due to the "holy water." They begged him for a refill. The rabbi was only too happy to oblige, and gave them another complimentary bottle (that he refilled from his sink!).

He actually used this trick with a few couples, who all reported that the "holy water" had improved their *shalom bayis*. Word spread, and before long Rabbi Dressler became known as a miracle worker.

Now the rabbi was faced with a dilemma. On the one hand, his "holy water" had restored peace and harmony to so many Jewish homes. On the other hand, the *Yerushalmi*[114] teaches that if someone learned one

---

113. *Bava Basra* 160a.
114. *Shevi'is* 10:3.

mesechta of Gemara and people honor him for knowing two *mesechtos* of Gemara, he must confess that he only knows one *mesechta*. Responsa *Chaim She'al*[115] explains that the reason for this halachah is that it is improper for him to undeservedly benefit from the honor of the Torah. Must Rabbi Dressler confess to those who consider him to be a kabbalist that he really does not know anything about Kabbalah, and that his water is not really holy?

The *Shulchan Aruch*[116] states that it is forbidden to mislead people in a way that they will think more highly of someone than he actually deserves. In this case Rabbi Dressler, by dispensing a "magical" potion for *shalom bayis,* certainly led people to believe that he was actually more "holy" than he really was. Is he in violation of *geneivas da'as*?

A In *Parashas Mikeitz*, Yosef refrained from revealing his true identity to his brothers, yet when he seated them at his table for a meal he arranged them according to their ages. *Rashi*[117] explains that Yosef would tap on his goblet as if it possessed special powers, and he announced, "Reuven, Shimon, Levi, Yehudah, Yissachar, and Zevulun are all from the same mother, and should sit in that order. Binyamin has no mother (as Rachel Imeinu had already died), and neither do I, so he should sit next to me!"

The brothers were astounded by Yosef's "mystical powers." Of course, Yosef had no intention of convincing his brothers that he was a necromancer. He merely wanted to arouse them to *teshuvah* and give them the opportunity to atone for having sold him as a slave. Even if his brothers would be misled that he had amazing powers, Yosef was still justified in behaving as he did.

---
115. Vol. 1, 71.
116. *Choshen Mishpat* 228:1.
117. *Bereishis* 43:33.

The prohibition of *geneivas da'as* is limited to doing or saying something for the purpose of giving a false impression. If one does something for a constructive purpose and, in the process, onlookers mistake his action and attribute undeserved honor to their benefactor, then that does not fall under the prohibition of *geneivas da'as*.

Similarly, in Rabbi Dressler's case, he had no intent to benefit from his reputation as a kabbalist. He is not seeking financial gain. He merely wants to restore *shalom bayis* to the lives of his congregants. There is no need to confess that he is distributing ordinary tap water. Hashem should help his water continue to work wonders!

פרשת ויגש
Parashas Vayigash

Occupational Hazards

וַיַּרְא אֶת הָעֲגָלוֹת
And he saw the wagons
(45:27)

Q Dov hailed a cab to take him downtown and notified the driver of the address of his destination. The driver turned on the meter and began to drive. Twenty minutes later, they were still about a half a mile from their destination, and traffic had come to a standstill. It seems that there was an accident ahead and only one lane was open. Dov knew that if he would get out and walk he would save both time and money, so he asked the driver to let him out. The driver claimed that he was only in this traffic jam because of Dov, and now he would have to waste his time getting out of it without being paid?! Is Dov allowed to disembark and just pay the meter until this point, or does he have to pay what it would have cost him to reach his destination?

A The Gemara in *Bava Metzia*[118] states that if one hired a boat for shipping and he unloaded his packages halfway into the trip, he has to pay for only half the shipping costs, and the boat owner only has a right of complaint. The Gemara wonders: If the boat owner can find another passenger at this point, why does he have the right to complain? If the owner of the boat cannot find another passenger, why shouldn't the shipper have to pay the full fare? The Gemara answers that although the boat could be hired by someone else, there is wear and tear on the boat from the additional loading and unloading. According to this Gemara, if the cab driver will not receive another fare while he is sitting in traffic, Dov should have to pay the entire fare.

In truth, there is a difference between the two cases. In the case of the boat, the one who hired the boat wants to unload halfway into the trip, for his own reasons. In our case, there are external factors that are preventing him from completing his trip. The *Shulchan Aruch*[119] described the following scenario: Someone hired a donkey for two days for the purpose of traveling to a specific destination, and on the return trip, the river overflowed its banks and detained his return for an extra day. If the rental was per day, then he has to pay for three days. If he rented it for the trip, or the owner knew where he was traveling, and he knew that sometimes the river overflowed, the renter does not have to pay for the extra day. The *S'ma*[120] explains that the rule is that any expected circumstance is the liability of the owner, since he is the one who has to solicit money from the renter, and he should have stipulated specific terms.

The *Nesivos HaMishpat*[121] explains the difference between whether the rental was per day or if was according to the destination: If he rented the animal per day, he could use the animal for any purpose he desires during that time and therefore he has to pay for that. If, however, he agreed to go to a specific place, he is not allowed

---

118. 79a.
119. *Choshen Mishpat* 310:3.
120. §12.
121. §8.

to use the animal for other purposes. Therefore, if he cannot reach his destination, he should not have to pay for the extra time.

Our case is similar to hiring by the location. The driver may claim that he was hired for a specific destination and does not want to travel elsewhere. The traffic jam is something that could be anticipated, and the driver should have stipulated in advance that he refused to allow Dov to leave in the event of traffic. If the driver did not do so, it is his loss.[122]

In addition, one who travels by taxi is interested in arriving at his destination without delay. If he can reach his destination faster by walking, it is as if he stipulated that in case of traffic, he may choose to walk, and he does not have to pay for the portion of the trip that he did not travel in the taxi.

In summary, Dov is allowed to leave, and does not have to pay the driver for the time he will have to waste sitting in traffic. If, however, there is a custom that the passenger does have to pay the fare until the destination, the custom would prevail.

Whose Wedding Is This, Anyway?

וְחֻפִּים
And Chuppim
(46:21)

Q Yehudah is a *chassan* who does not have a penny to his name. When he became engaged, his mother's brother, Uncle Shmuel, promised Yehudah that he would cover

---

122. If, however, Dov stays in the cab, he has to pay because he is gaining an advantage that as soon as traffic allows, he can immediately continue traveling. See *Nesivos HaMishpat* §9.

all the wedding expenses. As the wedding date approached, Uncle Shmuel called Yehudah and made it clear that he would fulfill his promise only if Yehudah would not invite his father to the wedding. Yehudah's parents had been divorced and his father had treated his wife terribly before the divorce. It would cause Uncle Shmuel and his sister, Yehudah's mother, much pain if Yehudah's father attends the wedding, and Uncle Shmuel insists that he will not pay for anything if that is the case. What should Yehudah do?

A The Gemara[123] cites Dama ben Nesina as the epitome of one who honors his father, because he refused to wake up his father, despite sacrificing a very profitable business offer. The *Beis Yosef*[124] points out that the halachah states that a son only has to provide for his father at his father's expense. The son does not have to pay for his father's needs from his own pocket. If so, why wouldn't it be permitted to wake up his father in order to avoid suffering such a substantial business loss? He quotes the *Ran*[125] who asks this question, and gives two answers: A son does not have to spend his own money on his father's honor, but would have to lose all the money in the world in order not to cause his father pain. An alternate explanation is that a son does not have to spend his own money, but he would have to sacrifice a potential profit.

In our case, according to both criteria, Yehudah would have to invite his father. If he does not invite him, he will be causing his father great pain. In addition, he is not losing anything by inviting him; he is merely sacrificing his uncle's gift in order to honor his father.

On the other hand, it may well be that Yehudah does not have to invite his father. Although he is forbidden to cause pain to his

---

123. *Avodah Zarah* 23b.
124. *Yoreh De'ah* 240.
125. *Kiddushin* 13 (in the pages of the *Rif*).

father, and not inviting his father is certainly painful, inviting his father would be causing pain to his uncle, who is willing to pay for the wedding hall, the caterer, the band, the flowers, etc. His uncle still feels his sister's pain very acutely, and he certainly has no obligation to invite Yehudah's father, when that would cause him to leave the wedding that he paid for! If so, it is not Yehudah who is not inviting his father, but his uncle, who happens to be paying for the entire affair.

In addition, if Yehudah's father indeed mistreated his ex-wife, then he has brought this problem upon himself, and perhaps even Yehudah would not be required to invite him. The father is merely reaping the fruits of his behavior. וצ״ע.[126]

A Likely Story

וַיְלַקֵּט יוֹסֵף אֶת כָּל הַכֶּסֶף
And Yosef gathered all the money
(47:14)

Q Shlomo, the *gabbai* of the K'nesses Yaakov shul, was listening intently to the final *Kaddish* after Maariv one Motza'ei Shabbos. He noticed Calev standing next to him; he was obviously waiting to ask Shlomo something. As soon as the minyan ended, Calev wished Shlomo a *gut voch* and laid his request before him.

Calev had *davened* Minchah on Erev Shabbos with the minyan that started 20 minutes before sunset. Just

---

126. Editor's Note: I heard that Rav Zilberstein agreed that this last position is the correct one.

before Shabbos began, Calev was searching his suit for a tissue, at which point he felt a bulge in his pocket. He realized that he had forgotten to empty the cash from his suit, and he was holding $500, just minutes before Shabbos. He thought quickly: Where he could stash the money until after Shabbos? His eyes fell upon the donation slot in the wall. He quickly deposited his money into the slot for safekeeping, and now he wanted Shlomo to return his money to him.

Shlomo listened to the story, but he was not sure how to react. He asked Calev if he had any proof to support his claim, other then the fact that there was $500 in the donation box. Perhaps someone else had put the money into the slot, and Calev had merely witnessed someone else making a donation. Perhaps Calev had donated the money to the shul, and now he was having regrets. How could Shlomo possibly know what happened? Calev was taken aback. He realized now that he should have called over two witnesses to testify that he was merely putting the money there temporarily, but now he had no proof. Shlomo would like to believe Calev, but he has a responsibility to the shul, and he cannot surrender the shul's money to someone who cannot prove that it belongs to him. What should Shlomo do?

The Gemara in *Kesubos*[127] relates the following incident: A man handed seven pearls wrapped in a handkerchief to Rabbi Mysha for safekeeping. Unfortunately, Rabbi Mysha was *niftar* soon afterward, and he did not have the opportunity to relay instructions to his children before his death. The owner of the pearls and Rabbi Mysha's heirs approached Rabbi Ammi to decide what to do with the pearls, as the heirs had no knowledge that the pearls had been given to their father for safekeeping.

---

127. 85b.

Rabbi Ammi based his decision on three factors:

1. He knew that Rabbi Mysha was not wealthy, and therefore it was improbable that the pearls had belonged to him.
2. The man had accurately described the pearls and how they were stored, which would seem to be a clear indication that they belonged to him.
3. The final and decisive factor was whether or not the man frequented Rabbi Mysha's house. If he did, then it was quite possible that someone else had given Rabbi Mysha the pearls for safekeeping and the man had merely witnessed this taking place. In that case, his claim that the pearls belonged to him could not be upheld.

In Shlomo's case, it would seem that only two of these three conditions were met.

1. A shul does not usually receive such large cash donations, anonymously inserted into the donation slot.
2. Calev correctly identified the money by its amount and the denominations of the bills.

The third condition, however, was not met; Calev was a frequent visitor in the shul, and therefore it was possible that he had merely seen someone else putting the $500 into the slot. Therefore, Calev has no right to ask for the money.

Even if the Rav of the shul feels that Calev is telling the truth, according to halachah he may not return the money to him because Calev does not have any proof, and the *Shulchan Aruch* states that we cannot issue rulings based on impressions.

Nevertheless, the Rav still has the license to do with the money as he sees fit, as all donations to the shul are given with the understanding that they will be used at the Rav's discretion. Therefore, the solution would be to invite Calev to provide some service for the shul, for which he will be paid $500, since as it stands, he does not the right to have the money returned to him.

פרשת ויחי
Parashas Vayechi

Looks Can Kill

בֵּן פֹּרָת עֲלֵי עָיִן
A charming son to the eye
(49:22)

Hashem had granted Michel fabulous success in his business; Michel was doing exceptionally well. He had always loved fish, so he decided to invest in an aquarium to enhance his home. Michel filled the aquarium with very beautiful and exotic fish. Subsequent to his purchase, he decided that such an exhibit was too beautiful to keep all to himself, and he wanted to invite all of his friends to experience the wonders of Hashem's creation.

His wife was concerned that displaying the expensive fish to the public might cause the fish to die due to *ayin hara*.[128] Michel assured her that the *pasuk*[129] explic-

---

128. The Gemara states a precedent for *ayin hara* affecting animals; *Shabbos* 53a prohibits leading a horse in the public domain on Shabbos when one has placed a fox's tail between its eyes. The tail's function is to prevent *ayin hara*.
129. *Bereishis* 48:16.

106 / SEFER BEREISHIS

itly qualifies that *ayin hara* does not affect fish, as Yaakov Avinu blessed Yosef's children that they should multiply like fish. The Gemara[130] explains Yaakov Avinu's metaphor to mean that just as fish in the sea are not subject to *ayin hara*, Yosef's children should not be affected by *ayin hara*.

Michel's wife countered that perhaps the Gemara is only referring to fish in the sea, which are underwater and therefore go unnoticed. Isn't it possible that the blessing doesn't include fish on display in an aquarium?

Michel and his wife wish to determine if they should be concerned about *ayin hara*.

The *Toras Chaim*[131] quotes this Gemara, which seems to say that fish are removed from *ayin hara* because they are hidden by the water. He points out that this would appear to be difficult to understand, as fish often swim close to the water's surface and are clearly visible from above. Accordingly, why would fish not be subject to *ayin hara*?

The *Toras Chaim* explains that *ayin hara* is the function of a damaging spark coming out of a person's eyes that has a negative influence and damages the object viewed by the *ayin hara*. If there is interference between the object and the person's eye, then the *ayin hara* cannot reach or affect the article, even if it is seen. Hence fish, although visible, are covered with water and are not subject to *ayin hara*.

According to the *Toras Chaim*, it would seem that Michel's aquarium is safe from *ayin hara*.[132] However, Michel should be concerned about *ayin hara* from a different aspect: People may be so impressed by Michel's acquisition that they may cast an *ayin hara* on Michel's wealth!

---

130. *Berachos* 20a.
131. *Bava Metzia* 84a.
132. See *Shem MiShmuel, Mishpatim* 675.

PARASHAS VAYECHI / 107

The Gemara in *Eruvin*[133] states that if a person becomes very wealthy without having exerted himself — e.g., by receiving an inheritance or by having discovered a treasure — his assets are in jeopardy of being lost due to *ayin hara*. The Gemara advises protecting his assets by using a portion of the money for a mitzvah. For example, he should buy a *Sefer Torah* or *tefillin*, and in that merit his wealth will be sustained.

Therefore, instead of Michel decorating his home with an aquarium, he would have been better off investing his money in a beautiful *Sefer Torah*. If that expense is too great for him, then he should purchase a library of attractive *sefarim* that will beautify Michel himself, as well as his home.

Attendance Mandatory

וַיַּעַל עִמּוֹ גַּם רֶכֶב ...
And he brought up with him both chariots ...
(50:9)

Q Dr. Frank lives in a quiet community in Northern *Eretz Yisrael*. He works in a hospital in Tel Aviv and has ample opportunities to offer his neighbors rides in his car on his way to work.

One afternoon, as he was about to leave the neighborhood on his way to work, he noticed two men standing at the side of the road, apparently waiting to hitch a ride. Dr. Frank had only one space left in the car and told the men that he could take only one of them.

---

133. 64a.

Peretz, the taller of the two, explained that his only brother's wedding would take place that evening, and it was very important to him to be there. The *chassan* would also be very upset if his brother missed his wedding. Peretz explained that he could not afford to wait for the bus, as the next bus was only scheduled to leave in another hour, and since it had so many stops on the way, he would arrive at the hall after the wedding was over.

Levi, the other would-be traveler, claimed that he was really in a hurry to get to Tel Aviv. Unfortunately, his brother had passed away a few hours earlier, and Levi had to attend the funeral. He could not imagine missing the funeral of his brother with whom he had shared so much of his life.

Dr. Frank was speechless. He could not decide which man had priority to reach his desired destination, and which one would have to forgo attending an event that was so important to him. Which man should he take?

The Gemara[134] teaches that if a *kallah* and a *niftar* arrive at an intersection at the same time, the *kallah* is to be given the right of passing first. The Ramban explains that a *kallah* takes precedence to a *niftar* in all instances, whether it be right of passage, to take care of her needs, or to support her from communal funds.

The rationale behind this privilege is that a *kallah's* needs are to honor the living, while honoring a *niftar* is honoring the dead. Accordingly, it would seem that the brother who wants to attend the wedding should take priority over the brother who wishes to attend the funeral.

However, the comparison is not necessarily accurate. If Dr. Frank would be transporting the actual *chassan* or *kallah*, he or she would certainly have priority. In this case, the *chassan* is already

---
134. *Kesubos* 17a.

present at his *chasunah*. The issue is whether his brother will be in attendance at his wedding or not. In that case, it would seem that Levi, who wishes to attend his brother's funeral, deserves to travel with the doctor, for three reasons:

1. Although it is very important to attend the wedding of a sibling, and Binyamin the son of Yakov Avinu actually named two of his children to commemorate the fact that he and his brother Yosef did not attend each other's *chuppah*,[135] it is not a mitzvah for a brother to be in attendance. On the other hand, if someone passes away, his brother becomes an *onen*,[136] who is exempt from fulfilling positive mitzvos, as he now carries an obligation to bury the deceased. Even a Kohen who must otherwise safeguard his *kedushah* is obligated to attend his brother's funeral. The *Rambam*[137] derives from this halachah the importance of the mitzvah of mourning for a deceased relative.

2. Escorting the *niftar* is the brother's personal mitzvah. The brother must sit *shivah*, and he exempts his minyan from saying *Tachanun* for the duration of the *shivah*. The brother of the *chassan*, although his joy is immense, does not share in the *chassan's* mitzvah (and does not have any exemption from *Tachanun*).

3. A *niftar* does not plan his moment of death in advance. Levi did not have the ability to plan his transportation in due time. Conversely, Peretz knew about his brother's wedding weeks, if not months, earlier. Why did he wait for the last minute to arrange transportation, as he did? One would suspect that he and his brother are not so close, after all.

   Peretz should step aside and allow Levi to accept the ride with the doctor.

---

135. See *Rashi, Bereishis* 43:29.
136. *Yoreh De'ah* 341.
137. *Hilchos Avel* 2:6.

Acidic Speech

אֱלֹקִים חֲשָׁבָהּ לְטֹבָה
God intended it for good
(50:20)

Yaakov owned the only wine shop in the small village of Pentov. He held an inventory of 100 barrels of fine wine. One day a visitor rode into town with a wagon loaded with 100 barrels of wine. He was interested in opening a business. The entire population of the city used fewer than 100 barrels a year, so it would be impossible for the city to support both merchants. Unfortunately, the visitor was not a paragon of faith in Hashem or of good *middos* and he decided to stoop to a lowly scheme.

He hired two townspeople to loiter in the town square and carry on a conversation where all passersby could hear them. The subject of their discussion would be, what a shame it was that 30 of Yaakov's barrels had turned to vinegar! The cunning plan worked and word spread quickly throughout the small town.

Two days later the men carried out a similarly staged conversation, except this time, it was 60 barrels that had spoiled. By the end of the week, they were overheard saying that Yaakov was so unfortunate that all of his inventory had turned completely to vinegar. Soon everyone was talking about Yaakov's 100 barrels of vinegar, including the town's children! Of course, before long, the talk of the town became a reality, as Hashem has empowered people's speech to affect the subject of their conversation.[138] Yaakov was stuck with 100 barrels

---
138. *Moed Kattan* 18a.

of vinegar and had no wine left to sell. The visitor was euphoric, as he now had a monopoly on the village's wine market.

Not so fast! Hashem had mercy on Yaakov. Hashem brought a rare skin disease upon the villagers that caused them to scratch incessantly, which only made the disease worse. The doctors insisted that the only way to heal themselves would be to bathe in very strong wine vinegar, the sooner the better. There was not a single bottle of wine vinegar available in town, aside from Yaakov's barrels. Yaakov sold his entire stock for twice the price of wine. Although Yaakov's stock remained vinegar, he was able to reap Hashem's blessing, not only despite the spoilage but specifically due to the spoilage, and for twice the estimated profit.

This story serves to remind us that Hashem is in absolute control, and no one can hurt anyone else if it is not decreed upon him by Hashem, no matter what kind of devious scheming he may employ. All of his plans will amount to nothingness, and Hashem's plan alone will endure.

Could Yaakov sue the person who maligned his wine, causing him a complete loss, to pay him at least *b'dinei Shamayim*, or, since in the end there was no loss at all, Yaakov has no claim against him?

*A*It would seem obvious that one who caused a loss that resulted from a person's speech that affected someone else through spiritual means, as in our case, would not be obligated to pay *b'dinei adam* (in the earthly courts).

As far as an obligation *b'dinei Shamayim*, the rule of damages in such cases is, if at the time that the damage was caused there was no loss because subsequently, the item was equal to or exceeded its original value, no payment would be required. Even though it would have been considered a loss under ordinary circumstances, if the current situation is such that there was no loss at all, then there is nothing for which to pay. If, however, there was definitely a loss at the time the damage was done, and only subsequently the loss was never realized because circumstances changed, then it is subject to an argument between the *poskim*. The *Mekor Chaim*[139] maintains that there is no obligation to pay, while other *poskim* maintain that the original damage cannot be exempted retroactively.[140]

It would seem that the same argument would apply in Yaakov's case, as well. However, the *Mekor Chaim* was only discussing a case where the question was whether there was an obligation *b'dinei adam*. Our discussion is whether there is an obligation *b'dinei Shamayim*, and therefore, perhaps even the *Mekor Chaim* would agree that there would be sufficient reason to require payment.

On the other hand, the *poskim* argued in a case where one did a physical act of damage. In Yaakov's case, people merely spoke words that caused the wine to spoil, and in the end it became apparent that "Hashem intended it for the good"[141] and sweetened the bitter liquid to provide sustenance for all. Perhaps in such a case all the *poskim* would agree that there would be no obligation to pay.

---

139. *Siman* 33.
140. See *What If*, Vol. 1, p. 430, where there are a series of similar questions.
141. *Bereishis* 50:20.

ספר שמות

Sefer Shemos

פרשת שמות
Parashas Shemos

A Timely Gift

וַתְּחַיֶּיןָ אֶת הַיְלָדִים
And they caused the boys to live
(1:17)

Shammai and Yocheved's joy knew no bounds when they were blessed with a beautiful and healthy baby boy, after a labor that lasted more than 24 hours. Still, Yocheved was completely worn out and felt that she needed to spend a few days in a convalescent home for new mothers to help her recuperate before returning home. Unfortunately, their tight budget simply did not allow it.

The baby's *bris* was celebrated in a local shul, and was well attended by family and friends. Uncle Yehudah noticed that his niece Yocheved looked wan and pale due to her exhaustion, so he cornered Shammai to inquire how they were managing. Shammai confided in his wife's uncle that Yocheved badly needed a break, but that they just could not afford it. Uncle Yehudah pulled out his checkbook and asked how much it cost for a day in the convalescent home. Shammai replied that it cost $150. His uncle wrote out a check right then and there for $450 to cover a three-day stay.

Yocheved enjoyed three days of nutritious meals and peace, quiet, and relaxation. By the time she packed her bags to go home she felt refreshed, with renewed energy. Yocheved went to check out and pay the bill. At the desk they asked her if she had supplemental medical insurance, and Yocheved replied that she did. They informed her that she was entitled to a three-day stay, fully covered by her insurance. Shammai submitted his wife's receipt and was fully reimbursed for her stay.

The question that remained was whether or not they should return Uncle Yehudah's generous gift. After all, he had given the check specifically to cover her stay in the convalescent home. Of course, they had plenty of other expenses as well, and could really use the extra money. On the other hand, perhaps Yocheved should stay on for another three days to help her recover even more strength. What should they do?

A The Mishnah in *Maseches Pe'ah*[1] states that if a wealthy man was traveling from one place to another and ran out of available funds, he is allowed to take *leket, shich'chah,* and *pe'ah* (gifts that are given to the poor) in order to sustain himself for the duration of his trip. Despite the fact that he may have many resources at home, he is considered temporarily poor, since for the moment he has nothing with which to support himself. Even when he returns home, he does not have to return the amount that he took, because he is similar to a poor man who became wealthy, who has no obligation to repay the *tzedakah* that he received. This is the ruling of the *Shulchan Aruch*,[2] as well. This

---
1. 5:4.
2. *Yoreh De'ah* 253:4.

halachah proves that an individual who received *tzedakah* is evaluated according to his level of need at the time he received the donation.

In this case, at the time that Uncle Yehudah wrote the check, Shammai and Yocheved had no idea that they were entitled to a free stay in the convalescent home, and therefore had the status of poor people. They only subsequently discovered that their insurance would pay for it. Had Yocheved not stayed in the convalescent home, she may never have known. Therefore, Uncle Yehudah's gift was certainly a fulfillment of the mitzvah of *tzedakah* and would not have to be returned.

Another reason to allow them to keep the money is because the Mishnah in *Shekalim*[3] states that if a collection was made to redeem a captive, any excess money is to be given to the captive. If extra money was collected on behalf of a poor person, it is to be given to that poor person. Even though the donors were only collecting for a specific need, the poor man is allowed to keep the additional money that was collected on his behalf. In this case as well, although Uncle Yehudah gave the check for a specific need, Shammai and Yocheved are entitled to keep any money that remains.

One the other hand, the *Yerushalmi*[4] states that if a community collected money to cover burial expenses for a *niftar* who was presumed to be poor, and it was later discovered that he had actually possessed the resources to cover the funeral expenses, the money is returned to the donors, as the entire collection was a mistake. In this case as well, Uncle Yehudah's contribution seems to have been a mistake, as Yocheved was already entitled to a three-day stay in the convalescent home for new mothers.

In truth, the cases are not similar. A *niftar* has no other needs, with the exception of his burial. If he already had those needs covered, it is as if the community collected for a poor person who was

---
3. 2:5.
4. Ibid., 2:5.

really wealthy. Shammai and Yocheved, in contrast, have many other expenses, and therefore may keep Uncle Yehudah's generous gift to help them defray the costs of their other needs.

The Right Name at the Right Time

וַיִּקְרָא אֶת שְׁמוֹ גֵּרְשֹׁם
And he named him Gershom
(2:22)

Q A young man named Yehudah miraculously escaped the clutches of the Nazis in Germany. After much trial and tribulation, he reached the shores of the United States, guided by Hashem's hand. Unfortunately, his family remained behind, in mortal danger in Europe. Soon afterward, Yehudah married and his wife gave birth to a baby boy. Yehudah is unsure if he should call the baby Paltiel (lit., *Hashem saved*), to thank Hashem for saving him from the horrific inferno of Germany, or if he should call the baby Yerachmiel (lit., *Hashem, Who has compassion*), as a plea for Hashem to save his Jewish brethren from their horrific situation.

A Moshe Rabbeinu called his first son Gershom, as he said, "I was a stranger in a strange land."[5] At the time, Moshe Rabbeinu was a refugee in Midyan, fleeing

---
5. *Shemos* 18:3.

Pharaoh's wrath. The *Meshech Chochmah* explains that the Torah is extolling Moshe's greatness: Although Moshe had been raised in Pharaoh's home and barely knew his Jewish brethren, he still felt an exceptional connection to them. Even though Moshe lived and had married in Midyan, he considered Mitzrayim, where his people were suffering terribly, to be his homeland. He was pained by their plight to the extent that when he named his first child, he did not have the presence of mind to thank Hashem for saving him from Pharaoh (as he did when he named his second son Eliezer), but rather, he named his child after the fact that he was distanced from his brothers. Although Moshe Rabbeinu was saved from Pharaoh's sword with open miracles, his first attention was to his brothers in Mitzrayim, as he bore their pain from afar.

Accordingly, it would seem appropriate for Yehudah to name his child Yerachmiel as a sign of supplication to Hashem to spare his relatives from their terrible oppression, before naming a child in gratitude for his own salvation.

Lasting Impressions

וְשַׂמְתָּ אֶת הַדְּבָרִים בְּפִיו
And put the words in his mouth
(4:15)

Q Aharon loves his rebbi. Whenever he reviews the rebbi's *shiur* with his *chavrusa* and repeats his rebbi's explanation, Aharon imitates the rebbi's voice nearly perfectly. He feels that his rebbi's voice awakens within him a spirit of *yiras Shamayim*. However, his friends think that Aharon is being an impressionist, and think that it is strange for him to imitate the rebbi. In fact, they consider it to be quite disrespectful. Aharon's intent is to be anything but disrespectful. Is it improper for Aharon to continue imitating his rebbi publicly?

The *pasuk*[6] tells us that Yitzchak Avinu did not recognize Yaakov because his arms were hairy, like those of Eisav, and therefore he blessed him, thinking that he was Eisav. This is despite the fact that Yitzchak recognized that the person who stood before him had Yaakov's voice. The *Netziv* in his *sefer Ha'amek Davar* explains that in Yitzchak's mind there was no contradiction between the two identifying features, because he thought that Eisav was intentionally trying to speak like Yaakov in order to bring Yitzchak to a state of *ruach hakodesh*. When Yitzchak would hear Hashem's Name in Yaakov's voice, which was constantly used for Torah and *tefillah*, it would facilitate Yitzchak reaching a higher spiritual level, allowing him to bestow his blessings upon Eisav. Yitzchak approved of "Eisav's" idea, and he blessed him.

Moreover, the *Rambam* and the *Me'iri* explain the Mishnah in the beginning of *Eduyos*[7] that teaches that Hillel HaZaken intentionally mispronounced a word, because that was how he had heard his rebbeim say it. Hillel learned from Shemayah and Avtalyon, who were both converts. They had difficulty saying the word *hin* and pronounced it *in*. Hillel also said *in*, in order to perpetuate his rebbis' words. Hence, there is a precedent to imitate one's rebbi, even if the rebbi mispronounces a word, providing that the student's intent is for the sake of Heaven.

The *Noda B'Yehudah* would serve as the *chazzan* on Yom Kippur at the Ne'ilah service. Among the congregants was a poor man who knew how to imitate the Rav's rendition of *"Me'chalkel chaim b'chesed."* The next day, the poor man went to collect donations,

---

6. *Bereishis* 27:23.
7. 1:3.

and at each house he would perform his rendition of the Rav's tune, together with the Rav's gestures. People were very amused and they increased their donations. The community leaders saw this as an affront to the Rav's honor, and warned the collector that if he continued this behavior, they would drive him from the town.

The man had no choice but to visit the *Noda B'Yehudah* himself, and he explained his dire situation to the Rav. He promised that he meant no disrespect. He just wanted to make people happy and earn some extra money thereby. The Rav was not upset or insulted. On the contrary, he gave the man his written permission to continue to sustain himself with the Rav's *"Mechalkel chaim."*

Accordingly, Aharon could continue his imitations, and should simply explain to his friends that he is not being disrespectful, but is doing so out of love for his rebbi.

פרשת וארא
Parashas Va'eira

Keep Your Cool

וַיִּבְאַשׁ
And it became foul
(7:21)

Q Yeshivas Ohel Zelig is located in a rural area, far away from the noise and distractions of city life. Due to the yeshivah's isolated location, the *bachurim* do not have access to any stores or food establishments. Anyone who wishes to purchase an item from the closest supermarket writes his order in a notepad that the yeshivah provides, and once a week there is a delivery. The boys organized a rotation to accept the deliveries and check that everything ordered has arrived. The boy on duty stores those items that require refrigeration, and then returns to his learning until the distribution of the items at the evening break.

One week the order arrived as scheduled, and it was Simcha's turn to process the order. He checked everything carefully and put the perishables into the refrigerator before returning to the *beis midrash*. Two days later, there was a very foul odor emanating from the refrigerator. It seemed that the fridge was on the fritz. Simcha had not noticed that it was not cold, and now all of the food that the boys had purchased for Shabbos was spoiled. Does Simcha have to pay for the spoiled food?

A Simcha did not directly damage the food. Had he not stored the food in the refrigerator, it also would have spoiled. He merely failed to refrigerate the food in order to prevent its spoilage. Therefore, his act is a *grama* (causative) at best, and *beis din* could not obligate him to pay.

In truth, however, this case is not so simple. It was Simcha's responsibility to refrigerate the food, so had he left the food outside to spoil, he would have had to pay. This is similar to the case of the *Nachlas Tzvi*,[8] who discusses someone who had hired a wagoner to deliver *esrogim* to his home before Succos. He intended to sell the *esrogim* to the members of his community. The wagoner forgot to deliver the box of *esrogim* until after Succos. The *Nachlas Tzvi* was asked if the owner of the *esrogim* has the right to claim damages from the wagoner, or if the latter could simply suffice with a sincere apology for the now-worthless merchandise.

The *Nachlas Tzvi* opines that the wagoner must pay for damages, as would any worker who was hired to work with perishable merchandise. The *Rema*[9] and the *Shach*[10] rule that if someone hired workers to remove his flax from soaking but the workers decided to renege on their original agreement, and it was too late to hire other workers and the flax was ruined, then the workers must pay for the loss. This is true even if the flax was not completely ruined, but had only deteriorated. Why are the workers responsible for the deterioration, when we find that the *Shulchan Aruch*[11] states

---

8. 291:21.
9. *Choshen Mishpat* 333:6.
10. Ad loc. §39.
11. *Choshen Mishpat* 363:1.

that if someone stole fruit and it began to rot, the thief is allowed to return the fruit to its owner without any further liability?

The difference is that the workers were hired specifically to save the flax from becoming ruined. Therefore, they are held responsible for not having done the job for which they were hired. The same is true in the case of the *esrogim*. The wagoner was hired specifically to deliver the *esrogim* in time to be sold. Hence, by delivering the *esrogim* late, his liability is the result of not having done the job for which he was hired.

In this case as well, it makes no difference if Simcha had put the food into a broken refrigerator or if he had left the food out altogether. Even if his part in the damage was merely *grama*, he definitely did not do the job for which he was responsible. His inaction is similar to that of the workers who left the flax to soak for too long. Simcha should have realized that there was no cold air in the refrigerator, and should have made an alternate arrangement to sustain the perishable items. Therefore, he must pay. However, if the refrigerator had been working at the time that the items were stored, then it would not be considered Simcha's fault, and he would not have to pay for the food.

Privileged Animals

הִנֵּה יַד ה' הוֹיָה בְּמִקְנְךָ
Behold, the hand of Hashem is on your livestock
(9:3)

Q In the summer, Berel volunteers at the zoo, feeding the animals. His job is to feed the horses, the donkeys, the camels, and the cows. The animals of each species are all just as hungry as the others, and Berel can choose which animals he wishes to feed first. Is there any hierarchy in the halachah as to which animals have priority over the others?

A Moshe Rabbeinu told Pharaoh that the hand of Hashem would afflict the cattle that were left in the fields: the horses, the donkeys, the camels, the cows, and the sheep. Rav Yaakov Kamenetzky explains why the Torah lists these animals in that order. The Gemara in *Berachos*[12] states that punishments are meted out from the smallest to the largest. Hence, the snake was cursed before Chavah, and Chavah before Adam. When Moshe informed Pharaoh that pestilence would strike in Mitzrayim, he mentioned the horses first because they are nonkosher animals. The donkeys are next because they are also not kosher, but they have special status, as a firstborn donkey has sanctity and must be redeemed from the Kohen. A camel has an advantage because it has one sign of a kosher animal; i.e., it chews its cud. Last on the list are the cows and sheep, because they are actually kosher.

This demonstrates that a camel actually has an advantage over other nonkosher animals by virtue of the fact that it has one sign of purity.

Accordingly, it would seem that when it comes to feeding the animals, one should feed them in the opposite order of the *pasuk* above, from the most important to the least important: The kosher animals should be fed first, followed by the camels that have one sign of purity. Afterward Berel should feed the donkeys, which have some measure of sanctity, and finally the horses, which have no special status other than being unkosher.

However, there is a *Tosefta* in *Bechoros*[13] that would seem to give special importance to the donkey, in contrast to all other nonkosher animals: In all of the nonkosher animals, there is none other than the donkey that carries the obligation of (redeeming) a firstborn.

---

12. 61a.
13. 1:3.

Based on this inference, why was the donkey considered less important than the camel when the plague struck in Mitzrayim?

Rav Yaakov Kamenetzky explains that in Mitzrayim, the donkeys had not yet acquired their status of having their firstborn sanctified, as they had not yet assisted the Jews in carrying out the wealth of Mitzrayim when the Jews were freed. At that point, the donkeys were not as important as the camels, which have one sign of purity. The signs of purity were already known, as Noach differentiated between kosher and nonkosher species in regard to the quantity of each category of animals that entered the *Teivah* (Ark). The fact that they would eventually become holy gave the donkeys an advantage over the horses, but not over the camels, which chew their cud.

Now, however, that we have already been given the mitzvah of *pidyon petter chamor*, Berel should feed the donkeys before the camels.

In summary, Berel should feed the kosher animals first, the donkeys second, the camels third, and the horses last.

A Sweet Pitch

בָּרָד כָּבֵד מְאֹד
A very heavy hail
(9:18)

Q After his *aliyah* to the Torah, it is customary to shower a *chassan* with candies on the occasion of his *aufruf*.[14] As one such barrage of candies was thrown at the *chassan*

---

14. The source for this *minhag* can be found in *Berachos* 50b and *Maseches Semachos* Ch. 8.

from the ladies' section, one of the candies veered from its intended course, as the ladies' section was quite a distance from the *bimah*. The candy had apparently been launched with great gusto because when it made a direct hit on the *gabbai's* glasses, the lens did not survive the impact. *Baruch Hashem*, the *gabbai* did not suffer any injury. Mrs. Schmidtkorn came forward and confessed that it was her candy that broke the *gabbai's* glasses, and she extended her sincere apologies.

After Shabbos, the *gabbai* asked Mrs. Schmidtkorn to pay for the replacement lens. Mrs. Schmidtkorn claims that it was an accident, and that the damage was a matter of course (pun intended) in the *aufruf* celebration. Hence, she feels that she should not have to pay. Who is correct?

A person is always considered forewarned and is therefore responsible to pay for any damages that he inflicts, whether accidental or otherwise.[15]

Nevertheless, in this case Mrs. Schmidtkorn should not have to pay, for two reasons:

The *Rema*[16] cites that there was a custom that young men would ride on horses and joust in order to amuse a *chassan* and *kallah*. If in the course of their merriment one were to damage the other, there would be no obligation to pay for damages, as the damage was inflicted in the context of merriment.

The *Rema* rules similarly in *Hilchos Purim*[17]: If someone damages his friend in the course of the Purim merriment, he is exempt from paying damages. The *Mishnah Berurah* explains that this exemption is limited to unintentional damage only, which was perpetrated in the context of the Purim merriment, and only if the damage was not excessive.

---
15. *Choshen Mishpat* 421:3.
16. Ibid., 378:9.
17. 695:2.

The women should all certainly be very careful to avoid hurting anyone with the candies, perhaps by throwing the candies in an arc, as opposed to a line drive. However, if damage did result from having thrown the candy in the *chassan's* honor, no payment is required. Since throwing candies is certainly an accepted custom, one cannot be liable to pay for the damage that she caused.

An additional reason to exempt Mrs. Schmidtkorn might be if the *gabbai* himself was at fault! If the reason his lens was hit was because he had been looking in the direction of the ladies' section when a hailstorm of candies was expected to be launched, then the *gabbai* was negligent by exposing himself to possible damage. In that case, he would be responsible for his own loss, and he would not deserve compensation.

פרשת בא
Parashas Bo

A Potentially Dangerous Snack

אִישׁ לְפִי אָכְלוֹ
Everyone according to what he eats
(12:4)

Q Sruli had recess in the middle of the morning, and before he went out to the school yard to play, he took a package of pretzels from his knapsack so he could have a snack before returning to class. Many times his stomach would growl in the hour and a half before lunch if he did not eat during recess. As Sruli opened his package of pretzels, the sensitive antennae of the other boys in his class informed them of their classmate's snack, and before Sruli could say *borei minei mezonos*, he was surrounded by a group of friends with outstretched hands. Each of them requested just two pretzels and Sruli did not know what to do. He wondered if he was allowed to share with them. On the one hand it would be uncomfortable to refuse their requests, as they will consider him a stingy boy. On the other hand, if he gives all of them pretzels, he will not have enough for himself and he will be giving them food from a "meal that is not sufficient for its owner," which the *Rambam*[18] considers to be related to stealing. What should Sruli do?

A If the story is about children under bar mitzvah, Sruli could share with them if he wants to, since the boys are not obligated in mitzvos, and Sruli is not responsible for their *chinuch*. If, however, bar mitzvah boys are involved, it would seem that there is no alternative but to explain apologetically that sharing with them would involve an *aveirah*, and he is therefore unfortunately unable to oblige.

Had the bar mitzvah boys not yet been mitzvah observant, and they would inevitably say bad things about Sruli and hate him, it would seem that Sruli should give them pretzels in order to prevent them from violating the prohibition of hating a fellow Jew. Although they will be sinning by depriving him of his food, that sin is one that the boys brought upon themselves by asking Sruli for the pretzels, as Sruli would have to give them some pretzels in order to avoid their disparaging him. In contrast, their violation of hating a fellow Jew would be worse for Sruli, because he would cause the boys to violate that prohibition.

This is similar to the *psak* of Rabbi Shlomo Zalman Auerbach[19] that when one has contact with a not-yet-observant Jew, and not offering refreshments would lead to resentment of observant Jews, one may indeed provide refreshments even though his guest will neglect to make a *berachah*. Since offering food in such a case is only providing an opportunity for an *aveirah* (eating without a *berachah*), and not offering the food will cause a worse *aveirah* — i.e., hatred — providing the food is no longer considered an act of

---

18. Ch. 4, *Teshuvah*: 4.
19. *Minchas Shlomo*, Vol. I, 35.

assisting an *aveirah*. On the contrary, it is an act of preventing a more serious transgression.[20]

In summary, whether or not he has to share depends on the age of his friends, and whether his refusal to share will cause them to violate a greater sin.

What Motivated You?

וְהָיָה לְךָ לְאוֹת עַל יָדְךָ
And it shall be for you a sign on your arm
(13:9)

Q Reb Avraham was passing through town on business and he was looking for a minyan for Shacharis. He was directed to the local shul, and was greeted warmly by the men who came to *daven*. Unfortunately, Reb Avraham noticed that many of the men had serious problems with their *tefillin*. Being a man of action, he spoke to the Rav and arranged to have a *sofer* visit the shul and give a *shiur* on various problems that develop in aging *tefillin*. Afterward, the *sofer* would accept people's *tefillin* for repairs.

The *shiur* was a big success. The *sofer* described what a precious mitzvah *tefillin* is, and the eternal spiritual implications of not having properly donned *tefillin*. The attendees took it to heart, and many pairs of *tefillin* were repaired and replaced.

Did Reb Avraham perform a mitzvah between man and Hashem, and therefore his reward is assured to him

---

20. See also *Chazon Ish, Shevi'is* 12 §9.

in the World to Come, or is his mitzvah classified as *chesed*, whose fruits are to be enjoyed even in this world[21]?

After Pinchas slew Zimri, Hashem told Moshe Rabbeinu to tell Pinchas that Hashem was giving him a "covenant of *shalom*."[22] The Gemara in *Sanhedrin*[23] explains that Hashem told Moshe, "Go initiate *shalom* to Pinchas." What does that mean?

The *Einei Yitzchak* explains that we know that the reward for mitzvos is given in the Next World. The exception to this rule are the "fruits," or dividends, of mitzvos between man and his fellow man. Pinchas had accomplished a double agenda; he had purged a terrible *chillul Hashem* and he had saved the entire Jewish nation from a terrible punishment. Which of these aspects had driven Pinchas to do his deed? Was it mostly out of zealousness for Hashem's honor, or was it mainly out of compassion for the nation? The difference between these two motivations would decide as to whether Pinchas's reward would await him in the Next World or if he would reap its benefits even in this world. Hashem revealed that Pinchas, the grandson of Aharon HaKohen, had followed his grandfather's example to bring peace to the Jewish people, and therefore he deserved to enjoy the covenant of peace even in this world.[24]

According to the *Einei Yitzchak*, if Reb Avraham was mainly motivated by his *ahavas Yisrael* to arrange the *tefillin* revolution in town, his mitzvah is classified as *gemilus chassadim*, and he will certainly enjoy the dividends of his mitzvah in this world in addition to his full reward that awaits him in the World to Come.

---

21. *Pe'ah* 1:1.
22. *Bamidbar* 25:12.
23. 82b.
24. Editor's Note: See *What If*, Vol. 2, "Free Mitzvah," p. 124, with the *Netziv's* insight that mitzvos between man and his fellow man do not require intent.

The Honor of Performing a Mitzvah

וְכָל פֶּטֶר חֲמֹר תִּפְדֶּה
And every first-issue donkey you shall redeem
(13:13)

Q Yitzchak purchased a donkey in order to perform the mitzvah of *pidyon petter chamor* (redeeming a firstborn donkey). Afterward, it occurred to him that perhaps instead of doing the mitzvah by himself, he should offer others the opportunity to buy a share in his donkey so that they, too, could merit a share in this rare mitzvah. Yitzchak had learned the *Magen Avraham*[25] which cites the *Sefer Chassidim*,[26] who writes that there was a man who built a beautiful shul. Members of the community asked to donate money toward the building so that they, too, could share in the mitzvah. The man refused their offers because he wanted the shul to memorialize only him and his offspring. In the end, the man's family was completely wiped out.[27]

---

25. 154 §23.
26. 503.
27. The *Chasam Sofer* (*Toras Moshe, Parashas Yisro*) explains that the man was not faulted for wanting to perpetuate his family's name. Indeed, *Chazal* (*Pesachim* 50b) teach that a person should always be involved in Torah study and mitzvos even if he has an ulterior motive, as eventually he will achieve a level of performance purely for the sake of Heaven. The reason the man was punished was because he precluded others from taking part in the mitzvah. The *Chasam Sofer* notes that this is also why Yisro criticized Moshe Rabbeinu for adjudicating the entire Jewish nation alone and not allowing others to take part in the mitzvah of judging the people. Yisro warned Moshe that he would wither from this practice, as did the man in the *Sefer Chassidim's* episode.

On the other hand, maybe allowing others to join in the fulfillment of a mitzvah applies only before someone has acquired the mitzvah for himself. Once a person has already made preparations to perform the mitzvah by himself, perhaps it is improper to share it and thereby show a lack of honor and regard for the mitzvah.[28]

The Gemara in *Pesachim*[29] teaches that when the Jews would come to the *Beis HaMikdash* to bring the *korban Pesach*, the Kohen who would accept the blood of

---

28. Similarly, it is related that Rabbi Yonason Eibishitz's *chavrusa* was sentenced to death for having committed an act of vandalism. Rabbi Yonason approached the prison guard and negotiated to arrange his friend's release, in return for a large sum of money. Next Rabbi Yonason approached the community leaders and asked them to raise the required sum for the mitzvah of *pidyon shevuyim*. When he realized that it would take time for them to raise the entire sum, Rabbi Yonason decided to use the money he had received as a dowry to cover the guard's fee. The guard released the prisoner and had him taken to a safe place to hide.

A little while later the community collectors arrived at Rabbi Yonason's home to deliver the money, but Rabbi Yonason would not accept their money, as he had already claimed the mitzvah for himself.

The next morning, the officials were outraged that the prisoner had disappeared. The guard denied having any part in the escape, but a few days later he noticed that he was being followed. He quickly put the escape payment together with his other valuables and secretly delivered them to Rabbi Yonason's house. He hurriedly informed the Rebbetzin that he had to leave town for a few days until things calmed down. If he returned, he was sure that the Rav would return the money to him. If he did not return, then the money would be theirs.

Not long afterward, the news arrived that the corpse of the guard had been discovered. When Rabbi Yonason returned home, his wife joyfully informed him that their money had come back to them with interest! The Rav burst into tears, as he understood that in Heaven they had rejected his mitzvah, and hence, the money had been returned. He fasted and asked in a dream why his mitzvah had not been accepted. The reply was that it was because he had refused to allow others to have a share in the mitzvah, and had wanted to keep it for himself.

Although Rabbi Yonason had already done the mitzvah and could no longer include the community retroactively, perhaps since they had already collected the money before his money was delivered, they already deserved a share in Rabbi Yonason's mitzvah.

29. 65b.

the sacrifice after its slaughter would not proceed directly to the *Mizbei'ach* to sprinkle it on the wall of the *Mizbei'ach*, but would pass it to a Kohen who was standing next to him, the first in a line of Kohanim. Each one would pass it one closer to the *Mizbei'ach*, and the last Kohen in the line, closest to the *Mizbei'ach*, would sprinkle the blood. The reason for following this procedure was to include many people in the mitzvah, thus enhancing the honor shown to Hashem.

Despite the fact that the first Kohen who collected the blood could have poured it himself, he nevertheless allowed others to take part in the mitzvah and passed on the mitzvah to others, in order to enhance the mitzvah. Perhaps the same would be true in our case, as well. Not only is allowing others to take part in the mitzvah not a disgrace to the mitzvah, but on the contrary, it is a greater honor to Hashem than merely doing the mitzvah by oneself. Therefore, Yitzchak should include others and grant them the opportunity to take part in his mitzvah.[30]

---

30. Editor's Note: It seems that Rav Zilberstein understood that the Kohanim **chose** to pass the blood along toward the *Mizbei'ach* as a fulfillment of doing the mitzvah publicly, and not because they had been instructed to do so. Hence, in our case as well, Yitzchak may choose to include others in his mitzvah.

Perhaps another proof to his decision may be brought from the *Tevuas Shor,* who writes that a father may honor someone else to perform his son's *bris milah* even if the father could have performed the mitzvah himself. Even though it is preferable to do the mitzvah personally, rather than through an agent, when one **honors** someone else to do the mitzvah, it is not degrading to the mitzvah. On the contrary, one is showing that he considers the mitzvah an honor that he is according to someone else. Perhaps this concept would apply in our case as well.

# פרשת בשלח
Parashas Beshalach

(Not) A Time to Sing

> אָז יָשִׁיר מֹשֶׁה
> Then Moses ... chose to sing
> *(15:1)*

Q Motty was planning a bar mitzvah reception for his eldest son. He hired Menachem, a talented musician, to fill the hall with his melodious gift of song. Motty was expecting 300 guests to attend.

The day before the reception, Motty met his cousin, Izzy. Izzy reminded Motty that he was an accomplished guitarist and vocalist, and proposed that he would be more than happy to play and sing at the bar mitzvah the following evening — free of charge. Motty was embarrassed to tell Izzy that he had forgotten about him and had already hired someone else, so he gladly accepted Izzy's generous offer and called Menachem to settle with him.

Menachem was very sympathetic, but he informed Motty that he would still have to pay the entire fee, as if he had actually performed at the bar mitzvah. After all, had Motty canceled well in advance, Menachem could have accepted a different job. One day's notice is certainly not enough time to cancel a musician.

Motty understood Menachem's position, but he was not convinced that he had to pay the musician's entire fee if he did not even perform. The two agreed to meet to discuss the matter with Rav Stein the day after the bar mitzvah to determine how much Motty had to pay.

It turned out that only nine guests arrived to join in the *simchah* on the night of the bar mitzvah! Only together with the bar mitzvah boy did they have a minyan. The reason for the sparse turnout was that the hall at which the bar mitzvah was being celebrated was in the center of Yerushalayim and on that day, one of the *gedolei hador* had been *niftar*. His *levayah* was attended by hundreds of thousands of people. Traffic came to a standstill for hours. Most of Motty's guests attended the funeral procession instead of attending the bar mitzvah. In any event, the roads were impassable.

When Motty and Menachem met at the Rav's house the next day, Motty had a new claim to exempt himself from paying Menachem's fee. Even if Motty had not canceled on the musician, Menachem would not have been able to attend, since there was no way for him to travel to the hall! Therefore, why should Motty have to pay just because he canceled Menachem's booking in advance of this development. Is Motty right?

A Two principles in the halachos of hiring a worker apply to this question:

1. When one hires a worker, and at the time he was hired he could have found employment elsewhere, and subsequently the worker is informed that his services are not needed,

PARASHAS BESHALACH / 139

but by that time he can no longer find employment elsewhere, the halachah is that the employer must pay the worker's wage, as he is responsible for causing the worker a loss.[31] However, the would-be employer only has to pay the wage of an idle worker, not the price that they originally agreed upon. The worker would have been willing to deduct a certain amount from his wage for the privilege of not having to work at all, and that amount may now be deducted from his salary. There is an opinion that that amount is half of the worker's wage.[32]

2. If the worker is unable to work because of prevailing circumstances, whether unforeseen or not, the employer does not have to pay the worker at all. An exception to this rule would be if the employer was aware that the circumstance may arise, and the worker was not.[33]

In this case, Motty's cancellation should have obligated him to pay Menachem as much as a worker who was excused from working should be paid. However, the fact that Menachem would have been prevented from performing in any event would seem to be ample reason to say that Motty's cancellation did not cause Menachem any loss, since even if Motty had not canceled, Menachem would not have been able to perform and would not have been paid.

This point is actually a dispute between the *Rema*[34] and the *Sha'ar HaMishpat*. The *Rema* rules that as soon as the employer breached his contract he is obligated to pay, regardless of the subsequent circumstance that would have made the employment unfeasible. The *Sha'ar HaMishpat* maintains that there is no reason for the employer to pay for a job that would have been canceled in any event.

In Motty's case, perhaps even the *Rema* would agree that he is exempt from paying. The *Rema* only spoke about a case

---

31. *Shulchan Aruch, Choshen Mishpat* 333:2.
32. Ibid.
33. *Taz* ad loc.
34. *Shulchan Aruch, Choshen Mishpat* 334:1.

in which the worker is prepared to perform the job for which he was hired. In our case, Menachem himself would not have wanted to come and sing at such a sad time, when hundreds of thousands of people were escorting such a great Torah giant and paying their last respects amid tears and mourning. Menachem himself would have preferred to join the tremendous entourage than to perform at the bar mitzvah celebration.

Rav Chaim Kanievsky agreed to all of the above, but added that regardless of that reasoning, since Motty was holding the money, the burden of proof would be upon Menachem, and as stated the final halachah is a dispute between the *poskim*. Therefore, Motty is not required to pay.

All for the Boss

לֶחֶם מִן הַשָּׁמָיִם
Food from Heaven
(16:4)

Q Shalom had recently been dismissed from his place of employment and was forced to find a different slot in the workforce. Shalom thought long and hard if it would be better for him to start his own business or to seek employment with someone else. The advantage of being hired by others is, obviously, that he will have a set, steady salary, which will give him a certain sense of security. If he turns entrepreneur, he has no idea how successful he will be, but he will certainly be encouraged to work on his *bitachon* in Hashem. Which path is the preferable one?

ALavan beseeched Yaakov Avinu to continue working for him, and encouraged Yaakov to name his price.[35] Yaakov responded that he did not seek anything from Lavan, but he would take the spotted and speckled sheep that would be born in Lavan's flock. The *Radak*[36] explains that while Lavan wished to pay Yaakov a steady salary in return for his shepherding, which would offer Yaakov financial security, Yaakov preferred to leave his wage undefined. Yaakov wanted to be dependent solely on Hashem.

Accordingly, it would seem that it is preferable for Shalom to open his own business, because doing so will force him to develop a closer relationship with Hashem, as Shalom will sincerely turn to Hashem to help him succeed in making a living. In a similar vein, the Gemara in *Yoma*[37] relates that Rabbi Shimon bar Yochai's students questioned why Hashem made the *mahn* fall daily instead of once a year. Rabbi Shimon answered with a parable. A king had an only son. The king gave his son an allowance once a year, and consequently the son would visit his father only once a year. The king was dissatisfied with this arrangement, so he decided to give his son only enough money for one day at a time. This caused the son to frequent the palace every single day! If Hashem had given the Jews a year's supply of *mahn*, they would not have had the constant impetus to strengthen their connection with Hashem, to ensure that they would, indeed, merit their daily allowance of *mahn*.

The *Megaleh Amukos* was the Rav of Cracow. For personal reasons, he decided to move his residence to a different city, and none of his students' earnest pleas could sway his decision. After he had already made all the necessary preparations for the upheaval he abruptly changed his mind and decided not to move, after all.

---

35. *Bereishis* 30:20.
36. Ibid.
37. 76a.

When his *talmidim* asked him why he had canceled his plans, he answered that it was in the merit of a *din Torah* that had come before him the previous evening. There was a resident of Cracow, a great *talmid chacham*, who suffered from dire poverty. He barely eked out a living by selling crackers that he baked by himself each night. One day a wealthy man who was deeply touched by the *talmid chacham's* struggle and commitment proposed to sign a *Yissachar-Zevulun* agreement that would provide the *talmid chacham* with ample *parnassah* and allow him to dedicate his time to learning. The contract was signed.

Three months later, the wealthy man was walking in the marketplace and saw the *talmid chacham* selling crackers! The wealthy man asked him to explain himself, and the *talmid chacham* replied that he had withdrawn his agreement to the wealthy man's proposition. The two came before the *Megaleh Amukos* for a *din Torah*.

The wealthy man insisted that he held a signed contract, and the *talmid chacham* had no right to renege. The *talmid chacham* explained that although he had signed the agreement, he regretted having done so and wished to annul their agreement. When he had to bake crackers in order to earn a living, he would *daven* to Hashem that the dough should turn out good. Afterward he would *daven* that the crackers should bake to be crisp and tasty. They should not be overbaked or underbaked, nor should they burn. After the baking, he would *daven* that Hashem should send him customers to buy his crackers. All of this developed an extremely close relationship between him and Hashem. Ever since he received a steady income from the wealthy man, he felt that his relationship with Hashem was lacking, and therefore he wanted to return to his previous position.

The *Megaleh Amukos* concluded that he desired to remain in a city that could hold such a unique *din Torah*.

The Gemara in *Sanhedrin*[38] explains that when the dove brought Noach an olive branch after the *Mabul* (Flood) to indicate that the waters had receded, it was actually also conveying a personal *tefillah* to Hashem: May my sustenance be as bitter as an olive, as long as it comes from Hashem's hand, rather than being as sweet as honey, but from the hands of man!

One who runs his own business feels more dependent on Hashem, whereas an employee feels that his sustenance comes from his boss. That was exactly how the dove felt when it was fed by Noach.

However, if a person feels that his *bitachon* is weak, and if he opens his own business he will have to invest all of his energies to succeed, that might push him further away from Hashem. He may find that he has less time to learn or attend minyan and will be driven to compromise his integrity. In that case, it would certainly be better to work for an employer so that he will not be faced with such difficult challenges.

Keeping the Peace

רְאוּ כִּי ה' נָתַן לָכֶם הַשַּׁבָּת
See that Hashem has given you the Shabbos
(16:29)

Q Asher, a newly married *avreich* (*kollel* student), was invited to his father-in-law's home for Shabbos Chol HaMoed Succos. At the *seudah*, he opened a new bottle of cola. Before he even finished pouring his drink, one of his brothers-in-law protested and accused him

---
38. 108b.

of being *mechallel Shabbos*! He charged him with transgressing the *melachah* of *mechatech* (cutting to size — by separating the plastic ring from the bottle cap) and *makeh b'patish* (putting the final touches on a utensil — making the bottle cap usable by separating the ring).

Asher chided him in a relaxed voice, saying that the brother-in-law should have judged him favorably; Asher had already separated the ring from the bottle cap before Shabbos.

Asher's wife, Chavah, who was sitting right next to her husband, was quite taken aback. Later, she questioned her husband about his behavior, since they both know very well that the ring had not been separated before Shabbos. She didn't understand why he responded as he did.

Asher explained that there is a dispute between the *poskim* as to whether or not one may open such a bottle on Shabbos.[39] His Rav taught him that it is acceptable to follow the lenient opinion. However, he knew that if he would tell his brother-in-law the truth, he would not accept it without giving him an argument. Therefore, in order to preserve the pleasant atmosphere, he decided to alter the truth.

Did Asher act properly?

A The Gemara in *Beitzah*[40] tells the story of Hillel HaZaken who brought a *korban olah* to the *Beis HaMikdash* on Yom Tov.[41] Hillel found himself surrounded by students of Shammai, who asked him what he intended to do with the

---

39. See *Orchos Shabbos* Ch. 12:18. Those who permit it reason that the cap is fully formed before the plastic ring is attached, and even afterward it is clear that the ring is an external attachment. Therefore, it is not *makeh b'patish*. Every person should consult his Rav to determine whether he may be lenient to open bottles on Shabbos, and to understand the different types of bottles that may or may not be opened on Shabbos.
40. 20a.
41. Every male who appears in the *Beis HaMikdash* for the *shalosh regalim* (three Festivals) is obligated to bring a *korban* as an *olas re'eyah*.

animal. Shammai maintained that one is not allowed to bring an *olah* on Yom Tov; rather, one must wait until Chol HaMoed to do so. Hillel calmly answered that the animal was a female, and he was bringing it as a *korban shelamim*.[42] To prove his point, Hillel wagged the animal's tail as if to show them the gender. The students accepted Hillel's response and left him alone.

Rashi explains that Hillel, in his great humility, altered the truth for the sake of peace. Hillel understood that the students of Shammai would not tolerate Hillel's bringing an *olah* on Yom Tov without an argument, at best. Therefore, Hillel deftly sidestepped the issue by fabricating a fictitious excuse.

Hillel taught, through his behavior, that one may alter the truth in order to avoid arguments and altercations. That is exactly what Asher did.

Actually, Asher's case was not as serious as the incident with Hillel. Hillel was the *gadol hador*, and his actions would set a precedent for others to behave likewise. For that reason, the students of Shammai were anxious to argue with him and prevent others from following his example. Even so, Hillel altered the truth in order to avoid *machlokes*.

In Asher's case, there was no point in continuing the argument. Asher had already opened the bottle in accordance with his Rav's ruling. His brother-in-law had already satisfied his obligation to rebuke Asher, albeit not in the proper way, according to his understanding of the halachah. To continue arguing at this point would serve no purpose, unlike the *machlokes* between Hillel and Shammai, which had serious ramifications.

In the future, Asher should certainly be careful not to open bottle caps in the presence of his brother-in-law, so that he will not be put in a position where he will have to say something that is not true.

---

42. An *olah* can only be a male. A *shelamim* can be brought on Yom Tov even according to Shammai, since it is not completely consumed on the *Mizbei'ach*, and its owner is allowed to eat its meat, as opposed to an *olah*, which is completely consumed and therefore has no (physical) human benefit on Yom Tov.

פרשת יתרו
Parashas Yisro

Out of Order

זָכוֹר אֶת יוֹם הַשַּׁבָּת לְקַדְּשׁוֹ
Remember the Shabbos day to sanctify it
(20:8)

Q Zev had just undergone surgery and had to spend Shabbos in the hospital. He was still very weak and not completely lucid. The entire Shabbos he could not eat or drink. Half an hour before Shabbos was over, he began to feel a little stronger. Suddenly, someone called out that he was making *Havdalah*. The *Shulchan Aruch*[43] writes that if one must, he could *daven* Maariv on Shabbos after *Plag HaMinchah* (the last eighth of the day) and make *Havdalah* as well, with the exception of the *berachah* on the fire. However, he is not allowed to do *melachah* until it is actually night. Zev thought that he had better go listen to *Havdalah*, because he was unsure if he would have another opportunity to do so.

---
43. *Orach Chaim* 293:3.

After Zev heard *Havdalah*, he realized that he had not made *Kiddush* the previous night! Perhaps he should make *Kiddush* now. The *Shulchan Aruch*[44] states that if someone did not make *Kiddush* on Friday night, he may still make *Kiddush* the entire following day. Then it dawned on him that he had just heard *Havdalah*. How could he make *Kiddush* after *Havdalah*? That would certainly be a contradiction. It is similar to the case brought in the *Shulchan Aruch*[45] that if someone *davened* Maariv while it is still day (after *Plag HaMinchah*),[46] and then he realized that he had not put on *tefillin* that day, he may no longer put them on. If so, perhaps Zev can no longer make *Kiddush*?

This scenario is discussed by the *Aderes*, in *Cheshbonos Shel Mitzvah*. Initially, he argues that there is still an obligation to make *Kiddush*. Even if this person made *Havdalah*, he is still obligated to observe Shabbos for the remainder of the day. Hence, he is still obligated to remember the Shabbos with *Kiddush*, as the Gemara[47] explains that whoever is obligated to keep Shabbos has an obligation to make *Kiddush*. According to this understanding, we can appreciate the words of the *Shulchan Aruch* stating that one is able to make *Kiddush* the **entire** following day, meaning until the day's end, even if one may have already recited *Havdalah*.[48]

Subsequently, the *Aderes* retracts, because the essence of *Kiddush* is to sanctify the Shabbos, and one could satisfy the basic requirements of the Biblical obligation by simply greeting someone with a "Good Shabbos."[49] If so, in the words of *Havdalah* he has

---

44. 271:8.
45. *Orach Chaim* 30:5.
46. *Krias Shema* must be repeated after nightfall.
47. See *Berachos* 20b.
48. According to this reasoning, perhaps he would have to make *Havdalah* again after having made *Kiddush*, in order to separate between Shabbos and the weekdays.
49. The obligation to recite the *berachah* of *Kiddush* over wine is of Rabbinic origin.

already stated that Hashem separated between the holy and the mundane, between Shabbos and the six workdays. Accordingly, he has already satisfied his (Biblical) obligation of *Kiddush* with these words, and therefore would not have to make *Kiddush* "again" under the circumstances.

Rav Shlomo Zalman Auerbach[50] writes that someone who made *Havdalah* after *Plag HaMinchah* on Shabbos can no longer make up the nighttime *Kiddush*. Even though it is still very much Shabbos, with regards to *Kiddush* and *Havdalah*, he has already made this time into night.[51]

Zev will have to wait until next Shabbos, when he will be obligated to make *Kiddush*.

Valuable Wine

זָכוֹר אֶת יוֹם הַשַּׁבָּת לְקַדְּשׁוֹ
Remember the Shabbos day to sanctify it
(20:8)

Q Akiva was opening his bottles in preparation for Shabbos and discovered that he was out of wine. It was too late to go to the store, so he borrowed a bottle from his neighbor, Shalom. As Akiva was pouring the wine for *Kiddush*, he noticed that the wine smelled spoiled and was not fit for *Kiddush*. He was not comfortable returning it to his neighbor, so he just placed it in the cabinet and used grape juice instead. On Sunday, he called the company to complain about the malodorous beverage, and they sent him a free case of wine as a gesture of goodwill.

---

50. *Minchas Shlomo*, Vol. I, 3.
51. See *Shemiras Shabbos Kehilchasah*, 47 §31.

When Shalom found out what had happened, it dawned on him that it had really been his bottle of wine, and although he had lent it to Akiva, expecting him to return a different bottle, that was because he thought Akiva was going to drink it. He never intended to lend him a bottle that had potential to generate an entire case of wine. Shalom therefore feels that the case belongs to him. Akiva doesn't agree with his logic. Who is right?

To answer the question with a question: Does Akiva have to return even one bottle of wine to Shalom, or can he claim that since the bottle was spoiled, he never received an item that would obligate him to return something in its place?

The *Shulchan Aruch*[52] writes that one who buys eggs that were found to be unfit for consumption can void the sale and ask that his money be refunded. The *Shulchan Aruch* adds that that is *not* the accepted custom, and the custom supersedes the halachah. Thus, the customer would have to take the loss.

In our previous volume,[53] Rav Elyashiv was quoted as saying that the custom of the *Shulchan Aruch* is relevant only to an egg merchant, as he can claim that he could have sold the egg to someone else. In a case where the egg would have been used personally by the owner, a borrower would not have to replace the egg, as the lender himself would have thrown it out when he tried to use it.

Perhaps in our case as well, Akiva should not have to return a bottle of wine to Shalom, since Shalom would have poured the bottle down the drain anyway. However, if Shalom would have returned the wine to the store for a replacement, then Akiva would have to replace this bottle, as well. On the other hand, Shalom only lent the bottle to Akiva to use for *Kiddush*, not to generate profit, and if so, maybe Akiva should give the entire case to Shalom. וצ"ע.

---

52. *Choshen Mishpat* 332:19.
53. *What If,* Vol. 1, "The Yolk Is on Whom?" page 276.

To Understand a Mitzvah

כַּבֵּד אֶת אָבִיךָ וְאֶת אִמֶּךָ
Honor your father and your mother
(20:12)

Q The Torah is comprised of two kinds of mitzvos: mitzvos that are between man and Hashem, and mitzvos that are between man and his fellow man. What kind of mitzvah is *kibbud av v'eim*? On one hand, perhaps it is a mitzvah between man and Hashem: Just as Hashem wants us to keep Shabbos and eat matzah on Pesach, Hashem wants us to accord honor to our parents. Alternatively, one could argue that it is a mitzvah between man and his fellow man: After all, our parents brought us into this world and dedicated themselves to raising us from infancy to adulthood. We certainly owe them a great debt of gratitude. Maybe the mitzvah to honor one's parents is a way of repaying that debt. The *Minchas Chinuch*[54] asks this very question in the following manner: If one did not honor his parents, must he request their forgiveness for the fact that he failed to observe this mitzvah, or is it sufficient to do *teshuvah* to Hashem?

A The *Chayei Adam*[55] writes that this mitzvah is a form of repaying a debt. *Chazal* state in the Gemara *Yerushalmi*[56] that all of a son's obligations that he fulfills to his parents

---
54. Mitzvah 33 §3.
55. *Klal* 67.
56. *Pe'ah* 1:1.

are to repay his debt for all of the kindness that they bestowed upon him. One who does not honor them is called a wicked person, as it is written, *a wicked borrower who does not repay*.[57] The *Zohar*[58] explains that this debt includes loving them intensely, the way they loved him, and not considering them to be a burden.

Similarly, the *Sefer HaChinuch*[59] explains that one of the fundamentals of this mitzvah is to recognize and bestow kindness upon those who have given to us, and not to be among those who lack gratitude. One should contemplate the fact that his parents are responsible for his existence, and thus it is truly fitting that he honor them with all of his abilities and do whatever he can for them. Not only did they bring him into this world, but they also raised him with tremendous effort. When he will acquire this attribute, he will extrapolate and realize his obligation to Hashem, Who is the Source of all life.

The *Rambam*[60] explicitly states that the mitzvah of *kibbud av v'eim* is among the mitzvos *bein adam la'chaveiro* (between man and his fellow man).

In contrast, the *Ramban*[61] writes that the *Aseres HaDibros* are comprised of five mitzvos that concern man and his Creator, among them *kibbud av v'eim*, and five that concern interpersonal relationships. Honoring a parent is tantamount to honoring Hashem, as a parent is Hashem's partner in bringing a child into the world.[62]

The *Chida*[63] asks why Yaakov Avinu was punished for not having honored his parents during the years that he spent in Lavan's house. Couldn't Yitzchak have forgiven Yaakov for not having accorded him honor while he was away from home? The *Chida* answers, based on the *Sefer Chassidim*, that even though a father has the right to forgo the honor that he is due, that is

---

57. *Tehillim* 37:2.
58. *Ki Seitzei* 281, 1-2.
59. Mitzvah 33.
60. In his commentary to the Mishnah in *Pe'ah* 1:1.
61. *Shemos* 20:12.
62. *Kiddushin* 30b.
63. *P'nei David, Parashas Vayeishev*.

only concerning that which is between man and man; *bein adam la'Makom*, between man and Hashem, the person is still obligated to honor his parent!

According to this *Chida*, it seems that *kibbud av v'eim* is both a mitzvah between man and man and also between man and Hashem.

Tosafos in *Maseches Bava Metzia*[64] questions how the Gemara could say that the mitzvah to honor one's parent does not supersede the mitzvah to return a lost item, when a previous Gemara explicitly states that a mitzvah that concerns money cannot supersede a mitzvah that is a prohibition. Similarly, it would seem that *kibbud av v'eim* would have that same advantage over the mitzvah of *hashavas aveidah*. The *Shitah Mekubetzes*[65] offers two answers to this question. The first answer is given according to the understanding that the mitzvah of honoring parents is similar to a restriction, as it is an obligation between man and Hashem, while the second answer understands that it is an obligation between man and man. The second answer states that the mitzvah of *kibbud av v'eim* is also of a monetary nature, since the point of the mitzvah is to benefit one's parents. This clearly means that the mitzvah of *kibbud av v'eim* is a mitzvah between man and man. Therefore, one would have to ask his parents for *mechilah* if he did not honor them, in accordance with the opinions that it is a mitzvah between man and man.

In summary, some opinions hold that the mitzvah to honor one's parents is a mitzvah between man and Hashem. Other opinions say that it is a mitzvah between man and man. The *Sefer Chassidim* says that the mitzvah has both facets, and is both a mitzvah between man and Hashem and a mitzvah between man and man.

---

64. 30b.
65. 32a

פרשת משפטים
Parashas Mishpatim

Sudden Impact

בַּעַל הַבּוֹר יְשַׁלֵּם
The owner of the pit shall make restitution
(21:34)

Q Asher was driving down his block when he spotted Shmuli walking to shul. Asher pulled over and kindly offered Shmuli a ride. Shmuli gratefully settled into the passenger seat and thanked Asher for his *hachnasas orchim*. When they reached the shul, Shmuli, eager to start *davening*, flung open his door without looking, not realizing that at that very moment someone else had pulled into the parking space next to them. The car crashed into Shmuli's open door and bent it forward. In addition, the moving vehicle's headlight and the side mirror were smashed. Does Shmuli have to pay for the damages, or is the other car's driver responsible to avoid colliding with objects in his path?

A The Gemara in *Bava Kamma*[66] states that if a man placed a jug in a public area, and someone subsequently tripped over the jug and smashed it, the one who tripped does not have to pay for breaking the jug. On the contrary; if he was hurt by tripping over the jug, the one who put the jug there has to pay for personal injury. In Shmuli's case, the car door is comparable to the jug that the moving vehicle "tripped" over, and Shmuli is responsible to pay for the damages.

The Gemara questions why the person who tripped is not to be faulted for being unaware that there was a jug in his path. The Gemara gives several answers. The answer that is cited by the *Shulchan Aruch* is that people are not accustomed to paying attention where they step when they are walking. In this case, that would certainly not apply, as a driver must always concentrate on the road. There is, however, another reason to exempt the driver, which does apply in our case: By the time the driver saw Shmuli's door open, it was already too late. He did not have enough time to brake, and therefore he cannot be held accountable.

Regarding the headlight and the mirror, since Shmuli is guilty of having placed an obstacle in a public domain, he is categorized[67] as one who dug or uncovered a pit in a public place, and who is exempt from damages caused to inanimate objects. Hence, he would not have to pay for the damages to the driver's car.

The *Bircas Shmuel*[68] and the *Chazon Ish*[69] disagreed as to whether one who "dug a pit" is obligated, *b'dinei Shamayim*, to pay for inanimate objects that were damaged, or if he is fully exempted. Accordingly, Shmuli might have an obligation to pay for the headlight and mirror, *b'dinei Shamayim*.

The exemption from paying for damages to inanimate objects would not cover the damages to Asher's car door, as the car door

---

66. 27a.
67. See *Bava Kamma* 2a. There are four categories of damages: an ox, a pit, a person, and a fire. Each category has its own set of rules that are discussed at length in the Gemara.
68. *Bava Kamma* 2 §32.
69. Ibid., §7.

was not damaged independently, but by the moving vehicle. The moving vehicle is categorized as an oncoming fire, which is not exempt from responsibility for damage to inanimate objects. *Tosafos*[70] explains that there is no difference between someone who brings a fire to consume his friend's property, and someone who brings his friend's property to be consumed by a fire. In this case, Shmuli introduced the car door to the moving vehicle, and therefore has to pay for Asher's damaged door. He would do well to be more careful in the future.

Return Policy

כָּל אַלְמָנָה וְיָתוֹם לֹא תְעַנּוּן
You shall not cause pain to any widow or orphan
(22:21)

Q Rabbi Yaakov Eliezer Schwartzman related the following fascinating incident: Many years ago in Beis Medrash Govoha of Lakewood, a widow cooked for the yeshivah. The *bachurim* were not overly enthusiastic in approving of her culinary skills, and they complained to the venerable Rosh Yeshivah, Rav Aharon Kotler, that something had to be done to improve the situation. Rav Aharon sympathized with their plight, but reminded them that it is forbidden to cause pain to a widow.

One Shabbos night after a full week of particularly disappointing meals, two *bachurim* decided to teach the

---

70. Ibid., 56a.

cook a lesson, and they removed the cholent pot from the *blech* and hid it in the basement. When Rav Aharon discovered what they had done, he ordered the two *bachurim* to return the pot to the *blech*, as that would only be a violation of the *issur d'Rabbanan*[71] (Rabbinical prohibition) of *chazarah*, while causing pain to a widow is forbidden *mi'd'Oraisa*.

Rav Zilberstein asked Rabbi Schwartzman if perhaps Rav Aharon had instructed the *bachurim* to have a non-Jew return the pot to the *blech*.[72] Rav Schwartzman verified that although a non-Jew was available to replace the pot on the *blech*, Rav Aharon specifically ordered the *bachurim* to do it themselves, in order to impress upon them the severity of their actions. By instructing them to return the pot, the *bachurim* were shocked into the realization of the magnitude of what they had done. It was a one-time ruling in order to teach them how careful one must be of others' feelings in interpersonal relationships.

The Rosh Yeshivah's ruling was revolutionary, as one may not violate an *issur d'Rabbanan* in order to prevent a violation of a mitzvah *d'Oraisa*. For example, on

---

71. *Chazal* forbade returning a pot to the stove on Shabbos unless five conditions are met:
    1. The food is fully cooked.
    2. The food is still hot.
    3. The heat source is covered.
    4. The pot was in his hands since it was removed.
    5. He had intent to return the pot when he removed it.

    The reason for the prohibition is that *Chazal* were concerned lest someone stoke the coals in order to reheat the food and also because returning the pot to the fire resembles the act of cooking. See *Orach Chaim* 253:2.

72. The *Beur Halachah* (253:5 *d"h le'hachem*) cites the *Pri Megadim* that in case of great need one may be lenient and ask a non-Jew to replace a pot of fully cooked food, as returning the food is an *issur d'Rabbanan* and asking a non-Jew to do so is also an *issur d'Rabbanan*. Although the *Chazon Ish* disputes this ruling, perhaps Rav Aharon relied on the *Pri Megadim* to avoid causing pain to the cook.

Rosh Hashanah, one may not remove a *shofar* that is hanging from a tree, even if refraining from doing so will prevent him from being able to perform the mitzvah *d'Oraisa* of *shofar*. What could have been Rav Aharon's basis for such a decision?

Perhaps since the pot of cholent belonged to the yeshivah, the *bachurim* had no right to remove it from the *blech*, thus prohibiting its return. The Gemara[73] has a principle that one cannot confer a forbidden status upon property that does not belong to him. However, the *Beur Halachah*[74] cites Rabbi Akiva Eiger, who writes that one **can** confer a status onto his friend's property, rendering it forbidden, if he does so with an action; e.g., someone moves his friend's pot from the stove to the floor.

The Gemara in *Shabbos*[75] does permit one who put dough into the oven on Shabbos to peel the dough off the oven wall in order to prevent it from baking.[76] Although peeling off the dough on Shabbos is prohibited *mi'd'Rabbanan*, it is permitted in order to prevent baking on Shabbos, which is a violation of an *issur d'Oraisa*. However, this leniency would not apply in the *yeshivah bachurim's* case. Rav Yisrael Salanter[77] considered the following case: If someone accidentally left a pot of meat with milk on the stove before Shabbos, would it be permitted to remove the pot from the fire on Shabbos, despite the fact that the raw meat is *muktzeh*, before it cooks and he transgresses the prohibition of cooking milk and meat together? He compares this scenario to the Gemara's case of peeling the dough on Shabbos, but he rejects the comparison on two counts:

1. Peeling dough from the oven wall was forbidden by *Chazal* merely because it is inappropriate behavior for Shabbos. This cannot be compared to moving *muktzeh*, which is a prohibition

---
73. *Pesachim* 90a.
74. 253:2 *d"h v'lo hinicham*.
75. 3b.
76. In the time of the Gemara, bread was baked by sticking dough onto the oven's wall and taking it off after it was baked.
77. *Even Yisrael*, p. 81.

enacted to distance people from desecrating the Shabbos *mi'd'Oraisa*.

2. Perhaps the Gemara permits transgressing a *d'Rabbanan* that relates to Shabbos only in order to prevent a *d'Oraisa* violation of Shabbos. That does not prove that it would be permitted to disregard the prohibition against moving *muktzeh* in order to prevent a violation of cooking milk and meat.

By the same logic, one would not be allowed to violate the prohibition of *chazarah* to prevent causing pain to a widow. *Chazarah* is also prohibited in order to safeguard the *d'Oraisa* of cooking, and is therefore more stringent than the prohibition of peeling dough. In addition, paining a widow is not a violation of Shabbos.

Rav Aharon may have relied on the opinion of the *Ran* quoted by the *Rema*,[78] which states that the prohibition of *chazarah* applies to pots that were removed from the stove before Shabbos. Pots that were removed on Shabbos may be returned to the stove even if they were placed on the floor, provided that the other conditions of *chazarah* are met.[79] Even though the *Ran's* opinion is not *halachah l'ma'aseh*, it can be used in conjunction with other factors to allow *chazarah* on Shabbos.

In addition, the *Beur Halachah* cites some *Rishonim* who permit *chazarah* even if the pot was placed on the ground, providing that the one who removed it from the stove intended to replace it afterward. Although the *bachurim* had no such intent, since the pot did not belong to them, their lack of intent cannot confer a forbidden status, as lack of intent is not considered an action.

In the face of the tremendous *aveirah* of paining a widow, it seems that Rav Aharon ruled that one may rely on these opinions in order to impress upon the *bachurim* how serious their actions were.

---

78. *Orach Chaim* 253:2.
79. The pot is fully cooked, still hot, and there is a *blech*.

Mis(ter) Understanding

הָשֵׁב תְּשִׁיבֶנּוּ לוֹ
You shall return it to him repeatedly
(23:4)

Q Raphael and Daniel boarded the bus together at the Central Bus Station in Ashdod. The bus' final destination was Tzefas, but it was to make several stops along the way. Raphael settled into his seat and watched as Daniel placed the laptop computer that he was carrying into the overhead compartment and took the seat below it.

When the bus arrived in Netanya, Daniel got off the bus. Raphael continued on to the next stop, but before he alighted he noticed that Daniel's computer was still in the overhead compartment. Raphael knew Daniel and realized that he had an opportunity to fulfill the mitzvah of *hashavas aveidah*. Raphael quickly picked up the computer, got off the bus, and called Daniel as soon as he reached his home.

Daniel picked up on the first ring, and Raphael thanked him for giving him the opportunity to return his lost item. Daniel didn't understand what Raphael was talking about. Raphael reminded him that he had forgotten the computer on the bus, and that he had taken it home for Daniel to collect at his earliest convenience.

Daniel cried out that the computer was not his at all! While he was waiting on line to board the bus, he noticed a man struggling with numerous bags, and offered to help him onto the bus. The man had gratefully handed Daniel his computer to take onto the bus, and since Daniel sat next to him, the computer was stored over their seats.

Raphael turned on the computer and quickly discovered the owner's identity. The owner was Yehudah Shapiro of Tzefas. Raphael phoned him immediately to tell him where his computer was. Yehudah was very relieved. He had been searching for his computer all day. He told Raphael that he needed his computer desperately, as he was in the middle of a project, and therefore, Raphael should please return the computer as soon as possible.

Raphael was aghast. Why should **he** have to make the trip to Tzefas to return the computer? After all, he was only trying to perform the mitzvah of *hashavas aveidah*. In such a case, the owner of the item is responsible for collecting his property.[80] Yehudah countered that, as a matter of fact, Raphael had actually stolen his computer, albeit unintentionally, and it is incumbent upon a thief to return whatever he stole.[81] Who is responsible to reunite the owner with his computer?

A principle in halachah states that generally, any moveable property that is found in someone's possession is assumed to belong to him.[82] Rav Shimon Zelaznik quoted Rav Isser Zalman Meltzer, who explained that it is this

---

80. The *sefer Pe'er Hador* cites this ruling from the *Chazon Ish* (Vol. IV, p. 217).
81. The *Shulchan Aruch, Choshen Mishpat* 367:1 writes that a thief does not have to pursue his victim to return the item, unless the thief swore falsely to deny that he stole. Otherwise, he can simply inform the owner that he can come to collect his property. However, the *Shach* adds that if the thief transferred the property to a different city, he must return it to the place from which he stole it. The *Nesivos HaMishpat* writes that even in such a case, the thief does not have to deliver the merchandise if he intentionally stole it, as *Chazal* designed this special dispensation to encourage thieves to do *teshuvah*. (See *Sma* 367 §2.) If, however, he only stole accidentally, his behavior is not included in that enactment and he should have to deliver the item.
82. *Shulchan Aruch, Choshen Mishpat* 133:1.

principle that allows us to believe every *chassan* who says that the *kiddushin* ring he possesses is actually his, and therefore his marriage is valid.

Accordingly, since Raphael saw Daniel holding the computer, he had a halachic basis to assume that it belonged to him. It was natural for him to conclude that Daniel had left his computer on the bus, and that a mitzvah of *hashavas aveidah* was incumbent upon him. Even if the truth was otherwise, Raphael is not to be faulted for acting in accordance to halachah.[83] A person only has to exercise intellectual gymnastics in judging others favorably, but not when it comes to *hashavas aveidah*.

If orphans found a cow in their father's yard and, assuming that it was part of their inheritance, they slaughtered and ate the cow, only to discover afterward that the cow belonged to someone else, they are required to pay only two-thirds of the value of the cow. They are not held completely responsible, as they cannot be blamed for thinking that the cow, which was in their father's possession, actually belonged to someone else.[84]

In summary, Raphael had no choice other than to take the computer and try to return it to its owner. He was not a thief, but one who was trying to return a lost item to its owner. Therefore, he has no obligation to expend time, money, or energy to deliver the computer to Yehudah. Yehudah will have to arrange the delivery himself.

---

83. See *Ketzos HaChoshen* 25 §1.
84. *Bava Kamma* 112a.

Kosher Loopholes

מִדְּבַר שֶׁקֶר תִּרְחָק
Distance yourself from a false word
(23:7)

Q If Gershon claims in *beis din* that Asher owes him money, and Asher admits to part of Gershon's claim, Asher must swear that he is telling the truth regarding the remainder of the claim against him. However, this halachah is limited to cases where the admission is worth at least a *perutah*[85] and the value of the remainder of the claim is at least two *ma'ah*[86] of silver.[87]

If the remainder would be exactly two *ma'ah*, would Asher be allowed to admit that he owes a little more than he really does in order to reduce the remainder to less than two *ma'ah* and avoid having to swear, or would that be a violation of the prohibition against lying?

A The *Chidushei HaRim*[88] raises this question, and initially compares it to the following case in *Maseches Shevuos*.[89] Naftali owes Shimon $100, and Shimon claims that the debt is really $200. If Naftali will admit that he owes $100, he will have to swear that he does not owe the additional $100. Naftali is not allowed to deny the debt completely in *beis din* and pay Shimon the $100 afterward, thereby avoiding having to swear, because the Torah commands us to distance ourselves from falsehood. If so,

---

85. A *perutah* is the value of 1/40 of a gram of silver.
86. One *ma'ah* is equal to 32 *perutos*. Two *ma'ah* = 64 *perutos*.
87. *Shulchan Aruch, Choshen Mishpat* 88:1. This is relevant as far as one's *mi'd'Oraisa* obligation. *Mi'd'Rabbanan* he would have to swear regardless of the remainder.
88. *Choshen Mishpat* 88 §14.
89. 31a.

perhaps in this case as well, Asher is not allowed to lie in order to avoid taking an oath. He is obligated to tell the truth. Moreover, if by lying he will be spared the oath, that would be unjust, since by telling the truth, he would be obligated to swear.

Moreover, if *beis din* knew that Asher really denies the full two *ma'ah* of Gershon's claim, they would obligate Asher to swear. This camouflage is falsehood, and should be included in the prohibition against lying.

However, the *Chidushei HaRim* concludes that it should actually be permitted, as a person's admission is as potent as "100 witnesses," and a person can create obligations upon himself even when they are detrimental to others.

By obligating himself to pay the extra *perutah*, *beis din's* exempting Asher from an oath will be halachically accurate, since his denial is truthfully on less than two *ma'ah*.[90]

Hidden Costs

מִדְּבַר שֶׁקֶר תִּרְחָק
Distance yourself from a false word
(23:7)

Once his parents were no longer able to live independently, Levi engaged the services of Boruch the real-estate broker to sell their apartment. Boruch looked over the property and asked Levi how much he wanted to sell it for. Levi replied that he wanted $500,000 for the apartment. Boruch thought for a moment, and then

---

90. The *Chidushei HaRim* cites additional proofs to support his conclusion.

164 / SEFER SHEMOS

proposed that Levi allow him to sell the apartment for as much as he could, and he would not charge him a penny. Levi would receive his half-million dollars, and if Boruch succeeded in selling it for more than that, he would keep the difference. Levi didn't really have the time or inclination to deal with such matters, so he decided to accept Boruch's offer.

Boruch showed Levi's parents' home to Binyamin. Binyamin was very impressed with the property and asked him the price. Boruch replied that the home cost $550,000, and there was no broker's fee involved. Binyamin agreed to the price, and they made an appointment for that very afternoon in a lawyer's office to draw up a contract. At the closing, Boruch informed Binyamin that he needed the payment to be divided into two separate checks. One check would be for $500,000 and the other for the remaining $50,000. At this point Binyamin became suspicious that perhaps his money was not going to be transferred to Levi in its entirety. Eventually, the truth emerged that the $50,000 was intended for Boruch to pocket in return for his involvement.

Binyamin was outraged at the fact that Boruch would charge such an exorbitant fee after he had specifically stated that he was not charging anything. Binyamin made it clear to Boruch, and everyone else in earshot and beyond, that he had no interest in dealing with such people, and he stormed out of the office.

Several weeks later Boruch discovered that Binyamin had bought Levi's house without involving him. Binyamin simply approached Levi and paid him the original price without having to take on a broker's fee. Levi readily agreed, and the two closed the deal without informing Boruch.

Boruch now insists that since he was responsible for attracting the buyer who eventually purchased the apartment, he deserves to collect his $50,000 since that was his fee for the deal. Levi claims that since he only received $500,000, he should not have to pay Boruch anything, since Boruch agreed not to charge him anything unless he sold the house for more than that. Binyamin is outraged again, since Boruch promised that he would not charge him anything. How should this matter be settled?

A The *Rema*[91] rules that one who agreed to accept a service or a favor from another cannot claim retroactively that it must have been offered for free since he did not request it. He must pay for the benefit that he received. The *Gra*[92] notes that the source that a beneficiary must pay for the benefit he received is the Gemara in *Bava Metzia*.[93] That Gemara states that if one planted his friend's field without having been asked to do so, and the field was scheduled to be planted, the owner of the field is required to pay for his benefits, even though he did not necessarily wish to pay the planter to do so. This is also the source for the obligation to pay a broker's fee.

In this case as well, Binyamin is required to pay Boruch for his services in leading him to purchase Levi's parents' home. Even if Boruch promised that he would not charge a broker's fee, his "generosity" was conditional on the price of $550,000, with the intent of pocketing $50,000. It is obvious that Boruch had no intention to work without being paid. Therefore, Binyamin certainly has to pay for Boruch's services. However, since Boruch acted deceptively, claiming that he was not charging a fee, he should only be paid at the lower end of the pay scale that is customary for a broker's fee in that community.

As far as Levi's obligation to pay, if it is customary for the seller to pay a commission as well, he would also have to pay Boruch, but if there is no such custom, he would not have to pay.

---

91. *Choshen Mishpat* 264:4.
92. Ad loc. §13.
93. 101a.

פרשת תרומה
Parashas Terumah

Almost the Same

וְכֵן תַּעֲשׂוּ
And so shall you do

רש"י: לְדוֹרוֹת
Rashi: In [future] generations

(25:9)

Q Simcha signed a contract with a builder to construct a new house for him. The builder asked Simcha how he wanted the house built, and Simcha responded that he wanted it to be just like his neighbor's house. A few months later the construction was completed. The house really did look exactly like his neighbor's house. However, upon measuring, Simcha discovered that his house was actually smaller than his neighbor's house by about 20 square feet. The builder claimed that he was aware of the discrepancy, but he had intentionally built the house smaller because he thought that it was nicer that way. He had only Simcha's best interests in mind. He explained that although he was supposed to build the house using the neighbor's house as a guide, that only referred to the form, but not to the dimensions. Is the builder right?

A This question was brought to the Tchebiner Rav to decide. The Rav wanted to exonerate the builder based on the *Mizrachi* in *Parashas Terumah*. *Rashi*[94] explains that Hashem wanted the furnishings of the *Beis HaMikdash* to be built in future generations in the same form as He had asked them to be built at the time of the construction of the *Mishkan*.

The *Ramban* points out that the dimensions of the *Mizbei'ach* in the *Mishkan* were five *amos* by five *amos*, yet Shlomo built the *Mizbei'ach* for the *Beis HaMikdash* to be 20 *amos* by 20 *amos*. The *Mizrachi* resolves the difficulty, that the *pasuk* stating *and so you shall do* is relevant only to the proportionate dimensions, but not to the actual size. If so, perhaps Simcha's words were also limited to having his house built in the form of his neighbor's house, but not to the exact size.

The *Shulchan Aruch*,[95] however, does not agree with this conclusion. One who agrees to lease a house "like this" to his friend has to provide a house the same size as the model that he was shown. The renter cannot claim that he was referring to the location; he must provide a house with the same dimensions.

The difference between the *Mizrachi* and the *Shulchan Aruch* is obvious. The essence of a house is to provide living space. Therefore, the size of the house is integral to its function. The significance of the furnishings of the *Beis HaMikdash* were not dependent on their size, and therefore it was sufficient to keep them proportionate.

The builder will have to compensate Simcha for not having honored their agreement.

---

94. *Shemos* 25:9.
95. *Choshen Mishpat* 312:17.

Dangerously Armed

וְעָשִׂיתָ אֶת נֵרֹתֶיהָ שִׁבְעָה
And you shall make its lamps seven
(25:37)

Q Not everyone is as lucky as Avi's in-laws, as he is an even more wonderful son-in-law than they could ever have dreamed of having. Fortunately, they are well aware of Avi's sterling character and his dedication to his family, and they try to show their appreciation at every opportunity. When Avi's wife, Aliza, gave birth to their fifth child, Avi's mother-in-law surprised them with a gorgeous seven-armed silver candelabra that she delivered in time for Aliza's first Shabbos at home after the birth.

Avi felt somewhat ambivalent about this gift. On the one hand, he was overwhelmed with *hakaras hatov* for his mother-in-law's generosity. The candelabra was very expensive and exquisite. On the other hand, the *Shulchan Aruch*[96] rules that one is forbidden to duplicate the *Menorah* that stood in the *Beis HaMikdash*. One may fashion a *menorah* with any number of arms, except seven. This holds true even if it is not made of gold, does not contain the various details with which the *Menorah* was fashioned, or is not the same size as the *Menorah* in the *Beis HaMikdash*. Obviously, Avi's mother-in-law was unaware of this halachah.

Avi called his rebbe to ask advice on how to proceed. The rebbe told Avi that he should thank his mother-in-law profusely for the beautiful, generous gift and tell her how much he loves it. However, he must

---
96. *Yoreh De'ah* 141:8.

also inform her that he may not use such a candelabra, as it is prohibited by halachah. Avi followed his rebbe's advice. Not only was his mother-in-law not insulted, but she respected his integrity. She was impressed that even if he was presented with such a valuable gift, he would follow the halachah over all.

Avi was now concerned whether he was allowed to return the candelabra to the store, or if he had to be concerned that someone else would buy it, despite the fact that it would be forbidden for them to do so. Can he return it?

A The *Pischei Teshuvah*[97] cites the *Bechor Shor* who writes that the *Menorah's* arms did not have to be arranged in a straight line, and therefore, any seven-armed *menorah* is forbidden, regardless of its shape. The *Pischei Teshuvah* concludes that although others differ, one should be stringent in this matter since it is something that is forbidden *mi'd'Oraisa*.[98]

In addition, the *poskim* argue as to whether the prohibition is only directed against making such a *menorah* or if it also includes owning such a *menorah*.[99]

The question is whether the owner of the silver store may claim that he follows the lenient opinion and does not have to negate the sale. The *Pri Megadim*[100] says that unless the stringent opinion is accepted as halachah, one cannot insist that the sale be negated. The *Chaim She'al*[101] rules that one may negate the sale even if the halachah states the item is permissible, but *le'chatchilah* one would not have purchased the item because of the dissenting opinion. The *Mishpat Shalom*[102] explains that these two opinions do not differ: The *Pri Megadim* is discussing someone who

---

97. Ad loc. §14.
98. See also *Darchei Teshuvah* §56.
99. See *Beis Yosef* and *Shulchan Aruch*, and *Darchei Teshuvah* §52.
100. *Orach Chaim* 467 §24.
101. Vol. 1, 74 §35.
102. 232 §12.

personally wants to follow the stringent opinion, even though it is halachically permissible, while the *Chaim She'al's* ruling is regarding a matter in which the one dissenting opinion should be followed *le'chatchilah*.

In Avi's case, many *poskim* rule stringently and state that one may not own a seven-armed candelabra, and therefore, even the *Pri Megadim* would agree that one could annul the original sale. Accordingly, the *menorah* still belongs to the silver store, and Avi may return it to them, regardless of whether the store will sell it to anyone else.

Rav Elyashiv ruled in a similar case that when someone bought a suit and discovered that it contained *sha'atnez*, the suit may be returned to the store. Since he never intended to buy a suit that contained *sha'atnez*, the original sale was never valid, and the store retains possession of the suit. Rav Elyashiv added that it would be *middas chassidus* (an act of piety) not to return the suit if someone else may buy it and violate the prohibition against wearing *sha'atnez*. In Avi's case, where there are *poskim* who permit owning such a candelabra, perhaps Rav Elyashiv would agree that even one who acts with piety may return the candelabra to the store.

Rav Chaim Kanievsky[103] was asked by someone who just became aware of the halachah against owning a seven-armed candelabra and whose wife had lit her candles in such a candelabra for 30 years, if there was room for leniency. Rav Chaim answered that once his mother, the Chazon Ish's sister, had bought such a candelabra and brought it home. The Chazon Ish instructed her to return it to the store.

In summary, Avi may return the candelabra for a full refund without concern that someone else may purchase it.

One of the most famous questions ever raised on the topic of

---
103. *Derech Sichah*, p. 267.

Chanukah is attributed to the *Beis Yosef*, although in truth, the question is actually discussed by earlier commentaries on the Gemara. The question is: Why do we celebrate eight days of Chanukah? If we are trying to commemorate the miracle that the amount of oil that was found was sufficient for just one day and it miraculously burned for an additional seven days, then the miracle only lasted for seven days. Why do we celebrate an extra day of Chanukah?

The *Beis Yosef* gives three answers to this question, although there are literally hundreds of other answers. The answer that Rav Elyashiv praised highly is that of the *Sho'el U'meishiv*[104]: Had *Chazal* enacted a seven-day holiday, many people might have transgressed the Biblical prohibition against fashioning a seven-armed *menorah*, similar to that of the *Beis HaMikdash*. Therefore, *Chazal* established Chanukah for eight days, based on additional reasons to extend it for an extra day, so that the *menorah* should have eight lights.

A Bad Shidduch?

וְיִהְיוּ תֹאֲמִם מִלְמַטָּה
And they shall be even at the bottom
(26:24)

Q Meir was walking down a busy street when he noticed a Shoe World shopping bag. It seemed that someone had dropped it on the sidewalk. Meir opened the bag and found a box of brand-new shoes. After consulting with his Rav, Meir understood that based on the

---
104. *Kamma* Vol. 3, 71.

circumstances of his find, he was not obligated to attempt to find the owner of the shoes, yet he went beyond the letter of the law and posted signs, hoping to return the shoes. After a few weeks, Meir realized that the chances of locating the owner at this point were almost nil, so he decided to open the box of shoes to see if he could keep them for himself or give them away. Meir picked up one of the shoes and discovered to his delight that it was a size 11: just his size! Unfortunately, as he continued to unpack the box, he realized that the shoes were actually a mismatch. The right shoe was a size 11, but the left shoe was a size 10 ½. Both of Meir's feet are size 11. Meir's thoughts raced in his mind. If the shoes were mismatched, then in all probability their sale was an error. When the customer would realize the mistake, he would surely go back to the store and return them. If so, perhaps the shoes still belonged to the store, since they were destined to be returned. The store owner could not possibly have given up hope of their recovery because he was totally unaware that they were lost!

Does Meir have an obligation to return the shoes to the store? If Meir is allowed to keep the shoes, could he ask the sales associate at Shoe World to switch one of the shoes for him so he could have a matching pair? Since he did not actually purchase the shoes from the store, does he have a right to make such a request?

A The *E'ven Yisrael*[105] writes that even if merchandise was found to be defective, the sale is still valid unless the customer wishes to return his purchase. In Meir's case, it is possible that Shoe World received the mismatched shoes from the manufacturer, and is happy that the customer never came to

---
105. *Hilchos Mechirah* 15:1.

negate the sale. Accordingly, the sale of the shoes is valid, and Meir would be allowed to keep the shoes. He may not try to exchange the shoes at the store, as the store has no obligation to Meir, since he did not purchase the shoes from them.

On the other hand, it could be that Shoe World is also stuck with two mismatched shoes; i.e., the other halves of the pairs for the shoes that Meir possesses. In that case, the owner of the store is waiting for the shoes to be returned, but would have no obligation to Meir, as he can claim that he will wait until the real owner comes back to the store to claim his money, or alternatively, other shoes that he chooses.

It is also possible that the owner already acquired one of the shoes, and only the shoe with the wrong size has to be returned. Thus Meir would only have to return one of the shoes, if he knew which one it was, and could ask Shoe World for the shoe that matches the one he is allowed to keep. Actually, Shoe World has no obligation to give Meir the matching shoe. Even though Meir is allowed to keep the shoe that he found, he has no claim on the shoe that remains in the store. Since Meir never bought the shoes, the store owners have no obligation to him. Shoe World may continue to hold it until the original customer comes to claim it. In addition, Meir cannot insist that the store give him the single shoe, based on the claim that they have no use for it and have nothing to lose by giving it to him, because the store has the identical claim to Meir! What use does *he* have for the single shoe; he should just give it to them so they could sell it to a different customer together with its match.

Going even further, there is a fourth possibility: Maybe the customer knew that the shoes were mismatched and purchased them at a significant discount. Perhaps the original customer's left foot was slightly larger than his right foot, and he intentionally bought mismatched shoes. Therefore, Meir has acquired this intentionally mismatched pair and has no right to exchange them without the store owner's express permission. This possibility seems the most likely, as sales people are generally careful to check that they did not separate a pair of shoes.

Therefore, Meir should just give the shoes back to the store, since he has no use for a mismatched pair of shoes.

פרשת תצוה
Parashas Tetzaveh

Presents of Mind

וְהָאֲבָנִים תִּהְיֶיןָ עַל שְׁמֹת בְּנֵי יִשְׂרָאֵל
And the stones shall be according to the names of the sons of Israel
(28:21)

It was Simchas Torah, and it was time to auction off the various *aliyos* and *kibbudim* (honors) for Yom Tov and throughout the year. In the Bnei Chesed shul they had a custom of selling *pesichah* to one person for the entire year. Actually, the *pesichah* was given to the Rav, but the Rav would make a special *mi shebeirach* during every *pesichah*[106] for the one who bought it for him.

Mendel bought *pesichah* for $2,500 and announced that he would give the *mi shebeirach* to his new son-in-law, Zalman. Three months later, Zalman's *shidduch*

---

106. The *Zohar* (*Parashas Vayakhel*) explains that at the time that the *Sefer Torah* is taken out of the *aron kodesh* to be read for the *tzibbur*, the Heavenly gates of mercy are opened and Hashem's love is awakened. Hence, it is an opportune time for *davening*.

tragically did not merit to be an eternal one, and the couple decided to divorce.

The next Shabbos, the Rav performed *pesichah*, and made his usual *mi shebeirach* for Zalman, the now ex-son-in-law. After *davening*, Mendel approached the *Rav* and requested that from now on, instead of making a *mi shebeirach* for Zalman, he should make it for Mendel's daughter, without mentioning Zalman.

Is Mendel allowed to rescind the *mi shebeirach* after he already bestowed it upon Zalman? The *Rivash*[107] writes explicitly that when one receives a present from his friend, the present belongs to him, even if subsequently their relationship deteriorates. Would that apply to this case as well, or is it obvious that Mendel only intended to give Zalman the *mi shebeirach* as long as he was still his son-in-law?

𝒜 Someone once donated an exquisite *paroches* to a shul. It had his name and his wife's name beautifully embroidered on it in gold lettering. Years passed, and unfortunately, the man and his wife divorced. The man asked the *gabbai* to remove his ex-wife's name from the *paroches*, as she was no longer his wife. The *gabbai* came to ask Rav Zilberstein if he should accede to the man's request.

Rav Zilberstein asked Rav Elyashiv, who responded that if the man did not want his name to be embroidered next to the name of his former wife, then he should remove his own name from the *paroches*! Once the husband had given instructions to embroider his wife's name on the *paroches*, he has in effect given her a present and he cannot revoke that present just because they are no longer married.

This ruling may seem applicable to this case as well, but in truth, the two cases are not the same. In the case of the *paroches*,

---
107. *Siman* 301.

the husband gave an outright present to his wife, and therefore he cannot revoke the present at a later date. When a father-in-law buys something for his son-in-law, his true intent is to benefit his daughter. His entire relationship with the son-in-law is rooted in the father's love for his daughter and his desire to see her success and happiness. A *mi shebeirach* for the son-in-law is really the father's way of blessing his daughter. Now that they are no longer married, and the daughter has no benefit from the *mi shebeirach* anymore, it is clear to everyone that the *mi shebeirach* was never intended to be given under such circumstances. (Mendel had even announced that he was giving the *zechus* to his **son-in-law**, and Zalman no longer holds that title.)

When someone gives his friend a present, he does so because of their friendship. Even if their relationship deteriorates, it cannot undo that which was true at the time that the present was given. In contrast, Mendel never intended to give a gift to his son-in-law, but rather to his daughter. Therefore, he may request that his daughter's name be mentioned in the *mi shebeirach* instead of that of her former son-in-law.

Broken Heart

עַל לִבּוֹ לִפְנֵי ה' תָּמִיד
On his heart constantly before Hashem
(28:30)

Q Libby was a mere 17 years old when she had a pacemaker implanted to ensure her heart's top performance. The operation was successful, and she felt great. The pacemaker did not interfere at all with her day-to-day living and the doctors assured her that she had no limitations. She went to a top cardiologist who also assured her that she was completely healthy, needed no follow-up care, and could continue to live with the pacemaker for 120 healthy years.

Based on the doctor's words, Libby felt no inhibitions in the *shidduch* process, and married a wonderful boy named Mordechai. After the wedding, Mordechai discovered that his new wife had a pacemaker, which she had neglected to tell him about. He felt cheated that she would try to hide such an obvious handicap, and he insists that Libby accept a *get* from him.

Libby maintains that she is not guilty of any deceit. She is completely fit and healthy, and she is as capable as any Jewish girl of being a wife and mother. She implored him to consult with her doctors to verify her words.

Can Mordechai claim that his marriage to Libby was a mistake? If their marriage was, in fact, a mistake, does she need a *get*?

A The definition of a defect is not determined by the doctors' opinions, even if we accept the premise that what they are saying is true. The *Rambam*[108] and the *Shulchan Aruch*[109] have a different guideline:

> Anything about which the residents of a country have concurred to consider a defect for which an item can be returned to the seller is grounds to annul the sale. If a certain quality is present in the merchandise, and common consensus is that it is not a defect, the merchandise cannot be returned unless the buyer stipulated in advance that he

---

108. *Hilchos Mechirah,* Chapter 15.
109. *Choshen Mishpat* 232:7

does not wish to purchase such an item. The reason for this is because when one does business, he does so based on the custom of the land.

Therefore, it would have to be determined whether or not most people consider a pacemaker to be a defect. If most people would consider a pacemaker to be a defect, then that would be the determining factor in this case, as well.

However, even if it is determined that the *kallah* had a defect, she would still need a *get*. Although initially Mordechai would not have married her had he known about the pacemaker, he would certainly not have divorced her for that reason had her need for a pacemaker only arisen after their marriage. Anything that is not grounds for divorce after marriage cannot be sufficient reason to annul the marriage, even if it is subsequently discovered that it existed before they married.[110]

The *Beis Shmuel*[111] rules that if a woman had a defect which she hid from her *chassan* before they married, then she could be given a *get* against her will, since she acted improperly by hiding it from him.

In summary, it must be determined whether people consider someone who has a pacemaker to be handicapped. If it is considered a defect, since Libby did not disclose her deficiency to her prospective husband, she does need a *get* in order to end the marriage, and Mordechai could give her a *get* against her will, under the circumstances.

Hopefully, though, he will come to terms with the situation, and this will not prove necessary.

---

110. See *Kehillas Yaakov, Yevamos* 44, from where this decision is extrapolated.
111. *Even HaEzer* 117 §24.

The Flood Is Over

מִמָּתְנַיִם וְעַד יְרֵכַיִם יִהְיוּ
From the hips to the thighs shall they be
(28:42)

Q Mendy needed a new pair of black slacks. He found a nice pair that accommodated his narrow waist, but was two inches too short for him. The salesman pointed out that the slacks already had a finished hem which could be let down, and then they would fit him perfectly. Mendy purchased the pants, and brought them to his local dry cleaners for alterations. He clearly told the seamstress that he needed the pants lengthened two inches. She promised to have the pants ready the following day.

The next day when Mendy came to pick up his altered slacks, he tried them on to make sure that they were done properly. He had not even closed the waistband when he realized that instead of lengthening the pants two inches, she had shortened the pants two inches, making them four inches shorter than Mendy needed, and now they were beyond repair, as she had cut off the excess fabric. (The seamstress was accustomed to shortening pants as opposed to lengthening them, and had simply made an irreversible error.)

The pants were still in perfect condition — just not for Mendy. Does the seamstress have to pay for ruining his pants, or, since anyone that size could still wear them, is she not to be charged for doing any damage?

A It would seem that the seamstress is guilty of ruining Mendy's pants, as she altered them contrary to his specifications. Even if she only did so accidentally, a person is responsible for damages he causes, even unwittingly.[112] This is especially so in this case, where she is to be faulted for not having been careful in following Mendy's instructions.

The *Nesivos HaMishpat*[113] rules that if someone damaged an item that only has value to its owner, but is worthless to anyone else, there would be no obligation to pay. According to this ruling, if someone broke his friend's glasses, he would not have to reimburse him for them, as the prescription lenses do not have any market value. However, the Chazon Ish[114] and the *Minchas Shlomo*[115] both write that one would have to pay in such a case, since to the owner this item has value, and he spent money to acquire it.

Mendy's case would seem to be the opposite. These pants would be wearable for a good percentage of the population; it is Mendy's tall and slight build that makes the pants worthless to him. Perhaps the fact that the market value remains intact would indicate that no damage has been done.

In fact, the seamstress has the status of a paid watchman, and thus is required to pay for not returning the item intact, regardless as to whether it is considered damaged or not. A paid watchman is responsible for damages (even according to the above *Nesivos HaMishpat*), even if the item only has value to its owner, as in the case of a pair of glasses that were broken. The seamstress must reimburse him in full for his new and now-unwearable pair of pants.

---

112. *Bava Kamma* 5a.
113. 148 §1.
114. *Bava Kamma* 6:3.
115. *Tinyana* 135.

Parashas Ki Sisa

Precious Time

וְשָׁמְרוּ בְנֵי יִשְׂרָאֵל אֶת הַשַּׁבָּת
And the Children of Israel shall observe the Shabbos
(31:16)

Q A righteous woman was pained by the fact that there are Jewish women who do not light candles in honor of Shabbos. She came up with an idea: She would visit hospitals on Friday afternoon and distribute candles to the patients. The problem was that she had no other time to cook properly for Shabbos, and her family's Shabbos menu would certainly suffer. Her family shared her feelings and encouraged her, despite the fact that their Shabbos menu would be affected. Does bringing merit to many have precedence over her mitzvah to prepare befitting Shabbos meals?

A The Gemara in *Eruvin*[116] records that the Jews are assured that Eliyahu HaNavi will not come to herald the Redemption on Erev Shabbos or Erev Yom Tov, as the

---

116. 43b.

Jews are preoccupied. *Rashi* explains that they would have to put aside their Shabbos preparations in order to greet him, and that would be improper. What could be a greater benefit to all Jews than Eliyahu's arrival? Yet, Eliyahu HaNavi, whom we await daily with all of our heart, will not come on Friday in order to avoid disturbing Shabbos preparations. Certainly, then, this woman, who is not obligated to distribute the candles, should not put aside her Shabbos preparations, for which she is obligated.

One could contend that this logic does not apply in this case. The *She'arim HaMetzuyanim BeHalachah* questions why it wouldn't be worthwhile to skip a Shabbos meal in order to hasten Eliyahu's arrival by even one day. After all, there are issues of life and death to be considered, which would even allow one to work on Shabbos; it would certainly be worth skipping a meal! Why should preparations for Shabbos be so important as to delay Eliyahu's arrival?

He explains that the above-mentioned Gemara is referring to a time when the Jewish people are at peace, but in times of travail, when lives are at stake and when people may lose their faith, Eliyahu HaNavi could even come on Erev Shabbos!

The Chofetz Chaim compared our times to a raging fire. It does not matter what quality of water we use to extinguish the fire; we must use whatever is at our disposal. Just as Eliyahu will come in wartime even on Erev Shabbos, even though our Shabbos preparations will suffer, so too in our times it is necessary to do outreach, even on Erev Shabbos, and even if it will have a detrimental effect on our Shabbos preparations.

Another argument that could be made is that Shabbos candles are Shabbos preparations as well, and are another way of honoring the Shabbos. The righteous woman's question would nevertheless still be relevant to other aspects of outreach.

When Rav Chaim Kanievsky was asked this question, he said that the woman should go even on Erev Shabbos. As far as the fact that Eliyahu HaNavi will not appear on Erev Shabbos, he can always come afterward. In contrast, this woman, who has no other time to do this mitzvah of outreach, or even the mitzvah of visiting the ill, can therefore do so even at the expense of her Shabbos menu.

Kiddush Hashem vs. Tznius

וְאִישׁ לֹא יַעֲלֶה עִמָּךְ
And no man may ascend with you
(34:3)

רש"י: אֵין לְךָ יָפֶה מִן הַצְּנִיעוּת
Rashi: There is nothing better than modesty

Q Reb Aharon accompanied his mother to the hospital on the day she was scheduled to have surgery. After they wheeled his mother into the operating room he turned on his laptop and started typing. The other people in the waiting room were surprised: His mother is undergoing surgery, and all he can think about is work?! Reb Aharon noticed the people staring at him, but remained silent. He removed a pile of documents from his briefcase so that the audience would understand that he had some very pressing business to tend to.

After a while, someone looked over his shoulder to see what was on the screen, only to discover that the only thing on the screen was a *daf* of Gemara. Reb Aharon had been learning the entire time! The man could not contain himself, and asked Reb Aharon why he had not shown everyone that he was learning.

Reb Aharon replied that he preferred to learn discreetly in order to fulfill the verse, *walk humbly with your God*.[117]

The man responded that if Reb Aharon would show everyone that he was learning, he would make a *kiddush Hashem* instead of a *chillul Hashem*, as he almost did. In addition, people could follow his example and make the most of their time!

Who is right?

The *Rambam*[118] writes: The Sages taught[119] that it is a sealed promise that one who toils in his learning secretly will become wise, as it is written, *With the modest ones is wisdom*.[120]

Similarly, the Gemara in *Succah*[121] teaches from the *Tanna* that the Torah is compared to a thigh[122] to teach us that just as a thigh must be covered, so too Torah study should remain concealed. Similarly, Rabbi Elazar explained that the *pasuk* that requires one *to walk modestly with Hashem* is referring to those who participate in the mitzvos of making weddings and funerals. Even though those mitzvos are almost always done in the public eye, nevertheless one should be careful to hide his involvement as much as possible. Accordingly, a mitzvah that does not require publicity should certainly be done discreetly.[123]

The *Shulchan Aruch*[124] lists giving *tzedakah* secretly as the highest level of *tzedakah*.

On the other hand, the *Rashba*[125] writes that it is proper to publicize those who give *tzedakah*. This is the behavior of the righteous, to publicize their deeds in order to give reward to those who

---

117. *Michah* 6:8.
118. *Hilchos Talmud Torah* 3:12.
119. The source of the *Rambam* is *Yerushalmi Berachos* 5:1.
120. *Mishlei* 11:2.
121. 49b.
122. See *Shir HaShirim* 7:2.
123. See *Rashi* for elaboration.
124. *Yoreh De'ah* 249.
125. Responsa 581, quoted by the *Rema* 249:13.

do mitzvos. The Torah itself publicizes those who did mitzvos (for example, Reuven seeking to save Yosef). Certainly we should follow the Torah's example, as well.

How does this correlate to walking modestly with Hashem?

The *Divrei Malkiel*[126] writes that it is better to do a mitzvah publicly in order to be an example for others, and by doing so, one will see the fruits of his labor even after he has passed away, because he will accrue merit for the others who have followed his example. Those mitzvos whose punctilious observance is commonplace are better when done in private, since there is no benefit to others seeing him. Yet a mitzvah that has been forsaken should be done publicly in order to teach others to emulate him. *Chazal* have taught, "At a time of gathering, scatter, and at a time of scattering, gather."[127] This means that it is better to learn in private in order not to be boastful of his learning, but when everyone is keeping to themselves, and no one is learning in the public eye, then it is a mitzvah to learn in front of everyone. The loss sustained by his making himself obvious to the public will be outweighed by the merit of those who will learn from him and follow in his ways. He will be among the *mezakei harabim*, whose merit, *Chazal* say, is eternal.[128]

Rabbi Chaim Palagi[129] cites the example of Avraham Avinu circumcising himself in public to establish that it is preferable to do mitzvos in a way that sets an example for others to follow.

In the beginning of *Parashas Vayeira, Rashi* explains that Avraham consulted Mamre concerning performing *bris milah*, and that is why Hashem appeared to Avraham on Mamre's estate. *Tosafos* asks, Why would a *tzaddik* like Avraham, who withstood ten trials, ask advice concerning Hashem's command? Certainly Avraham did not question whether or not he should perform the *milah*; rather, Avraham Avinu was uncertain if he should perform the mitzvah in public or privately. Mamre advised Avraham to

---

126. In his introduction.
127. *Berachos* 63b.
128. *Bava Basra* 8a.
129. *Re'eh Chaim, Parashas Lech Lecha*, p. 11.

do so publicly, in order to set an example for others to follow.

Rabbi Palagi adds that this may be the intent of the *pasuk* urging us to walk modestly "with Hashem." When one is alone with Hashem, he should act modestly, but not when there are others who could learn from his example.

This is also the ruling of the *Mishnah Berurah*[130]:

> An average person who is in the presence of great people should not hesitate to do mitzvos and learn Torah in front of them. However, if it is possible, it would be preferable to perform the mitzvah in private. If he is among people who might learn from him, it is better to do the mitzvah in their presence, so that they could emulate his example.

Nevertheless, his intent should be for the sake of Heaven, and not to glorify himself. Reb Aharon should indeed reveal the true nature of his pastime to the onlookers.

Publicizing Those Who Do Mitzvos

וְאִישׁ לֹא יַעֲלֶה עִמָּךְ
And no man may ascend with you
(34:3)

רש"י: אֵין לְךָ יָפֶה מִן הַצְּנִיעוּת
Rashi: There is nothing better than modesty

In the previous case, when Reb Aharon was learning unobtrusively, and someone else noticed what he was doing, may the one who observed him publicize his

---
130. *Siman* 1 §6.

true deeds so that others might learn from this example?

A The *Chasam Sofer*[131] writes that we learn from the ways of Hashem that one who does a mitzvah in private is to be publicized. Reuven, for example, schemed in his heart to save Yosef's life and no one else knew his true intent. Yet the Torah reveals that Reuven wanted to return Yosef to his father. The *Rashba*[132] derives from this point that it is a mitzvah to engrave the names of the donors on shul furnishings in order to publicize their generosity.

Similarly, the Gemara in *Mo'ed Kattan*[133] states that when one learns Torah in private, his Torah announces him to others. The *Midrash Tanchuma* on the *pasuk, Can a man hide in concealments and I not see him,*[134] says in the name of Rabbi Binyamin bar Levi: Hashem says, "If a man sat in the corner of his house to learn Torah, I will show him to other people."

If Hashem publicizes those who serve Him in private, perhaps it is proper for people to do so as well.

---

131. *Derashos,* Vol. I, 64a.
132. Responsa 581.
133. 16b.
134. *Yirmiyah* 23:24.

פרשת ויקהל
Parashas Vayakheil

Public Relations

לֹא תְבַעֲרוּ אֵשׁ
You shall not kindle fire
(35:3)

Q Simcha had a wonderful idea. He lives in a neighborhood that has an *eiruv*, so on Shabbos afternoon he brought a big bag of candy to a busy public park and gathered a large group of children to say *Tehillim* out loud with him. (It is amazing what one can accomplish with a bag of candy, but the children's *Tehillim* was infinitely sweeter than the confections in the bag!) Interestingly, not only did Simcha attract the children, but their parents as well, many of whom were not (yet) religious, who approached to observe the scene. Some of them even pulled out their cameras to capture pictures of the heartwarming event.

Simcha wants to know what he should do next Shabbos. Should he continue to gather the children to say *Tehillim*, despite the photographers, or perhaps any merit that is accrued by the *Tehillim* is counterbalanced by the desecration of Shabbos that it is causing?

On Chanukah 5771 there was a terrible fire that scorched the Carmel forest near Haifa in *Eretz Yisrael*. As Shabbos was approaching, the firefighters knew that they would have to remain in the area to continue lifesaving measures. One of the firefighters in the area had an ongoing *chavrusa* with a *kollel* member. In addition to his already having made great strides in his Shabbos observance, he had also enrolled his children in Torah schools. This particular fireman asked the *kollel* member to meet him at the location where many of the firemen were based to make *Kiddush* for them on Shabbos night and deliver a *shiur*. He encouraged his *chavrusa* to come, saying that his fellow firemen had promised that they would travel from all over the Carmel to attend the *shiur*.

The *kollel* member was afraid to accept the offer. Many firefighters would desecrate the Shabbos by traveling to be in attendance, and they would be neglecting their firefighting and emergency exercises, as well. Especially on such a Shabbos when they might think that all activities are permitted, the Shabbos desecration would be rampant.

Rav Zilberstein asked Rav Elyashiv, who responded that although the *shiur* would serve a great purpose, if the *kollel* member knows that it would cause *chillul Shabbos*, he should cancel it. In addition to the firemen desecrating Shabbos in order to attend the *shiur*, there will also be a massive *chillul Hashem*. It would be as if he was condoning the *chillul Shabbos* that the *shiur* will cause. As painful as it is to cancel the *shiur*, he cannot be indifferent to *kedushas haShabbos*.

If it would only be a question of one or two firemen who would travel of their own volition to attend the *shiur*, that would not justify canceling the *shiur* for the firemen who are already present. However, since many firemen will desecrate the Shabbos en masse, it would constitute a *chillul Hashem*, and it would be forbidden to deliver a *shiur* under these circumstances.

In Simcha's case as well, if one or two people would photograph the scene, but the fact is that many children would be drawn to say *Tehillim*, the Shabbos desecrators cannot deprive the children of their mitzvah. However, since many people were attracted to take pictures, Simcha would create a *chillul Hashem* by reenacting the scene, as it would seem that the holy laws of Shabbos are not important to him.

A possible solution would be for Simcha to precede the recitation of *Tehillim* with an announcement to his dear brothers explaining that the *Tehillim* is very necessary to create merits for Jews all over, as *Chazal* have taught that *Tehillim* protects us from harm. By the same measure, keeping Shabbos is very important, and taking pictures on Shabbos prevents the children's prayers from reaching the heavens. He should implore them to refrain from taking pictures. Such an announcement will dispel any misunderstanding as to how precious Shabbos is, and then the *Tehillim* can continue, even if a few individuals would disregard Simcha's pleas and continue to snap pictures.

From Rags to Riches

כָּל מֵרִים תְּרוּמַת כֶּסֶף
Every man who separates a portion of silver
(35:24)

Q Henchie Weintuch was a special girl with a star-bright personality. When she became engaged, her entire seminary shared in her joy. Her *chassan* was a true *ben Torah* with sterling *middos* and *yiras Shamayim*. The only thing that was missing in this perfect *shidduch* was greenery (read: $). Henchie lived with her mother and did not have much of a relationship with her father since her parents had divorced many years earlier. Henchie's mother had difficulty making ends meet, and providing for her daughter's wedding was out of the question. When Henchie called her father to tell him that she was engaged, she asked if he would help her financially, but she received no response, as he had deliberately hung up the phone at that point in the conversation.

Rav Elya Kahn, the dean of Henchie's seminary, organized an urgent meeting of the teachers to discuss Henchie's plight. The seminary had a *hachnasas kallah* fund that could contribute a certain amount, and in addition, most of the teachers took on financial obligations to help raise the minimal expenses.

To everyone's surprise, on the day following the *tena'im*, Henchie's father had a change of heart. He called Henchie and asked her to visit him together with her *chassan* and his parents. At their meeting, Mr. Weintuch agreed to give much more than just the minimal expenses.

Now Rav Kahn wants to know whether he and his staff are still obligated to contribute toward Henchie's wedding expenses, or perhaps now that Henchie's father is taking care of his daughter's needs, they no longer have an obligation, despite their prior commitments. Maybe they should honor their pledges by contributing to a different *kallah* in need. What should they do?

A The Mishnah in *Maseches Shekalim*[135] states that if a collection was made for a particular poor person, and they collected more than was required, the excess money

---

135. 2:5.

should be given to that poor person. The *Yerushalmi* cites a difference of opinion in a case where they collected for a person who was thought to be poor, but was subsequently discovered to be financially secure.

The *Pischei Teshuvah*[136] quotes the *P'nei Aryeh*, who ruled in a case of someone who pledged to donate to a poor man, but before the man could deliver his donation, the poor man became wealthy. The *P'nei Aryeh* ruled that the donor could annul his pledge in *beis din* by regretting having made the pledge in the first place, but not because of the fact that the poor man became wealthy, because that was an unexpected occurrence.[137] If the donor did not annul his pledge, he would still have to honor his commitment without delay, but the recipient would not be allowed to use the money, because that would be tantamount to one who receives *tzedakah* when he really does not deserve it. Rather, the money should be transferred to a different poor person, at the discretion of the recipient.

Rav Wosner[138] writes that he struggled to understand the *P'nei Aryeh's* ruling. How could it be that the donor is obligated to give, yet the recipient is prohibited to receive? If the recipient may not take, then there should be no obligation to give, either.

The *Pischei Teshuvah* also records a case of the *Chasam Sofer* that involved a widow with seven children. Several generous individuals took upon themselves to provide support for the woman and her orphans for a period of three years. After two years, the woman married a wealthy individual who provided for all the

---

136. *Yoreh De'ah* 258 §7.
137. There are two mechanisms by which a Rav or a *beis din* can annul a vow: 1) If the person regrets having made the vow in the first place. This is called *charatah*, regret. 2) If circumstances changed in a way that had the person realized at the time of the vow that the vow would affect him even under such circumstances, he would never have made the vow. This is called a *pesach*, an opening. If the circumstance that arose is something that was completely unexpected, then it cannot be used as a *pesach* because he was not lacking realization at the time of the vow, since the new circumstance could not have been foreseen.
138. *Shevet HaLevi*, Vol. 5, 143 §4.

children's needs. No further donations were needed. As for their pledges, the *Chasam Sofer* ruled that if someone obligated themselves to support a poor person, as long as the money had not yet been given, and the poor man died or became wealthy, there is no need to annul the original pledge. They may certainly give their *tzedakah* elsewhere, or even dismiss their original commitment. It is clear that they never obligated themselves to give under such circumstances.

In our case as well, there would not be an obligation for the seminary teachers to honor their original commitments to Henchie, but it would be an act of piety to give the intended money to other poor *kallos*.

פרשת פקודי
Parashas Pekudei

Something Went Wrong

אֵלֶּה פְקוּדֵי הַמִּשְׁכָּן
These are the reckonings of the Mishkan
(38:21)

Q Ivdu was heavily advertising their Chinese Auction all over town, and people were clamoring to buy tickets like *chametz* after Pesach. The proceeds would fund Ivdu's widespread *kiruv* projects, which targeted not-yet-observant Jews throughout the West Coast. The drawing was set for Motza'ei Shabbos Chanukah, and all ticket representatives had to have their stubs submitted by the first day of Chanukah.

Dov Firman had sold nine booklets of raffle tickets and was about to send in the stubs, when he realized that somehow, one booklet had been misplaced. The worst part was that he had no idea to whom he had sold those tickets. He frantically called Ivdu's office to notify them that he was missing 200 ticket stubs.

Mendy Gross, Ivdu's executive director who was in charge of organizing all the details of the Chinese Auction, beseeched Dov to search his house for the missing book. Dov did make a concerted effort to discover the whereabouts of the missing stubs, but he simply could not unearth them. Motza'ei Shabbos Chanukah arrived, and a large crowd of people gathered in the designated hall to watch the drawing. Two hundred tickets were still missing when a very pressured Mendy drew the winning tickets. Afterward, when the frenzied preparations had finally come to an end, and Mendy had a moment to breathe, his conscience gave him no rest. How in the world could he return the money for the 200 missing tickets that were not entered into the drawing? Even worse, perhaps the entire raffle was invalid, as not everyone who was entitled to participate actually had a chance to win. By this point, all of the stubs had already been discarded. Is there any way to provide retribution for what had been done?

A The *Chavos Ya'ir*[139] was asked a similar question. Eleven men had each purchased lottery tickets for a price of two silver coins. The prize was a silver goblet. After one of the men's tickets had been drawn, someone checked the remaining lots and found that one of the men's names had inadvertently been omitted. The men whose names had not been chosen demanded that the lottery be redone, as the original drawing had been unfair since one of the men had not been given a chance to win. The man who had won claimed that the other men had actually increased their chances to win by only having 10 lots, instead of 11. The man whose name had been omitted was willing to accept four silver coins from the winner in order to consent to the outcome. The *Chavos Yair's* petitioner wanted to determine if such a lottery was valid.

---

139. *Siman* 61.

The *Chavos Ya'ir* ruled that the lottery was null and void. Although each side had a logical claim, there is one factor that they did not take into account. A lottery that is done properly is infused with Divine intervention. If the lottery was flawed, one cannot claim that the one who won was chosen with Hashem's consent. Each person can contest that had the lottery been run properly, he would have won, whether through his *tefillah* or through predestined *mazel*.

Responsa *Mishneh Halachos*,[140] based on the words of the *Chavos Ya'ir*, writes that the lottery is to be disqualified only if one would-be participant demands a redrawing. Even if the reason nobody protested is that they did not know that it was not held fairly, the lottery would still be binding. However, the question that remains is whether one would have to inform those left out what had actually taken place.

Even if the lottery was not valid, Ivdu would still not have to return the money that was given to them as *tzedakah*. Rav Moshe Feinstein writes[141] that when a raffle has no limitation placed on the amount of tickets that are available for purchase, one can purchase tickets with *ma'aser* money, as each ticket has no market value.[142] Seemingly, the ones who purchased tickets do not specifically intend to purchase a lottery ticket. They mainly intend to give *tzedakah*, regardless of the fact that they would receive a lottery ticket in appreciation for their donation. The Gemara in *Rosh Hashanah*[143] states that a Jew who gives *tzedakah* as a merit for his son's life to be prolonged is still considered a *tzaddik*. *Tosafos* points out that this would appear to contradict the Mishnah in *Pirkei Avos*,[144] which teaches that one should not perform mitzvos with the intent of receiving remuneration. *Tosafos* explains

---

140. Vol. 3, 193.
141. *Orach Chaim* Vol. 4, 76.
142. Since there may be an infinite number of tickets, the chances of winning may be very slight, rendering the tickets almost worthless.
143. 4a.
144. 1:3.

that even if the child did not survive, *chas v'shalom*, the Jew would not regret having given *tzedakah*. In this case as well, even if the Chinese auction was not conducted properly, the donors would not regret having given the *tzedakah*.

In summary, it seems that the results of the Chinese auction are valid. Since it is impossible to redo the lottery, as all the stubs were by now discarded, it is logical to conclude that the donations would not have to be returned, as the money has gone to *tzedakah*, and each donor would assumedly want their money to remain with this very worthy cause, even if the Chinese auction could not be held, for whatever reason. Therefore, the lottery is considered valid.

False Representation

אֵלֶּה פְקוּדֵי
These are the reckonings
(38:21)

Q Mayerville was a community known for its *chesed*, and its crown jewel was the large *gemach* that lent considerable sums to those in need. The *gemach* had guidelines that delineated how much money one could borrow, with a maximum of $8,000 per loan. Most of the money came from people who made temporary deposits as loans to the *gemach*, while some of the money was simply donated. There were several managers who each had the authority to sign over a loan, as well as to accept deposits.

Shimmy, a longstanding member of the community, approached his friend Eli, who was one of the managers of the *gemach*, to beseech him for a desperately needed loan. Shimmy broke down crying as he explained that he was deeply in debt after having married off his seven daughters, and his creditors gave him no rest. He feared for his health if the situation continued as it was.

Eli was very moved by his friend's plea, and asked him how much he wanted to borrow. Shimmy replied that he needed $70,000 in order to return to an even keel, and promised to pay back part of the loan every month. Eli explained that the most he could lend him was $8,000, and sincerely apologized that he could not be of greater assistance.

Two days later, Dov knocked on Eli's door, wishing to deposit money in the *gemach*. Dov handed over $70,000. Eli understood that this was more than a mere coincidence, and after Dov left, Eli joyfully called Shimmy and told him that he had $70,000 available for a loan. Although Eli had given Dov a receipt for the money, he did not enter the deposit in the *gemach* records, and he hoped that Shimmy would replace the money before anyone realized that it was missing.

Six months passed and Dov approached one of the *gemach's* managers to withdraw his deposit. The manager carefully checked the ledger, but could not find any evidence that Dov had made a deposit. Dov produced his receipt that bore Eli's signature, and a phone call to Eli revealed the entire story.

The *gemach* manager called Shimmy to collect the loan, but Shimmy did not have the means to repay more than his steady monthly payment. Eli admitted that he acted irresponsibly and reprehensibly, and would willingly pay Dov for misappropriating his deposit, but he also did not have the money to pay back everything at once. It would be a year before he could repay the entire $70,000 loan.

The *gemach's* managers claimed that they never received Dov's money, and therefore bear no responsibility to repay him. Dov countered that he had a receipt from the *gemach* for his deposit, and wants to be paid back immediately. Eli felt very guilty, and agreed to pay Dov back a small sum every month, but only up to $62,000, as he had the right to lend Shimmy $8,000. Who is right?

Even though Eli must pay the entire $70,000, as he was negligent with Dov's money, if Eli does not have the entire sum available at the moment, the *gemach* is required to pay Dov the entire amount. The fact that the *gemach* authorized Eli to accept deposits on their behalf obligates them to accept responsibility for money people deposit with him. The moment that Dov followed the *gemach's* guidelines by depositing his money with Eli and receiving a receipt for his deposit, the *gemach* was required to honor the receipt written by their representative. The fact that Eli did not register the deposit in the *gemach's* books is a problem between Eli and the *gemach*, and is not Dov's concern.

This situation is no different than if someone were to deposit his money in a bank, receiving a receipt for the transaction, and instead of putting the money into his cash drawer, the teller slipped the money into his own pocket. The bank would certainly have to replace the money, as it hired the teller to accept the money on its behalf. The bank is responsible for its employee's transactions and cannot claim that it never received the money. The teller stole from the bank, and the bank has to deal with him, independent of its responsibility to the client.

In truth, there is a difference between a bank teller and a manager of a *gemach*, because the manager is working not only for the *gemach*, but on behalf of all those who deposit money in the *gemach*, as well. The depositors can claim that they never intended to take responsibility for mistakes that the managers make, and since the money belongs to the depositors, they do not have to pay Dov for Eli's misappropriation.

A bank, in contrast, does not work the same way. A bank is a business that profits from its deposits and loans. It does have to pay for its employee's mistakes. The bank's clients knew that there are usually profits (e.g., interest, when permitted) and possibly losses. If a teller steals money from the bank, and the bank has to use people's deposits to cover withdrawals until it can divert funds from elsewhere, no one can claim that the bank cannot use its money for that purpose.

A *gemach* is not a business. No one receives a salary, nor do they have the right to invest people's money. Each manager, therefore, has personal liability for the mistakes that he makes, and no depositor has to cover for someone else's loan.

Therefore, Eli will have to pay Dov from his own pocket, and the *gemach* carries no liability.[145]

As far as Eli's claim that he had the right to lend Shimmy $8,000, that would only be true if he had recorded the loan in the *gemach's* ledgers. However, since he lent the money surreptitiously, that is not called a loan, but rather a *geneivah*. When transactions take place under the table, it is usually a sign that they just were not meant to be!

---

145. Editor's Note: One might wonder why the *gemach* would not have to pay Dov from donations that it had received. Perhaps it is because those who donated to the *gemach* did not do so with the intent to cover such losses.

The Same Pocket

וְאֶת הָאֶלֶף . . .
And from the one thousand ...
(38:28)

Q In some Sephardic shuls, they auction off the *aliyos* to the highest bidder. At times women participate by bidding from the women's section in order to buy an *aliyah* for their male relatives. At one such session, a man bid 1,000 shekels for *Maftir Yonah* (the third *aliyah* at Minchah, on Yom Kippur), and a woman outbid him when she called out, "1,200 shekels." The woman wound up buying it for that price, and gave the *aliyah* to her husband. That was when they discovered that the man that she had outbid had been none other than her husband! Now the woman wants to claim that she bought the *aliyah* under false pretenses. Had she known that her husband had bid 1,000 shekels, she would have had no reason to outbid him, as he would have received the *aliyah* anyway. Is she allowed to subtract the 200 shekels from her final bid?

A The *Rema*[146] writes that if someone pledged money to *tzedakah* by mistake the pledge is not valid. If so, perhaps the woman in our case made a mistake that is considered accidental and she should not have to pay.

However, it would seem that the *Rema* is talking about a mistake involving the pledge itself. For example, if someone accidentally pledged the wrong coin to *tzedakah*, that pledge would

---
146. *Yoreh De'ah* 258:2.

not be valid. In this case, the woman certainly wanted to donate 1,200 shekels to the shul, and that was her pledge exactly; the only thing she didn't know was against whom she was bidding. That is not considered a mistaken pledge; she probably agreed in her heart that the shul should keep the extra money, and she will pay willingly.

The Gemara in *Maseches Ta'anis*[147] tells the story of Abba the doctor who received regards from the Heavenly yeshivah every day. One day Abaye sent a pair of rabbis to test him. After the doctor had invited them to eat and drink, he laid down bedding for them. Early the next morning, the rabbis folded up the bedding and took it with them to the market place. The doctor met them in the market, and they asked him how much he thought the bedding was worth. He reported its value, and when they asked him how he could be so certain of the price, he responded that that is how much he paid for it. They confessed that the bedding was his, and that they had taken it from him. They asked him what he thought when he discovered that his bedding had been taken. He responded that he understood that the rabbis must have had to redeem captives and had been too embarrassed to tell him. The rabbis beseeched him to accept his bedding back, but he answered that he had already designated it for *tzedakah*.

Perhaps this would apply to this case as well. Even though she had made a particular mistake, once she decided to give the shul that sum of money, she has agreed that even under such circumstances the shul could keep it.

---

147. 21b.

ספר ויקרא
Sefer Vayikra

פרשת ויקרא / Parashas Vayikra

A Gift in the Mouth

וְקָמַץ מִשָּׁם מְלֹא קֻמְצוֹ
And one of whom shall scoop his threefingersful from it
(2:2)

Part 1

Q Yoel is an oral hygienist who runs a busy private practice. Many people visit to have their teeth cleaned, and in the course of his work, Yoel often notices that they are in urgent need of dental care. Yoel is familiar with a group of highly professional dentists and he regularly refers these patients to them. In return, he receives a 10 percent commission for his referrals. He completely trusts these dentists to pay him the proper amount.

A patient came to Yoel and he realized that the man required an extensive and expensive series of dental procedures. He referred the patient to one of the dentists within the group, and the patient scheduled an appointment, mentioning that he had been referred by Yoel.

When the patient arrived for the appointment and introduced himself to the dentist, they realized that they were childhood friends who had lost touch. As a matter of fact, the patient had been extremely helpful to the dentist when he had fallen upon difficult times. The least the dentist could do was to treat his benefactor for free, so that the treatment, which should have cost $2,000, became a gift of *hakaras hatov*.

When Yoel followed up on the patient, he heard the entire story. He understands the dentist's motivation, but he still feels that he should not lose his commission just because the dentist decided to give his patient a present. The dentist explained that he agreed to give him 10 percent of what he billed the patient, and in this case, that amount was zero. Is he required to pay Yoel his commission?

It seems that Yoel does not deserve to be paid, since the dentist did not receive any payment for his services, and their agreement was that he would pay him 10 percent of his fee. Although the patient may have benefited from a $2,000 treatment, Yoel is not charging **him** a commission; the dentist pays the commission, and he only "lost" on the deal.

The *Sha'ar Ephraim*[1] writes that if a broker closed a deal, and subsequently the parties involved decided to back out and forgave each other for any claims that they had on each other, they would still have to pay the broker his fee. That would apply in this case as well, had the dentist given an estimate of $2,000 and subsequently decided not to charge for his work. Here the dentist never intended to charge for his services, and hence Yoel referred a non-paying patient to the dentist.

---

1. *Siman* 150.

Part 2

Q A few weeks later, Yoel referred a patient to the same dentist, and the patient was so pleased with the dentist's work that he also brought his son for treatment. Is Yoel entitled to collect a commission for the son's treatment as well?[2]

Another variation of this question would be if a broker introduced a buyer to someone who was selling his house, and the seller also showed an additional house to the buyer, and both houses were sold. Would the broker be entitled to collect a fee for both houses?

A The *Maharsham*[3] cites the *Ma'amar Mordechai*, who discusses the case of someone who suggested a house to a potential buyer, but in the end, the house was sold to someone else. The potential buyer was not dissuaded, and proceeded to buy the house from the one who had just purchased it. They cite the *Responsa Shev Yaakov*,[4] who ruled in such a case that if the broker was instrumental in persuading the second buyer to purchase the house before it was originally sold, the broker would deserve to be paid as a *maschil* (introducer) and receive one-third of his fee. If the broker was not instrumental in the sale, then he would not deserve payment.

In this case, Yoel was instrumental in introducing both parties. Perhaps he should be paid as an introducer.

The *Avnei Nezer*[5] records a similar question: A *shadchan* suggested a *shidduch* between the daughter of a wealthy businessman

---

2. Editor's Note: It would seem that one could ask the same question, whether Yoel would deserve a commission for other treatments that were not yet needed at the time of the referral.
3. *Mishpat Shalom, kuntres acharon* 185:6.
4. 13.
5. *Choshen Mishpat Siman* 36.

and a boy from a similar home. The *shadchan* invested all of his talents to convince the families that their children were a perfect match. In the end, the girl became engaged to someone else, but she had a younger sister. Other *shadchanim* suggested that the boy would be a good match for the younger sister, and they became engaged. Now the original *shadchan* claimed that since he had laid the groundwork by introducing the families and extolling the boy's virtues, he should be paid one-third of the *shadchan's* fee, as an introducer.

The *Avnei Nezer* responded that the *shadchan* does not deserve to collect anything from the girl's family, as a *shadchan* is actually working for the *chassan* and the *kallah*, even if the parents generally pay on their behalf. In this case, the original *shadchan* never did anything on behalf of the younger sister, and therefore he cannot claim a fee from her or because of her.

In Yoel's case, he never intended to refer the son, only the father. Perhaps that would be sufficient reason that he should not receive a commission for the son's treatment.

He does not even have a claim to be paid as an introducer. The entire discussion of whether one could collect as an introducer is only relevant when he would not be paid otherwise. When he is already being paid for his services, as in Yoel's case, by collecting a commission for the father's treatment, there is no source that indicates that he should be paid for additional jobs that resulted from the original referral.

The *Shevet HaLevi*[6] issued a similar ruling in the case of an agent who brokered a house rental. The negotiations on the rental eventually evolved into a sale. Does the agent deserve to collect a commission on the sale of the house? The *Shevet HaLevi* ruled that since the agent was hired to arrange a rental, he cannot claim a fee for the sale. Although the agent was asked to close the deal on the house, the transaction was limited to renting the house and he was only indirectly involved in the fact that the house was eventually

---

6. Vol. 10, 268.

sold. He certainly deserves their appreciation, but it is very unclear if he can actually claim anything more than that.

How Does This Sound to You?

וְנֶפֶשׁ כִּי תֶחֱטָא וְשָׁמְעָה קוֹל

And if a person will sin: And if he accepted a demand (lit., and if one shall sin, and heard a voice)

(5:1)

Q Nosson was a *chazzan* in Congregation Shirah Chadashah, and he decided to engage the services of a voice specialist to enhance his singing capabilities. Tragically, his teacher had abandoned Torah observance and was no longer *shomer Shabbos*. In addition, he lived some distance away. However, the man had come highly recommended, so Nosson felt that he would be the best choice. After a few sessions, the teacher was very pleased with Nosson's progress, but felt that there were still some areas that could use some polishing to improve his overall performance.

That Shabbos, Nosson was the *chazzan* for Mussaf. After davening, when everyone came over to give him a warm "*yasher ko'ach*," he was shocked when he was greeted by his voice teacher! It was clear to Nosson that the man had not walked to shul. Nosson did not know what to say, except to ask the man what he was doing there. The teacher responded that he had found that the best way to diagnose weak points is to listen to a real-time performance. He simply committed his notes to memory and promised to share his findings at their next session.

Nosson is doubtful if he could attend the next session because one is not allowed to benefit from Shabbos desecration.[7] Should Nosson cancel the session?

One is not allowed to take benefit that is born of direct *chillul Shabbos*. For example, one may not eat food that was cooked on Shabbos.[8] In this case, Nosson is not directly benefiting from *chillul Shabbos*. His teacher's visit to the shul merely served the teacher to study his student's weaknesses. Nosson's benefit will be from the lessons he attends, and the visit is not considered a direct benefit.

However, it is definitely a *chillul Hashem*. Imagine if someone were to hire a contractor to build him a house, and the contractor dug up the grave of the customer's father to see what kind of materials were used in the burial, in order to duplicate them in the house that he would build. Would anyone agree to use such a contractor after he had shown such utter disrespect to that person's father? Certainly after the teacher had trampled Hashem's Shabbos and shown absolute disdain for the relationship between Hashem and His people, it would be highly inappropriate to consult him for voice training. That would seem as if Nosson had no feeling for Hashem's honor. Nosson may not go for additional lessons until the instructor has done *teshuvah*.

---

7. *Shulchan Aruch, Orach Chaim* 318:1.
8. See ibid.

Breaking Even

וְהֵשִׁיב אֶת הַגְּזֵלָה
And he shall return the stolen item
(5:23)

Q A boy in his early teens developed the bad habit of taking money from his parents, without their permission, to buy candies in a local store. After he learned *Bava Kamma* and realized the severity of his stealing, he never stole again, but he felt that he did not have the strength of character to confess his crime to his father. It would be too embarrassing, and it would cause his father pain.

One day, one of the boy's relatives sent him a cash gift that exceeded the value of all that he had stolen. His father received the gift on behalf of his son, and called his son in yeshivah to tell him. The son came home from yeshivah after several weeks, and his father had forgotten to pass on the gift to his son.

The son did not forget. He wants to know if he can decide in his heart to let the gift cancel out his debt to his father for all the money that he had taken without permission, or if his confession is absolutely necessary.

A The *Shulchan Aruch*[9] states that if the one stolen from knows that his money was taken, the thief has not fulfilled his obligation of returning the money until his victim is aware that the money has been returned.

Rav Yitzchak Koppelman, the Rosh Yeshivah of Lucerne, explained in the name of his rebbi, Rav Shimon Shkop, the

---
9. *Choshen Mishpat* 355:1.

rationale behind this halachah. As long as the victim does not realize that the money has been returned, he does not have the use of that money. He will not try to spend more than what he thinks he has, and therefore the money cannot be considered "returned."

Accordingly, it depends what the father did with the son's gift. If the father spent the money, it can be considered as if it was returned, since the father made full use of the sum. If, however, the father put it aside, and merely forgot to give it to his son, the father also did not have use of the money, and it cannot be considered as if it were returned. Although the father owes his son a similar sum to what the son owes him, as long as the father is not told, it cannot be considered that the son has undone his deed.

Therefore the son should tell his father as follows: "Dad, you received a gift on my behalf and you forgot to give it to me. I decided that you should keep the money as a gift, because I am afraid that I may have taken some of your money without asking permission." In that way, it will certainly be considered returned.

פרשת צו
Parashas Tzav

Don't Sell Yourself Short

וְלָבַשׁ הַכֹּהֵן מִדּוֹ בַד
And the Kohen shall don his fitted tunic
(6:3)

רש"י: שֶׁתְּהֵא כְמִדָּתוֹ
Rashi: So that it should be like [the Kohen's] measurement.

Q Shimmy has a difficult time making ends meet, and he does not have enough money to buy a new suit for Shabbos. He is still wearing his wedding suit, which looks quite worn out by this time. One day, a package arrived on Shimmy's doorstep. The return address was that of his uncle in California. Shimmy opened the box and found that it contained a magnificent new suit. A label stating that it had already been checked for *sha'atnez* was affixed to an inner pocket. A small card inside read: In honor of the Holy Shabbos.

Shimmy excitedly tried on the new suit, but to his dismay, he found that the suit was a little short for him. The pants didn't really make it down to his shoes, nor did the sleeves reach his wrists. Most people would not wear such a suit, although some people might. Shimmy wondered if it would be preferable to wear his old, worn-out suit for Shabbos, as at least it fit him well, or if perhaps he should wear the beautiful new suit, even if it was not exactly his size.

The *Torah Lishmah*[10] writes that it is better to wear an old suit that fits the person well, rather than to wear a beautiful new suit that is too short. He proves his assertion from the *Rambam's*[11] words concerning the special garments worn by the Kohen when he served in the *Beis HaMikdash*. "The garments worn by the Kohen should be new, beautiful, and drape the wearer in the manner of important people, as it is written, *as an honor and a glory*.[12] If the garments were too long or too short, the Kohen's service would be invalidated. If the garments fit but were worn out, the service is nevertheless valid."

One may infer from the *Rambam* that an old suit that fits well is superior to a new suit that is too short. An old garment is still acceptable for service in the *Beis HaMikdash*, while a garment that is too short is not. Accordingly, Shimmy should stick to his old suit.

Perhaps one could challenge this conclusion from the *Ramban's*[13] explanation as to why a short garment is unacceptable. He writes that if part of the Kohen's body remains exposed, it would be tantamount to missing a garment, at least on that part of the body, and a Kohen who is not wearing his complete vestments is not fit to serve. According to this explanation, this would only apply to a Kohen's service, but not to a Shabbos suit.

---

10. 99.
11. *Hilchos Klei HaMikdash* 8:4.
12. *Shemos* 28:2.
13. *Sefer HaMitzvos, Lo Sa'aseh* 64.

However, the *Minchas Chinuch*[14] infers from the juxtaposition of the *Rambam's* words that a short garment shows a lack of honor and glory because such clothing is not beautiful, not because it is considered lacking. If so, the *Torah Lishmah's* proof is still intact according to the *Rambam*.

Nevertheless, if Shimmy wears his wedding suit during the week as well, then he should wear the new suit on Shabbos. *Chazal* derived from the *pasuk*[15] that enjoins us to honor the Shabbos, that one should have special clothes for Shabbos.[16] The *Mishnah Berurah* cites the *Arizal*, who states that it is even preferable for a person to have a complete change of clothing for Shabbos, including undergarments. If Shimmy will wear the same clothing for Shabbos as he does during the week, he may forget that it is Shabbos! In such a case, it would be preferable to wear the new, albeit shorter, suit for Shabbos.

Golden Dust

וְלָבַשׁ בְּגָדִים אֲחֵרִים
And don other garments
(6:4)

Q On Erev Rosh Chodesh Nissan, Chaim was busily involved in putting his heart and soul into baking *mehudar* matzos for Pesach. In the course of his work his shirt, pants, and shoes also got involved in baking matzos for Pesach, and now it was time to *daven* Minchah. Would it be

---
14. *Mitzvah* 150.
15. *Yeshayah* 58:13
16. *Shabbos* 113a.

considered disrespectful to *daven* in such a state, or, since his clothing bears testimony to his mitzvah observance, he could *daven* without cleaning his clothing?

AThe *Shulchan Aruch*[17] states that it is proper to designate honorable clothing for *davening*. Indeed, among the eight matters that one should devote attention to before *davening*, the *Rambam*[18] lists attending to one's attire. The *Aruch HaShulchan*[19] compares the clothing that one wears for *davening* to the garments that the Kohanim wore in the *Beis HaMikdash*. If one has the means, he should certainly be stringent in this matter. In any event, it is a worthy practice to reserve special trousers for *davening* in case his pants become dirty. In addition, one should have a clean pair of shoes prepared for his meeting with Hashem.

Rav Elyashiv was always very meticulous that his clothes should be clean. The Gemara in *Shabbos*[20] prohibits a *talmid chacham* from wearing stained clothing. *Rashi* explains the prohibition as referring to an oily stain. Rav Elyashiv maintained that nevertheless, a *ben Torah* must be scrupulous to be free of dirt and dust, as well.

One Erev Pesach, on the night of *bedikas chametz*, Rav Elyashiv exerted himself to check his entire home, which included bending down to the floor in order to thoroughly check all cracks and crevices. As a result, his clothing became dusty. One of the grandchildren, who knew how particular the Rav was concerning the cleanliness of his clothing, offered to brush off the Rav's clothing. The Rav declined the offer and explained that the dust on his clothing was not considered "dirt," but rather "mitzvah stains," as the Gemara[21] points out that it is a praise for the sons of Aharon to wade in the blood of the *korbanos* (sacrifices) up until their knees.

---

17. *Orach Chaim* 98:4.
18. *Hilchos Tefillah* 5:1.
19. *Orach Chaim* 96 §5.
20. 114a.
21. *Pesachim* 65b.

Similarly, Rav Chaim Kanievsky ruled that a painter who is painting the walls of a shul, intending to beautify the House of Hashem, can *daven* without changing his clothing, as his clothes are not considered dirty.

However, this leniency would only seem to apply when changing one's clothes for *davening* would be difficult. It should not be relied upon initially. Rabbi Yishmael taught[22] that one should not serve his master in the same clothing that was worn while cooking. For this reason, the Kohen who removed the ashes that accumulated on the *Mizbei'ach* would wear inferior garments in order to keep his superior garments clean for other services that he would perform in the *Beis HaMikdash*. It becomes apparent that although it is a mitzvah to remove the ashes from the *Beis HaMikdash*, it would not be appropriate to subsequently serve in the *Beis HaMikdash* while wearing clothing that had become soiled with ashes.

The *Ben Yehoyada* adds that the *pasuk* only teaches that the Kohen had to change his clothing in order to remove the ashes. Rabbi Yishmael explains that the reason for this action was to preserve the clothing, lest one think that it is appropriate to intentionally dirty his clothing in the process of the mitzvah in order to honor the mitzvah. Rabbi Yishmael stresses that there is no such requirement.

Hence, even if one's clothing became dirtied in the process of a mitzvah, even one so exalted as removing the ashes from the *Beis HaMikdash*, it is still inappropriate to stand and serve Hashem in those garments if one has the opportunity to change to clean clothing. The same should apply to *davening* as well, if one can clean his clothing in preparation for *davening*. If Rav Elyashiv had been going to *daven*, he certainly would have cleaned off the dust as well.

---

22. *Shabbos* 114a.

A Friend Indeed

לְמֹשֶׁה הָיָה לְמָנָה
It was a portion for Moshe
(8:29)

Part 1

Thirteen years had gone by in the blink of an eye, and now Meir's oldest child, Yechezkel, was celebrating his bar mitzvah. Meir had rented the shul's social hall and hired an exclusive caterer to wine and dine his guests in honor of his *simchah*. However, on the day of the bar mitzvah, the city was hit with the worst blizzard that it had weathered in 30 years. Heaps of snow covered the entire city, and the streets were not safe for driving. Fortunately, Meir and most of his guests lived in close proximity to the shul, so they were able to walk to attend the bar mitzvah. The caterer, on the other hand, whose kitchen was miles away, was unable to transport the food that he had prepared. Meir felt very uncomfortable because he had nothing to offer his guests who had trekked through the snow in his honor. One of Meir's friends, Shlomo, was scheduled to make a bar mitzvah for his son two days later, and his wife had baked for weeks and had an abundance of cookies and cakes in the freezer. He sensed Meir's distress and, after obtaining his wife's wholehearted permission, graciously offered to donate all of his delicacies to Meir's *simchah*. The guests helped to arrange the platters, and the bar mitzvah was a smashing success. When Meir asked

Shlomo how much he owed him for the refreshments, Shlomo refused payment, and said that he would find a way to replace that which had been eaten. *Mi k'amcha Yisrael* (What a nation)!

What would be the halachah if Shlomo had asked to be paid? Obviously, he could ask Meir to pay even if he did not negotiate a price beforehand, as the *Rema*[23] rules that if someone offers his friend a meal, he may charge him afterward, and the recipient cannot claim that he thought it was a gift. The question is, how much could Shlomo charge for the food that he provided? Could he charge the price of a caterer, as Meir benefited as if the bar mitzvah were catered, and saved on the caterer's fee that he had initially intended to pay? Moreover, Shlomo will now have to hire a caterer for his own bar mitzvah, since his wife does not have enough time in a mere two days to bake again for all her bar mitzvah guests. On the other hand, Meir could claim that Shlomo is not a professional caterer, nor does he have the overhead that a caterer does. Therefore, Meir should only have to pay for the ingredients plus the hours of work it took to bake the delicacies. The fact that Shlomo will now have to hire a caterer for his own bar mitzvah is merely a *grama*. What could Shlomo charge?

A Since Shlomo is not in the catering business, he cannot charge more than the value of homemade food. If he had wanted to be paid as a caterer he would have had to stipulate that in advance, before he provided the food. This is similar to the case described in the *Shulchan Aruch*:[24] Two men were walking in the street. One of them was carrying a barrel of wine, and the other was carrying a barrel of honey. The barrel

---
23. *Choshen Mishpat* 246:17.
24. Ibid., 264:5.

that contained the honey developed a crack, and before the honey spilled out, the other man poured out his wine in order to rescue his friend's honey. The halachah is that the owner of the wine can only ask to be paid for the service he provided, but he cannot charge for the wine that he lost in the process, unless he stipulated as such to his friend, or in front of *beis din*, before spilling out the wine.

Just as the owner of the wine cannot charge his friend to cover his losses unless he negotiates in advance that he would provide the service only if he were paid for his wine, Shlomo can charge a caterer's rate only if he arranged with Meir to pay him such a price. Nevertheless, even if Meir is not obligated to, it would still be proper for Meir to contribute toward Shlomo's expense in hiring a caterer, an expense that came about as a result of Shlomo's generosity.

Part 2

Q Who must sustain the loss of all the food that the caterer prepared and was unable to deliver? Does Meir have to pay for everything that was prepared for his *simchah* and that is now sitting in the freezer? The caterer cannot be blamed for being incapable of delivering the food, as the streets were impassable. Perhaps Meir can claim that he never received the goods and therefore should not have to pay.

A The first issue that has to be determined is who owns the food that is now being stored in the caterer's freezers. Does it belong to the caterer, or to Meir? When someone orders food, and the work has already begun, does the unfinished product already belong to the one who ordered it, or does it belong to the producer until the item is delivered? That would seem to be the crux of this question, as well. If the food belongs to the caterer, Meir would not have to pay for the food that was never delivered, whereas if the food belongs to Meir, he would have to pay for the food that he bought, regardless of its location or its usefulness to him once his affair is over.

The *Shulchan Aruch*[25] writes that if someone contracted a craftsman to produce a certain product for him, intending to then buy it from him, if afterward the one who ordered this item does not want to buy the product and it is perishable, he still has to pay for the item.

The *Sma* and the *Shach* rule that if the craftsman used his own materials, the craftsman must sell the item to someone else, and the one who ordered the item only has to pay the difference between how much he would have paid for it and the amount for which the craftsman actually sold it.

The fact that the craftsman has to invest effort in selling the item indicates that the item indeed belongs to him, and the one who ordered the item merely has to cover the losses that he caused the craftsman by withdrawing from their deal. Accordingly, it would seem that the food still belongs to the caterer, and since Meir was not the cause of the caterer's losses, he would not have to pay.

Moreover, Meir has no interest in acquiring the food until it is actually served on the tables. Until that point, the food is still the caterer's responsibility. What would have happened if the food had been ruined while it was still in the kitchen? As long as the food has not been served, the caterer has still not finished producing the item for which he was hired, and therefore does not deserve to be paid.[26]

---

25. Ibid., 338:8.
26. Had the caterer been serving in his own hall and he was ready to serve the food, but the guests could not arrive due to inclement weather conditions, then the halachah might be different. צ״ע.

PARASHAS TZAV / 223

פרשת שמיני
Parashas Shemini

Expensive Tastes

יַיִן וְשֵׁכָר אַל תֵּשְׁתְּ
Do not drink wine and intoxicating beverages
(10:9)

Q Chaim worked very hard to prepare for Shabbos. He personally bought the meat and fish, as well as a host of other delicacies. It was only after he arrived home from shul on Friday night that he realized that he had forgotten to buy wine for *Kiddush*.

Chaim turned to his neighbor Naftali and asked if he could have a bottle of wine for *Kiddush*. Naftali surveyed his liquor cabinet and found that he had one extra bottle of wine. He gave it to Chaim without mentioning the price of the bottle, in accordance with the halachah in *Shulchan Aruch*,[27] as such speech is inappropriate on Shabbos.

---
27. *Orach Chaim* 323:4.

Chaim assumed that the bottle cost about $10, and set out after Shabbos to pay Naftali for the wine. Chaim extended the $10 bill to his neighbor and asked if that would cover the cost of the wine. Naftali could not help but smile. He said that Chaim was close in his estimation, and was only off by one zero. When Chaim asked Naftali to explain, Naftali revealed that the bottle of wine had been an expensive French import, valued at $100.

Chaim's jaw dropped. He asked Naftali why he had not told him the price of the wine, and Naftali defended himself by saying that he was not allowed to discuss prices on Shabbos.

Does Chaim have to pay $100 for the wine he drank?

The *Yam Shel Shlomo*[28] records the case of a man who borrowed a sword from his friend, thinking that it was a simple sword. The borrower accepts responsibility for the entire value of the sword, even if he only discovered later that it was a very valuable antique. This is similar to someone who borrowed a piece of jewelry that contained a precious stone that was worth 100 gold pieces. He cannot claim that he thought the stone was only worth one or two gold pieces. The only exception to this rule would be if the owner misled the borrower into thinking that the borrowed item was less expensive than it really was. In that case, the borrower can claim that he never accepted responsibility for such an expensive item.[29]

The *Shach*[30] argues with the *Yam Shel Shlomo's* comparison between a sword and a precious stone. Precious stones are often expensive, and the borrower, who lacked expertise in evaluating stones, should have taken into account that the stone may be very valuable. A sword, in contrast, is not generally an expensive item,

---
28. *Bava Kamma* 6:34.
29. See ibid., 62a.
30. *Choshen Mishpat* 72 §40.

and therefore the borrower is not to be held responsible for not having realized that the sword was an expensive antique.

One could contend that Chaim's case is dependent on the differing opinions of the *Yam Shel Shlomo* and the *Shach*. According to the *Yam Shel Shlomo,* Chaim agreed to pay for the wine, even if he did not realize its true value. According to the *Shach*, Chaim may claim that he never dreamed that the wine was so costly.

However, the truth is that Chaim should only have to pay for an average bottle of wine, according to all opinions. Chaim was specific when he asked for a bottle of wine **for Kiddush**. If Naftali gave Chaim an expensive bottle of wine without revealing its aristocracy to Chaim, Naftali is guilty of negligence.

Had Naftali mentioned that he had an exceptional wine, even without noting its price, Chaim would have understood that he was not taking a standard bottle of wine. Then Chaim would certainly have to pay the true price of the wine. Since Naftali handed over the wine without mentioning anything, he should have realized that Chaim would underestimate the wine's true value, and hence Naftali was negligent. It is therefore sufficient that Chaim pay the price of a normal wine used for *Kiddush*, or slightly more than that, since he did benefit from the wine's superior quality.

Even though Chaim enjoyed the luxury of drinking the expensive wine, and the *Rema*[31] writes that one who benefited from eating his friend's food is required to pay for that benefit, in our case, where Chaim specifically asked for wine for *Kiddush*, he was not interested in any other benefit, and therefore does not have to pay.

---

31. *Choshen Mishpat* 264:17.

Half a Hechsher

וּלְהַבְדִּיל בֵּין הַקֹּדֶשׁ וּבֵין הַחֹל
And in order to distinguish between the sacred and the profane
(10:10)

Q Shimshon was offered a job as a *mashgiach* (kashrus supervisor) at a restaurant that was not known for modestly dressed clientele. Shimshon himself will not have to see any of the immodesty, because he will be working in the kitchen. The question is whether it is appropriate to give a *hechsher* to such an immodest place.

A The *Megillah* tells us that Achashveirosh made a point at his party "to do according to each man's pleasure."[32] The Gemara[33] explains, "To do the will of Mordechai and Haman." *Rashi* elaborates that Mordechai and Haman were in charge of the drinks at the king's party. This would seem to be very peculiar. How could Mordechai have agreed to oversee the feast at which the Jews had sealed their own fate, when he himself had told them not to attend? Rav Chaim Kanievsky explained that Mordechai wanted to minimize their sin by keeping the wine pure of any *aveirah* and by overseeing other kashrus issues.

According to this reasoning, perhaps Shimshon should take the job so at least these people will not be violating the laws of kashrus, in addition to their other problems.

In truth, there is no proof from Mordechai at all. Mordechai didn't tell the Jews that he was going to supervise the kitchen at the party. Perhaps he did so discreetly. If Shimshon gives this establishment a *hechsher*, they will advertise his supervision as if he approves of everything that happens on the premises.

---

32. *Esther* 1:8.
33. *Megillah* 12a.

The *Da'as Torah*[34] was asked if the prevailing custom in his time to close the kosher butcher shops during the Nine Days should be abolished, as there were people who, with the absence of kosher meat, would buy nonkosher meat instead. Wouldn't it be preferable to open the kosher shops in order to save them from eating *tereifah*? His answer is based on the principle of the *sefer Akeidas Yitzchak*,[35] who writes that a big sin that is done privately is borne only by the individual who did it. A small sin that has public approval is borne by the entire congregation and they will all be punished for it. Therefore, it is better that individuals should eat *tereifah* than to allow that which is forbidden (eating meat during the Nine Days) and transform their sin into a public one.

Even though the *Akeidas Yitzchak* relates to someone who approves of the sin itself, and in our case the *mashgiach* is only validating the kashrus of the food and not the other activities of the establishment, nevertheless, it is still bordering on public approval of their activities, and giving a *hechsher* is inappropriate.

No Good Deed...

אַךְ אֶת זֶה לֹא תֹאכְלוּ
But this is what you shall not eat
(11:4)

Q Metugan is a large food corporation that donates hundreds of free meals daily to the poor. One of the recipients of these meals was given food that had spoiled, but he did not realize it until he fell ill in the middle of the

---

34. *Orchos Chaim*, 551 §30.
35. *Bereishis* 20.

night. He is demanding compensation for the suffering that Metugan caused him by serving him food that caused poisoning. Metugan certainly only had the best of intentions and had no idea that the food was unfit for consumption. Does the company have to pay?

Rav Zilberstein[36] quotes the Chazon Ish,[37] who writes that one who feeds his friend's animal poison can be categorized as one who sends a fire to damage his friend. A person who sets a fire to cause damage is just like someone who directly inflicts damage, and he can be obligated to pay for medical expenses, etc.[38] Accordingly, Metugan should have to pay for having served the man spoiled food.

Arguably, however, Metugan should be exempt, for the sake of the public good. If people will sue corporations for their charitable activities, firms will stop being philanthropic. A doctor who acts responsibly but accidentally causes harm to a patient does not have to pay, even though according to the strict halachah he really should be obligated.[39] Nevertheless, the *Chachamim* exempt him from payment because of the benefit to society, so that he will not be afraid to tend to patients. Perhaps the same should apply to corporations, as well.

Rav Elyashiv did not agree, as the Gemara provides an exemption only for doctors and for people who return a lost item, not generous donors. Therefore, Metugan should have to pay for the man's damage (only definite losses, with no additional compensation).

---

36. See *Chashukei Chemed, Shevuos*, p. 190.
37. *Bava Kamma* 14 §9.
38. *Choshen Mishpat* 418:17 (loss, pain, shame, loss of work, medical bills).
39. *Shulchan Aruch, Yoreh De'ah* 336:1.

פרשת תזריע
Parashas Tazria

Due Honors

וּבַיּוֹם הַשְּׁמִינִי יִמּוֹל
And on the eighth day ... shall be circumcised
(12:3)

Part 1

Q Binyamin was blessed with a healthy baby boy. Since Binyamin's father was unfortunately unwell and bedridden, Binyamin invited his uncle to be the *sandek* at the *bris*, as a second choice.

The day of the *bris* arrived. The baby was carried into the hall, and had already been placed on the uncle's knees in preparation for the great mitzvah of *bris milah*. Suddenly, the door to the hall opened and everyone turned around. Binyamin's father had arisen from his sickbed! The *simchah* of the mitzvah had infused him with new vigor to the point that he was able to rise from his sickbed to attend the *bris*.

Binyamin was in a quandary. He had certainly wanted his father to be the *sandek*, but he never dreamed that in his father's weakened state, there was a possibility that his father would attend the *bris*. Now that the baby was already on his uncle's knees, how could he ask his uncle to step aside? On the other hand, Binyamin wants to do the mitzvah of honoring his father. What should he do?

The *Rema*[40] writes that once someone had accorded the honor of *sandek* he may not rescind the offer. However, the *Taz* explains that the reason one may not reconsider is because it is considered a breach of integrity. In a case where a *tzaddik* or a very close friend had just become available for the *bris*, and it is general knowledge that had they been available at the time that the first person received the offer, the baby's father would surely have chosen the *tzaddik* or the close friend, there is no breach of integrity, and the father may indeed adjust his choice for *sandek*.

In this case it is clear to everyone that Binyamin would not have chosen his uncle over his father, and therefore Binyamin may honor his father with *sandek*.

There is a similar ruling in *hilchos chalitzah*.[41] If the eldest brother is not present to perform *chalitzah* with his deceased brother's wife, a younger brother is chosen in his stead. Even if *beis din* had already gone through the entire lengthy procedure that preceded the *chalitzah* with the younger brother, and then the eldest brother appeared in *beis din*, *beis din* would start the entire procedure again, substituting the eldest brother. The reason for this is because the Torah is particular that *chalitzah* be performed by the eldest brother, if possible.

In Binyamin's case as well, there is a mitzvah *d'Oraisa* to honor one's parents whenever possible. It is therefore appropriate to

---

40. *Yoreh De'ah* 264:1.
41. *Even HaEzer* 161, *Pischei Teshuvah* §3.

PARASHAS TAZRIA / 231

substitute his father to act as *sandek* since that has now become an option.

If Binyamin is concerned that the uncle may be insulted, he need not fear, as he will be following the Torah's directives, so the uncle has no reason to be insulted. Even if the uncle nevertheless feels slighted, his misplaced feelings are not to be considered an impediment, as they contradict Hashem's will.

There is a precedent for this behavior in the *Shulchan Aruch*, in the laws of *Krias HaTorah*.[42] When there is no Kohen present, a Yisrael may be called for the first *aliyah*. If after the Yisrael was called for the *aliyah*, a Kohen entered the shul, the *aliyah* is to be given to the Kohen instead of to the Yisrael. There is no disgrace to the Yisrael, since by rights the *aliyah* belongs to the Kohen, and the Yisrael cannot take it away from him. In Binyamin's case as well, the uncle should not feel slighted, since the honor of *sandek* rightfully belongs to Binyamin's father.

Part 2

Q What would have been the halachah if instead of choosing his uncle as the replacement *sandek*, Binyamin had honored one of the *gedolei ha'dor*, and Binyamin's father entered the room right before the *bris*? Would Binyamin's father take priority even in such a situation?

A In such a case, Binyamin would not be able to give the honor to his father, as both Binyamin and his father have an obligation to honor the *gadol ha'dor*.[43]

---

42. *Orach Chaim* 135:6.
43. See *Shulchan Aruch, Orach Chaim* 472:5. A *talmid chacham* who is unusually proficient has the halachah of one's rebbi, even if the *talmid chacham* has not yet taught one anything.

We find that even Eliyahu HaNavi had to honor a *gadol* many generations after Eliyahu was taken from this world. The Gemara in *Berachos*[44] records that Rabbi Yose was traveling on the road, and he entered one of the ruins of Yerushalayim in order to *daven Shemoneh Esrei*. Eliyahu HaNavi appeared on the scene, and waited at the doorway for Rabbi Yose to finish *davening*. When Rabbi Yose finished, Eliyahu greeted him by saying, "Shalom to you, Rebbi."

Rabbi Yose replied, "Shalom to you, my Rebbi and my master."

Eliyahu continued, "My son, why did you enter the ruin?"

"To *daven*," Rabbi Yose replied.

Eliyahu taught Rabbi Yose that he should have *davened* on the road instead.

Rav Elyashiv asked why Eliyahu accorded Rabbi Yose the title of Rebbi (lit., *my teacher*). It is not apparent that Eliyahu actually learned anything from Rabbi Yose. Rather, we are to learn from this episode that since Rabbi Yose was the *gadol hador*, Eliyahu HaNavi was obligated to honor him, and therefore, he called him Rebbi.

In addition, in such a case there is no assumption that Binyamin would have accorded the honor to his father rather than to the *gadol hador*, and therefore it would be improper to take the honor away from the *gadol* in order to give it to his father.

---

44. 3a.

פרשת מצורע
Parashas Metzora

Safe Keeping

כִּי תָבֹאוּ אֶל אֶרֶץ כְּנַעַן ... וְנָתַתִּי נֶגַע צָרַעַת בְּבֵית אֶרֶץ אֲחֻזַּתְכֶם

When you arrive in the land of Canaan ... and I will place a tzaraas affliction upon a house in the land of your possession

(14:34)

Q Menashe realized his longtime dream of purchasing a home. Five years later, he was climbing a ladder to change a light bulb, and he noticed there was a crack on top of one of the doorways. He also spotted some paper stuffed into the crack. Menashe took a thin wire and was able to take the paper out of the crack. To his surprise, the paper turned out to be three $100 bills.

Menashe wants to know what to do with the money. Does he have to trace all the owners of the house since it was built and ask them if they left any money in the house? If nobody claims the money, does it belong to the previous owner? Perhaps the previous tenant lost the money, and Menashe's house acquired the money for him before the owner gave up hope of finding it, which would mean that Menashe has an obligation to return it to him. On the other hand, maybe Menashe could just keep the money for himself. What does Menashe have to do?

It seems that Menashe is allowed to keep the money for himself. The Gemara in *Bava Metzia*[45] states that if someone finds a lost item in his house, the item belongs to him, because the previous tenants certainly cleared the house of any of their belongings, and if something had been there, they would have found it. *Tosafos* writes that if the item was found in a deep hole, we cannot rely on the fact that it would have been found by merely sweeping the premises. The *Shach*[46] explains that according to *Tosafos,* the homeowner could certainly keep it since the original tenants gave up hope when they were unable to find it. Even if the item had an identifying marking, the *Nesivos HaMishpat*[47] writes that if the item was rusty and had obviously been there for some time, the owner certainly gave up hope of recovering his item, and the one who finds it may keep it.[48]

The previous tenants did not acquire the money by virtue of the fact that it was sitting in their house, because they had very little chance of ever finding it. In such a situation, one's property cannot acquire an object on his behalf.[49]

Menashe may thus keep the money.

---

45. 26a.
46. *Choshen Mishpat* 260 §11.
47. §7.
48. See *Shulchan Aruch, Choshen Mishpat* 265:5.
49. See ibid. 260:1, *Rema* 232:18.

Buried Treasure

כִּי תָבֹאוּ אֶל אֶרֶץ כְּנַעַן . . . וְנָתַתִּי נֶגַע צָרַעַת בְּבֵית אֶרֶץ אֲחֻזַּתְכֶם

*When you arrive in the land of Canaan ...
and I will place a tzaraas affliction upon
a house in the land of your possession*

(14:34)

Q The Segals were an elderly couple who lived in a one-story house in upstate New York for as long as anyone could remember. They were too old to leave their home, and the neighborhood children would deliver their groceries and run errands for them. Eventually they passed on to the Next World and left their house to their two sons. The sons promptly sold the house to a developer, who had the house demolished in order to build a bigger and better home.

The bulldozers knocked the old house down with ease and proceeded to level the land, leaving piles of sand all around. After the bulldozers had left for the day, the neighbor's children came to play in a sandpile that had risen between their house and the empty lot. As the boy was digging deeply in the sand he pulled out a piece of paper, which he discovered to be a $100 bill. He continued to dig more earnestly and pulled out bill after bill. He ran to call his father and to their amazement, they found a total of $700,000 that was buried in the sand.

Suddenly, the developer arrived at the scene, taking in the sight of the father and his children sitting in the sand with piles of money. No sooner did he hear the story than he demanded that they surrender the money to him, as the money had been found on his property.

The neighbor refused to hand over the money. In his opinion, the developer had only bought the property, but not the treasure that was buried there. The money is like any other unidentifiable lost item, and should belong to the one who finds it.

Eventually, the Segal sons heard about the discovery, and they, in turn, felt that the money belonged to them. After all, they had inherited their parents, and they certainly never intended to sell the money together with the property. The neighbor claims that there is no proof that the money belonged to the senior Segals, and perhaps may have belonged to earlier owners, but there is no way to trace them. The Segals were known to be of very modest means, and it did not make sense that they owned so much money, especially without telling someone about it.

Who should get the money? The sons are claiming it as an inheritance; the developer is claiming that he bought it together with the property; the neighbor is claiming that he found a lost item. Who is right?

A The Gemara in *Bava Metzia*[50] states that if someone found an object in a mound of rubble or in an ancient wall, he is allowed to keep it because he can claim that it belonged to the Emorites (the original residents of *Eretz Yisrael*). In our case, one cannot claim that the dollars belonged to the Indians, because the first dollars of this kind were printed in 1928. (Prior to 1928, dollars were printed differently.) In addition, if the date on the bills does not precede the date that the Segals moved into their house, it makes sense that they left them there.

The neighbor's claim that the Segals were known to be of modest means is indicative that he is not well versed in *Mishlei*,[51] where the wisest of men writes, *Some pretend to be rich and have nothing,*

---
50. 25b.
51. 13:7.

but others act poor and have great wealth. Rashi[52] explains that someone who acts as a pauper may indeed be very wealthy.

There is room to argue that even though the money may have belonged to them, they may have relinquished their ownership. This can be supported by the fact that they did not mention the money in their will. They must have given up hope of bequeathing it to their children; i.e., maybe they forgot where they had hidden it. The *Shulchan Aruch*[53] rules that if someone finds something that had obviously been forgotten by its owner for a very long time, and the owner must have given up hope of recovering it, the finder may keep it even if the item can be identified by markings or by the location in which it was found. There is, however, no proof that this is true in our case. Due to their advanced age they may have simply forgotten to write it in their will, even though they were well aware of the money's existence and location.

If the Segals only came to live there subsequent to the printing of the dollars, and the house was owned previously by untraceable tenants, perhaps the money may have belonged to the previous owners. This is also supported by the fact that the money was omitted in the will. In such a case, the money would belong to the one who found it, because of the likelihood that it was a lost item, in line with the aforementioned Gemara in *Bava Metzia*.

Hence, the money should belong either to the neighbor who found it, or to the developer. That question would be dependent on the argument between the *Levush* and the *Nesivos HaMishpat*. The *Rema*[54] writes that if a trader bought a metal utensil with the understanding that it was tin and he sold it as tin, and only discovered afterward that it had actually been gold or silver, he cannot contest the sale claiming that it was a mistake. The trader never owned the gold or silver because he did not know of its existence. The *Pischei Teshuvah*[55] cites the *Levush*, who explains that a person

---

52. *Menachos* 85b.
53. *Choshen Mishpat* 262:5.
54. 232:18.
55. §8.

cannot own something that he had no intent to acquire. Therefore, if he bought a bar of gold, but he thought that it was tin, he does not own the gold.

The *Nesivos HaMishpat* brings forth a different understanding. The gold is considered lost from him or anyone else because it does not stand to be discovered. If, however, the question would arise on an item that is destined to become known, then the trader would have acquired it for himself.

In our case, according to the *Levush*, the developer did not acquire the money together with the property, because he had no intent to do so; it would therefore belong to the neighbor. According to the *Nesivos HaMishpat*, it depends: If the developer would have eventually come across the money during the course of the excavation, then the money would belong to him; if he would not have found it, then it belongs to the neighbor.

Cannot Part With Art

וְטָח אֶת הַבָּיִת
And plaster the house
(14:42)

Q Nachman the painter arrived at Tzvi's house to give him an estimate for painting his house. Nachman inspected the premises and quoted a price that Tzvi thought was unreasonable. The haggling went on and on, but the two could not settle on a price that they both felt was fair. Finally, Nachman made Tzvi an offer. During his tour of the house, Nachman had noticed a painting in the living room. He agreed to paint the entire house in return for the painting. Tzvi did not attribute any special value to the painting, so he agreed.

Nachman did an exceptional job painting the entire house. When Tzvi's wife found out that her husband had agreed to pay for the job with the painting in the living room, she absolutely refused to part with it. To her, the painting was very valuable, even though her husband could not appreciate it. She insisted that her husband pay Nachman with money or anything else, but she would not part with the painting. Nachman wants the painting that he was promised, and he refuses to accept anything in its stead. What should they do?

The Gemara in *Avodah Zarah*[56] states that if someone hired a worker and stipulated that he would pay him with merchandise, the goods do not belong to the worker until he makes a *kinyan* (an act of legal acquisition) on them. The *Rosh*[57] questions this, as a worker's salary does not require a *kinyan*. Just by working for his employer he has already earned his salary. Why should he be required to do anything more than that? The *Rosh* deduces from this Gemara that when an employer hires a worker in return for merchandise, the employer still retains the option to pay him the cash equivalent instead. The worker has acquired his salary, but the option of object or cash belongs to the employer. The worker owns the merchandise only after he has actually made a *kinyan* on the object itself.

The *Rema*[58] writes this ruling in *Shulchan Aruch*, as well, that an employer who hired someone and promised him an object for

---

56. 63b.
57. 5:2.
58. *Choshen Mishpat* 332:4.

his salary can decide later to pay him in cash since the worker never acquired the object with a *kinyan*.

The *Ketzos HaChoshen*[59] adds a crucial point. The reason the worker still requires a *kinyan* is because his work is considered as if he paid for the object, and merely paying for an object cannot transfer ownership. However, it does create a moral obligation, and if the employer wants to retract, he must accept a *Mi shepara* from *beis din*.[60] The *Nesivos HaMishpat* differentiates between whether the employer promised the object *"as payment"* for the job, or if he promised to give him the object *"when the job is completed."* In the latter scenario the object was not actually promised as a direct payment for the work, and would thus not invoke a *Mi shepara*.

In our case, according to all opinions there is no *Mi shepara*, as the *Beis Yosef* explains that when someone pays for an item, and the owner is unable to supply the merchandise for reasons that are not his fault (*oness*), no *Mi shepara* is warranted. When Tzvi's wife opposed the sale because she wanted the painting, it is beyond his capability to honor his commitment, and he would not receive a *Mi shepara*. He may pay Nachman the value of the painting instead.

---

59. §4.
60. See *Choshen Mishpat* 204:1. In a *Mi shepara*, *beis din* declares that He Who punished the generation of the Flood will punish those who do not keep their word.

פרשת אחרי מות
Parashas Acharei Mos

An Expensive Dip

וְרָחַץ בַּמַּיִם אֶת בְּשָׂרוֹ
And he shall immerse himself in water
(16:4)

The Rebbe Rabbi Shimon of Lelov traveled from *Eretz Yisrael* to America to attend the *aufruf* of his grandson. On Shabbos morning one of the Rebbe's attendants apologized to the Rebbe; the *mikveh* they had designated for the Rebbe's use was not operable, and he directed the Rebbe to an alternate *mikveh* in the vicinity. As the Rebbe left the *mikveh* building, instead of proceeding to the shul where the *aufruf* was to take place, the Rebbe went to *daven* in the shul above the *mikveh*. Everyone was amazed: Why would the Rebbe, who had traveled all the way from *Eretz Yisrael* to attend his grandson's *aufruf*, *daven* in a different shul and miss the *aufruf*?

After *davening*, the Rebbe's mysterious behavior became clear. As the Rebbe had left the *mikveh* building, he noticed a small sign that hung over the door. It read: "The use of this *mikveh* is reserved for those who *daven* in this shul." The Rebbe did not want to be guilty of stealing, and therefore, he attended *davening* there to justify his use of the *mikveh*!

Was the Rebbe obligated to act as he did, missing his grandson's *aufruf*, or could he have sufficed with payment to the *mikveh* after Shabbos, and merely refrained from doing so out of piety?

It would seem that the Rebbe's behavior was an act of *chassidus* (piety). The intent of the *gabbai* who hung the sign was not to coerce people to *daven* in the shul, but to prevent outsiders from frequenting the shul's *mikveh*. Perhaps the *gabbai* wanted to encourage people to *daven* in the shul by offering the privilege of using the *mikveh*. Certainly, if the *gabbai* had known that someone had used the *mikveh* by mistake and would miss his grandson's *aufruf* if he *davened* in the shul that owned the *mikveh*, the *gabbai* would not expect that person to adhere to the sign's restriction. Therefore, as a matter of strict halachah, the Rebbe could have gone to *daven* in the shul where the *aufruf* was to take place.

This is especially so since after Shabbos the Rebbe would have the opportunity to pay for having used the *mikveh*. Moreover, even if someone who intentionally used the *mikveh* without permission would have to pay, one who used the *mikveh* by mistake should not have to pay, simply because a *mikveh* does not usually charge men who immerse on Shabbos, and therefore the *mikveh* is not intended for rent. The man who benefits from the *mikveh* without causing the shul any loss is therefore exempt from paying, based on the principle of *Zeh ne'he'neh v'zeh lo chaser*.[61] Even if the person took a little of the *mikveh* water with him, all the water will be drained away after Shabbos in any case, and therefore there was no loss.

---

61. When one benefits from his friend's property without causing a loss, one does not have to pay (see *Bava Kamma* 20a).

The Winning Ticket

עַל שְׁנֵי הַשְּׂעִירִם גֹּרָלוֹת
Lots upon the two he-goats
(16:8)

Q Michel was a staunch supporter of Eizer Refuah, and in appreciation for one of his donations, the organization sent him a booklet of raffle tickets. He did not even remember about the raffle until he received a phone call from Mr. Zilber, the dean of Eizer Refuah, informing him that he had won a 26-speed mountain bike. Mr. Zilber invited Michel to their office to accept the valuable bicycle. Michel asked where their office was located, and was surprised to hear that they were located in Chicago, hundreds of miles from Michel's home. It was absolutely not worth Michel's time to travel to Chicago to claim his prize, as valuable as it might be, not to mention the travel expenses, so Michel just tossed his winning ticket into the wastepaper basket at the side of his desk.

Boruch, Michel's coworker, overheard Michel's conversation and readily understood why Michel had thrown away the ticket. When Michel stepped out of the office, Boruch stealthily slipped the winning ticket into his own pocket.

Boruch hurried home and called Eizer Refuah's office. He complained to the secretary that if the organization wanted to maintain good public relations with their donors, they should not even consider suggesting that the non-local raffle winners travel to Chicago to collect their prizes. That was simply ludicrous! He insisted that such behavior shows a lack of decency and gratitude, and they should definitely have the prizes delivered to the winners' doorsteps. Finally, he concluded with a firm order to deliver the 26-speed bike promptly, if they wanted to continue to benefit from his generosity!

The secretary put the call through to Mr. Zilber who apologized profusely and promised that a special messenger would arrive at Michel's house the following afternoon.

The next day a representative of Eizer Refuah rang Michel's doorbell. As Michel went to answer the door, Boruch, who had been waiting near Michel's house, came up behind the delivery man. Before anyone had a chance to say anything, Boruch announced that he was responsible for the delivery of the bike. He claimed that since Michel had thrown away the raffle ticket, he lost his claim to the prize, and he, Boruch, who had retrieved the ticket from the garbage, is now the proud owner of the brand-new mountain bike!

Michel was taken aback. He was certain that the prize should belong to him. After all, it was his ticket that had won, not Boruch's. How could Boruch attempt to usurp his prize? The representative of the organization chimed in that if Michel had thrown away the ticket, and had no intention of claiming the prize, then perhaps the organization deserves to keep it and use it for a subsequent raffle.

Who should keep the prize?

*A*While it is true that Michel relinquished his ownership of the raffle ticket, that does not give Boruch the right to claim the prize. Eizer Refuah would never agree to award a prize to someone who did not donate to them, and hence did not participate in their raffle![62] Boruch has acquired the right to keep the winning ticket, but not to claim its prize. Only the real winner could claim that right.

Even if Michel renounced his prize, now that the bicycle had been delivered to his home, he has reacquired it, and the organization should certainly agree to let him keep it in order to maintain their reputation and to encourage their donors to continue to support their activities.

Now the question becomes whether Michel has any obligation to Boruch for his hand in arranging for the bicycle to be delivered to him. Perhaps he deserves a broker's fee, or at least some token of acknowledgement of his effort.

In truth, one has to pay only for benefits for which one would normally pay. A benefit that people do not usually pay for cannot make one liable for payment.[63] This is especially true in this case, since Boruch was only acting in his own interest and not on behalf of Michel.[64]

Nevertheless, it would be appropriate for Michel to present some token of gratitude to show his appreciation. The daughters of Yisro told their father that they had been rescued by an Egyptian man.[65] The *Midrash* asks, "Was Moshe Rabbeinu [who saved them] an Egyptian? Rather, this is comparable to someone who was bitten by a serpent and ran to the river in order to soak his wound. When he reached the riverbank he saw a child drowning, and quickly drew him out of the water. The child began to thank his rescuer for saving his life. The man replied that he should thank the serpent that caused him to come to the river in the first place! Similarly, when Yisro's daughters began thanking Moshe for his intervention, he maintained that they owed their salvation to the

---

62. Editor's Note: If Boruch had bought the ticket from Michel, he would have acquired the privileges to which the owner of the ticket was entitled. Since Boruch only acquired the paper, he is not entitled to that which the ticket represents.
63. See *Ketzos HaChoshen* 129 §9.
64. See *Nesivos HaMishpat* 158 §8.
65. *Shemos* 2:19.

Egyptian whom Moshe had killed in defense of his fellow Jew, which forced him to flee to Midyan, where Yisro lived."

Rav Chaim Shmulevitz[66] cites this *Midrash* as the source to prove that one owes a debt of gratitude even if his benefactor had no intent to provide the benefit, and even if his participation was indirect. Accordingly, Michel should show his appreciation to Boruch, since it was due to his intervention that the bicycle was delivered.

---

66. *Sichos Mussar* 2:32.

פרשת קדושים
Parashas Kedoshim

Older Parents

אִישׁ אִמּוֹ וְאָבִיו תִּירָאוּ
Every man: Your mother and father shall you revere
(19:3)

Q Zaydie Frankel was not allowed to eat salt. His doctors had repeatedly warned him, but Zaydie did not agree with their assessment. Without salt, his food had no taste. He begged his children to please put a little salt in his food. His sons responded that salt was dangerous to his health, but Zaydie was not convinced, and he continued to plead with them to allow him to enjoy his meals. Should the children accede to their father's requests?

A The *Sefer Chassidim*[67] records the story of a patient whose doctor had informed him that drinking water together with a particular food would be very dangerous

---
67. 234.

for his particular condition. The patient could not control himself, and asked his child for that food and some water. He threatened the child that if he would not satisfy his request, not only would he not be forgiven in this world, but he would not be forgiven in the World to Come either. Nevertheless, the *Sefer Chassidim* concludes that the child should not give his parent the food!

What would the halachah be if the foods did not pose any danger to the father's **life**, but they could merely have a negative impact on the father's health? Should the son still refuse to capitulate to his father's request?

There are three opinions on the subject. The *Mahari Molcho*[68] says that the son should give his father what he wants. The *Yad Shaul* says that the son should not give the father what he wants. The *Kol Gadol*[69] also says that the son should not give his father the food, because his father will, in retrospect, regret having eaten it, and since the child's intent is for his father's benefit, he is not violating *kibbud av* by not giving in to his father's temporary desire.

It would seem that the *poskim* are not really disagreeing with one other, but rather, each one is discussing a specific case. The *Mahari Molcho* permitted the son to give in to his father in a case where drinking cold water could cause the father to contract a minor illness, e.g., a cold and a sore throat. If the father is complaining of thirst, it is logical that the son could accede to the father's request for cold water, because thirst is also painful. The discomfort of a cold and sore throat is not much greater than the pain of thirst, so the son is allowed to grant his father's request to trade one pain for another. If withholding a food is more painful to the father than the indigestion that will result, especially when the father is asking his son and wants his wishes to be fulfilled, the son could most likely give in to the father.

The other *poskim* are referring to cases that will bring the father to infirmity, even if it is not life threatening. For example,

---

68. Cited in *Birkei Yosef, Yoreh De'ah* 240:70.
69. 54.

if the father is a diabetic and requests something sweet that will most likely cause damage to his body, then the *poskim* forbid the son to grant the request.

If a father asks his son to buy him a package of cigarettes, if each cigarette actually endangers the father's health, the son may not listen. If, however, the father is in good health, and this pack will not dramatically affect the father's health, even though one should certainly not smoke, once the father has asked the son to buy him the cigarettes, the son should listen to his father.

If the salt will actually endanger Zaydie's health, then the children have no choice but to deny his request.

An Irregular Story

וְלֹא תִגְזֹל
And you shall not rob
(19:13)

Q Yeshivas Ner Nachshon instituted a rule that in order to maintain health standards each *bachur* was required to provide his own personal hand towel. Yankel noticed his friend Shimshon drying his hands on a towel that had "Diamond Hotel" emblazoned across the center of the towel. The Diamond Hotel was located just two miles from the yeshivah. Yankel was extremely disturbed to think that his friend would use a towel that did not belong to him. His consternation was exacerbated when Yankel realized that Shimshon had a whole stack of various sizes of those towels neatly arranged on his shelf in his dorm room.

Yankel determined that if he would approach Shimshon to try to convince him that he had a mitzvah to return the stolen towels, Shimshon was not likely to listen. Yankel decided that he himself would simply return the towels to the hotel the next time he was in the area.

Shimshon was very surprised to find his towels missing, and since he was clueless as to their whereabouts he had no choice but to visit his home and replenish his supply of towels ... from the Diamond Hotel! Yankel was amazed at Shimshon's audacity. Did he think that he could take towels from the hotel whenever he needed them? Yankel stealthily removed the towels from Shimshon's closet when no one was looking and returned them to the hotel, as well. This pattern continued, until one day Shimshon decided to hide under his bed to see who had been stealing his towels. Sure enough, Yankel eventually crept into the room to perform his "mitzvah," but this time he was caught! Shimshon was shocked that Yankel would engage in such behavior, but Yankel justified his actions by claiming that he had merely been returning the stolen towels to their rightful owner. He insisted that Shimson should thank him for saving him from such a serious *aveirah*.

Not only did Shimshon not apologize, but he demanded that Yankel pay him for stealing his towels! Yankel could not believe his ears. Who was accusing whom of stealing?

Shimshon explained that the Diamond Hotel had placed an order for thousands of towels with a new manufacturer. Somewhere along the line there had been an error, resulting in hundreds of defective towels. The manufacturer took responsibility for the defect and had replaced the towels, free of charge. The hotel owners had sold the irregular towels at a very discounted price; hence Shimshon had plenty of towels from the Diamond Hotel. Now that Yankel had "returned" the towels to the hotel and they had been mixed into the hotel's laundry, there was little hope of finding them. Shimshon demanded that Yankel pay for all of his towels that were missing due to his overzealousness.

Yankel maintains that it was not his fault. He could not have known that the towels actually belonged to Shimshon. He was only trying to save Shimshon from an *aveirah*. He feels that if Shimshon wants his towels back, he should arrange it with the hotel's management. Can Yankel be excused for jumping to conclusions, when he only had his friend's best interest in mind?

A The *Ketzos HaChoshen*[70] writes that if someone passes his friend's item on to someone else because he thought that it belonged to the other, it is not considered stealing. Although one is obligated to pay for damages that he caused, even accidentally, that does not apply to one who accidentally stole something by giving it to someone else, as described. Perhaps one could claim that this would apply in Yankel's case, as well.

In truth, this is not the case, as Yankel did not steal accidentally. He had no right to take Shimshon's towels. He should have judged his friend favorably, as the Torah dictates,[71] until he was able to confront him directly to ask him how the towels had found their way into his closet. Had he tried to rebuke Shimshon for his behavior as the Torah commands, he would have discovered the truth, and he certainly would not have returned the towels to the hotel where they were mixed into the hotel's laundry.

---

70. 25 §1.
71. *Vayikra* 19:15.

Even if Yankel thought that confronting Shimshon would be counterproductive, as he was convinced that Shimshon had stolen the towels and would not accept Yankel's rebuke, Yankel still should have consulted a Rav before taking the law into his own hands.

Although Rochel Imeinu had the best of intentions when she stole her father's idols,[72] she was nevertheless punished in that she did not merit to raise her child Binyamin. The *Sefer Chassidim*[73] explains that regardless of her good intentions, she was guilty of not having consulted with Yaakov Avinu as to whether she was correct in taking such action.[74] Especially when it involves taking someone else's property, one should refer the issue to a Rav who can rule whether such action is appropriate. As Yankel did not do so, he is liable for having willfully stolen Shimshon's property, and now he has to pay for it.

All That Glitters

לֹא תַעֲמֹד עַל דַּם רֵעֶךָ
You shall not stand aside while your fellow's blood is shed
(19:16)

Q A seasoned antique dealer had an extensive collection of fake antiques. He traveled to a distant marketplace and offered all the items for sale at a very low price, as

---

72. As explained in the *Zohar HaKadosh*.
73. *HaChadash* 924.
74. Editor's Note: In contrast, before Pinchas took swift action to end Zimri's *chillul Hashem*, he was careful to consult with Moshe Rabbeinu, even though he knew the halachah.

he claimed that he was closing his business. He hoped to find some unsuspecting customer to buy his entire lot.

Robert was walking through the marketplace and the antique seller piqued his interest. Robert inquired if the merchandise was indeed worth the asking price. The salesman assured him that this was a once-in-a-lifetime opportunity that was available for one day only, and only for cash. Robert requested that the dealer wait for him to return with the money, and urged him not to sell the merchandise to anyone else.

Shlomo watched the entire exchange. After Robert left, he asked the salesman if he really intended to sell such marvelous antiques for such a low price. The salesman whispered to Shlomo, asking him not to say anything, as all the merchandise was fake!

Shlomo realized that he had a mitzvah to warn Robert not to fall prey to the salesman's deception. (The mitzvah of not standing by when your friend's blood is being spilled applies to saving someone from monetary damage, as well.[75] This is in addition to the mitzvah of returning lost property.) He ran across the marketplace to locate Robert.

When Shlomo found Robert, he informed him that the antiques were not real, and that he should not allow himself to be swindled. Robert asked Shlomo if the merchandise was worth half the price being asked. Shlomo thought that Robert didn't understand him, and asked him why he would even consider buying false antiques. Robert whispered that he understood Shlomo's concern, but he asked him not to say anything, as Robert's money was also counterfeit!

Now Shlomo wants to know if he has an obligation to try to warn the salesman who had tried to take advantage of an unsuspecting customer.

---

75. See *Chofetz Chaim, Rechilus* 9:1.

The Chofetz Chaim[76] writes that if a prospective father-in-law promises his future son-in-law a generous dowry, and someone discovers that the father-in-law has no intention of keeping his word, there is a mitzvah (under certain conditions) to warn the unsuspecting son-in-law that he is being deceived. However, the Chofetz Chaim adds that this would be true only if the son-in-law is not guilty of deception, himself. If the father-in-law is also being deceived, then the deceptions "cancel each other out."

Accordingly in this case, Robert and the salesman would seem to "deserve" each other, and Shlomo would not have to get involved.

However, it seems clear that the Chofetz Chaim only meant to say that in a case where the two parties are misrepresenting themselves to the extent that they are equally matched, neither party would deserve a warning. In Robert's case, the seller's merchandise does have some value, and the buyer intends to pay nothing for it. Therefore, even if the seller is being dishonest and does not deserve to have his merchandise protected for him, as he will just use it to try and swindle someone else, it is still a mitzvah to prevent Robert from violating the prohibition of stealing.

Moreover, once Shlomo knows that Robert possesses counterfeit money, he has an obligation to rebuke Robert for possessing forged currency. If he can, Shlomo should confiscate the fake money and destroy it. If he cannot do that, he should threaten that he will publicize the fact that Robert possesses counterfeit money.

---

76. Ad loc. §8.

A Waity Decision

וְהָדַרְתָּ פְּנֵי זָקֵן

And you shall honor the presence of a sage

(19:32)

Q In 5774, a *tefillah* rally was organized in Yerushalayim, with hundreds of thousands of people in attendance. The members of a certain community chartered a bus to Yerushalayim. Due to the tremendous crowds, the bus was parked quite a distance away, and the driver waited there to return his passengers to their homes after the gathering would end. A small group of passengers, among them several *talmidei chachamim,* misunderstood the arrangement, and they mistakenly walked to the other end of the city to catch the bus. One of these *talmidei chachamim* was scheduled to deliver a *daf yomi shiur* later that evening. Due to the heavy traffic conditions, the bus would have to make an arduous detour around Yerushalayim in order to collect the group. It would cause a delay of an hour and a half!

Some of the passengers protested that the bus driver should keep to his original route and allow the wayward group to find their own way home. The man who had chartered the bus felt otherwise. He believed that they had an obligation to honor their important passengers and were also required to ensure that the *daf yomi shiur* take place. He instructed the driver to make the detour.

Now the bus leader wants to know if he acted properly or if he was guilty of taxing the other passengers unfairly.

The honor of the community and *tircha d'tzibbura* (burdening the congregation) are very serious matters. The *Rema*[77] rules that a *chazzan* should not wait for individuals who *daven* a long *Shemoneh Esrei*, even if they are important people, because doing so is *tircha d'tzibbura*. Similarly, if a minyan has already gathered, they should not delay the *davening* in order to wait for a Rav or other important person to arrive. The *Mishnah Berurah* adds that common practice is to wait until the Rav finishes his *Shemoneh Esrei*, as most people *daven* too quickly and their pace would not afford the opportunity to those who *daven* word by word to say *Kedushah* with the *tzibbur*.

The *Maharik*[78] writes that if a *Sefer Torah* has already been opened in preparation for *Krias HaTorah* and a Kohen is still *davening*, the congregation should not wait for him. Although giving the Kohen the first *aliyah* is a fulfillment of the mitzvah to sanctify the Kohen,[79] this requirement is waived in deference to the congregation's honor and the difficulty involved in waiting.

The *tzaddik* Rabbi Zerach Braverman accorded the honor of *sandek* at his son's *bris* to his rebbi, Rabbi Yehoshua Leib Diskin (known by his acronym, the Maharil Diskin), the Rav of Yerushalayim at the end of the 1800's. Rav Braverman began to prepare for the *bris* immediately after the *vasikin* (sunrise) minyan. Although it took quite some time to make the necessary preparations, the Maharil Diskin had still not arrived. Realizing that his *rebbi* must still be *davening*, Rav Braverman took the honor of *sandek* for himself, and did not wait for his rebbi to arrive. When Rabbi Yehoshua Leib heard that they did not wait for him to come, in order not to delay the performance of the mitzvah, he was very pleased, and he blessed Rav Braverman with a heartfelt *berachah*.

---

77. *Orach Chaim* 124:3.
78. Quoted in the *Beis Yosef, Orach Chaim* 135; see *Shulchan Aruch se'if* 7 and *Magen Avraham*.
79. *Mishnah Berurah* 135 §9.

Delaying the other passengers for an hour and a half is certainly taxing to the *tzibbur*. Therefore, it would have been proper not to delay their travel.

However, once the bus leader decided to go pick up the group at the expense of everyone else, he would not be required to ask them for forgiveness, as he made a mistake in the process of doing a mitzvah,[80] and everyone understands that his misjudgment stemmed from his honor for the Torah.

Soon There Will Be a Beis HaMikdash

כִּי כָל אִישׁ אֲשֶׁר בּוֹ מוּם
For any man in whom there is a blemish
(21:18)

Q Levi Cohen visited the doctor and complained about pain in his fingertip. After some testing, the doctor concluded that Levi was suffering from a narrowing of the blood vessels in his finger, and since there was no cure, suggested that Levi amputate the end of his finger. Levi, being a God-fearing Jew, decided to consult with his Rav before proceeding with such a step. Perhaps Levi should continue to endure the pain, because if he will amputate the end of his finger, when the *Beis HaMikdash* will be rebuilt (quickly in our days!) he will not be able to serve as a Kohen in the *Beis HaMikdash* because he will

---

80. *Rambam, Hilchos Shegagos* 2:8.

be blemished. There is nothing life threatening in not amputating; it is just painful. What should he do?

Some Rabbanim wanted to dismiss the question, because in the future all defects will be healed, as is explicit in the Gemara in *Sanhedrin*.[81] The *Rambam*,[82] however, writes, "Don't think that in the days of Mashiach the nature of the world will change or there will be a difference in the Creation; the world will continue to function normally .... The *Chachamim* stated that the only thing that will change is the Jews' autonomy." The *Vilna Gaon*[83] noted that the *Rambam* seems to contradict what he himself wrote in *Hilchos Teshuvah*,[84] where he rules that all the prophecies were referring to the days of Mashiach. The *Gaon* answers that there are two eras that are called Mashiach's times. The days of Mashiach ben Yosef, which if the Jews are worthy will precede the days of Mashiach ben David. In these earlier days the world will continue according to the nature that exists today. Only in the time of Mashiach ben David will all defects be healed. Therefore, there might be reason for a Kohen not to maim himself, lest he not be able to serve in the *Beis HaMikdash* in the days of Mashiach ben Yosef.

The *Avnei Nezer*[85] records the case of a boy who was born with a crooked leg. A specialist assured the parents that he could straighten the leg with a cast, if it was put on immediately, while the baby's bones were still soft. He asserted that if they would wait until after the *bris milah*, it would already be too late. On the other hand, if they would put on the cast immediately, the baby would be too weak to undergo the *bris milah* on the eighth day. Are they allowed to set the leg in a cast in order to correct the baby's defect, at the expense of not making the *bris milah* on time?

---

81. 91b.
82. *Hilchos Melachim* 12:3.
83. Ad loc.
84. 8:7.
85. *Yoreh De'ah* 321.

The *Avnei Nezer* responded that if the doctors are correct in their evaluation, it is clear that it is permitted to go through with the procedure. One is not required to spend a fortune in order to perform a positive mitzvah.[86] It follows that one certainly does not have to leave the child with a defect in order to perform such a mitzvah on time.

In our case, where the *Beis HaMikdash* service is unfortunately not yet in place, and — unlike the mitzvah of *milah* — the failure to perform the service in the *Beis HaMikdash* does not involve the penalty of *kares*, Levi is definitely allowed to amputate his fingertip, since his suffering is considered more than he would have to spend on a positive mitzvah.

Not only is there no obligation not to remove the fingertip, but on the contrary, he should have it removed, because his pain disturbs him from learning Torah and doing mitzvos.

---

86. *Orach Chaim* 656, only up to one-fifth of one's assets.

Parashas Emor

A(n) (Un) Hairy Situation

לֹא יִקְרְחוּ קָרְחָה בְּרֹאשָׁם
They shall not make a bald spot on their heads
(21:5)

Q Beirush knew he badly needed a haircut. When he passed a new barber shop that was advertising an introductory offer, he decided to take advantage of the lower price and try a new barber. He sat down in the chair and took off his glasses. The new barber was quick and in just a few minutes he was done. Beirush replaced his glasses and checked his reflection in the mirror. He was aghast. His *peyos* had disappeared!

Beirush gasped and demanded an explanation. The barber apologized and explained that he was a recent *ba'al teshuvah* and had mistakenly cut Beirush's hair as he had been accustomed to do. Beirush was too embarrassed to be seen in public. While he was looking for something to cover his face so he could make it home, the barber turned to him and quietly informed him that he expected to be paid for the professional haircut he had given him. He felt the lack of *peyos* didn't detract from the general success of his efforts.

Beirish couldn't believe his ears. The barber wanted to be paid for the haircut!? He would never agree to have his hair cut like this if he had been offered any amount of money! If anything, the barber should pay Beirush for the humiliation he will suffer until his *peyos* grow back. Does Beirush owe the barber any compensation, or vice versa?

Beirush certainly does not have to pay. The barber caused Beirush severe anguish. Although the haircut was executed in stages, and the *peyos* only came off at the end, and until that point the barber did deserve to be paid, nevertheless, the entire haircut is considered one unit, and Beirush does not have to pay for the barber's work. The haircut is of no benefit to Beirush; it is an act of damage and a badge of shame.

On the contrary, the barber must pay Beirush for giving him such a haircut. Although he does not have to pay for causing embarrassment, since he did not have malicious intent,[87] the barber would have to compensate Beirush for loss of work if Beirush is too embarrassed to appear at work without *peyos*.[88] The *Shulchan Aruch*[89] rules that one would have to compensate for loss of work, even in our day and age.[90] The *Rema* cites the *Rosh's* opinion that nowadays one would not have to remunerate for loss of work, but there is nevertheless an obligation to appease the damaged party for a sum that *beis din* deems fair.

---

87. See *Choshen Mishpat* 421:1.
88. See *Bava Kamma* 86a.
89. *Choshen Mishpat* ad loc.
90. See ibid., 1:2 that in our days we do not have the authority to obligate payment for shaming.

Even though Beirush cannot bring himself to attend shul and will lose the opportunity to perform many mitzvos, the barber's liability doesn't extend that far. The *Alshich*[91] explains the *pasuk* that the one who damaged "only has to pay for loss of work"[92] as meaning that he does not have to pay for loss of mitzvos. The reason for the exemption is because that is something that will need to be settled between them, by Hashem Himself!

To Fix or Not to Fix

וּמַכֵּה נֶפֶשׁ בְּהֵמָה יְשַׁלְּמֶנָּה
And a man who strikes an animal life mortally shall make restitution
(24:18)

Part 1

Q Yuval, an old-time *Yerushalmi*, is the proud father of five sons who all light Chanukah candles outside. Instead of buying a glass box for each *menorah*, Yuval ordered a large glass case with shelves. This arrangement worked very well until the fifth day of Chanukah, when Nati was walking down the sidewalk, chatting on his cell phone. He did not notice Yuval's glass case until his briefcase banged into it. Luckily, only the glass on that side was broken, Nati immediately knocked on Yuval's door to

---
91. *Shemos* 21:19.
92. Ibid.

confess and apologize. Nati asked Yuval to notify him as to the price of the repair so he could pay for it. Yuval wasted no time, and called down a glazier to repair the damaged case. He told Yuval that it would cost $50, and he would fix it before nightfall.

An hour later, Sruli, one of the neighbor's teenagers, who was involved in an intense ball game, smashed his ball into the glass on the other side of Yuval's case. Yuval called the glass repairman to inform him that the other side of the glass box now needed to be repaired, as well. The repairman said that he would fix the second side for an additional $30 Since he was already coming down for the first repair, the second repair was less expensive.

The question now became, how much do Nati and Sruli have to pay? Should Nati pay $50 and Sruly $30, as that is how much damage each one caused, or perhaps, since each one's act of damage was identical, they should split the cost at $40 each? Is their financial obligation determined based on the moment they caused the damage, or on when they are actually supposed to pay?

The *Shach's*[93] opinion is that when one damages his friend's property he is obligated to fix that which he ruined. The obligation is not merely to pay the cost of the repair, but rather to actually repair the damage. If the damage cannot be repaired, then he would have to pay the depreciation of the item.

The Chazon Ish[94] explains that according to the *Shach*, if at the time of the damage it cost $40 to fix the item, and at the time of the repair the price of the repair went down to $10, or vice versa, the one who damaged would pay whatever the actual repair cost.

---

93. *Choshen Mishpat* 95 §18 and 387 §1.
94. *Bava Kamma* 6 §3.

In contrast, the Chazon Ish cites *Rabbeinu Yonah*,[95] who maintains that one who damages only has to pay for the item's depreciation but does not have to repair the item. *Rabbeinu Yonah's* ruling is based on the Gemara in *Bava Kamma*.[96] If Reuven's ox digs a pit on Shimon's property, Shimon is responsible for any damage caused by the pit. This is because Shimon is required to fill in the pit, as Reuven only has to pay for the damage that his animal caused. According to this opinion, writes the Chazon Ish, one who inflicted damage has to pay the cost of the damage at the time it was inflicted, even if the price went down later.

Moreover, according to *Rabbeinu Yonah*, the one whose property was damaged may decide that he does not wish to repair his property, and he may keep the cash, instead. This can be proven from the Gemara in *Bava Kamma*[97] that states that if one hit his friend, he is obligated to pay for his friend's medical expenses. The victim may not ask for the medical costs in advance, as the assailant can counter that he is concerned lest the victim keep the money for himself and refrain from seeking the treatment that he requires. In that case, the resulting handicap will serve as a constant reminder of the assailant's misdeed, which is something that he does not deserve.

Had one not been able to ask for repair costs of property in advance, the Gemara would not have to discuss whether he could do so in cases of personal injury. In addition, personal injury is the exception, whereas in cases involving property damage, one could ask for the amount of money the repair would cost, even if he chooses not to fix his property.

Based on the above opinions, it would seem that according to the *Shach*, who holds that the obligation is to repair the damage, Nati and Sruly would each have to pay the cost of the actual repair, which comes to $40 per glass. Conversely, according to *Rabbeinu Yonah*, who maintains that the obligation is to pay for

---

95. *Shitah Mekubetzes, Bava Metzia* 5a.
96. 48a.
97. 85a.

the depreciation of the item, Nati's damage is valued at $50, and Sruli's damage is only $30.

One could argue that in this case, even the *Shach* would agree that Nati should pay $40 and Sruli, $30. The *Shach* only discussed a case where the price of the repair went down. In this case, the price never changed. The first window still costs $50, and the second window is only less expensive because the repairman is already coming out. Therefore, each person should pay the price of his respective repair. וצ"ע.

Part 2
It Was an Acci-Dent

Q Chaim was trying his best to parallel park and accidentally bumped Yehudah's car, leaving a nice-sized dent in it. The truth is that Yehudah's car already had a dent in that place, but it was not as big before. The new dent makes Yehudah's car worth less, but on the other hand, Chaim did not create a greater repair cost. The body shop does not charge more for fixing a bigger dent, as opposed to a smaller one. Does Chaim have to split the repair cost with Yehudah, or does he have to pay for the car's depreciation? Perhaps Chaim does not have to pay at all, since he didn't cause Yehudah to have to pay anything more to fix his car?

A This question would seem to be dependent on the *machlokes* between the *Shach* and *Rabbeinu Yonah* (directly above, Part I of this question). According to the *Shach*, when one inflicts damage, his obligation is to repair that which he ruined. In this case, one cannot repair the new dent without fixing the old dent as well. Hence, although Chaim caused Yehudah's car to go down in value, he did not add anything to the cost of repairing the car. Therefore, he should not have to pay.

According to *Rabbeinu Yonah*, one has to pay the cost of the actual damage that he caused. Yehudah will decide whether or not to fix the car, but that is not Chaim's concern.

However, one could argue that even according to *Rabbeinu Yonah*, Chaim should not have to pay. *Rabbeinu Yonah* only argued on the *Shach* when someone damaged something that has to be repaired. In that case, the person caused damage and must reimburse the owner, independent of whether the item will be repaired or not. In a case where someone damaged something that was already damaged, and the victim was planning on fixing the item anyway, there really is no additional damage. Therefore, in such a situation there would be no obligation to pay, even if temporarily the car is worth less. וצ"ע.

פרשת בהר
Parashas Behar

Deafening Silence

וְלֹא תוֹנוּ אִישׁ אֶת עֲמִיתוֹ
And each of you shall not aggrieve his fellow
(25:17)

Q The Torah prohibits a Jew from verbally abusing his friend, as the *pasuk* says, *Each of you shall not aggrieve his fellow*. Rashi explains that this is the source that one may not upset his friends with words. Does this prohibition apply even to a case where one does not speak, yet causes pain with his silence?

A Responsa *Chikrei Lev*[98] records the story of a *gabbai* who became upset at a congregant who refused to honor a pledge. The *gabbai* arose in shul and swore that until the pledge was paid, the congregant's name would be omitted from the customary *Mi shebeirach*[99] after his friends and relatives received *aliyos* to the Torah.

---
98. Vol. 4, *Yoreh De'ah* 80.
99. Lit., *He Who blesses*; a prayer invoking Heavenly blessings.

The *Chikrei Lev* writes that the oath is not binding, as one cannot swear to violate a mitzvah,[100] and the *gabbai* swore to violate the prohibition of verbal abuse. The omission of the congregant's name is sure to cause embarrassment, as if he was cut off from the community. The *Chikrei Lev* continues to support his opinion that one who hurts his friend with silence is equivalent to one who does so with speech. He cites the *Yerei'im*,[101] who writes that one who shows his friend an unhappy face is also guilty of abusing him.

It seems that the *gabbai* would be guilty of "abuse" because he is formally omitting this person's name from the *Mi shebeirach*. If, however, the *gabbai* would not have made the omission an official policy, nobody would have attributed any malicious intent and hence there would be no abuse. Everyone would assume that it was just a mistake.

There was a man whose father was a *gadol baTorah*, yet, when he made a wedding for his own son, he intended to honor someone other than his father to officiate at the wedding. Rav Elyashiv told Rav Zilberstein that the *chassan's* father was in violation of the prohibition against shaming one's father![102] Everyone would notice that the grandfather had not been given his due honor at his grandson's wedding. The same would be true of a son who does not attend his father's wedding!

Obviously, one could violate the prohibition of verbal abuse by not saying anything, as well.

---

100. *Shavuos* 27a.
101. 51.
102. *Devarim* 27:16.

פרשת בחקתי
Parashas Bechukosai

Fare Is Fair

וַאֲכַלְתֶּם לַחְמְכֶם לָשֹׂבַע
And you will eat your bread to satiety
(26:5)

Q Fishel is a one-man *chesed* organization. He receives deliveries of unserved meals from various catering halls and distributes them to the poor. One afternoon, Fishel opened the door to his apartment and found a box outside containing 150 fresh rolls. Fishel assumed that they were extra rolls from someone's *bris* that were intended for distribution.

Fishel called a local yeshivah and asked the administrator if he would like to serve the rolls for supper. The *bachurim* usually ate sliced bread, but if the rolls were available, they would certainly enjoy them. Sure enough, the *bachurim* polished them off with gusto.

Later that night, Fishel discovered that a mistake had been made. His neighbor, Yosef, had ordered the rolls for a *sheva berachos seudah* he was celebrating that night.

The delivery man from the bakery had accidentally placed the rolls at the wrong door! Yosef hastily made other arrangements, but the question remained: Who must pay for the rolls? Fishel, who assumed that the rolls were designated for distribution? The delivery man, who dropped off the rolls at the wrong door? The *bachurim* who ate the rolls and enjoyed them? Perhaps nobody has to pay, and the bakery must absorb the loss?

A Fishel cannot be held accountable, since he behaved as he usually does, and he had every reason to believe that the food placed by his door was a regular delivery intended for distribution. He had no reason to suspect that the rolls belonged to his neighbor.

The delivery man receives payment for his work, so he has the status of a paid watchman. He is responsible to ensure that the rolls arrive at the proper destination. Since he placed them in a compromising position, he should have to pay.[103]

Do the yeshivah boys also have to pay? Perhaps this is comparable to the case of the orphans who slaughtered and ate a cow in their father's yard, and later discovered that the cow belonged to someone else. The halachah[104] in that case is that they have to pay the price of meat on sale (two-thirds). They do not have to pay full price because they can claim that had they known that it was not their father's cow, they would not have eaten the meat. Nevertheless, they have to pay two-thirds because it is normal for people to purchase meat at a sale price, even if they would not have eaten meat otherwise.[105]

---

103. Even though he could not have known about Fishel's *chesed* activities and is not liable for having placed the box in front of Fishel's door, that would only exempt the delivery man from his obligation for having damaged the rolls, but would not release him his obligation of being a paid watchman. The reason he has to pay is not because he put them at Fishel's door, but because he did not put them at Yosef's door!
104. *Choshen Mishpat* 341:4.
105. *Sma* ad loc.

In this case, the yeshivah boys could have eaten the normal fare that the yeshivah usually prepared for them and refrained from engaging in the luxury of eating fancy rolls. Therefore, we cannot obligate them to pay even two-thirds. However, since they did enjoy the rolls, as a compromise, the boys should each pay for one-third of a roll, and the delivery man should pay for two-thirds of each roll. Truthfully, though, the delivery man should be told that it is not proper to charge the boys for the rolls they thought they were getting for free, and therefore it would be appropriate (although not an obligation) for him to pay the entire cost himself.

Davening With Heart

וְאִם תֵּלְכוּ עִמִּי קֶרִי
And if you behave casually with Me
(26:21)

Q Hillel lives in a city with only one Orthodox shul. Unfortunately, the people who come there to *daven* do not seem to appreciate what *davening* is about. They talk to their friends when they are supposed to be talking to the King of all kings. They discuss worldly topics that never have a place in a miniature *Beis HaMikdash*. Hillel finds it difficult to have *kavanah* when *davening* there, but he has no other option at this point in his life. Would he be better off *davening* at home without a minyan, where he will be able to have more *kavanah*, or perhaps it is still preferable to *daven* with this minyan where he can also hear *Kaddish*, *Kedushah*, and the Torah reading?

A The Gemara in *Avodah Zarah*[106] states that a person can learn only in a place that his heart desires. The *Gilyonei HaShas* cites the *Radvaz*[107] who writes that the same is true for *davening*. One has to feel comfortable in his surroundings in order to *daven* well. The *Radvaz* continues that it is written in *sefarim* that when a person listens intently to his rebbi and gives him his heart, their spirits will be bound to each other. The rebbi's influence will rest upon him, and he will have an addition to his soul. This is the meaning of the *pasuk, And your eyes will behold your teachers.*[108] Rabbi Yehudah HaNasi said that had he seen his teacher's face, he would have become even greater.[109] This is the reason that Rabbi Yose said that a person does not merit to learn from just anyone.[110] It is also for this reason that one is allowed to travel elsewhere to learn Torah, even against his father's wishes.[111] The same is true for *davening*, as well. When a person looks and sees his friends or relatives, or his rebbi, or those with whom he feels a connection, his soul will be awakened to have total *kavanah*. The *Radvaz* writes that had he not been too afraid to say so, he would suggest that it is preferable for a person to *daven* alone than to *daven* among people with whom he does not feel comfortable.

The *Radvaz* did not decide that one should follow his decision, as he was fearful to issue such a ruling. The *Mishnah Berurah*[112] writes that one should not refrain from *davening* in a shul that has members who are sinners, which would seem to contradict the *Radvaz*. However, the *Mishnah Berurah* may have been referring to those who are not careful in other mitzvos, but are at least not

---

106. 19a.
107. Responsa Vol. III, 410.
108. *Yeshayah* 30:20.
109. *Eruvin* 13b.
110. Ibid., 47b.
111. *Yoreh De'ah* 240.25.
112. 90 §28.

disrespectful to the *davening*. In Hillel's case, perhaps it would be better for him to *daven* at home. .וצ״ע

Rabbi Yeshayah Cheshin was a *maggid shiur* in the Etz Chaim Cheder in Yerushalayim. He would tell the following story to every boy on the occasion of his bar mitzvah.

An epidemic broke out in the city of Asstra. The Rav and his *beis din* decreed a day of fasting and prayer. They announced that anyone who knew of anything suspicious in the city should come and notify *beis din* so they could determine what sin had to be rectified in order to put an end to the plague.

There was one Jew in town who did not join the community in shul. In light of the situation, and in consideration of *beis din's* announcement, two men decided that they would try to discover the man's secret. Perhaps he was somehow connected to the cause of the epidemic. They followed him all day but did not notice anything peculiar. They continued to watch him throughout the night until eventually, in the middle of the night, they saw him leaving his house stealthily and exiting the city! The two men followed him silently until he entered the forest and disappeared from view. The men returned to the city.

The next day, they came to the Rav to report what they had seen. Who knew what the man was doing in the forest at midnight! The Rav decided that he would personally go to monitor this man's activities. That night, the Rav accompanied the two community members, and this time they followed the suspect into the forest. They watched as the man stopped, sat down on the ground, and began to recite *Tikkun Chatzos* while wailing uncontrollably. The trio's hearts melted from the experience. One thing they could not understand, however, was that they seemed to hear someone else saying *Tikkun Chatzos* together with the man, yet they did not see anyone else.

When he finished his *Tikkun Chatzos*, the Rav approached him and asked him who had said the *Tikkun* with him. The man tried to avoid answering the question, but the Rav decreed, with the authority he had as the city's Rav, that the man reveal his secret. When the man realized that he had no choice, he told the Rav that he had practiced this custom of heartfelt mourning for the *Beis HaMikdash* for a long time, and that he had been given a gift from Heaven; every night Yirmiyahu HaNavi would come to the forest and say *Tikkun Chatzos* together with him. The Rav inquired why he didn't *daven* that the epidemic should end. Since he had the tremendous merit of saying *Tikkun Chatzos* together with Yirmiyahu HaNavi, Hashem would certainly listen to his prayers. The man said that he would ask Yirmiyahu the following day.

The next day, the man returned with an answer from Yirmiyahu. The *navi* revealed to him that in truth, the *Beis HaMikdash* should have been destroyed 40 years earlier, but since people were careful not to speak idly in shuls, the *Beis HaMikdash* continued to stand for an additional 40 years, despite the wickedness of the people of that generation. When people began to talk in shul, the *Beis HaMikdash* was destroyed. All of the tragedies that were visited upon the Jews are a result of idle chatter in shul!

The Rav decided to call the entire city together to meet in the biggest shul. The Rav spoke about the sanctity, awe, and honor that are due to a shul. Then he told them the events that had transpired in wake of *beis din's* announcement, exhorting them with Yirmiyahu's message as well. They all broke down crying and resolved that they would take special care not to speak of mundane matters in shul, especially when wearing *tefillin*. Immediately, the epidemic ceased, to the great joy of the Jews.[113]

---

113. Brought in the introduction to *Divrei Mishpat* by Rabbi Chaim Auerbach.

Wholesale or Retail

וְהֶעֱרִיךְ אֹתוֹ הַכֹּהֵן
And the Kohen should evaluate him
(27:8)

Q Yechezkel wrote a wonderful *sefer* and gave the manuscript to Tuvia for editing. Yechezkel promised Tuvia 30 copies of the *sefer* as remuneration for his editorial expertise. Tuvia added insightful comments, corrected mistakes, and polished the *sefer* until it shone with a professional editor's touch. When the *sefer* arrived from the printer, Yechezkel decided that he preferred to pay Tuvia in cash instead of with the *sefarim* that he promised him. How much does Yechezkel have to pay? Does he have to pay Tuvia according to the *sefer's* list price, or does he only have to pay based on the price he charges the distributor?

A The *Ketzos HaChoshen*[114] writes that when an employer promises to pay for a job with merchandise, and after the job is completed the employer wishes to pay cash instead, he is subject to a *Mi shepara*.[115] In our case there would not be a *Mi shepara* because the *sefarim* were not yet printed at the time the job was completed, and therefore the worker did not acquire them as far as obligating the employer to deserve a *Mi shepara*.

The *Ketzos HaChoshen* also writes that if an employer promised to pay with something that had not yet been produced, he

---

114. *Choshen Mishpat* 332 §4.
115. A declaration from *beis din* that "He Who punished the generation of the Flood…will punish those who do not keep their word."

still must pay what he promised. Such a case is not worse than any case where someone promises to pay with an item; even though the worker has not acquired the item by working, the employer still has to pay the worker the value of the item, if not the item itself. The value is estimated according to the item's value at maturity; i.e., if he promised to pay him with fruits, he would have to pay the value of fully grown fruits. The *Ketzos HaChoshen* explains that this was why the arrangement was binding when Yaakov made an arrangement with Lavan that Yaakov would be paid with sheep not yet born to Lavan.

The *Nesivos HaMishpat*[116] argues that the employer only has to pay the value of the item at the time that the job was finished, because that is when payment is due. *Maharil Diskin* writes that in his opinion the employer has to pay the value of the item at the time of their agreement.

In our case, it would be dependent on the aforementioned *machlokes*. According to the *Ketzos HaChoshen*, Yechezkel has to pay the market price of the *sefarim*. The *Nesivos HaMishpat* would contend that it is sufficient to pay the value of the *sefarim* at the time the job was finished, and according to the *Maharil*, at the time of the agreement. However, since there was no value at that time, it would seem that, according to this opinion, Yechezkel would have to pay based only on the price paid by the distributor.

---

116. Ad loc. *Chidushim* §5.

ספר במדבר

Sefer Bamidbar

פרשת במדבר
Parashas Bamidbar

Name Change

בְּמִסְפַּר שֵׁמוֹת
By number of the names
(1:2)

Q Elliot Friedberg entered Motty's *sefarim* store bearing an expensive set of antique leather-bound *machzorim*. He wanted to have them embossed with his *kallah's* name so he could present them to her in advance of the upcoming Yom Tov. He spelled out her name in Hebrew, שרה פרידברג, on a slip of paper, and entrusted the salesman with his *machzorim*. He was assured t0hat they would be ready in an hour.

An hour later, Elliot arrived to collect his *machzorim*. He checked the name and his face fell. Instead of printing the name שרה, the man had embossed שירה. Elliot pointed out to the clerk that they had made a terrible mistake. The man apologized profusely, and added that he would certainly not charge Elliot for the service.

Elliot was outraged. He had no use for an expensive set of *machzorim* with the wrong name printed on them. He accused the man of defacing his *machzorim* and insisted that the man pay for the damage he had done. The printer examined the cover carefully to see if there was some way to erase the extra letter, but didn't find any solution. He did, however, notice something else. He asked Elliot which *nusach* he *davened*, and Elliot, not knowing what difference that made, responded that he *davened nusach Ashkenaz*. The printer triumphantly opened the cover of one of the *machzorim*, and pointed to the *nusach*: *Eidot Ha'Mizrach*. Elliot had accidentally bought the wrong *nusach*! Even if the printer had printed the name properly, Elliot would have had no use for the *machzorim*.

Elliot was not dissuaded. He insisted that his mistake was not the printer's concern. The printer ruined the *machzorim* that he was hired to emboss. Elliot felt that since the printer had stamped the wrong name on the *machzorim*, he should be obligated to pay for them. Who is right?

The Gemara[1] states: If someone leased a field in return for a set amount of the produce, and before the harvest, the yield was attacked by locusts or the like, the obligation to pay may be affected. If all the fields in the area were hit, the lessee may deduct from his payment according to the percentage that was damaged. If only this field was damaged, the owner of the field can attribute the loss to the lessee's misfortune, and the lessee would have to pay the entire amount.

The Gemara discusses a case where the owner of the field leased the field for the purpose of being planted with wheat, and the lessee planted barley instead. Subsequently, all of the fields in

---

1. *Bava Metzia* 105b.

the area were completely ruined due to weather conditions. Does the lessee have to pay for the lease? On the one hand, even if the lessee had planted wheat, it never would have reached harvest. Therefore, it should not matter that he planted barley, since the entire area's crops were ruined, so why should he have to pay? On the other hand, the field owner may claim that had the lessee followed their agreement, his harvest could have survived, because the owner *davened* that the wheat should grow successfully and Hashem would have listened to his *tefillos*. Since he had planted barley instead, the *tefillos* were not able to be accepted, as there was no wheat to grow successfully. The Gemara concludes that the field owner's claim is indeed valid, and the lessee has to pay for the entire lease.

One can infer from this Gemara that had the field owner not had a special claim that his *davening* would have averted the decree, the lessee would have been able to defend himself by saying that the fact that he planted the wrong crop is irrelevant. In any event, the harvest would have been ruined, and he would not have had to pay. In this case as well, the *machzorim* would have been unusable in any event, and the printer should not have to pay for imprinting the wrong name.

Whereas the owner of the field can claim that had the field been planted properly, there would not have been any loss because his *tefillos* would have been answered, Elliot cannot claim that had the printer printed the correct name, the *machzorim* would have changed their *nusach*! Therefore, the printer's claim is valid, and he does not have to pay for defacing the *machzorim*. Elliot will have to shop more carefully in the future.

The Gift of Pidyon Haben

וְלָקַחְתָּ חֲמֵשֶׁת חֲמֵשֶׁת שְׁקָלִים
And you shall take five shekels each
(3:47)

Q The *Yerushalmi*[2] queries: "Why is the price of *pidyon haben* set at five *sela'im*? Rabbi Berachya and Rabbi Levi quote Reish Lakish: Since Yosef, the firstborn of Rochel, was sold for 20 silver pieces, let everyone redeem their firstborn for 20 silver pieces (5 *sela'im* = 20 silver pieces)."

The *Meshech Chochmah*[3] wonders about this reasoning; it seems to be a punishment for the fact that the brothers sold Yosef. If so, why should the tribes of Yosef (and Binyamin) have to give five *sela'im*? And to whom? To none other than the tribe of *Levi*, the one who sold him!?[4]

A The *Meshech Chochmah* explains that perhaps the *Yerushalmi* is only giving the reason for the price; i.e., the brothers decided that the value of a firstborn is five *sela'im*. The *Yerushalmi* never intended to explain the reason that *pidyon haben* is given to the Kohen.

Perhaps it can be explained that *pidyon haben* is meant to atone for Yosef's sale, despite the fact that the Kohen is descended from the one who sold Yosef. Nevertheless, when the Jews, among

---
2. *Shekalim* 2:3.
3. *Shemos* 13:13.
4. See *Bereishis* 49:6 and 37:19, and *Rashi* to both.

284 / SEFER BAMIDBAR

them the firstborns, worshiped the golden calf, the tribe of Levi remained steadfastly true to Hashem and His Torah; they put their lives on the line in order to preserve the Jewish people. At that moment the tribe of Levi was considered reborn, and they were no longer the same Levi who had sold his brother to Egypt. That is why it is not undeserving that they merit the money garnered from the *pidyon haben*.

The *Meshech Chochmah* himself writes that the mitzvah of *pidyon haben* was already in force during the first year following *Yetzias Mitzrayim*, even though Aharon and his sons were not yet chosen to be Kohanim. It is unclear as to whom the *pidyon haben* money was given during this time. Perhaps the money remained holy or was used to purchase animals to be brought as offerings. If so, the mitzvah of *pidyon haben* is independent of giving money to the Kohen. Only after the Kohanim were chosen did Hashem designate that they should receive the money as one of the Kohen's 24 gifts.[5]

The original question can be answered that *pidyon haben* is not given to the descendants of Levi, but to Hashem. Hashem chose to give it to the Kohanim for their faithfulness to Him, similar to *gezel ha'ger*[6] that is given to the Kohanim as an atonement.

---

5. Hashem rewarded the Kohanim with 24 gifts. See *Bamidbar* Ch. 18.
6. One of the 24 gifts awarded to the Kohanim is *gezel ha'ger*: If someone steals from a convert who subsequently died leaving no heirs, the stolen item or its value is to be "returned" to the Kohen.

Tzedakah, Tzedakah

וְלָקַחְתָּ חֲמֵשֶׁת חֲמֵשֶׁת שְׁקָלִים
And you shall take five shekels each
(3:47)

Rabbi David Friedman of Karlin was one of the greatest *talmidei chachamim* in Lithuania. He was already at a very advanced age, yet he continued to learn with incredible diligence. When a collector from Novaradok came to visit the Rav, he did not have the audacity to interrupt the Rav, so he waited in the corner of the room. He stood for a while, until finally the Rav lifted his gaze from the *sefer* he was studying and noticed that he had a visitor. The Rav asked the man who he was and why he had come. The collector stated his purpose, and received a few coins as a donation. The Rav went back to his learning.

The collector was transfixed by the scene of the great Rav who learned with such obvious pleasure, and he continued to watch the Rav. A few minutes later, the Rav noticed him and again asked who he was and why he had come. The collector identified himself again as the collector from Novaradok, and again the Rav gave him a donation! The collector did not know what to do. A few minutes later the scene repeated itself. The collector understood that something was wrong, and told the Rav that he had already given him twice. The collector was merely lingering to watch the Rav learn.

Rav David Karliner began to cry. He apologized for having forgotten that the collector had already identified himself, and that he had forgotten having given him the money. The Rav admitted that he suffered from

286 / SEFER BAMIDBAR

forgetfulness. However, he thanked Hashem that he had not forgotten anything that he had learned even half a century ago. Torah, he could not forget!

What would the halachah be if someone was given *tzedakah* twice because the donor forgot that he had already given? Is the collector allowed to keep the money, or does he have to inform his benefactor that he has already given him?

A Rav Chaim Kanievsky quoted the *Yerushalmi* in *Pe'ah*,[7] that if a poor man left the city and subsequently returned to collect a second time, whoever gives him has given — i.e., he is considered as having given *tzedakah* — but the one who takes is accountable for his actions. The *Yerushalmi* is telling us that the poor man has acted improperly by returning a second time, but that the donation is his nevertheless.

It would seem that the *Yerushalmi* is discussing a case where the poor man had the ability to collect elsewhere to satisfy his needs. If, however, he is desperate to collect specifically in this place, it would be correct to donate to him again.

In a case where the donor suffers from short-term memory loss, it is incorrect to solicit him again, and the poor man is accountable for his actions. If, however, the donation is very small, it might be presumed that the donor is not particular about having given twice.

---

7. 8:5.

פרשת נשא
Parashas Nasso

Shamefully Yours

וְהִתְוַדּוּ אֶת חַטָּאתָם
And they shall confess their sin
(5:7)

Q During *Aseres Yemei Teshuvah*, Binyamin sat down to make an honest accounting of his deeds in preparation for Yom Kippur. He remembered that he had once disgracefully made a disrespectful comment about one of the Rabbanim in the community, but he was now too embarrassed to ask forgiveness in person. Instead, he wrote an almost-anonymous letter explaining that he had slighted the Rav's honor and now he was asking for forgiveness. Binyamin signed the letter "Binyamin ben Leah" and dropped it into the Rav's mailbox. Is that method sufficient to ask forgiveness, or does Binyamin have to overcome his shame and appear before the Rav in person?

The *Yerushalmi*[8] quotes Shmuel who said that one who sinned against his friend has to admit his guilt to him. The *Ein Yaakov* comments that according to this, the common custom of sending a messenger to appease someone who was insulted before the one who insulted him asks for forgiveness is incorrect. The one who insulted him should come personally and ask for forgiveness.

The *Derech HaMelech*[9] attempts to show a precedent for this common custom from the fact that Yosef's brothers sent messengers to him saying that their father had commanded him to forgive them, and only later did the brothers approach Yosef directly. The *Derech HaMelech* then retracts, as the messengers who were sent were the sons of Bilhah and Zilpah, who also had to beg Yosef's forgiveness. This would not prove that one could send an intermediary who does not need to ask forgiveness himself.

The *Yafeh Mareh* writes that there is no necessity for someone to personally ask *mechilah*. If the insulted party would forgive the insulter without being petitioned, that would also be sufficient. As long as he forgives, it is not necessary for the guilty party to shame himself by asking for *mechilah* in person.

Rav Chaim Palagi[10] cites support for the *Yafeh Mareh's* point from the fact that Aharon HaKohen used to make peace between Jews by visiting each one separately and acting as if he had been sent by the other one. He would tell each one how contrite the other one was, until they agreed to forgive each other. Obviously, the petitioning in person is not a prerequisite.

These two proofs, from Yosef's brothers and from Aharon HaKohen, need examination. We do not really find that Yosef's brothers asked to be forgiven; rather, they were afraid that Yosef would try to take revenge. Yosef never said that he forgave them, and yet the brothers were satisfied with his promise that they had nothing to fear. That is because they never asked to be forgiven.

---

8. *Yoma* 8:9.
9. *Hilchos Teshuvah* 2:9.
10. *L'Chaim B'Yerushalayim* on the *Yerushalmi* in *Yoma*.

Likewise, we do not find that Aharon HaKohen asked each Jew for forgiveness. He merely sought to assuage their hurt feelings so that they could come to forgive each other.

The *Mateh Moshe*,[11] the *Shiyarei Knesses HaGedolah*,[12] the *Bach*, and the *Elya Rabbah* all quote the *Ein Yaakov* as halachah. The *Pri Chadash* agrees with the *Yafeh Mareh*. The *Mateh Ephraim*[13] adds that in case of difficulty, or if the petition for *mechilah* will be more effective if delivered by a messenger, one would be allowed to resort to this method. This is the ruling of the *Mishnah Berurah*[14] as well.

The *Pele Yo'etz*[15] suggests that one could even write a letter, as writing is a good solution for all embarrassing situations.

However, this entire discussion is relevant to a person who sends an agent on his behalf. An anonymous letter, however, would not suffice. If someone spoke disparagingly against someone, and does not invest anything more than a postage stamp, he has not shown any remorse. The Rav who receives such a letter would feel uncomfortable forgiving an unknown individual for some undisclosed insult to his honor. Could that possibly be considered having appeased someone who was wronged? If anything, Binyamin has just added more insult than before.

If Binyamin knows that the Rav will certainly forgive him with all of his heart, a letter may suffice. If the Rav is not necessarily expected to simply forgive his anonymous offender, then Binyamin would have to disclose his identity in order to truly ask for forgiveness. וצ"ע.

---

11. 848.
12. 606 §4.
13. 606:1.
14. 606 §2.
15. "*Teshuvah.*"

Call for Peace

וּמָחָה אֶל מֵי הַמָּרִים
And erase it into the bitter waters
(5:23)

Q Tragically, Avi and Rochel had been married for just 10 months, and Rochel wanted out of the marriage — and fast. Avi admitted that he had acted extremely improperly, but he desperately wanted a second chance. He begged Rochel to go with him for marriage counseling to help him change his ways, but Rochel, backed by her father, was adamant in her decision.

One of Avi's neighbors knows that Avi is really a good person and is just confused about how one is meant to treat his wife. With some good counseling, Avi could be a wonderful husband and father. Avi's neighbor tried to convince Rachel's father that Avi could change. In the course of the conversation, he mentioned that the previous tenants of the couple's apartment had also divorced, and perhaps if the couple moved to a different apartment their fortune would change, as well, as *Chazal* teach, מְשַׁנֶּה מָקוֹם מְשַׁנֶּה מַזָּל.[16] The father-in-law was not moved. The neighbor tried a different tactic. He suggested that perhaps the couple's *mezuzos* were defective and were a factor in causing the friction between the couple. Upon hearing this, Rochel's father agreed to have the *mezuzos* checked.

The *mezuzos* were found to be exceptionally *kosher*. The neighbor wants to know if he would be allowed to erase a letter from the word בֵּיתֶךָ, *your home*, in order to

---

16. Based on *Rosh Hashanah* 16b, that changing one's location can tear up a Heavenly decree.

"prove" to Rochel's father that with a new *mezuzah* there was still hope to save the marriage. Would one be allowed to erase a letter from a *mezuzah* under extenuating circumstances, in order to restore marital harmony between husband and wife? In this case, it is not even Hashem's Name being erased. Would Avi's neighbor be allowed to employ this tactic?

A The *Mishnah Berurah*[17] cites the *Rambam*[18] that one who defaces any *kisvei kodesh*[19] has violated the command of לֹא תַעֲשׂוּן כֵּן לַה׳ אֱלֹקֵיכֶם — *You shall not do this to Hashem, your God.*[20] The *Acharonim* explain that this applies to *tefillin* and *mezuzos*, as well.

An apparent exception to this prohibition is found in the halachos of having a woman drink from the *sotah's* bitter waters. Hashem allows His Name to be erased together with other *pesukim* in order to test the *sotah's* loyalty to her husband and thereby, it is hoped, restore *shalom bayis*.[21]

Perhaps in this case there would be leniency to allow one to erase a letter from the *mezuzah*, based on the *Rema*.[22] The *Rema* explains that the Torah never permitted one to violate a prohibition, i.e., erasing Hashem's Name, for the sake of *shalom bayis*. Rather, since the prohibition against erasing Hashem's Name applies only when the erasure is by nature a destructive act, when one does so as a constructive act, in order to restore *shalom bayis*, it could be permitted,[23] as in the case of the *sotah*. Other prohibitions do not necessarily have the same leniency.

---

17. 154 §24.
18. *Sefer HaMitzvos, Lo sa'aseh* 65.
19. Literally, *holy writings* that contain either the Name of Hashem or *divrei Torah*, which may not be erased. .
20. *Devarim* 12:4.
21. *Nedarim* 66b.
22. Responsa 100 §10.
23. A Rav should be consulted in any case regarding the care to be taken with Hashem's Name.

Accordingly, it would seem that since the neighbor wishes to erase a letter from the *mezuzah* for a constructive purpose, perhaps this act could be sanctioned.

However, since it is not unequivocally clear that the erasure is actually warranted, he cannot simply decide to erase a part of the *mezuzah* based on his thinking that he is accomplishing something constructive. The Torah only permitted erasing Hashem's Name in the case of a *sotah,* where the Torah declares that the couple's *shalom bayis* will be restored if she is found to be innocent. In our case, the erasure will not actually ensure *shalom bayis,* but it will only extend the opportunity to possibly save the marriage. One cannot permit erasing a *mezuzah* in such a case.

Rather, the neighbor should ask the *sofer* to give him an invalid *mezuzah* and then tell Rochel's father that the *mezuzah* on the couple's bedroom door had been found to be *pasul*. In such a case, one could alter the truth in order to promote peace.[24]

The Zechus to Give

עֲגָלָה עַל שְׁנֵי הַנְּשִׂאִים
A wagon for each two leaders
(7:3)

Q Eli Goodman was the *rosh kollel* in the newly opened Riverstone Kollel. The *beis midrash* was mostly furnished, but the *kollel* still needed 10 tables. Eli set out for the local shul and made an appeal between Minchah and Maariv. He passionately described with great eloquence

---

24. *Yevamos* 65b.

the sanctity of a table that serves *talmidei chachamim* in their learning. He promised that anyone who merited to donate a table to the *kollel* would have earned himself a very precious mitzvah. He concluded that he was looking for 10 people who were each willing to donate a table at the cost of $200 each.

Eli figured that if he received pledges for five or six tables, he would consider himself fortunate. He proposed that anyone who wished to donate a table should raise his hand as a sign of commitment. He was amazed when he saw 20 men eagerly raise their hands to take advantage of this golden opportunity.

After a minute, an argument erupted. Some men said that Eli should make a lottery to see who would have the *zechus* to donate a table. Others claimed that it would not be fair to exclude anyone from sharing in the mitzvah. They suggested that each person should donate half the cost of a table. Which solution should they choose?

A The *pasuk*[25] tells us that on the day that the *Mishkan* was erected the *nesi'im* brought a gift of six wagons. The *Sforno* wonders why each *nasi* didn't bring an entire wagon on his own. He answers that they wanted to attest to their friendship by offering a present together, each *nasi* with a partner. In the merit of their unity, they would be worthy of having Hashem's Presence rest upon the *Mishkan*.

Since we find a precedent for sharing one's donation with a partner, perhaps that would be the appropriate practice in this case, as well. However, there seem to be two reasons that the concept mentioned in the *Sforno* should not be applied to Eli's case. In the case of the *nesi'im*, each *nasi* was the prince of his tribe. Each one's donation was representative of the unity of the entire nation.

---

25. *Bamidbar* 4:3.

That itself would bring to fruition the goal of the *Mishkan*, that Hashem's Presence would rest among *Bnei Yisrael*. This would not be the case if each pair merely donated their own table to the *kollel*.

In addition, each *nasi* had planned to offer a wagon with a partner. In our case, each donor intended to donate an entire table, as Eli had requested. As each man raised his hand, he never intended to share the *zechus* with someone else.[26]

It would seem that the first 10 men to raise their hands had already claimed their opportunity to donate, but nobody knows who was first. Therefore, the suggestion to draw lots[27] seems to be the most practical, because in that way each winner will be able to donate according to his original undertaking.

---

26. See *Yoreh De'ah* 258:13 that one can obligate himself to give *tzedakah* by merely deciding in one's heart to do so.
27. See *Choshen Mishpat* 174 that cites the lottery system as a valid way of deciding how to divide property.

פרשת בהעלותך
Parashas Behaaloscha

A Really Nice Gift

כִּי נְתֻנִים נְתֻנִים הֵמָּה לִי
For presented, presented are they to Me
(8:16)

Q Yishai and Shoshi sat down during the week of their *sheva berachos* to open the piles and piles of envelopes that they received at their wedding. They opened one envelope and were shocked to find that it contained a check for $2,500. The check was signed by Shimon Fried, a friend of the *kallah's* family. Yishai asked his new wife why she thought he would write them such a nice check. She had no idea. She suggested that maybe he heard that she was marrying such a wonderful yeshivah *bachur*, so he decided to give generously. She could not think of any other explanation. Without giving it another thought they tossed it into the pile of checks headed for the bank.

A few weeks later, Yishai received a phone call from a man who introduced himself as Yankel Fried, the son of Shimon Fried, *z"l*. Yankel inquired as to which kind of business Yishai was in.

The *chassan* answered that he doesn't own a business; he learns in *kollel*.

Yankel explained that he was reviewing his father's last checkbook and he noticed that he had written them a check for $2,500. His father was very old, and he thought it possible that there was some mistake.

Yishai apologized and offered to return the entire amount of the gift if that was indeed what he was required to do, according to halachah.

Yishai and Yankel want to know if the money should be returned. Shimon Fried did not have any mental health issues, and Yankel has no proof to support his theory that the check was written in error. Nevertheless, it would appear that there may be a mistake due to Shimon's advanced age, as only a close relative would write such a generous check, even if he was very wealthy. Must the money be returned?

Had the check been written for $100,000, there would be no doubt that the check would have to be returned. Even if Mr. Fried was known to be mentally stable, writing such a check for a wedding present proves otherwise, as one of the signs of a person lacking mental acuity is that he recklessly disperses assets,[28] and Yankel could certainly ask for the money to be returned. On smaller sums, however, each case would have to be considered based on its specific circumstances.

In our case, although circumstantial evidence shows that one does not usually give such a large sum, we cannot decide money matters based on circumstantial evidence. The Gemara in *Bava Basra*,[29] quoted by the *Shulchan Aruch*,[30] states that even if we find

---

28. *Chagigah* 4a.
29. 193a.
30. *Choshen Mishpat* 408:2.

a camel in the throes of a fit, with a dead camel at its side, we cannot assume that the crazed camel killed it, until there are kosher witnesses. This is because of the rule that one who wishes to claim money from his friend bears the burden of proof.

Similarly, we have a rule that something that is in doubt cannot overturn something that is a surety. The Gemara in *Avodah Zarah*[31] brings the opinion of Rabbi Yochanan, that even a likelihood cannot overturn something that until now was known for sure. For example, an idol that broke by itself is still forbidden to be used. Since we know it was previously worshiped, and it is doubtful whether it was nullified, we cannot permit benefit from its remains. This is true even though it is more likely that an idol worshiper, who witnessed that the idol could not even protect itself from falling apart, probably nullified the idol in his heart. This probability cannot change its previous status that we know to have been true. Therefore, the *suspicion* that perhaps Mr. Fried made a mistake cannot undo the *fact* that he gave the check as a present.

Another point to consider is the Gemara in *Bava Metzia*[32] that states that when one gives his friend money, either as a payment or as a loan, and the recipient found that he received additional money that could not be attributed to a mistake, he may assume that the money was given intentionally, and he does not need to return it.

In our case as well, Yankel cannot take the money from the couple when he himself is in doubt and they have possession of the money. Rather, we will rely on the fact that it may very well have been a generous gift. Perhaps he intended to very substantially enhance Yishai's *kollel* stipend in honor of his wedding.

---

31. 41.
32. 63b.

A Recipe for Disaster

הַבָּשָׂר עוֹדֶנּוּ בֵּין שִׁנֵּיהֶם
The meat was still between their teeth
(11:33)

Q Yoni opened a day center geared to the elderly. He offered a full day of activities, including a communal lunch, for which he was interested in hiring a cook. One day, he spotted an advertisement from an agency that hired out foreign workers. The ad read: "Foreign workers, according to halachah." The receptionist at the agency explained that this meant that they were trained in the various halachic implications of their employment.

Yoni was excited. This was exactly what he was looking for. He asked if they had someone who could cook professionally. The receptionist put him through to Shimon, who promised Yoni that he did, indeed. Yoni asked if the cook was familiar with the laws applicable to a kosher kitchen. Shimon assured him that the cook was well versed in the various dietary laws involved in cooking. He insisted that the advertisement was quite accurate when it stated that their employees work according to halachah.

Yoni hired the worker, who proved to be a professional chef who produced delicious and nutritious meals for everyone in the center.[33] Yoni signed a one-year contract with him.

Two weeks later, Yoni decided to inspect the cook's activities in the kitchen. He found him preparing a

---

33. A Jew had turned on the stoves and ovens each morning to avoid the problem of *bishul akum*.

PARASHAS BEHA'ALOSCHA / 299

chicken dish. Suddenly, the chef unwrapped a stick of butter and threw it into the pot of chicken!

Yoni was shocked and sharply rebuked the chef. The chef was unperturbed. He smiled and confidently explained to Yoni that the butter greatly enhanced the flavor of this particular recipe. He assured Yoni that after he tasted it, he too would agree!

Yoni gasped, horrified. He reprimanded the chef, insisting that he must have been taught not to mix milk with chicken. The chef maintained that he was taught that it is forbidden to mix milk with chicken or meat. But butter is not milk!

Yoni realized that the chef had spoken in all innocence. He truly did know about the halachos of kashrus. He had merely made a mistake, concluding that the law did not apply to butter as well as to milk.

Yoni contacted Shimon to terminate the chef's employment. He also refused to pay for the first two weeks because he felt that he had not received that which he had been promised. How could Shimon advertise that his workers were capable of keeping the halachah, when the chef had proven that he did not know the very basics of the laws of milk and meat?! Not only had he *treifed* up the entire kitchen, but he had served forbidden food to the members of the entire center!

Shimon had a ready response. According to him, the chef had only erred in a single halachah. He really was familiar with the rest of the practical halachos. Although Shimon admitted that there had been a glitch in the system, he asserted that the responsibility for the tragedy fell squarely on Yoni's shoulders. How could Yoni have left a non-Jew alone in the kitchen for two weeks without any supervision? Did he think that the chef had *semichah*?! Had Yoni ensured that the chef was watched, he would have noticed the problem right away.

Shimon contended that Yoni should pay for the two weeks of services rendered, and that he should uphold the contract for the duration of the year.

Who is right?

A The chef did his job in good faith (no pun intended). He cooked well, and was careful not to use any nonkosher ingredients. He merely added butter to the chicken out of ignorance, causing the elderly people to violate an *issur d'Rabbanan*.[34] The *Shulchan Aruch*[35] rules that if someone sold a food that was prohibited *mi'd'Rabbanan*, and the customer accidentally ate it, the seller is not required to refund the customer's money. The *Nesivos* explains that if one mistakenly ate a food that was prohibited only *mi'd'Rabbanan*, no *teshuvah* is required. The Rabbinical enactment was only to prohibit eating the food, and since he did not intentionally violate their decree, he does not require atonement. Hence, the food he ate was completely kosher, and the customer has to pay for his benefit.

Therefore, Yoni would have to pay the chef's salary and uphold his contract, since the chef did not cause anyone to sin, according to the reasoning of the *Nesivos*.

Although many *poskim*[36] argue with the *Nesivos*, in Yoni's case it is clear that he cannot claim that he hired the chef erroneously. The *Gemara* in *Bava Metzia*[37] asserts that if one seeks to impoverish himself, he should hire workers and leave them without supervision. Leaving a non-Jew alone in a kosher kitchen, however well versed he may be in the dietary laws, is a sure recipe for disaster. Yoni was negligent in leaving the chef to his own devices and relying on him to adhere to the many and varied requirements necessary to run a kosher kitchen.

---

34. See *Yoreh De'ah* 87. Fowl cooked with milk is prohibited only *mi'd'Rabbanan*, as opposed to meat cooked with milk, which is prohibited *mi'd'Oraisa*.
35. *Choshen Mishpat* 334.
36. Such as the *Mishpat Shalom, Ein Yitzchak, Asvan D'Oraisa*, and others.
37. 29b.

Some *Rabbanim* disagreed with Rav Zilberstein's conclusion and claimed that Yoni was misled. Yoni was very specific in his requirement that he wanted a cook who was capable of running a kosher kitchen. The chef the agency sent did not fit that bill. In addition, even if the senior citizens do not require atonement for what they ate, the chef was still not what Yoni was promised, as far as the parameters of *mekach ta'us*.

In summary, Rav Zilberstein maintains that Yoni has to pay Shimon as well as the chef, and continue the chef's employment. Some Rabbanim differed and justified Yoni's claim that he was misled, and thus he would be exempt from payment as well as from honoring the contract.

A Loan on Time

קֵל נָא רְפָא נָא לָהּ
Please, God, heal her now
(12:13)

Q Reb Shmuel was a very dedicated and accomplished *kollel* member, and a true *talmid chacham*. He was marrying off his fourth child and needed a loan to help him cover the wedding expenses. A friend mentioned to him the name of a wealthy businessman who frequently and magnanimously lent money to *talmidei chachamim*. Reb Shmuel made an appointment and asked the man if he would loan him money to cover the expenses of his daughter's upcoming wedding. The man, true to his reputation, replied without hesitation that he would be happy to lend Reb Shmuel $10,000. Reb Shmuel was elated. Suddenly, the man burst into tears, Reb Shmuel was confused. What had triggered such a reaction? When the man calmed down, he told Reb Shmuel that he had just received a phone call from his son's doctor. His son was, unfortunately, very sick. He implored Reb Shmuel to *daven* for his son's complete and speedy recovery. Reb Shmuel readily agreed to do so.

After Reb Shmuel left the man's home he began to think. Was it possible that praying for his lender's son would constitute *ribbis* (interest paid on a loan)? On the one hand, one is required to *daven* for any fellow Jew who has a problem, so why should the lender's son deserve less consideration than anyone else? On the other hand, Reb Shmuel has no connection to this man other then the fact that he benevolently loaned him money. He never would have even known about the son's illness had it not been for the loan, so he would never have known to *daven* for him. Would Reb Shmuel *davening* for the boy be a violation of the prohibition against *ribbis*?[38]

A One is obligated to *daven* for a sick person as soon as he becomes aware of the person's illness, regardless of whether or not he knew the person beforehand, or whether or not he was asked to *daven* for him. The *Sefer Chassidim*[39] writes that all Jews are responsible for one another, and therefore, if one person is in pain, everyone else is obligated to share that pain with him. David HaMelech exemplified this behavior, as he writes, וַאֲנִי בַּחֲלוֹתָם לְבוּשִׁי שָׂק — *But as for me, when they were ill, my clothing was sackcloth.*[40]

---

38. See *Yoreh De'ah* 160:11, that merely greeting someone whom one would not normally greet (had it not been for the loan) is considered *ribbis*.
39. 753.
40. *Tehillim* 35:13.

PARASHAS BEHA'ALOSCHA / 303

The *Mishneh Halachos*[41] adds that this is included in the prohibition of not standing by idly while your friend's blood is being shed. Imagine if Don would lend money to Jack, who is not (yet) religious, and Don took advantage of the opportunity to ask Jack to put on *tefillin*. Would anyone suggest that Don had violated the prohibition of *ribbis*? All he did was ask Jack to do something that he should have done anyway.

Similarly, Reb Shmuel is obligated to *daven* for his lender's son in any event, and there is no concern that there is an issue of *ribbis*.

---

41. Vol. XIII, 211.

פרשת שלח
Parashas Shelach

Stretching Time

יוֹם לַשָּׁנָה
A day for a year
(14:34)

Q On the night that had been designated as the end of daylight savings time, the clocks were moved back at 12 a.m. to 11 p.m. Boruch had hired a musician to play at his son's bar mitzvah that evening between the hours of 9 p.m. and 12 a.m. At midnight the music stopped and the musician prepared to pack up his instruments. Boruch made his way over to the musician's stand and informed him that since the clocks had now changed, it was now only 11 p.m., and his guests were not yet ready to go home. He assumed that the musician was going to play for another hour. The musician explained that he had only agreed to play until 12 a.m.; obviously this was according to the clock at the time he had begun. Just then the manager of the hall came over to Boruch, and told him that he was ready to lock up, as the rental was only until 12 a.m.

Boruch's guests were still going strong. Does Boruch have to pay for overtime?

A Rav Wosner[42] discusses a similar question regarding someone who vowed to learn each night until 12:30 a.m. How late would he have to learn on the night that the clocks were changed? Rav Wosner explained that this person's pledge could be interpreted in three possible ways:

1. Perhaps he intended to learn for a certain number of hours. For example, if he started to learn at 10:30 p.m., and vowed to learn until 12:30 a.m., he intended to accept upon himself to learn for two hours.
2. Perhaps he intended to learn until half an hour after midnight.
3. He may have required a certain amount of sleep each night, and therefore set his limit at 12:30 a.m. on the clock.

Rav Wosner concludes that the deciding factor is indeed the intent of the one who made the vow.[43] However, this is only applicable to a personal vow, as *nedarim* (vows) are always interpreted leniently. This would not necessarily shed light on this question, where two parties are involved in an issue of *Choshen Mishpat*.

It would seem that since neither Boruch nor the musician foresaw that the clocks would be changed that night (because if they had, they certainly would have clarified their intent in advance), their agreement was most likely for the musician to be hired to play three hours of music, according to the prevailing time. In addition, the fee that they settled on is indicative that he was only hired for three hours, and if Boruch wants the musician to work longer, the burden of proof that they agreed upon an extra hour lies on Boruch.

As far as the *simchah* hall, the assumption is that the hall was rented for the evening, for as long as people wish to stay, unless a

---
42. *Shevet HaLevi*, Vol. 3, 138.
43. See *Yoreh De'ah* 218.

number of hours is specified in the contract. If people are staying out later because the clocks were changed, then Boruch would be allowed to use the hall until 12 a.m. standard time.

Hot Buns

לְהוֹצִיא דִבָּה
By spreading a report
(14:36)

Q The tantalizing aroma that wafted from the bakery was advertising hot and fresh-from-the-fryer doughnuts. Simcha, a young teen, loved the smell and taste of the doughnuts but had no money with which to purchase them. All he could do was stand next to the door and wistfully inhale their delectable smell.

Meir, the baker, noticed Simcha lingering by the door of the bakery, and judging from circumstantial evidence, Meir concluded that the coveted doughnuts were not within Simcha's budget. Meir motioned Simcha inside the bakery and told him gently that the bakery was closing at 10 o'clock, and if Simcha would come then, Meir would give him all the leftover doughnuts for free.

Simcha ran home as fast as his legs could carry him and gleefully told his brothers and sisters that they would each have their very own doughnut that night. At a quarter to 10, Simcha was already waiting outside the bakery, longing to pick up his treasure. At five

PARASHAS SHELACH / 307

minutes to 10, a man parked his car next to the bakery, and Simcha heard him telling his wife on his cellphone that he was going to bring home a dozen doughnuts for his family. Simcha's face fell, as he had already tallied that there were only 12 doughnuts left, and he had promised his siblings that he would bring them each a doughnut.

Sadly, Simcha's *yetzer hara* got the better of him, and he approached the man hesitantly to confide in him that if he was interested in buying doughnuts, the bakery down the block had doughnuts far superior to the ones in the bakery right here. The man thanked Simcha for the tip, and continued on down the block.

At 10 o'clock, Simcha gratefully collected the 12 doughnuts and joyfully distributed them at home. The deprived children thoroughly enjoyed the treasure. After the last crumbs were licked off the table, Simcha's conscience began to niggle at him. Perhaps he was guilty of stealing from the bakery. After all, he had repaid Meir's intended kindness by causing him a loss.

Does Simcha have to pay Meir for the doughnuts?

A Simcha is required to pay Meir for the 12 doughnuts, as Meir's gift was an absolute mistake. Had Meir only known that Simcha had convinced a potential customer to shop elsewhere in order to ensure that there would be leftover doughnuts, he never would have given Simcha a single crumb! Hence, Meir's promise to Simcha was null and void. Simcha and his siblings ate Meir's doughnuts, and now Simcha must pay for them.

One could argue that Simcha only prevented the man from buying the doughnuts, which is only a *grama* (damage that was merely caused, but not inflicted). Had Simcha subsequently not taken the doughnuts, he would not have had to pay for the fact that he caused Meir a loss, as *grama* is exempt *b'dinei adam*. By

10 o'clock, Meir had already given up on selling the doughnuts to anyone else, and therefore the doughnuts had no value to him. Perhaps that would be a reason enough to exempt Simcha from paying for them.

This scenario can be compared to the case of an armed robber who accosts a person. At that point, the victim relinquishes any hope of retaining ownership of his property, and if someone would take hold of the victim's property, it would not have to be returned. The exception to this halachah is the robber himself, who engendered the entire situation. He cannot claim that now that the victim relinquished his ownership he is allowed to take it from him, as the victim did so solely as a result of his hostile encounter with the hooligan.[44] The same is true in this case, as well. Meir despaired of selling the doughnuts, but only because Simcha prevented him from making the sale. Therefore, Simcha specifically would be singled out to have to pay for the doughnuts.

The *Chasam Sofer*[45] writes that if someone approaches a customer in a store and convinces him to make the purchase from him instead, it is tantamount to stealing.

The same should apply in this case, as well. Had Simcha not convinced the man to buy elsewhere, Meir would have sold out his doughnuts. Now Simcha has to pay for his misdeed. This is in addition to the fact that Simcha has to do *teshuvah* for speaking *lashon hara* about Meir's merchandise.

---

44. See *Nesivos HaMishpat* 361 §2.
45. Responsa *Choshen Mishpat* 79.

Knot So Simple

וְעָשׂוּ לָהֶם צִיצִת
And they shall make themselves tzitzis
(15:38)

Q Boruch sits next to Gidon in shul. One morning, Boruch noticed that one of the knots on Gidon's *tallis* had become loose. Not wanting to disturb the latter's *davening*, Boruch decided to tighten the knot himself. He uttered the words לְשֵׁם מִצְוַת צִיצִת, *for the sake of the mitzvah of tzitzis,* and pulled the strings taut. Boruch must have pulled with a little too much force, because one of the strings snapped off in his hand. Before Boruch had intervened, the *tallis* was completely *kosher lechatchilah*, but now the *tallis* was only kosher *bedi'eved* (de facto).[46] Does Boruch have to pay Gidon for having ripped his *tzitzis*? Boruch had only the best intentions. In addition, the *tallis* was still kosher. Even if Boruch has to pay, could he just pay for one string, even though one new string would look out of place when the other strings are darker from use?

A The *Nesivos HaMishpat*[47] writes that if one tried to benefit his friend and damaged him in the process, it would seem that he would have to pay for the damage. The *Mekor Chaim*[48] argues that since it is a mitzvah to help one's friend, one should be exempt from any damages, just as one who runs on

---

46. The *Mishnah Berurah* 12 §2 explains that if only one string tears, the *tallis* is still kosher. However, the strings cannot be transferred to a different *tallis* in their ripped state because *lechatchilah*, they must all be intact.
47. 291 §14.
48. (Sanalovitz) *Siman* 29.

Erev Shabbos is exempt from damages because he is running in the context of a mitzvah.[49]

However, the *Mekor Chaim* is not the accepted ruling in this case, as he himself mentions that *Tosafos*[50] does not agree with him, and the general rule is that a person is obligated to pay for damages he incurs under all circumstances.[51]

As far as the fact that the *tallis* is still kosher, perhaps one could compare this to the ruling of the *Maharim Mintz*.[52] The Gemara in *Bava Kamma*[53] states that if someone vowed to bring an offering on the *Mizbei'ach* and sanctified an ox for that purpose, and a thief subsequently stole the ox, the thief may replace the ox with a sheep if the ox is no longer available, as a sheep is also sufficient to satisfy the owner's vow. The *Maharam Mintz* deduces from this Gemara that if one stole a beautiful and expensive *esrog* and lost it, he can repay the value of a simple kosher *esrog*. The *Chacham Tzvi*[54] argues that the case of the ox and the case of the *esrog* are not similar. The owner of the ox could not have sold the ox once it was sanctified, as one is not allowed to sell a *korban*. Its sole use was to satisfy his vow, for which it is sufficient to offer a sheep. An *esrog*, in contrast, can be sold to someone else for its full market value. Therefore, one would have to pay the full value of the *esrog*.

Perhaps this case of the *tzitzis* would be dependent on this halachah, as well, as the *tzitzis* are still kosher, even if they are not in the preferred state to do the mitzvah.

As far as replacing just one of the strings, in *What If*, Vol. 1[55] there was a case of someone who borrowed a pair of earrings and lost one of them. The question was posed if it is sufficient to pay the value of one earring, or one would be required to pay the depreciation of the remaining earring as well. In this case Boruch

---

49. *Bava Kamma* 33a.
50. Ibid., 56a *d"h Kisuyei*.
51. Ibid., 26a.
52. 113.
53. 58a.
54. 120.
55. "Color Coordination," page 269.

was not considered a watchman, as the borrower of the earrings was, and therefore should not have to pay for the "depreciation" of the other strings solely because they do not match their new counterpart.

Perhaps Boruch would still be obligated to pay for the depreciation *b'dinei Shamayim*. However, it is probable that since there is no real loss other than the aesthetic value, even *Tosafos* would agree that since Boruch ripped them due to his good intentions, he should not have to pay, even *b'dinei Shamayim*.

In addition, the color of the strings is not really so significant, unless the old strings were really very dirty, in which case they certainly should have been changed in any event.

פרשת קרח
Parashas Korach

Space Management

וַיֵּעָלוּ מֵעַל מִשְׁכַּן קֹרַח
So they got themselves up from near the dwelling of Korach
(16:27)

Q Laizer and Mutty had been childhood friends as far back as they could remember. They continued on in the same yeshivah for high school and *beis midrash*. Eventually, they both left the *beis midrash* to join the workforce, but they were always careful to set aside as much time as they could for learning. They agreed to learn as *chavrusas* every night between the hours of 8 and 9, and were looking for an appropriate place to meet. A friend suggested a shul in the neighborhood that had an extensive *sefarim* library. Although the shul had many minyanim and *shiurim* throughout the week, the small library was available between 8 and 9. Laizer and Mutty found this arrangement amenable, and over time they completed quite a few *mesechtos*.

After a few years, a new development upset this convenient arrangement. Unfortunately, the 8:30

minyan for Maariv now had two *chiyuvim*[56] who wanted to *daven* for the *amud*, and they suggested forming two minyanim. One group would *daven* in the shul, while the other planned to *daven* in the small library. Laizer and Mutty asserted that they already had a claim to the library, as they had been learning there between 8 and 9 for years, and they felt that the minyan should go elsewhere. The problem was that unfortunately, there were no other rooms available in the vicinity. Who should have priority: the 10 men who want to *daven* there, or the *chavrusas* who learn there every night? In addition, if one of the adjacent rooms were to become available within a few minutes, could the *chavrusas* insist that the minyan wait so that their learning not be disturbed?

*A*It is logical that the minyan would take priority for two reasons: First, a *tzibbur* (congregation) has tremendous importance, as the Gemara reveals[57] that a *tzibbur* can annul Heavenly decrees even after the decrees have been signed and sealed. Second, the shul was built essentially as a *makom tefillah*, and not to function as a *beis midrash* for *chavrusas* to learn there.

One could argue that *tefillah* is only a mitzvah *d'Rabbanan*, and *davening* with a minyan is merely an enhanced *davening*, whereas learning Torah is a mitzvah *d'Oraisa*. Rav Moshe Feinstein[58] was asked if one should learn Torah late into the night if it will cause him to miss *davening* with a minyan the following morning. Rav Moshe derives from the halachah that states that one is required to travel four *mil* (72 minutes) along his way or one *mil* (18 minutes) out of his way to attend a minyan,[59] that *davening* with a minyan is

---

56. Men who have lost a parent within the year. It is a merit for the parent for the son to serve as *chazzan*.
57. *Rosh Hashanah* 17b.
58. *Igros Moshe, Orach Chaim* Vol. II, 27.
59. *Orach Chaim* 90:16.

an obligation. Therefore, attending minyan takes priority over the Torah study of individuals.

In this case, the *mispallelim* could *daven* with the other minyan. The only question is if the minyan will be split, and, if so, where the second minyan will *daven*. Perhaps someone should suggest to the *chiyuvim* that although being a *chazzan* is a merit for the *niftar*, the mitzvah of *chesed* in not disturbing the *chavrusas* is also very great. One *chiyuv* could wait for a different minyan, or he could *daven* with the first minyan and just say *Kaddish*. That might even serve to elevate the *neshamah* of the *niftar* even more than *davening* in a separate minyan and interrupting those who are learning.[60]

However, if the *chiyuv* refuses this suggestion, the *davening* of the *tzibbur* would take priority over the learning of the individuals. This would apply even if a different room would become available soon. In that case, Laizer and Mutty will have to search for a new location to continue their worthy partnership.

Pick It Up!

וַיִּקְחוּ אִישׁ מַטֵּהוּ
And they took, each man his staff
(17:24)

Q Ivdu is a wonderful organization that is dedicated to bringing Jewish children closer to their heritage. Among their varied activities they planned a Purim carnival, and they decided to borrow a cotton candy machine to enhance the atmosphere and attract a larger crowd.

---
60. See "*L'Ilui Nishmas*," p. 323.

An Ivdu representative contacted Shmuel Levy, who owned one such machine, and asked if they could use the machine on the Sunday before Purim. Shmuel was happy to lend his machine to such a worthy organization, free of charge, of course.

The carnival was a smashing success. Ivdu's carnival coordinator, Binyamin Stein, asked Shmuel to pick up his machine, which had been placed in their storage room. He mentioned that the storage room was in a state of disarray and was not a very safe place to store the machine. He urged Shmuel to collect his machine without delay. But Shmuel had other things on his mind, and even after Binyamin called him several times, he still didn't get around to picking up the cotton candy machine.

One week before Lag B'Omer, Shmuel suddenly realized that he needed his machine urgently for Lag B'Omer. He contacted Binyamin Stein, who promised to look for the machine. Days passed and Shmuel was concerned that Binyamin would not find it, so he purchased a new machine. The day before Lag B'Omer, Binyamin Stein called Shmuel to tell him that he had dug out his machine.

Shmuel has no use for two machines, and wants Ivdu to pay him the value of his old machine. After all, because they did not return it to him when he needed it, he had to purchase a new one. Ivdu claims that they did return the machine in time, and it was only Shmuel's procrastination that caused the machine to be lost, temporarily. Who is right?

Ivdu does not owe Shmuel anything, for two reasons:

1. The *Ketzos HaChoshen* and the *Nesivos HaMishpat*[61] both write that if the borrower informs the lender that he many come and collect his item, and the time of the loan

---

61. *Siman* 344, §2.

expires, the borrower has no obligation to watch the item for its owner. (The *Sma*, however, argues.) Therefore, it was not Ivdu's obligation to store and protect Shmuel's machine once they had asked him to come and pick it up.

2. Ivdu can present Shmuel with his machine at this point without any further obligation. Even one who had stolen *chametz* before Pesach and returns the stolen *chametz* after Pesach is absolved from paying.[62] This is true even if the *chametz* was not sold before Pesach, and is now forbidden to be used. Since the actual item was returned, its halachic status does not invalidate using it as a form of payment. The *Shach*[63] writes that the same is true regarding one who borrowed his friend's item. Furthermore, Ivdu is exempt even *b'dinei Shamayim*, as they were not negligent. This is especially true since Ivdu is not an individual, but a volunteer organization, and therefore they cannot be asked to pay even *b'dinei Shamayim*.

Getting Your Priorities Straight

אַךְ פָּדֹה תִפְדֶּה אֵת בְּכוֹר הָאָדָם
But you shall surely redeem the firstborn of man
(18:15)

Q | Meir is a young married man who learns in Yeshivas Ohr Hada'as in Yerushalayim. His parents live in America, and they repeatedly urged Meir and his wife to come

---

62. *Bava Kamma* 96b.
63. *Choshen Mishpat* 292 §9 and 363 §7.

to visit them for Succos. The couple agreed, and they purchased tickets well in advance.

On the 22nd day of Elul, Meir's wife gave birth to their firstborn son. According to the calculations of the calendar, the 31st day of the baby's life falls on Erev Shabbos, the 23rd day of Tishrei, which happens to be Simchas Torah in *chutz la'Aretz*.

Meir has a *she'eilah*. If he travels to America for Succos in order to fulfill the mitzvah of honoring his parents, the *pidyon haben* will have to wait until after Shabbos, which is the 25th of Tishrei, since he cannot do it on Yom Tov or on Shabbos.[64] If he remains in Eretz Yisrael, he would be able to make the *pidyon haben* on time, on Erev Shabbos, since he keeps only one day of Yom Tov. Which mitzvah takes precedence?

A The *sefer Tanya Rabasi*[65] writes that each day that a person allows to pass without redeeming his son, he is in violation of the positive commandment to redeem a firstborn. The *Magen Avraham*[66] writes that according to *Tosafos* in *Mo'ed Kattan*,[67] if he has not redeemed his son on time, he has violated the mitzvah once, but there is no additional violation as time passes.

On the other hand, the opinion of many *Rishonim* and *Acharonim* is that there is no prohibition to postpone a *pidyon haben* other than, "Once a mitzvah has come to your hand, do not allow it to linger."[68] Mitzvos are meant to be done with alacrity.

Accordingly, perhaps his travel is not justified, since, at the very least, it will cause him to delay the performance of this rare mitzvah.

---

64. See *Shulchan Aruch, Orach Chaim* 339:4. *Chazal* forbade making a *pidyon haben* on Shabbos because of its similarity to a business transaction.
65. 98.
66. 8b.
67. 568 §10.
68. *Mechilta*.

Responsa *Givas Shaul* writes explicitly that on Yom Tov one may not redeem his son, even on the second day of Yom Tov. Would the halachah be any different for a person who lives in *Eretz Yisrael* and is visiting *chutz la'Aretz*? Since no one else in *chutz la'Aretz* is allowed to redeem their child on the second day of Yom Tov, it would seem that he would also not be allowed to do so, just as he is prohibited from doing any other *melachah*, even if he is alone and no one will see him.[69]

Nevertheless, it would seem that Meir should visit his parents for Succos even though it will cause the *pidyon haben* to be postponed. Right now the mitzvah of *kibbud av v'eim* is in front of him, and therefore he should seize the opportunity to do the mitzvah that he can do now. If afterward he will be forbidden from making the *pidyon haben* "on time," that is not his fault. It is not his decision not to make the *pidyon haben* on the second day of Yom Tov or on Shabbos. He is merely following *Chazal's* directive.

---

69. *Mishnah Berurah* 496 §9.

פרשת חקת
Parashas Chukas

A Man's Real Station in Life

זֹאת הַתּוֹרָה אָדָם כִּי יָמוּת בְּאֹהֶל
This is the teaching regarding a man who would die in a tent
(19:14)

Part 1

Q Yehoshua commutes to work every day on a train from Be'er Sheva to Lod. He *davens* on the train each day with a minyan of men traveling the same route. On Mondays and Thursdays they *lein* from a *Sefer Torah* that is stored in a special *aron kodesh* on the train, and they even have a small *bimah*. Usually Yehoshua finishes *davening* before he has to disembark from the train. One Monday, however, he ran into a problem. The *leining* was *Parashas Netzavim*, which is especially long, and the train stopped in Lod during *shlishi*!

Yehoshua was in a quandary. The halachah clearly states[70] that one is not allowed to leave shul once the *Sefer Torah* has been opened for *Krias HaTorah*. One who disregards this halachah is considered to have abandoned Hashem, and it is written about him that he will perish![71] If Yehoshua remains on the train for the duration of the *aliyah*, he will miss his stop and would have to continue on to Tel Aviv, making him two hours late for work. What should he do?

A Responsa *Torah Lishmah*[72] records the following case: A man *davened* in a shul where it was customary for anyone who received an *aliyah* to make a generous donation to the shul. After each *aliyah*, the *gabbai* would make a loud *Mi shebeirach* and announce the person's pledge as a merit that the *Mi shebeirach* be accepted. This person was financially incapable of making any significant donation, yet, if he did not pledge to donate, he would be very embarrassed. To pledge, clearly intending not to fulfill the pledge, would be a terrible *aveirah*. Therefore, he does not want to accept any *aliyos*. The Gemara in *Berachos*[73] states that one who is called to the Torah and refuses is punished by having his life shortened. Does this man have to fear retribution for not accepting an *aliyah*?

The *Torah Lishmah* answers that the prohibition against rejecting an *aliyah* is only applicable when the motivation for the rejection is that the person lacks the proper regard toward the mitzvah. If the person's motivation stems from factors beyond his control, i.e., the shame that it will cause him, he has nothing to fear and he may choose not to accept the *aliyah*. (The *Torah Lishmah* adds that stinginess or the fact that he is at odds with the *gabbai* or the *chazzan* would certainly not be a valid reason not

---

70. *Shulchan Aruch, Orach Chaim* 146:1, *Mishnah Berurah* ad loc.
71. *Yeshayah* 1:28.
72. 428.
73. 55a.

to accept an *aliyah*, and would therefore not exempt him from being punished.)

Perhaps this case is similar; since Yehoshua means no disrespect toward the Torah and he must disembark solely to save himself from missing his station, he should not have to worry that he has violated this halachah.

However, the *Aruch HaShulchan*[74] very clearly states the contrary. One who is capable of exerting himself to stay may not leave during *leining*, even in cases of great need or distress. One should not leave even if he has to use the washroom, as *leining* has the same parameters as *Shemoneh Esrei*. The honor of the Torah is like the honor of the *Shechinah* (Divine Presence), and one must wait until after the *aliyah* (if at all possible).

According to the *Aruch HaShulchan*, it seems that one would not be allowed to leave shul during the *aliyah*, even if he was compelled to do so for reasons beyond his control, and Yehoshua would have to stay on the train.

Nevertheless, it appears that Yehoshua may disembark in Lod, and he will not be guilty of having abandoned the Torah. As Yehoshua alights from the train, he should continue listening from the platform. As the train closes its doors and begins to travel, Yehoshua will not be leaving the *Sefer Torah*; rather, the Torah will be leaving him. That is not the *aveirah* described. Yehoshua does not have to run after the train.

Rav Zilberstein asked Rav Nissim Karelitz if perhaps it would have been better to avoid the entire situation by changing train compartments before the *leining* began. Although Yehoshua would miss hearing even as much as he could, at least he would not have to leave during *Krias HaTorah*. Rav Nissim answered that he should definitely not leave before the *leining* begins.

---

74. 146:1.

Part 2

Q Mendy was *davening* fervently in the airport's designated shul, oblivious to the passage of time. Somehow he made a serious miscalculation, and during the *leining* he was surprised to hear an announcement for the final boarding call for his international flight. Would Mendy be allowed to leave during the *aliyah* to avoid missing his flight and losing the money that he spent on his ticket?

A Since this is a question that involves a serious financial loss, Mendy would be advised to continue to *lein* from his *siddur* as he runs toward the gate. Even though that cannot count for *Krias HaTorah*, it still serves to minimize his abandoning the *leining*, as he is showing that he really wishes to continue to listen to the words of the Torah. This is similar to someone who does not have a *Sefer Torah* who is instructed to *lein* from a *Chumash*, without making a *berachah*. This will serve as a reminder of the obligation of *Krias HaTorah*.[75]

L'ilui Nishmas

וְהִלְבַּשְׁתָּם אֶת אֶלְעָזָר בְּנוֹ
And dress Elazar his son in them
(20:26)

Q Zelig had been the *chazzan* for his minyan almost every day since his mother was *niftar* four months earlier. The only time he was not the *chazzan* was when someone

---

75. *Mishnah Berurah* 143 §9.

else in the minyan had a *yahrzeit*. Since the halachah states that one who is observing a *yahrzeit* has priority over a mourner to be the *chazzan*, on those days Zelig would *daven* in a different minyan so he could lead the *davening* for the *tzibbur*, thus bringing merit to his mother's *neshamah*.

One day, Zelig was about to begin serving as the *chazzan* when he was approached by someone else who occasionally *davened* in that minyan. The *tzibbur* had just completed *Pesukei D'Zimrah* and was about to start *Yishtabach*, and this man chose that moment to inform Zelig that he had a *yahrzeit* that day. He expressed his desire to be the *chazzan*.

Does Zelig have to step aside to allow the other man to *daven*? Perhaps Zelig can claim that had the man informed him before *davening*, Zelig could have found a different minyan, as he was wont to do when there was a *yahrzeit*. Now that he was already *davening*, it was too late to start looking for a different minyan. Perhaps the man observing *yahrzeit* should look for another place to *daven*?

A practical solution might be to institute a rule that anyone who has a *yarhrzeit* must notify the steady *chazzan* the day before, in order to reserve the right to be the *chazzan*. If he did not give notice, he cannot expect to be the *chazzan*. Barring that, what should be done at this point?

A It is certainly commendable that Zelig wants to be the *chazzan* to bring merit to his mother's *neshamah*, but in truth, he has no obligation to do so when someone else has priority. Granted, the person who has *yahrzeit* did not act properly. He should not have appeared at the last moment to ask to be the *chazzan*. Nevertheless, since the halachah states that someone who has *yahrzeit* has priority to *daven* for the *tzibbur*, and had he come on time he would have been allowed to do so, he does not forfeit his rights just because he came late. The fact that Zelig wants to be the *chazzan* beyond his requirement to do so should not cause the man with the *yahrzeit* to lose out. In addition, why should the father of the man who has *yahrzeit* have to lose his chance to have his son *daven* and increase his merits?

It should be noted that surrendering the job of *chazzan* to the other man would also be considered an act that brings merit to the *niftar*, perhaps even more so than being the *chazzan*! The Chofetz Chaim[76] writes that any mitzvah that a son does brings merit to the *neshamah* of the *niftar*. This mitzvah of allowing the other man to be the *chazzan* is certainly advantageous to the *niftar*, as it will cause Hashem to act with *chesed* and *rachamim* toward him. The *neshamah* will be looked upon favorably as one who raised a child to perform acts of kindness. This will awaken the Attribute of Mercy and be a source of merit for both of them.

As far as instituting such a rule for the future, only the Rav of the shul can enact such a rule. The Rav will decide if such a *takanah* is truly for the benefit of his congregation.

The *sefer Ana Avda*[77] records the following story:

The great *tzaddik*, Rabbi Tzvi Kovalsky, was an *avel* within the year of the *petirah* of his great father, Rabbi Binyamin Kovalsky. As is customary, Rav Tzvi was very particular to be the *chazzan* each day in order to continue to honor his father even after his *petirah*.

Rav Tzvi arrived at his shul on Rabbi Akiva Street in Bnei Brak and waited for an opportunity to be the *chazzan*. The minyanim there follow one after another, and one who wishes to lead the *davening* in the following minyan waits next to the *chazzan* of the

---

76. *Ahavas Chesed,* Part 2, Ch. 15 footnote.
77. The biography of HaRav Kovalsky.

previous minyan until they finish *davening*. As Rav Tzvi waited patiently next to the *chazzan*, he watched as an elderly gentleman lovingly closed his *siddur* and slowly wrapped up his *tefillin* and folded his *tallis*. The man was obviously weak, and he was scanning the crowd, hoping to find someone to escort him home. The man looked up and held out his hand to several people who had finished *davening*, but unfortunately, they were in too much of a hurry to take the man home.

Rav Tzvi, witnessing the scene, could not ignore the man's obvious and desperate need. As careful as he was to be the *chazzan* each day, he stepped toward the old man and offered him his arm, knowing full well that he would lose his turn.

The man grasped Rav Tzvi's outstretched arm, and the two left the shul to make the arduous trek to the man's home. Although it was only two blocks away, it took a long time, as the man walked heel to toe all the way. Rav Tzvi murmured, "This should be a merit for my father's *neshamah*!"

At last they reached the man's building, and the man thanked Rav Tzvi with great emotion, but Rav Tzvi was not yet finished. He continued to help the man up the steps to his apartment, step by step, until they finally arrived at his door. Only then did Rav Tzvi return to the shul in time to catch the last minyan, which already had a *chazzan*. That was the only time that Rav Tzvi missed out on *davening* for the *amud*.

That night, Rav Tzvi's saintly father appeared to him in a dream and told him emphatically, "I surrender and forgo all of your *davening* in front of the *amud*, if only you will continue to do such mitzvos instead!"

Zealousness

עֲשֵׂה לְךָ שָׂרָף
Make for yourself a fiery [serpent]
(21:8)

Q There was a shul (believe it or not!) where cell phones would ring during *davening*. It seems that many men who *davened* there suffered a mental block against shutting their phones before entering the miniature *Beis HaMikdash*.[78] This resulted in people having difficulty concentrating on their *davening*, which is why they came to shul in the first place.

Reuvy was a member of the shul who took the matter very seriously. He decided that he had to put an end to the noise pollution in shul. He installed a device that blocked cell phone reception in the shul!

Benny had a little extra time one morning and he decide to stay in shul after *davening* to learn that day's *daf yomi*. Before entering the shul he switched his cell phone to "vibrate," in case he received an important phone call. After half an hour, he stepped outside and checked his phone, only to discover that he had 10 missed phone calls from his stockbroker. Benny listened to the last message that the broker left him. The broker said that he had been trying desperately to contact Benny, as one of his stocks had begun to plummet, and he needed immediate instructions on how to proceed. Unfortunately, by now it was already too late.

It did not take long to realize that, strangely, there was no reception in the shul, and Reuvy's phone-blocker

---
78. *Megillah* 29a.

was discovered. Benny had lost a great deal of money due to Reuvy's phone-blocker, and he demanded that Reuvy reimburse him for his losses. Reuvy is convinced that he acted properly in his efforts to maintain the dignity of the shul. Benny claims that since he had already *davened*, he was justified in setting his phone to "vibrate," and his losses are completely Reuvy's fault. Who is right?

A First of all, it was wrong for Reuvy to have installed such a device in the shul on his own volition. He should have consulted the shul's Rav first, as the Rav is the only one who has the authority to sanction installing this type of system in the shul.[79] By acting on his own, without permission from the Rav (or from the *gabbai*, if there is no Rav), and not even informing the congregants about the fact that the shul's reception was blocked, Reuvy acted improperly. He should have taken into account that someone might have to receive an important phone call, either before or after *davening*, while his phone was switched to "vibrate," and in that case he would take the call outside the shul.

Moreover, perhaps a doctor or a Hatzolah member would arrive for *davening*, and would have to take an urgent call. Perhaps a wife who is due to give birth would have to reach her husband urgently.

Since Reuvy was negligent, it would seem that he has to compensate Benny for his losses, but only *b'dinei Shamayim*, as his part in the loss was only indirect.[80] Although the *Meiri*[81] writes that one is only obligated to pay for *grama* if he intended to do damage, in this case, Reuvy is considered one who intended to do damage! Blocking people's phone calls is something that is likely to damage them, as it did in our case. Even though Reuvy's intent was to protect the honor of the shul, this does not grant him an exemption, as he should have recognized the possibility of someone having to receive an important call.

---

79. See *Choshen Mishpat* 2:1.
80. See *Bava Kamma* 60a, that *grama* is exempt *b'dinei adam*.
81. Ibid., 56a.

In summary, Reuvy should have consulted the Rav for permission to install a reception blocking device, and should have put up a sign to let people know that such a device was in use. Since he did not do so, he must compensate Benny (*b'dinei Shamayim*) for the losses that he caused him.

פרשת בלק
Parashas Balak

To Return or Not to Return

כִּי הִכִּיתָנִי
That you struck me
(22:28)

Q The Goldenbergs purchased a rabbit as a pet, but they tended to mistreat the poor thing. Their neighbor, Mr. Fishman, who was a God-fearing Jew, tried to warn them about the prohibition against cruelty to animals, but his words fell on deaf ears, and they continued to cause pain to the rabbit. One day, the neighbor saw the rabbit leave the owner's yard and enter the nearby public park. Does he have a mitzvah to return the lost item to its owner, or could he could look the other way and thereby spare the rabbit from returning to its cruel owners?

[Under normal circumstances one may not ignore his friend's lost item because of the Torah's prohibition against doing so.[82]]

---
82. *Devarim* 22:1.

The *Shulchan Aruch*[83] writes that one may not raise goats or sheep in *Eretz Yisrael*, as the animals have a tendency to stray into other people's fields and damage crops. Nevertheless, the *Meshech Chochmah*[84] writes that if one found a sheep or goat, he has a mitzvah to return it to its owners. This is regardless of the fact that its owner is prohibited from owning such an animal! The mitzvah of *hashavas aveidah* still applies even if one ignored this halachah.

Accordingly, it would seem that in our case as well, the neighbor should return the rabbit.

However, this would not be the proper course of action in practice, for two reasons:

1. In the case of the *Meshech Chochmah*, the only one who is in violation of owning the animal is the owner himself. The one who found the sheep has the obligation to perform the mitzvah of *hashavas aveidah*. He has no connection to the sin of its owner. In our case, however, even Mr. Fishman has a mitzvah to save the animal from suffering. That mitzvah is not restricted to the owner of the animal. Anyone who sees someone's animal struggling under its load is also required to help its owner unload it. If so, the neighbor cannot return the animal to a place where it will suffer.

2. The *Meshech Chochmah's* words need elucidation. How could one return a lost item that will cause harm to the public? Would there be a mitzvah to return substances that its owner will use to harm his neighbors? Perhaps the *Meshech Chochmah* means that he should return the sheep on condition that it is slaughtered promptly, but not return it in a way that will cause the owner to continue to sin.

In our case, where Mr. Fishman cannot ensure that the rabbit will be treated kindly, he surely cannot return it.

---

83. *Choshen Mishpat* 409:1. This prohibition is no longer applicable.
84. *Devarim* 22:3.

It's Worth the Pain

מֶה עָשִׂיתִי לְךָ כִּי הִכִּיתָנִי

What have I done to you that you struck me

(22:28)

Q Nachshon watched as his wicked neighbor, Menashe, harnessed his horse and mule to his plow, and was about to commit the *aveirah* of plowing with two species together. Nachshon knows that his words will not prevent Menashe from sinning. The only way to stop him would be to wound one of the animals. Is Nachshon allowed to cause pain to the innocent animal in order to prevent an *aveirah*? Perhaps Menashe should be left to do what he wants (and earn a greater portion in *Gehinnom* in the process) rather than cause pain to the animal.

A The *Sefer HaChinuch*[85] explains that the reason for the mitzvah of not plowing with two species is because it is painful for animals to have to work with animals that are not of their own kind. Accordingly, one could argue that it does not make sense to cause pain to an animal in order to prevent an *aveirah* that causes pain to the animal.

Actually, we are not allowed to decide whether a mitzvah is relevant based on our understanding of the rationale behind the mitzvah. We are commanded to keep the mitzvos regardless of their reasons. Since a man is allowed to cause pain to animals for a constructive purpose, then certainly preventing an *aveirah* would justify injuring the animal.

The *Shach*[86] quotes an opinion that one has no obligation to prevent a *mumar*, a disbeliever, from committing an *aveirah*. Even

---
85. *Parashas Ki Seitzei.*
86. *Yoreh De'ah* 151 §6.

if Menashe is such a person, Nachshon may nevertheless harm the animal despite the *Shach's* opinion, and he does not have to worry about the prohibition against causing pain to the animals. The angel slew Bilam's donkey in order to save Bilam from shame,[87] even though Bilam was a *rasha* and his donkey was not at fault. That being the case, certainly one could injure an animal in order to save its owner from sin.

Even though Nachshon will be damaging Menashe's property, he is allowed to do so, as the *Rambam*[88] writes that it is proper to break a sinner's tools to stop him from sinning.

A person is obligated to forfeit all of his possessions in order not to violate a mitzvah, and if so, Menashe is certainly obligated to forfeit his animal's value if that will save him from sin.

A Good Investment

כִּי הִכִּיתַנִי זֶה שָׁלֹשׁ רְגָלִים
That you struck me these three times
(22:28)

Q Chezky was involved in a major car accident, but miraculously walked away without a scratch. As a token of gratitude, he put aside $30,000 to be used for *tzedakah*. Two petitions came before him and he has only enough money to help one of them. One is from a poor *kallah* who needs money for her wedding. The other is from a family who lives comfortably in France, but wants to

---

87. *Rashi, Bamidbar* 22:33.
88. *Peirush HaMishnah, Shevi'is* 5:6.

visit *Eretz Yisrael* in order to come closer to *Yiddishkeit*. They may decide to move there permanently, but in order to do so, they need a sponsor. To whom should Chezky allocate the funds?

A Bilam's donkey questioned him as to why he had struck him "three times." *Rashi* elaborates on the *pasuk* and explains that the donkey was hinting to Bilam that he would be unsuccessful in uprooting a nation that celebrates three times a year (Pesach, Shavuos, and Succos).

Rav Aharon Leib Shteinman asked why the donkey would choose the mitzvah of traveling to Yerushalayim for Yom Tov, rather than any other mitzvah, to extol the virtues of *Klal Yisrael*. Rav Shteinman noted that it is a very great *zechus* when people abandon their homes and businesses and place their faith in Hashem to protect their property as they travel to the *Beis HaMikdash*, where they can achieve great spiritual heights.[89]

Accordingly, Chesky should evaluate if his donation will make the crucial difference between whether or not the family from France will come to *Eretz Yisrael*. If his sponsorship will help them advance in their commitment to Torah and mitzvos, their needs would take priority. The *kallah* will marry in any event. Chezky's donation is not critical, as many people will be willing to donate to help a poor *kallah*. This would not be true for the family who wants to come to *Eretz Yisrael*. No one can estimate the far-reaching benefits of bringing this family closer to Hashem and His Torah.

---

89. See *Tosafos, Bava Basra* 21a.

פרשת פינחס
Parashas Pinchas

The Gift That Keeps on Giving

הִנְנִי נֹתֵן לוֹ
Behold! I give him
(25:12)

Chatzkel was a very wealthy man in many areas, including his financial portfolio. He was blessed with 10 wonderful children, and at last count, over 70 devoted grandchildren. Chatzkel was quite advanced in years, and at some point appointed his eldest son to manage his finances. Years passed, and Chatzkel became incapable of making any financial decisions. His son was unsure if he should uphold his father's custom that he had kept until that point. Every time a grandchild or great-grandchild was born to Chatzkel, he would give $1,000 to the parents of the baby. Now that Chatzkel has lost use of his faculties, should the son continue to give these gifts on his father's behalf? Certainly, if the father were capable, he would give the gifts. Can the son act as the father's agent to give gifts that his father would want him to give?

A The Gemara in *Bava Basra*[90] records the following occurrence: An only son traveled overseas and reportedly died there. His father, thinking that his son had died and that he had no heir, distributed his assets to others using the appropriate *kinyanim*. Eventually, the son returned, alive and well, and the father regretted having given away his property. Rabbi Shimon ben Menasya says that since the gifts were obviously given in error, the father is allowed to retract. From this halachah we learn a precedent that one could take away property when it is obvious to everyone what his mindset was at the time of the gift, even though he did not state his desires explicitly. In this case as well, it is obvious to everyone that the father would want to give the gift from his assets.

However, the comparison is not accurate. In the case written in *Bava Basra*, we are merely understanding that the gift was given under certain pretexts, as if he had stipulated that the gift was conditional. Once the son returned, the condition was not fulfilled and the gift is null and void. In our case, we are trying to **create** a gift based on our understanding of what Chatzkel would have wanted. There is no precedent that one could create a gift based on mere understanding, to the detriment of others.

On the contrary, the Gemara in *Shevuos*[91] says that we are not allowed to decide financial matters based on circumstantial evidence. Rabbi Acha rules that if one camel in a group of camels was having a fit, and one of the other camels was found dead, we can assume that the crazed camel killed him. The *Chachamim* argue, and that is the ruling of *Shulchan Aruch*[92] as well. Damages are paid based solely on clear proof and/or kosher witnesses.

---

90. 132a.
91. 34a.
92. *Choshen Mishpat* 408.

One could, however, prove this case from the Gemara in *Kesubos*[93] that states that if one lost his faculties, *beis din* will continue to take from his estate for *tzedakah*. The *Maharit*[94] explains that we evaluate that his desire is to continue to give the *tzedakah* that he is used to giving, in order to provide him with the merits of giving *tzedakah*. Perhaps in this case as well, we could make such an evaluation, with the same rationale.

Rav Zilberstein writes that he heard that this question was asked of Harav Shlomo Zalman Auerbach, and he ruled that the son may take the money from his father's bank account to give the gifts to the parents of the grandchildren.

Preserving Special Relationships

וּבְנֵי קֹרַח לֹא מֵתוּ
But the sons of Korach did not die
(26:11)

Q Reuvy had a very close relationship with his Rav. He would consult the Rav in all aspects of his life, be it halachah, *chinuch*, or proper *hashkafah*. Tragically, after 25 years their relationship ended because of a *machlokes*. Reuvy's older children are still very close to the Rav and consult with him frequently in their personal lives.

---

93. 48a.
94. Vol. I, 127.

It was time for Reuvy's first grandson to become a bar mitzvah, and Simcha, the boy's father, had a problem. Reuvy called his son Simcha and told him that he heard that Simcha was planning to invite the Rav to the bar mitzvah. He warned Simcha (in no uncertain terms) that if the Rav comes, he will not come, and he will never speak to Simcha again.

In the same vein, Simcha had a picture of the Rav on his living-room wall. His father informed him that as long as that picture was on his wall, his father will not enter his house, and he will have nothing to do with him. How is Simcha supposed to deal with his father's unreasonable demands? He wants to maintain his family ties as well as his relationship with his Rav. What should he do?

A The *Shulchan Aruch*[95] rules that if a father commands his son not to talk to someone specific and not to forgive them, the son should not consider his father's command. The *Shach* and *Taz* explain that it is forbidden to hate a fellow Jew (unless he is a sinner). If so, the father is in effect asking his son to commit an *aveirah*, which he has no right to do. Simcha is strictly forbidden to listen to his father, especially since their father's hatred is directed at their primary Rav, to whom they owe special honor.[96]

However, it is possible for Simcha to fulfill both his father's request as well as not to offend the Rav. On the day of the bar mitzvah, Simcha should accompany his son, bearing a tray of special delicacies, and pay the Rav the honor he deserves by visiting him before the party. That will take the place of the Rav's attendance at the party, and show the Rav that not only do they not share their father's feelings, but they wanted to have a personal bar mitzvah celebration together in the Rav's house, in honor of the Rav.

---

95. *Yoreh De'ah* 240:16.
96. Ibid. 242.

As far as the Rav's picture, it should be taken off the wall and placed on the shelf next to the *Shas*, so they can see it while they are learning. That will be an honor to the Rav, and not an offense.

Simcha should tell his father that he has fulfilled his wishes. He will not invite the Rav to the (public) bar mitzvah, and he has taken down his picture (in order to move it to an honorable place). In this way, everyone will be happy.

פרשת מטות
Parashas Mattos

Who Should Pay Whom

אַךְ בְּמֵי נִדָּה יִתְחַטָּא
But it must be purified with the water of sprinkling
(31:23)

Q Joey's parents were not (yet) mitzvah observant, and unfortunately, had hoped to pass this tradition down to their son. Joey, however, had begun to attend *shiurim* and was interested in returning to his roots. One day the topic of the *shiur* was the mitzvah of *tevilas keilim*,[97] and of course the boy wanted very much to take his parents' kitchenware to the *mikveh* in order to do the mitzvah. Unfortunately, his parents had never learned about the mitzvos and were opposed to their son's lofty ideas. They vehemently refused to have their utensils dunked into the *mikveh*.

---

97. See *Yoreh De'ah* 120. Metal or glass utensils that were manufactured by or purchased from a non-Jew and are to be used in preparing or serving food must be immersed in a *mikveh* before use.

A few days later, the parents went on vacation, and left their son at home, alone. Joey seized the opportunity and eagerly gathered all the kitchenware and brought it to the nearest *mikveh*. Unfortunately, in the course of his zealous *toiveling*-spree, several of the utensils were broken. The vast majority remained intact as he submerged them in the *mikveh*, washed and dried them, and returned them to their places in the cabinet. He did such a good job at reconstructing the layout of the cabinet's contents that when his parents returned, they did not notice a thing, even though some of their utensils were missing. Joey wants to know if he has an obligation to compensate his parents for the utensils that he broke.

According to the halachah, even though he certainly did his parents a great favor by *toiveling* their *keilim*, since the parents told him specifically not to do so, it would seem that he would have to pay, even though the utensils broke accidentally.[98]

Nevertheless, there are three reasons why Joey should not have to pay:

1. The son is a guarantor (*arev*) on his parents' mitzvah of *tevillas keilim*. The *Nesivos HaMishpat*[99] writes that not only *beis din* has the authority to force people to do mitzvos, but every Jew has an obligation to prevent his friend from sinning, even by force (if it will be effective). If one could physically prevent his friend from eating on utensils that had not been immersed, it would seem that he would not have to repay damage to his property either, if the damage occurred while ensuring that his friend not sin.

2. The son has "permission from *beis din*" to *toivel* his parents' *keilim*. Therefore, any damage that occurred as a result is

---
98. See *Bava Kamma* 26b, *Adam Muad L'Olam*.
99. *Choshen Mishpat* 3.

considered damage with *beis din's* permission. Even if he was partially negligent, he should still be exempt, because he was probably under pressure to perform the mitzvah, and it follows that he had *beis din's* permission to *toivel* in haste.

3. The *Mekor Chaim*[100] writes that if someone intended to do his friend a great favor, and in the end he wound up damaging his friend, no payment is required. A proof to this is the Gemara in *Bava Kamma*:[101] One who runs on Erev Shabbos and caused damage is exempt from paying, since he was running with "permission," for the sake of the mitzvah. Similarly, since there is a mitzvah to do your friend a favor, he should not have to pay for the coincidental damage caused.[102]

This is the appropriate ruling in our case as well.

Best-Laid Plans

אַךְ בְּמֵי נִדָּה יִתְחַטָּא
But it must be purified with the water of sprinkling
(31:23)

רש״י: טְבִילָה
Rashi: Immersion

Q Purim was only a few days away, and Leah's *mishlo'ach manos* preparations were in high gear. One of the people on her list was her daughter's speech therapist.

---
100. 29.
101. 32a.
102. Editor's Note: See "Knot So Simple," p. 310, that the *Mekor Chaim* is not the accepted ruling and is only brought here as an added reason to exonerate.

The therapist was a little weak in the area of mitzvah observance, and Leah hoped that the *mishlo'ach manos* would help bring her a little closer to *Yiddishkeit*. Leah planned to place a luscious cake that she had prepared onto an elegant footed cake plate and present it to the speech therapist together with a bottle of fine wine.

When Leah shared her idea with her husband, he gently informed her that there is a dispute between the *poskim* as to whether one who is presenting a food utensil as a gift may *toivel* the utensil or not. Perhaps since the giver is not using it for eating purposes, but to give as a gift, it is similar to someone who sells food utensils; he is not obligated to *toivel* them. The utensils are considered merchandise, and do not yet function as service utensils. Her husband explained that it was not proper to give an *untoiveled* utensil to the therapist, since she might not *toivel* it herself. Therefore, he advised Leah to *toivel* the cake plate, and use it once, herself.

Leah understood her husband's point, but felt uncomfortable giving a "used" cake plate as a gift. She was still trying to get used to the idea as she shopped. While mulling over her options, she suddenly had an idea. She reasoned that when she bought the cake plate, she could notify the salesman that she was buying the cake plate for the therapist, and then she could acquire it on her behalf. Once the cake plate belonged to the therapist, it could certainly be *toiveled* for her.

Leah had forgotten her cell phone at home, so she couldn't run this idea by her husband. However, she was sure it was acceptable, so she carried out her plan and proceeded to the *keilim mikveh* to *toivel* the therapist's cake plate. On the way, the shopping bag somehow slipped out of her hand, and the cake plate smashed on impact with the sidewalk.

The cake plate had been very expensive, and Leah could not afford to replace it. However, since the cake plate already belonged to the therapist at the time that it smashed, maybe Leah has to pay for having damaged the therapist's cake plate! At the very least, perhaps she has to ask for *mechilah* (forgiveness). On the other hand, Leah never received permission from her husband to buy the plate on the therapist's behalf. Maybe the plate never belonged to the therapist in the first place. What is Leah's obligation at this point?

A It would seem at first glance that Leah would have to pay the therapist for having broken the cake plate since it was already hers, and Leah was not careful enough when she carried it to the *mikveh*. There are, however, two reasons that Leah should not have to reimburse the therapist.

First, even though an unpaid watchman is liable for negligence,[103] Leah never accepted responsibility for the therapist's cake plate. She only acquired it on her behalf, so that she would be able to *toivel* it. Since she never accepted responsibility for the plate, she does not have the status of a watchman, and should not have to pay for having been negligent.[104]

Second, if Leah would tell the entire story to the therapist, that she had bought her an expensive cake plate, and had acquired it on her behalf, and that it was difficult for her to buy a new one, etc. it would certainly be expected that the therapist would be *mochel*. Accordingly, perhaps Leah does not even have to solicit the *mechilah*, as one does not have to ask *mechilah* for something that people are naturally *mochel*.

This can be proven from the *Tur*,[105] who explains that one does not have to return money to someone to whom he sold merchandise for less than one-sixth more than it was actually worth.

---

103. *Choshen Mishpat* 291:1.
104. See ibid., 291:2.
105. Ibid., 227.

The reason for this is because it is common practice to be *mochel* on such a small discrepancy. There is no obligation to solicit an express *mechilah* for having overcharged in such a case, since the assumption is that everyone is *mochel*. In this case as well, Leah does not have to ask for an express *mechilah*, nor does she owe the therapist any money. However, she will have to make do with a disposable cake plate.

פרשת מסעי
Parashas Mas'ei

A Time to Rejoice

אֵלֶּה מַסְעֵי בְּנֵי יִשְׂרָאֵל
These are the journeys of the Children of Israel
(33:1)

Chaim Friedberg was enjoying a quiet evening at home, sipping a cup of tea in the kitchen with his wife, when the sharp jingle of the phone interrupted their peaceful interlude. The caller buoyantly announced that Chaim was the lucky winner of the yearly Ezras Yisrael raffle, whose grand prize was an impressive $50,000. Chaim and his wife were overjoyed. He was invited to visit the Ezras Yisrael office the next morning to pick up his check.

Later that evening, Chaim's wife told her husband that she felt that they should use part of the money to visit their parents who lived overseas, since they had not seen them in several years due to budget constraints. Chaim immediately agreed, and excitedly contacted a travel agent to purchase airline tickets, as well as to arrange hotel reservations.

The next morning, a mortified spokesperson for Ezras Yisrael called Chaim. Unfortunately, he had some bad news. They were soooo sorry, but there had been a terrible error. Someone had misread the winning ticket, which actually belonged to Chaim Friedenberg, and therefore, Chaim Friedberg had not won anything at all. The disappointment was crushing. The first thing that Chaim did was call the travel agent to cancel the travel plans. However, it was a little too late, and he was informed that he would have to pay a cancellation fee.

Chaim called Ezras Yisrael and explained what had happened. He was not asking for any compensation for the distress that they had caused him, as he understood that Hashem had decreed that he should have to endure such aggravation. Yet, he felt that perhaps a Rav should be consulted as to whether the organization should have to pay the cancellation fee, since they had misled him into thinking that he had won the prize. Is Chaim correct?

A Rabbi Shlomo Eliezer Alfandri[106] records in his responsa the following case: Reuven agreed to sell his field to Shimon, at which point Shimon went to the bank and cashed in an annuity in order to procure funds for the purchase. He had to pay certain penalties for cashing in the fund before it had matured. Afterward, Reuven had a change of heart and decided not to sell the property. Shimon wanted Reuven to pay for the losses incurred in liquidating his annuity.

The question was brought to the Sages of Teveria who debated if Reuven had to pay. Rav Alfandri's opinion was that Reuven is

---

106. Responsa *Sabba Kadisha,* Vol. 3, *Choshen Mishpat* 37.

exempt, because even if Reuven instructed Shimon to prepare the money, he did not force him to cash in his annuity. Shimon should have been cautious and realized that there was a possibility that Reuven would withdraw from the deal, and he should have waited until he was certain that the deal would be satisfactorily completed before he caused himself to be forced to pay the penalties. By not doing so, Shimon is responsible for his own loss.

In this case as well, Chaim was a bit hasty in spending money that he did not yet possess. He should have waited until the check was in his hand. Had Chaim purchased tickets and made hotel reservations after he had already received the money, and *then* Ezras Yisrael had told him about the mistake, the organization would have much more of a liability for their lack of caution. Even in such a case they would not be liable in *beis din*, as they did not directly cause any damage.[107] They would only have an obligation to cover Chaim's losses *b'dinei Shamayim*.

Under the circumstances, Chaim's cancellation fee is part of the aggravation he was destined to endure.

An Eye in the Sky

אֶל אֲשֶׁר יֵצֵא לוֹ שָׁמָּה הַגּוֹרָל לוֹ יִהְיֶה
Wherever its lot shall fall, his shall it be
(33:54)

Q A large supermarket chain announced that they were having a special promotion in celebration of the store's anniversary. Those who spent over $50 could write their

---
107. See *Bava Kamma* 60a that *grama* is exempt.

names on their receipts and insert them into the raffle box in the front of the store. The owner of the receipt that was drawn would receive his entire purchase for free!

People came in droves to shop and enter the store's raffle. The checkout lines were very hectic, to say the least. One day, Rafi and Avi were standing one behind the other. Rafi spent $400 and was busy packing up his groceries while Avi checked out and only spent $100. Avi noticed that Rafi's receipt was still on the counter and decided to surreptitiously switch receipts with him. Avi quickly wrote his name on Rafi's receipt, and Rafi, who hadn't noticed the switch, wrote his name on the receipt with the smaller amount. Both of them slipped their receipts into the box and exited the store without drawing any attention from the crowd.

Of course, nothing in this world goes unnnoticed. If a person would always remember three things, he would never come to do an *aveirah*.[108] One of those things which a person should always be conscious of is that there is an Eye in the sky. As an aid to remember this, Hashem gave man the knowledge to create cameras, which record his actions forever. Avi forgot that in addition to Hashem's eye, the store's security camera had witnessed his *aveirah*. The store manager immediately decided that since the raffle was set up to return the purchaser's amount of sale, if Avi's name came up in the drawing, Rafi would receive the refund!

At the end of the day, the winning receipt was drawn, and sure enough, it had Rafi's name on it. That meant that it was Avi's purchase of $100 that had Rafi's name written on it! Now the store manager wants to know what to do. According to his logic, the purchaser

---

108. *Pirkei Avos* 3:1.

deserved to have his money returned, regardless of whose name was written on the ticket, and if so, Avi should really get his money back. Does Avi, the one who cheated, deserve to win?

As soon as Avi switched his receipt with Rafi, he forfeited his chance to win with that receipt and transferred his rights to Rafi! He entered into a lose-lose situation, and gave his friend Rafi two chances to win.[109]

Even if the manager believes that the prize is to return the money to the one who spent the amount listed on the receipt, Rafi purchased even more than the amount on the receipt and he deserves to get back the amount of the receipt that bears his name.

Avi should internalize the words of Shlomo HaMelech: סוֹף דָּבָר הַכֹּל נִשְׁמָע אֶת הָאֱלֹקִים יְרָא וְאֶת מִצְוֹתָיו שְׁמוֹר כִּי זֶה כָּל הָאָדָם — *The sum of the matter, when all has been considered: Fear God and keep His commandments, for that is man's whole duty.*[110] The *Targum* explains: In the End of Days, that which a person did in secret in this world will be publicized, and in the future it will become known to everyone. Therefore, one should be careful to do Hashem's mitzvos and keep His commandments faithfully in order not to sin secretly.

A person will be shamed beyond description for having sinned in this world. That thought itself is enough to safeguard a person from any transgression.

---

109. See *Bava Kamma* 28a for an example of someone who tried to trade something that belonged to him for something that he had no right to take from its owner. The Gemara says, "That which he has given is given but he receives nothing in exchange."
110. *Koheles* 12:13.

A Jewish Auction (Not Made in China)

אֲשֶׁר תִּתְנַחֲלוּ אֹתָהּ בְּגוֹרָל
That you shall divide as an inheritance by lot
(34:13)

Q A local *tzedakah* organization decided to raise funds by holding a Chinese auction. At the conclusion of the event, after all the winners had been selected, it was discovered that six people had won 30 of the prizes that were "auctioned," a highly improbable outcome, to say the least. Upon investigation, it was discovered that all these winners had put in their tickets last, and thus their tickets had been sitting on the top of each box. The boxes had never been mixed!

Is such an auction valid? Everyone had a chance to win, as the one who drew the names could have decided to mix the tickets in each box. Is mixing all the tickets an integral part of the lottery? If it was not done, perhaps such a lottery is fundamentally flawed and is therefore not considered valid.

A There are sources stating that mixing the lottery tickets is not absolutely necessary, and a lottery is valid even without it:

1. The Gemara in *Yoma*[111] states that the Kohen Gadol would dip his hands into the lottery and lift out both lots.[112] *Rashi*

---
111. 39a.
112. The Torah commanded that on Yom Kippur the Kohen Gadol should draw lots on two goats, to decide which one would be sacrificed to Hashem, and which

explains that the Kohen would grab the lots quickly. *Tosafos Rid* explains that he would first shake the lots, as is the custom of those who draw lots, in order to mix them and prevent him from choosing a specific one. It would seem that *Tosafos Rid* is telling us that the custom of those who draw lots is to first mix them. But at the same time it is obvious that it is not mandatory, for if it was, that should have been *Tosafos Rid's* reasoning for the Kohen Gadol doing so, and not as he writes that it is in order to avoid his intentionally picking a specific lot.

2. Similarly, the Gemara in *Bava Basra*[113] records the order of the distribution of *Eretz Yisrael* to the *Shevatim* when the Jews entered the Land with Yehoshua bin Nun. Elazar the Kohen Gadol wore the *Urim VeTumim*. Yehoshua and *Klal Yisrael* stood before Elazar and two boxes were placed in front of him; one box contained the names of the tribes, and the other the boundaries of each portion. Using *ruach hakodesh*, Elazar would deliberate and predict which tribes had been designated to receive which portion. Then he would mix the lots and choose exactly as he had predicted. The *Rashbam* explains that the lots were mixed in order that people should not claim that Elazar had purposely chosen according to his prediction. One could infer that if not for avoiding suspicion, it would be unnecessary to mix the lots.

3. The *Sifri*[114] records that Moshe Rabbeinu made two lotteries: (a) To decide which 70 people would be chosen as the *zekeinim* to assist him in leading the Jews[115]; (b) to decide which 273 *bechoros* would have to redeem themselves.[116] Moshe mixed

---

should be sent to Azazel (taken to the wilderness and pushed from a cliff).
113. 122a.
114. *Beha'aloscha, pischah* 95.
115. See *Bamidbar* 11:16.
116. See ibid., 3:46. There were 22,273 firstborn sons among the Jews, aside from those of the tribe of Levi. There were 22,000 Levi'im who were not themselves firstborn, and they "exempted" 22,000 of the other tribes' firstborn sons from redemption. Moshe had to make a lottery to decide which 273 firstborn sons were the additional ones, who were obligated to redeem themselves.

the notes, put them into a box, and told each of them to remove a paper. It sounds as if Moshe mixed the notes before he put them in the box. Why would he do that? Perhaps all it means is that Moshe folded the papers before putting them in the box. Then he put the papers in, and asked the people to choose. He did not, however, mix the notes inside the box.

Rav Chaim Kanievsky ruled that the aforementioned *Rashbam* is very likely a proof that mixing the lots is not necessary and is only done to avoid suspicion, as was the case in distributing the land.

However, the *Chavos Ya'ir*[117] writes that results of any lottery that is carried out improperly cannot be binding. If people are complaining that the lottery is unfair, then that would indicate that the lottery was not done properly. Accordingly, the lottery should be redone properly.

Vocational Hazard

וְאִם בְּפֶתַע בְּלֹא אֵיבָה הֲדָפוֹ
But if with suddenness, without enmity, did he push him
(35:22)

Q Little Dovy went to kindergarten. On the first day of school he came home with broken glasses. He apparently had a scuffle with another boy in the group, and his glasses broke. Can Dovy's parents ask the other boy's parents to pay their child's damage? Perhaps the teacher must pay for the glasses because she was supposed to watch the children.

---
117. Responsa 61.

A Neither the boy who broke the glasses nor his parents have to pay. The Mishnah in *Bava Kamma*[118] warns that a scuffle with a minor is a losing proposition. One who wounds a minor has to pay for the damages. Yet, if the minor damages someone else, he has no obligation to pay (and neither do his parents). A minor does not have the intellectual capacity required to be held accountable for his actions.

One could argue that the teacher is responsible. *Tosafos* in *Bava Kamma*[119] writes that if someone entrusts a house to someone else for safekeeping, the watchman has to be careful that the children present should not climb and jump in a way that will break objects. Logic would dictate that if someone needs to ensure that children not play wildly, they are responsible to make sure that they do not break each other's eyewear.

However, we cannot obligate the teacher to pay, as it is not practical to obligate her to watch the children to the extent that they should not break their classmates' glasses. She has to watch many children at the same time, and the children are all playing with one another. It only takes a second for one child to break someone else's glasses. It would be impossible for the teacher to be obligated to prevent such accidents.

The *Rambam*[120] writes that the extent of a watchman's responsibility is set according to the accepted norms of watching the item that is entrusted. Therefore, as long as the teacher acted according to the rules, without neglect, and in a way that normal kindergarten teachers do, she cannot be held accountable.

---

118. 87a.
119. 21b.
120. *Hilchos She'eilah U'Pikadon.*

ספר דברים

Sefer Devarim

פרשת דברים
Parashas Devarim

What Drives the Driver?

לֹא תַכִּירוּ פָנִים בַּמִּשְׁפָּט
You shall not show favoritism in judgment
(1:17)

Q Meir is an experienced intercity bus driver, and in the course of his work he often witnesses people running to catch the bus. Unfortunately, sometimes they even endanger themselves by recklessly dashing across streets; at times they even dart into the street in front of his bus! Meir wants to determine if he may deny such passengers the right to board his bus, in the hope that they will learn their lesson and obey traffic safety rules. If they will have to wait for the next bus, Meir hopes they will realize that their lack of regard for safety did not help them, and perhaps this will prevent such behavior in the future. On the other hand, maybe Meir has no right to penalize them. Should he suffice with a verbal reprimand?

A	Meir has to fulfill the mitzvah of *lo sa'amod al dam rei'echa*[1] (not to stand by while your friend's blood is being shed). He must teach those who disobey traffic rules that they are endangering themselves and others with their irresponsible behavior. He should not open the bus door for them even if they plead with him that they are in a desperate rush.

However, Meir can do so only if he is acting solely for the sake of benefiting the one denied boarding. If Meir merely intends to teach them a lesson out of anger or even as revenge for their lack of consideration, perhaps Meir would even have a mitzvah to open the bus's door for them, in order to exercise control over his own evil inclination.

Meir should consider: If the rushing passenger had been Meir's own son, would Meir also be willing to leave him standing forlornly at the bus stop to wait for the next bus? Perhaps that would be the litmus test, as to Meir's true intent.

The problem is, even though Meir is obligated to deny his own son access to the bus under such circumstances, his love for his son might overcome his desire to do what is right. That would not be reason to deny others to learn their lesson by letting them board the bus when he should not let them do so, simply because he has no such conflicting feelings toward them, as he does toward his son.

Even in cases where speaking *lashon hara* is permitted for a constructive purpose, there are several conditions that have to be met before one is actually allowed to speak. One of the conditions is that the speaker's intent be solely for the constructive purpose, not based on anger or negative motivation toward the subject of his speech.[2] The same guideline would apply in Meir's case, as well. Meir may only teach the would-be passenger a lesson if his intent is purely to benefit him, and not out of anger or revenge.[3]

---

1. *Vayikra* 19:16.
2. *Chofetz Chaim, Klal* 4, *Be'er Mayim Chaim* §43.
3. See also *Sma* 421§28 and the *Taz* as well.

The Gemara[4] teaches that one who wants to enjoy others' kindness should behave like Elisha the prophet did, and one who does not wish to benefit from others should act as did Shmuel the prophet.[5] It would seem that Elisha had an inclination to benefit from others, while Shmuel preferred not to resort to benefiting from other people's generosity. In fact, the *Lev Eliyahu*[6] cites the Alter from Kelm that both Elisha and Shmuel actually behaved contrary to their natural tendencies: Shmuel felt very comfortable to be the recipient of others' kindness, but he did not do so in order to control his nature. Elisha felt uncomfortable accepting a favor, yet he did so in order to break his natural inclination.

In Meir's case as well, if he is upset by the passenger's lack of care and therefore wishes to act insensitively to him, he should thwart his natural inclination by opening the door for him and welcoming him onto his bus. Only if his intent is to benefit the would-be passenger may Meir deny him the right to board.

Work Site or Vacation Site?

לְהָמָם
To confound them
(2:15)

Q Michoel needed a few peaceful days away from work, so he rented a room in the beautiful city of Tzefas. The room was very comfortable, but the morning after

---

4. *Berachos* 10b.
5. Shmuel would take his tent with him wherever he traveled in order to avoid accepting favors from anyone (*Berachos* 10b based on *Shmuel I* 7:17). Elisha, in contrast, accepted the hospitality of the couple from Shunaim (*Melachim II* 4:8 *ff*).
6. Vol. I, p. 264.

Michoel arrived, the neighbor brought a tractor and a jackhammer and began to demolish a ground-floor apartment in the building next door. Michoel contacted the owner and grumbled that the room was not fit for relaxation and rest. He demanded that he receive his money back for the duration of his rental. The owner told Michoel that it was his bad luck that brought the noise upon him, and refused to return the money. Which of them is right?

A It would seem that since the room is livable, albeit a "little" noisy, it is similar to the following case, which is brought in the *Shulchan Aruch*[7]: If someone rents a field that has its own water source, e.g., a well, and the well dried up so that he can only water the field by bringing buckets of water from the river, he cannot deduct from the rent, despite his inconvenience. The *Rema*, citing the *Mordechai*, adds that neither is he allowed to cut the rental period short. The *Maharam Padua* argues that he may stop the rental immediately, but the *Rema* concludes that the *Mordechai's* opinion should be followed. The *Nesivos HaMishpat* explains that since the problem arose once he rented the item, the owner can tell the renter that it is his bad luck that caused the problem.[8]

Similarly, in our case, Michoel would seem to have no claim against the owner. If, however, the owner knew that his neighbor was planning construction, rendering his apartment unfit to be a vacation rental, he cannot claim that it was the renter's luck; the owner rented out a defective room, and Michoel may back out of his contract.

One could ask, if the owner was aware of his neighbor's imminent renovations, would he have to provide Michoel with alternative accommodations?

---

7. *Choshen Mishpat* 321:1.
8. When one rents an item, it is as if he owns it for the period of the rental, and therefore it is his *mazel* that determines its fate.

The *Shulchan Aruch*[9] states that if someone rented a house and it collapsed, the owner does not have to rebuild it or replace it; rather, he can return the money for the duration of the rental. The Chazon Ish[10] writes that the building's collapse does not constitute grounds to negate the entire rental, because the building was strong at the time the contract was signed, and it only collapsed later. One could infer from the Chazon Ish's words that if the defect had been in existence at the time of the rental, the owner would have to provide alternative accommodations. Perhaps the same would be true in our case as well. וצ"ע.

Good Things Come in Small Packages

הִנֵּה עַרְשׂוֹ
Behold! His bed
(3:11)

Q Shimky was exceedingly short for his age, and his parents want to treat him with daily injections of a growth hormone in order to help him grow taller. The doctor assured his parents that the hormone had been approved in many countries, but has been in use for only about 10 years, so that no one really knows its long-term effects. He noted that this treatment may one day be found to be carcinogenic or otherwise harmful

---

9. *Choshen Mishpat* 312:17.
10. *Bava Kamma* 23 §10.

to the body. The parents want to know if it is better to take advantage of the drug, or to let "nature" take its course.

A The Gemara in *Bechoros*[11] lists being very short as a defect that separates a Kohen from other Kohanim and invalidates him from serving in the *Beis HaMikdash*.
In this case, if Shimky's shortness will make him obviously different from everyone else and he will suffer as a result of his appearance — e.g., his classmates will tease him or, when the time comes, he will have difficulty finding a *shidduch* — then perhaps it would be recommended that he take the growth hormone; the possibility that there may be long-term side effects should not detract from the certain immediate benefits of the treatment. In addition, since many people are already using this treatment, the rule[12] that *Hashem protects the simple*[13] would apply.

In the time of *Mahari ben Lev*, wealthy Jews would occasionally be taken captive and forced to do hard labor for the government. There was a certain man who was favored by the king's officers, and he had the opportunity to spare one such Jew from his servitude, but he was afraid that the king's soldiers might grab another hapless Jew in his stead. The *Mahari ben Lev*[14] was asked if the favored subject is allowed to use his influence in such a situation.

The *Mahari ben Lev* quotes the Gemara in *Yevamos*[15] that seven of Shaul's descendants were singled out to be killed.[16] How did they decide who would be killed? Rav Huna explained that the

---

11. 45b.
12. See *Niddah* 31b, *Yevamos* 72a, *Avodah Zarah* 30b.
13. *Tehillim* 116:6.
14. Vol. II, 40.
15. 79.
16. Shaul HaMelech had killed out the city of Nov, depriving the Givonim — who had supplied water and wood to the *Mishkan* in Nov — of their livelihood. As a result, Hashem brought a famine, which would end as soon as the Givonim forgave Shaul. The Givonim refused to do so unless seven of Shaul's descendants would be put to death.

descendants were led before the *Aron HaKodesh*. The *Aron* identified who was to be put to death, and who would live. Rav Chana bar Bizna questioned the *pasuk* that says that David had mercy on Mefiboshes, the son of Yonason who was the son of Shaul. Does "having mercy" mean that he did not pass him in front of the *Aron*? Is it permitted to show such favoritism at such a time? If it means that Mefiboshes was sent to be killed and David *davened* that he should be released, that is still considered favoritism! The Gemara concludes that perhaps it means that David *davened* that Mefiboshes should not be marked for death.

This Gemara teaches us that if a Jew was already taken to work for the king, and it is known that if he will be released someone else will be taken in his stead, one may not attempt to save the first one. If, however, the person has not been taken yet, one is allowed to try and save whomever he wants. On the other hand, if it is not definite that they will take another Jew, one would be allowed to free the first one, even though there is a possibility that they will catch someone else.

The *Mahari ben Lev* asked why this is different from the mitzvos of *shofar* and *lulav,* which are suspended on Shabbos because of the possibility that perhaps someone may come to carry them in the public domain when there is no *eruv*, and thus it is preferable to be passive and not perform the mitzvah. Perhaps it would be better for the king's friend to remain passive, due to the possibility that another captive may be taken.

He explains that it is proper to suspend the positive command of *shofar* and *lulav* in order to protect the Shabbos, which is a much more stringent mitzvah. The two men, on the other hand, are equally precious, so the possibility of another being caught is not enough to prevent saving the one who is in definite need.

Accordingly, in our case, where taking the growth hormone could possibly cause problems that are much more serious than being short, perhaps one would not be allowed to seek the definite gain for fear that something much worse may develop, just as the possibility of *chillul Shabbos, chas v'shalom,* is sufficient to suspend the mitzvos of *shofar* and *lulav.*

However, upon further examination, the cases are not comparable. The *Mahari ben Lev* was discussing whether to choose one mitzvah over another or one person over another. Our case is dealing with only one person. One is allowed to endanger himself for his livelihood, or the like.[17] Certainly one may also take a risk in order to save himself from other situations that are causing him difficulty.

Therefore, the parents may opt to give their young son the treatment.

In addition, Rav Elyashiv ruled that 10 years without any report of detrimental effects was long enough to allay concerns about the safety of the hormone treatment.

If the parents would ask if the treatment is *recommended,* the answer would be that it depends on the boy. If he has a healthy and strong self-image and will not be hurt socially or have difficulty finding a *shidduch,* it would be better not to take the treatment. However, if his personality is more fragile and his condition will cause him to suffer, then he should take the hormone.

---

17. *Nodah B'Yehudah, Tinyana, Yoreh De'ah* 10.

פרשת ואתחנן
Parashas Va'eschanan

The Lesser of Two Evils

לֹא תִשָּׂא אֶת שֵׁם ה' לַשָּׁוְא
And you shall not take the Name of Hashem ...in vain
(5:11)

Q Harry knows that his employee, Jonathan, is stealing supplies from the office. Harry would like to confront him with his discovery in order to prevent any recurrence, but he knows that if he corners Jonathan, the latter will "swear in the Name of Hashem" that he never stole anything. Harry knows differently. Harry also knows that even though Jonathan will not admit to his stealing, if he knows that he is suspected, he will certainly stop taking materials from the office out of fear that he is being watched. Should he confront his employee even if it will cause him to swear falsely, or should he allow Jonathan to continue to steal in order to spare him from a terrible sin?

The Mishnah in *Shevuos*[18] presents the following case: Reuven arranged with Shimon, a storeowner, to pay Levi, Reuven's employee. Subsequently Shimon claimed that he paid Levi, while Levi asserted that he had not been paid. The halachah is that Shimon swears that he paid, and then collects his repayment from Reuven. Levi then swears that he has not been paid, and he, too, collects his salary from Reuven. Ben Nannas argues with this halachah, for how could we authorize one of them to swear in vain?

The Mishnah appears to be difficult to understand. The entire world is punished because of someone who swears falsely.[19] How could we allow the entire world to suffer, just so that the innocent party should receive his money?

The *Rashba*[20] responds that this question is relevant every time someone is asked to swear in *beis din*. If he is telling the truth, the oath is extraneous, and if he is lying, how could we ask him to swear falsely and bring terrible consequences upon the entire world? The answer is that it is a mitzvah to swear in *beis din* and validate issues that are in doubt by swearing in the Name of Hashem. *Chazal* required people to swear in order to establish peace and put people's minds to rest, in the hope that if a person is not telling the truth, he will admit his lie rather than swear falsely when put to the test.

The *Shitah Mekubetzes*[21] quotes the *Radvaz* that one is allowed to make his opponent swear even if he knows that his opponent will swear falsely, although it is considered an extra measure of piety to retract at the last moment and not force him to swear falsely, thereby saving him from a terrible *aveirah*.

In this case, Harry may warn Jonathan that he is aware of his activities, despite the fact that this will cause him to swear falsely. The *Radvaz* only considers it an extra measure of piety to avoid compelling one's adversary to swear in a case where the

---

18. 45a.
19. 39a.
20. *Teshuvos Meyuchasos L'Ramban* 282.
21. *Bava Metzia* 2b.

adversary will swear falsely when the claimant will not benefit from insisting on the oath. In our case Harry will profit from the warning, because Jonathan will refrain from stealing in the future. Moreover, although Harry may indirectly be causing Jonathan to swear falsely, he is saving Jonathan from continuing to violate the prohibition against stealing.

Coming Home Late

כַּבֵּד אֶת אָבִיךָ וְאֶת אִמֶּךָ
Honor your father and your mother
(5:16)

Q: When *cheder* was over for the day, 13½-year-old Yanky joined an organized learning group in the shul next door to his *cheder*. One day, the program continued overtime until the scheduled time for Maariv arrived. The men in the shul asked Yanky to join them as a tenth man. However, his parents were expecting him home already, and he had no way to notify them that he will be home late. (Can anyone imagine a shul full of congregants without a single cellphone?) Can Yanky stay for Maariv to complete the minyan and return home in 15 minutes, or should he go home immediately to spare his parents any worry?

A: Yanky may not stay in shul even if that will cause the other nine men to miss *davening* with a minyan. In a similar vein, the *Beis Lechem Yehudah*[22] writes that a son

---

22. Glosses to *Shulchan Aruch* 240:15.

may not take upon himself an optional fast if he knows that doing so will upset his parents. To cause his parents pain of worrying about him is not an acceptable option for Yanky.[23]

Return Policy

מְלֵאִים כָּל טוּב אֲשֶׁר לֹא מִלֵּאתָ
Filled with every good thing that you did not fill
(6:11)

Q Mrs. Shulman sold eggs out of her apartment to the neighborhood women. She never advertised, except by letting her neighbors know that they could buy eggs from her whenever they needed, and word spread between them. Her sales were modest, commensurate with her investment.

One day Mrs. Shulman was talking to her neighbor Mrs. Shapiro, who lived on the same floor as she did.

---

23. Editor's Note: The Chazon Ish was once waiting to *daven* Minchah with a group of men in his *beis midrash*. After a half an hour of waiting, there were still only nine men. Finally a tenth man arrived, but before they could begin *davening*, Rabbi Shmuel Greineman, who was one of the 10, approached the Chazon Ish to ask for his direction. Rav Greineman had made an appointment to meet someone in the next quarter of an hour. The purpose of the meeting was not so crucial, but if he remained to *daven*, he would not be able to keep his appointment.

The Chazon Ish answered that someone who appreciates what it means to be truthful would not even ask such a question.

Rav Greinemen left to keep his appointment, and the minyan eventually disbanded. That day the Chazon Ish had to *daven* Minchah without a minyan, despite having waited over half an hour in order not to have to do so (*Ma'aseh Ish*, Vol. 3, p. 209).

It would seem that, in addition to the reason of the mitzvah of *kibbud av v'eim*, Yanky also must return home on time as an appreciation of what it means to keep his word, even at the expense of the minyan having to disband!

She mentioned to Mrs. Shapiro that the egg sale was a major headache for her. People bothered her all day long. She just wished that someone else would take the whole business off her hands!

Mrs. Shapiro was an industrious homemaker. She suggested to Mrs. Shulman that she allow her the opportunity to take over the business. Mrs. Shapiro said that she didn't mind if people knocked on her door at all hours.

Mrs. Shulman said that she would gladly give up her right to sell eggs, but only on condition that if she ever wanted to reopen her business, Mrs. Shapiro would return it to her. In other words, Mrs. Shapiro would then stop selling eggs in order to allow Mrs. Shulman to restart her business. Mrs. Shapiro readily agreed.

Mrs. Shapiro invested her talents as well as her money to expand and advertise her business. There was no one in the neighborhood who had not heard about her egg sale. Her sales grew considerably. In addition, she used the added volume to negotiate with competing suppliers, which lowered her cost price dramatically. The once-dull business had grown to be quite profitable.

A few years later, Mrs. Shulman knocked on Mrs. Shapiro's door and informed her that she would like to reopen her business, and asked Mrs. Shapiro to honor her commitment. Mrs. Shapiro claimed that the product she received is no longer the same product that she is being asked to return. The once marginally profitable egg sale had been transformed into a lucrative venture due to Mrs. Shapiro's hard work and ingenuity. Therefore, she claimed, the original agreement is no longer relevant, as it would be unheard of for Mrs. Shulman to reap the benefits of Mrs. Shapiro's tremendous investment of advertising, hard work, and negotiating with suppliers.

Both women agree that there is only enough business for one of them to run an egg sale on the same floor! Which woman deserves the rights?

A The Gemara in *Maseches Yoma*[24] relates that if a Kohen Gadol has to be replaced temporarily, his substitute has to withdraw when the original Kohen Gadol is ready to serve again. Nevertheless, *Tosafos* writes in *Maseches Nazir*[25] that if the substitute retained the position for several years, the original Kohen Gadol cannot usurp his it.

The *S'dei Chemed*[26] discusses the case of a *chazzan* who had tenure for *davening* Mussaf on Rosh Hashanah and Yom Kippur. For financial reasons, he had to relocate his family. Five years later, he returned to the city and wanted his old position to be returned to him. The *poskim* maintain that he cannot demand his previous position back, for the following reasons:

1. He left his position willingly. The fact that he had financial pressures is not considered as if he was forced to leave town. One may claim that he has the right to reassume his previous position only when he was forced to leave, but not when he did so by choice.

2. Moreover, after several years of absence, he certainly gave up hope of reclaiming his position. The *S'dei Chemed* adds that according to *Tosafos* in *Nazir*, after a few years the original Kohen Gadol cannot usurp the position from his replacement.

Perhaps according to this reasoning, Mrs. Shulman cannot ask to return to her prior position after so many years have elapsed, their agreement notwithstanding.

However, there are several differentiations between these two cases:

Tosafos is discussing a case where the Kohen Gadol was forced to leave his position, not where someone left willingly, stipulating

---
24. 12b.
25. 47a.
26. *Ma'areches Chazakah B'Mitzvos* 5:1.

that he reserves the right to return. *Tosafos* is also discussing a position in which the Kohen Gadol serves on behalf of the congregation. The *tzibbur* has become accustomed to the Kohen Gadol or the *chazzan*, as the case may be, and does not wish to switch their messenger as long as they have not yet become accustomed to his substitute. By the time a few years have passed, they have already become used to the replacement, and therefore the first one cannot return. This would not be relevant in a case where there was a financial obligation to give the original proprietor's business back to him.

Regarding Mrs. Shapiro's claim that she built up the business into a much greater venture than its predecessor, and since it is no longer the same business she does not have to return it, she is not in the right. No one induced her to expand the business. Mrs. Shulman can claim that she would be willing to return to her egg sale in its previous state. Does she have to lose her rights just because Mrs. Shapiro built up her small business into a more successful one?

Mrs. Shulman deserves to get her business back. Perhaps in the interest of good will, Mrs. Shulman should go beyond her obligation and offer Mrs. Shapiro some money in appreciation for her efforts in furthering the business venture.

פרשת עקב
Parashas Eikev

Getting Involved

וְאָכַלְתָּ וְשָׂבָעְתָּ וּבֵרַכְתָּ
And you will eat and you will be satisfied and bless
(8:10)

Q Mendy glanced up from his *sefer* to check the time and was startled to discover that he only had two minutes to run to the shul down the block to catch the last minyan for Minchah. He scolded himself for getting so involved that he had not noticed how much time had gone by. It took extra effort to concentrate on the first *berachah* of *Shemoneh Esrei*, and during the second *berachah*, Mendy suddenly remembered that before he had delved into his *sefer*, he had been eating lunch, and he had forgotten to *bentch*! If he continued to *daven Shemoneh Esrei*, more than 72 minutes will have gone by since he had finished eating, and it would be too late to *bentch*.[27]

---

27. See *Mishnah Berurah* 184 §20. If a person ate to the point of satiation, he may *bentch* until he is hungry again. If he only ate a small amount that did not satiate him, he may *bentch* until 72 minutes have elapsed, as until that point,

What should he do now? Should he *bentch* during *Shemoneh Esrei*? Maybe he does not have to *bentch*, as he is *davening Shemoneh Esrei* now, and one who is already involved in a mitzvah is exempt from doing other mitzvos.[28] If he can no longer *bentch* afterward because the allotted time has elapsed, then perhaps he is an *oness*. A third possibility might be to pause to go to the shul's kitchen and eat something to keep his meal going, which will give him an additional 72 minutes, and then he could *bentch* after he completes his *davening*.

What should he do?

The Gemara[29] teaches that one who is involved in one mitzvah is exempt from fulfilling a different mitzvah. The *Pri Megadim*[30] infers from the *Magen Avraham*[31] that even involvement in a mitzvah *d'Rabbanan* exempts one from a mitzvah *d'Oraisa*. Mendy, however, can not be exempted from *bentching* even though he is now involved in *davening* because he was negligent for not having *bentched* when he should have. If he does not *bentch* at this point, he will be blatantly transgressing the mitzvah to *bentch*.

In addition, the *Pesach HaDvir* writes that one who started doing a mitzvah *d'Rabbanan* is exempt from doing a mitzvah *d'Oraisa* at that time, even if he will not be able to do the mitzvah *d'Oraisa* afterward. The rationale for this exemption is that at the time the person started the mitzvah *d'Rabbanan*, he was not yet obligated to do the mitzvah *d'Oraisa*. In our case, Mendy was already obligated to *bentch* before he started *davening*. Hence, he cannot be exempted.

Rav Chaim Kanievsky ruled that Mendy should *bentch* between the *berachos* of *Shemoneh Esrei*, as *tefillah* is a mitzvah *d'Rabbanan*, and since *bentching* is a mitzvah *d'Oraisa* it therefore takes

---

his food has not yet been digested.
28. *Succah* 25a.
29. *Succah* 25a.
30. *Siman* 72.
31. §4.

precedence. Rav Chaim was incredulous that someone could even consider eating during *Shemoneh Esrei*.

The difference between pausing to *bentch* and eating during *davening* is that eating is not a mitzvah and is therefore an interruption to *davening*, while *bentching* is a mitzvah that can supersede *davening*.

Of course, this question would be relevant only if Mendy was no longer satiated by his meal. If he still felt full, then he can *bentch* even more than 72 minutes after his meal, in which case he can certainly finish his *davening* first.[32]

Bad Answer

וּקְשַׁרְתֶּם אֹתָם לְאוֹת
And you shall bind them for a sign
(11:18)

Q On the day Tzvi was scheduled to travel home from a business trip abroad, he was approached by his friend Avi, who asked if he had room to take a small package for him. Avi had bought his father two beautiful pairs of *tefillin*: one pair of regular *tefillin*, written according to the opinion of *Rashi*, and one pair of *Rabbeinu Tam tefillin*.[33] Tzvi obligingly replied that he had plenty of room, and he would be happy to take the *tefillin* with him.

---

32. Mishnah Berurah 184 §20.
33. *Rashi* and *Rabbeinu Tam*, who was *Rashi's* grandson, differed as to the order of the placement of the Torah sections that are placed inside the *tefillin*. Some people have a custom to wear *Rabbeinu Tam's tefillin* in addition to their regular *tefillin*.

Tzvi had a stopover in a European country known for its meticulous security. He prepared to have his luggage searched for illegal substances. The customs officer who searched his luggage immediately noticed the *tefillin* and sternly asked Tzvi what he was hiding in the black boxes. Tzvi explained that Jews are commanded to don the "black boxes" every day: one on the arm and one on the head. The officer continued to interrogate Tzvi: If he was only required to place one on his arm and one on his head, why was Tzvi carrying four boxes? Tzvi thought he would have difficulty explaining the nuances between the *shitos* of *Rashi* and *Rabbeinu Tam* to the customs officer, so he simply replied that one pair was for during the week, and one pair was for Shabbos!

The officer contacted one of his superiors, who happened to be a *frum* Jew. He asked if it was true that Jews wear *tefillin* on Shabbos. His superior told him that they certainly do not, and the officer thanked him for the information. To Tzvi's utter dismay, the officer confiscated the *tefillin* for further investigation, and Tzvi never saw them again. Does Tzvi have to pay Avi for the *tefillin* that were confiscated due to Tzvi's bungled response to the officer, or is it not considered his fault, as he could not have foreseen such an outcome?

𝒜 Tzvi's responsibility toward the *tefillin* is that of a *shomer chinam*, one who watches without being paid. His liability is limited to acts of negligence, and he would not have to pay if the *tefillin* were stolen or lost as long as Tzvi had watched them responsibly. He is certainly exempt for circumstances beyond his control. That said, Tzvi should not have to pay Avi for the loss of the *tefillin*, as the entire string of events that led to the *tefillin's* confiscation was completely unexpected, and Tzvi was merely a slight impetus, at best.

When the officer questioned Tzvi about the two pairs of *tefillin*, it would have been very difficult, if not impossible, to explain that there are two opinions in halachah, a facet of Judaism that probably does not exist in other religions, and hence, Tzvi's answer was not an act of negligence.

The Gemara in *Megillah*[34] records the story of Ptolemy II, the king of Egypt, who sequestered 70 Jewish scholars, each in his own room, without telling him why. Afterward, he approached each one separately and asked him to translate the Torah into Greek. Hashem placed into each one's heart the inspiration to write an identical translation, and every one of the scholars strayed from the true translation of the text in the same 15 places, lest the king deny the authenticity of the Torah. For example, they wrote, "I will make man," instead of "Let us make man," lest the king misconstrue the *pasuk* and conclude that there was more than one Creator, Heaven forbid. Another *pasuk* they changed was the name of the *arneves* (hare) in the list of non-kosher animals, because that happened to be the name of Ptolemy's wife, and Ptolemy would have misunderstood and thought that the *Chachamim* were trying to insult him by listing his wife with the animals.

Hence, we find a precedent for altering the facts in an instance where it would be impossible to convince others of the authenticity of the true explanation.[35] Perhaps in this case as well, since Tzvi felt he could not exactly explain that there is more than one opinion concerning Hashem's mitzvah to don *tefillin*, his answer to the customs officer was appropriate, and he is not held accountable for not realizing that the officer would attempt to verify if his answer was true.

Even after the officer phoned his superior to verify Tzvi's story, the *tefillin* were still far from being in peril. The superior

---

34. 9a.
35. An exception to this rule is that one may not alter a halachic ruling. See *Bava Kamma* 38a. Tzvi's alteration was not an alteration of the halachah, as the customs officer had no interest in knowing the halachah. He just wanted to ascertain that there was nothing dangerous or illegal involved.

should have understood that his officer was not trying to learn the halachos of *tefillin*, and he should have investigated the situation himself in order to avoid the unnecessary confiscation of the *tefillin*.

The Gemara[36] relates that Rava was once questioned whether one is allowed to make a *bris* on Shabbos. Rava answered that it is permitted, but on second thought Rava realized that if someone was asking such a question, to which the petitioner should have known the answer himself, then there must be a special reason he was asking. Upon further examination, Rava determined that due to the circumstances of the birth, the *bris* indeed had to be postponed until after Shabbos.

If someone is asked a peculiar question, he should inquire as to why the question is being asked. In this case, the *frum* superior should have had the sense to try to determine if a fellow Jew was in trouble for no real reason. Tzvi is not held responsible for the unfortunate outcome of his novel answer, especially since he answered under the pressure of being interrogated.

Even after Tzvi was caught in his lie, the *tefillin* did not have to be completely lost. They could have been X-rayed and returned.

In summary, the unfortunate turn of events cannot be attributed to Tzvi's part in the story. Even if Tzvi had received payment to take care of the *tefillin*, one could still claim that the subsequent events are not Tzvi's fault, and he would not have to pay for the *tefillin*.

---

36. *Niddah* 42b.

Is First Come Served First?

בְּשִׁבְתְּךָ בְּבֵיתֶךָ וּבְלֶכְתְּךָ בַדֶּרֶךְ
While you sit in your home, and while you walk on the way
(11:19)

Q Dovy, a member of Hatzolah, heard a call come over his radio for a wounded man who needed medical attention but was not in any danger as long as he would be tended to within a short period of time. Dovi responded and raced to the scene, but as he was about to enter the building, he noticed an old man who had fallen on the sidewalk. Dovy could tell that the elderly man was not injured, but the man asked Dovy to help him stand up and to walk him to the nearby bench so he could recover. Dovy knows that helping the old man will take him five minutes. From a halachic perspective, what should he do? Should he leave the case to which he was summoned in order to help the old man or should he apologetically leave the old man lying on the sidewalk in the hope that in another minute someone else will come by and help the man up?

A At which moment is a Hatzolah member considered "involved in a mitzvah"? Is it from the time that he starts heading toward his destination or only once he begins treating the patient?

The Gemara in *Succah*[37] discusses the source of the rule that one who is already involved in one mitzvah is exempted from

---
37. 25a.

performing a different mitzvah. It cites the *Baraisa* analyzing the the obligation to read the *Shema*: "While you sit in your home" excludes one who is involved in a mitzvah. "While you walk on the way" excludes a *chassan*. The *Ritva* explains that the *chassan* is not actually getting married now, because if he were, he would already be included in the exemption of one who is involved in a mitzvah. Rather the *Baraisa* is referring to a *chassan* who is on the way to get married and therefore preoccupied with his impending mitzvah. He is also included in those who are involved in a mitzvah.[38]

The *Amudei Aish*[39] writes that although traveling to perform a mitzvah is also a mitzvah, it is only a preparation for the mitzvah itself, and together they are not considered one long mitzvah.

Even if one would look at the traveling as the beginning of the mitzvah of *hatzalah*, perhaps once Dovy encountered the old man while already involved in the same kind of mitzvah, he should not pass over the mitzvah that has come to him first.[40]

Consider the following scenario:

A 16-year-old boy was crossing the street and was hit by a car. The boy was thrown quite a distance. With Heavenly grace, an intensive-care ambulance passed by within seconds of the collision, and bystanders flagged him down. The driver told them that he was already on his way to respond to a different call, but the people pleaded with him to attend to the boy who was just hit. The driver stayed and called for another ambulance to take the other call.

Did the ambulance driver act properly by treating the boy or should he have continued on to his initial destination?[41]

One might think that the ambulance should definitely have stayed with the boy because of the rule that one should not pass

---

38. The *Shulchan Aruch, Orach Chaim* 70:3, rules that in our times there is no exemption for a *chassan* to say *Shema*, as even under ordinary circumstances we do not have the proper level of concentration when we recite *Shema*.
39. Responsa, *Kuntras Mo'ed V'Shabbos* 5:21.
40. See *Yoma* 33b.
41. Assuming there was no greater threat to life in abandoning the first call.

over mitzvos.[42] However, the *Chacham Tzvi*[43] writes that this rule does not apply when both mitzvos are the same mitzvah, as in our case, where both were mitzvos of saving lives.

On the contrary, since the ambulance driver was involved in saving the first person, he should not have stopped to treat a patient who had not called for him, as one who is involved in one mitzvah is exempt from getting involved in another mitzvah.

If the boy could afford to wait for a different ambulance, or even if his status was just as desperate as the first patient, there would be a valid argument that the driver should not stop. However, if the boy's life is in danger and the first patient could wait, then it makes sense that the boy's *piku'ach nefesh* would outweigh the exemption of one who is involved in a mitzvah, and the ambulance driver should treat him first.

Another scenario to consider is if both patients are in similar conditions, and there is no threat to either of their lives by making them wait the extra time. In this case, the ambulance should continue to its original destination, because the patient for whom the ambulance was called has already been waiting for it to arrive. If another ambulance is sent at this point, the patient will wait much longer. The outcome would be unfair if one patient had to wait twice the length of time, and one patient did not have to wait at all. If the ambulance continues on, then both patients will have waited the same period of time.

The same should apply to Dovy and the older man as well; as there is no danger in having the older man wait, Dovy should apologize and attend to the original patient.

---

42. See *Yoma* 33b.
43. Responsa 106.

פרשת ראה
Parashas Re'ei

Free Rebate

עַשֵּׂר תְּעַשֵּׂר
Tithe you shall tithe
(14:22)

Q Miri gave a $500 check to a poor *kallah* to assist her in buying clothing for her wedding and deducted the sum from her *ma'aser* account. The *kallah* took the check to a clothing store and used it to help purchase the wardrobe she needed. Months passed, and Miri's check still didn't clear. Now, the check cannot be located. It is possible that the merchant passed the check on to his suppliers, or that he lost it himself. Does Miri have to give another $500 for *ma'aser*?

A Rav Elyashiv is quoted to have said that in such a case, she has fulfilled her obligation to *ma'aser*, even though the check never cleared.

The Gemara in *Gittin*[44] quotes the *Tanna* of the yeshivah of Rabbi Yishmael, that all who "shear" their assets to give to *tzedakah*

---
44. 7a.

are spared from the judgment of *Gehinnom*. This is comparable to two sheep that needed to cross a lake. One of the sheep had been shorn, and the other was very woolly. The shorn sheep walked through with ease, while his companion drowned. *Rashi* adds that just as a sheep who was shorn passes through easily, so too if one "shears" his assets for the benefit of *tzedakah* he will pass easily into the World to Come.

One may infer from this metaphor that unless one's assets have been decreased, they have not accomplished the mitzvah of *tzedakah*. However, in truth, Miri did "shear" her assets when she presented the $500 check. The poor *kallah* received the full value of Miri's generous gift. The fact that Miri's account was not diminished is due to the fact that someone else neglected to take the money. That does not detract from the fact that Miri gave the *kallah* the money that she needed to clothe herself. As far as Miri is concerned, she gave, and Hashem allowed her to retain her money.

A Matter of Heart

כִּי פָתֹחַ תִּפְתַּח אֶת יָדְךָ לוֹ ... דֵּי מַחְסֹרוֹ
You shall open your hand to him ... his requirement
(15:8)

Q A homeless person had nowhere to spend the night. He wants to know if it is permissible to go to the communal hospital and complain that he has chest pains in order to be admitted. That way he will be provided with a warm bed, a shower, and three nutritious meals. Is that considered stealing from communal funds?

A Even though it is the community's responsibility to ensure that the poor man has shelter and food to eat, nevertheless, the aforementioned scheme is stealing. The homeless person should bring his needs to the attention of the local Rav, who will look after the person's needs honestly without resorting to devious means.

If, however, the person is truly in need and there is no person or group who is in a position to help him, it may be permitted for him to feign chest pains, for the following reason:

The *Shulchan Aruch*[45] states unequivocally that every person must give *tzedakah*. If a person gives less than he should, *beis din* will force him to give an amount that they understand to be appropriate for him to give.

The *Rishonim*[46] argue as to whether or not *beis din* will confiscate belongings to that end as well. The *Shach*[47] quotes the *Bach's* ruling that *beis din* will even confiscate the person's money if he refuses to give it to *tzedakah*, but the *Shach* himself disagrees, as does the *Beis Meir*.[48]

The *Ketzos HaChoshen*[49] writes that a person's belongings are responsible to pay for his *tzedakah* obligations. The reason that *beis din* will not confiscate possessions in order to enforce *tzedakah* obligations is only because a person may choose the recipient of his *tzedakah*. The *Nesivos HaMishpat*[50] differentiates between absolute obligations — e.g., to a needy relative or the communal fund — and voluntary obligations to *tzedakah* — e.g., a personal pledge. The former are obligations that bind a person's assets, whereas the latter are not.

Accordingly, it might be permissible to feign chest pains since the community is obligated to shelter and feed their poor, and

---

45. *Yoreh De'ah* 248:1.
46. See *Ran, Kesubos* 18a in the pages of the *Rif*, and *Shulchan Aruch* ad loc., who is quoting the *Rambam*.
47. *Yoreh De'ah* ad loc. §4.
48. *Even HaEzer* 71 §2.
49. 290 §3.
50. §8.

therefore their resources have a responsibility to that end. Since this is an absolute obligation, they cannot claim that they wish to give their *tzedakah* elsewhere. Even though this bed is meant for a sick person, it is not considered depleting communal funds, but only transferring from one *tzedakah* to a different one.

It's Not an Expense — It's an Investment

נָתוֹן תִּתֵּן לוֹ
You shall surely give him
(15:10)

The *Ramban*[51] writes that one should never feel that he is losing out by giving *tzedakah*; on the contrary, one should look upon giving *tzedakah* as an opportunity to multiply his assets, as Hashem will repay him many times over. This is the lesson of the *pasuk*, נָתוֹן תִּתֵּן לוֹ וְלֹא יֵרַע לְבָבְךָ בְּתִתְּךָ לוֹ כִּי בִּגְלַל הַדָּבָר הַזֶּה יְבָרֶכְךָ ה' אֱלֹקֶיךָ בְּכָל מַעֲשֶׂךָ וּבְכֹל מִשְׁלַח יָדֶךָ — *You shall surely give him, and let your heart not feel bad when you give him, for in return for the matter, Hashem, your God, will bless you in all your deeds and in your every undertaking.*[52]

When one gives *tzedakah* begrudgingly, he violates the prohibition against having a heart that feels bad. The *Ha'amek Davar* explains that one should not even give the

---

51. *Hosafos* on *Sefer HaMitzvos* (*Shich'chas Lavim* 17).
52. *Devarim* 15:10.

slightest impression that he is not happy to give the *tzedakah*, as a heart that feels bad is apparent on one's face.

Zalman knew that old Solomon the miser always donates begrudgingly. Would it be forbidden to solicit a donation from him because of the prohibition of *lifnei iver*?

Certainly, one who scowls when giving *tzedakah* is even worse than one who merely lacks a positive attitude. The *Shulchan Aruch*[53] writes that one should give *tzedakah* with a pleasant countenance, with a joyous heart, and with a generous spirit. He should feel the petitioner's pain and impart words of encouragement. One who does the opposite has forfeited his reward. The *Shach* adds that even if the person donated great sums of money, he could still violate the prohibition of "having a heart that feels bad." Perhaps it would be better not to ask such a person for *tzedakah* at all. Should Zalman abstain?

If old Solomon would not give *tzedakah* altogether, he will have violated the even more severe prohibition against hardening his heart, in addition to losing out on the mitzvah of giving *tzedakah*. Therefore, it might seem that he would actually be better off giving the *tzedakah*, even if it is accompanied by a scowl, rather than not giving at all.

However, the matter is not that simple. The *Shevet HaLevi*[54] quotes the *Rambam*,[55] who writes that one is obligated to give *tzedakah* once one becomes aware of the poor person's need, if he has the potential to help him. The *Rashba*,[56] in contrast, maintains that one is only bound by the mitzvos regarding *tzedakah* if the poor man or his representative actually petitions him to give.

---

53. *Yoreh De'ah* 149:3.
54. Vol. 9, 199.
55. *Sefer HaMitzvos, Lavim* 232.
56. *Shevuos* 25a.

Rav Sternbuch[57] cites the *Maharil Diskin's* opinion, that one who refrained from donating *tzedakah* has only violated the prohibition of having a bad heart passively, whereas one who gave *tzedakah* with a bad feeling has actively violated the prohibition, which is obviously a greater sin.

For these reasons (the opinions of the *Rashba* and the *Maharil Diskin*), it seems that perhaps one should not solicit *tzedakah* from such a person, to prevent him from transgressing this sin.

The truth is, however, that one should approach even this type of person to donate, as every person has an obligation to give *tzedakah*. The one who solicits him is doing what he is supposed to do. If the donor chooses to give with a scowl, that is his *aveirah*, and one does not have to be concerned with the donor's shortcomings. One is only guilty of causing his friend to stumble when he is providing something that is solely an opportunity to sin. One who acts appropriately by collecting *tzedakah* for the needy is affording others the opportunity to perform a mitzvah. If his friend stumbles as a result, that is not the collector's responsibility.

Multiple Answers

לְמַעַן תִּזְכֹּר אֶת יוֹם צֵאתְךָ מֵאֶרֶץ מִצְרַיִם
So that you will remember the day of your departure from the land of Egypt

(16:3)

Q The father of one of the boys in Rabbi Katz's class gave the rebbi a set of *Mishnayos* to be used as an incentive. He suggested that Rabbi Katz ask his class a question

---

57. *Teshuvos VeHanhagos* 5:288.

and offer the *Mishnayos* as a prize to whoever answered correctly. If several boys answered correctly, then the *Mishnayos* would be raffled off among them.

Rabbi Katz posed the following question to his class: What is the *mitzvas asei* (positive commandment) that the Torah obligates us to fulfill every day?

(It is not the mitzvah of *tzitzis*, as only one who wears a four-cornered garment has to wear *tzitzis* on it. *Tefillin* are not worn on Shabbos and Yom Tov. *Berachos* in *davening* are only *d'Rabbanan*. *Bentching* is only applicable if someone ate bread. Learning Torah is a constant mitzvah without interruption. Hence the question is, indeed, a challenge.)

The answer to the riddle is based on the words of the *Rambam* in his introduction to his commentary on the *Mishnayos*, who writes that there is no other mitzvah that one is obligated to perform every single day, other than the mitzvah of saying *Krias Shema*. That is why Rabbeinu HaKadosh started the *Shas* with the mitzvah of *Shema*.

Only one student came up with the right answer. However, there were two other students who also came up with acceptable answers. One of them suggested that it is the mitzvah of *davening*, which according to the opinion of the *Rambam*, one is obligated to do every day; while the actual text of the *davening* is only *mi'd'Rabbanan* the act of *davening* is a *mitzvas asei*.[58] Another student proposed the mitzvah to remember *yetzias Mitzrayim*.[59]

These two answers are an apparent difficulty in the aforementioned *Rambam*, where he writes that only *Krias Shema* is obligatory every day. The *Pirchei Kehunah*

---

58. *Rambam, Hilchos Tefillah* 1:1.
59. *Rambam, Hilchos Krias Shema* 1:3.

resolves the apparent contradiction by pointing out that the mitzvah to *daven* is not explicit in the Torah, and is derived from the *pasuk and you shall serve...*,[60] which refers to *davening*. Regarding the mitzvah to remember *yetzias Mitzrayim*, the *Tz'lach* writes that according to the *Rambam*, that mitzvah is not counted among the 248 *mitzvos asei*.

Nevertheless, these two other answers are certainly valid, even if they are not what the rebbi was looking for. Should Rabbi Katz raffle off the *Mishnayos* among the three boys, or should the boy who discovered the *Rambam's* answer be awarded the prize without a raffle?

A The rebbi did not stipulate that the boys should answer the question specifically according to the *Rambam*, and essentially, the other two answers are correct, as well. Nevertheless, since the student who answered according to the *Rambam* has the *Rambam* to support his answer, and he had the Divine assistance to give that answer, his answer is superior to those of his friends, and he alone deserves the prize. At the same time, Rabbi Katz should award the other two boys a smaller prize for having given correct answers, as well.

---

60. *Shemos* 23:25.

פרשת שופטים
Parashas Shoftim

Early Bird?

צֶדֶק צֶדֶק תִּרְדֹּף
Righteousness, righteousness, shall you pursue
(16:20)

Q When Bracha Hoffman and Boruch Jacobs became engaged, their respective fathers met and agreed to buy the young couple an apartment. Each side committed to pay for half of the expenses, and pledged to try to find an apartment that would be suitable for the needs of their children. Rabbi Jacobs contacted a real-estate broker who described a very appealing apartment. The next phone call was to Mr. Hoffman to arrange a time to see the prospective apartment and to discuss the details. Mr. Hoffman mentioned that he had also heard of an apartment that sounded perfect for their children. The two set a meeting for later that evening to compare their findings.

The two *mechutanim* met. Each one had brought a layout of his respective apartment. It did not take long for them to realize that they had both heard about the same apartment! Two different brokers had suggested the same apartment, each to a different *mechutan*.

A week later, they closed the deal on the apartment. Now the question arose as to which broker deserved to collect the commission on the sale. Mr. Hoffman's broker had suggested the apartment first, before Rabbi Jacobs heard about it from his broker. Does he deserve the commission, or should both brokers divide the sum between themselves, as they both had a hand in the sale?

A This question was discussed by Rabbi Yisrael Grossman, in his *sefer Halichos Yisrael*.[61] He writes that when the fathers of the *chassan* and *kallah* buy an apartment for their children, they are considered like one person. Each side that receives an offer does so as an agent for the other, as that was their agreement. Therefore, when Mr. Hoffman heard about the apartment, it is as if Rabbi Jacobs heard about it as well, and when Rabbi Jacobs heard the offer from his broker, he was hearing about an apartment that had already been suggested to him. They are like two partners in business. When either partner earns a profit, it is shared because each one is acting on behalf of the partnership. Accordingly, the *Halichos Yisrael* concludes that Mr. Hoffman's broker deserves the entire commission.

However, with all due respect to Rabbi Grossman, it would seem that since neither *mechutan* has the right to act without permission from his counterpart, any offer has value only when it is actually heard by both *mechutanim*. Any suggestion that is heard by only one side is not relevant until the two of them can evaluate it together. Therefore, it would make sense that Mr. Hoffman's broker can only be considered as having suggested the apartment the evening that the two *mechutanim* met, and at that point, Rabbi Jacobs had already heard about the apartment from his own

---

61. 62.

broker. Accordingly, neither broker preceded the other in offering the apartment.

The obligation to pay a broker is derived from the halachah of one who enhances his friend's property. The property owner has to pay for the benefit that he reaped. In this case, neither broker actually benefited the *mechutanim* exclusively, since both proposals came to the table at the same time. Hence, the two brokers should share the commission on the apartment, because each *mechutan*, who is paying for half of the apartment, only has to pay half of the commission to the broker that he employed.

In summary, Rav Zilberstein maintains that the two brokers should divide the commission, while Rabbi Yisrael Grossman in his wonderful *sefer*, *Halichos Yisrael*, rules that the broker who suggested the apartment first should receive the entire commission.

One Fine Day ...

תָּכִין לְךָ הַדֶּרֶךְ
Prepare the way for yourself
(19:3)

Q The city had issued a warning to the residents that the bomb shelters should be completely emptied from any personal property, and any shelter that was found to contain storage would cause a fine to be imposed upon all the residents of that building. All the neighbors at 35 Ziditchov Street removed their *schach*, *succah* boards, and assorted paraphernalia from the communal shelter. One neighbor was too busy to remove his old broken couch and oven from the shelter. Sure enough, the city sent inspectors and found that the shelter had not been emptied. They issued a fine to every resident in the building. All the neighbors are demanding that the owner of the couch and the oven should pay everyone's fine. Does he indeed have to pay?

A The guilty neighbor must pay for everyone. He cannot claim that it is merely *grama*, because the shelter is communal property. Anyone who leaves his possessions there without everyone's permission has to pay rent for storing his belongings on his neighbors' property. In estimating the value of the rent, it would have to be at least the amount required to cover any losses that he caused the neighbors, including city fines.

Rav Chaim Kanievsky said that one who leaves his things in the shelter is a *rodef*,[62] because he is cluttering the shelter and thereby endangering lives. Any Rav should penalize the *rodef* to pay everyone's fine.

Coming Late for an Appointment

שֵׁן בְּשֵׁן
Tooth for tooth
(19:21)

Q Dr. Fine is a wonderful and dedicated dentist. If only his patients would all be just as wonderful! Dr. Fine ordered a crown for Mr. Kupp in Adar 5772, and despite the fact

---

62. One who pursues someone else to harm or kill him.

that the dentist's office called Mr. Kupp a few times to schedule an appointment to insert the crown, Mr. Kupp did not arrive for an appointment until Adar 5773. The doctor tried to locate the crown at that point, but after an entire year's time, he could not find it. Since Dr. Fine had to order another crown, he wants to know if he is permitted to charge Mr. Kupp for the lost crown in addition to the crown he installed.

First, it has to be established what the dentist's status is when he orders a crown for a patient. Does the dentist purchase the crown from the dental supply company and then sell it to the patient, or is he considered the patient's agent to purchase the crown, and the doctor is merely watching it for the patient before inserting it?

This would seem to be disputed among the *poskim*. The *Mahara Sasson*[63] writes that when one orders a *kesubah* from a *sofer* and the *sofer* writes it with his own materials, the *sofer* owns the *kesubah*, and he sells it to the husband. In contrast, the *Nesivos HaMishpat*[64] writes that if someone asks a craftsman to build him something, the craftsman is considered a worker and the object is the property of the one who ordered it. If he tells the craftsman to build something and "he will buy it from him," then the craftsman is a salesman. The Chazon Ish[65] concurs with the *Nesivos HaMishpat*.

The *Responsa Be'er Moshe*[66] details further guidelines as to when the craftsman is considered in the employ of the one who engaged his services. If the item that he fashions is suitable for anyone and the craftsman has a market to sell it to others, then he has the status of a vendor. If, however, the item that he creates is suitable only for the one who ordered it, e.g., custom-made

---

63. Cited by the *Ketzos HaChoshen* 339 §3.
64. 333 §15.
65. *Bava Kamma* 23:35.
66. Rav Moshe Danoshovsky, *Choshen Mishpat* 6:3.

cabinets, then he is considered a hired worker. Therefore, if one orders a *kesubah* from a *sofer*, the *sofer* is working for the one who ordered it. The *Mahara Sasson* refers to the *sofer* as a salesman only in regard to the obligation to pay him on time.

According to this, it follows that in the case of a crown that is custom made for this specific patient and is not saleable to anyone else, according to all opinions the dental supply company is working directly for the patient, and the dentist is merely an agent to procure the crown. Therefore, the patient has to pay for the lost crown as well.

Nevertheless, it would seem the dentist is still considered a paid watchman for the item with which he was entrusted — as are all paid craftsmen — and this is so especially since he is making a profit on the crown.

However, in this case, the dentist may very well be considered someone who is watching an item without being paid. The *Shulchan Aruch*[67] writes that all craftsmen are like paid watchmen, but once they instruct the customer to come pick up his items and pay his bill, or if they inform the customer that the job is done but he does not come to pick up his item, then the craftsman is merely considered one who watches something for free and has no liability if the item is lost. In this case as well, the dentist scheduled several appointments for Mr. Kupp to have the crown installed, and usually the patient is called the day before to remind him about the appointment. If the patient does not show up, the dentist can be considered only an unpaid watchman, and thus he is not liable for loss. Therefore, he may charge Mr. Kupp for both crowns.

---

67. *Choshen Mishpat* 306:1.

פרשת כי תצא
Parashas Ki Seitzei

Really Lost

וַהֲשֵׁבֹתוֹ לוֹ
And you shall return it to him
(22:2)

The drama began on a Motza'ei Shabbos at a crowded bus stop in Bnei Brak. The Goldsteins had spent a wonderful Shabbos with Mrs. Goldstein's parents, and were now waiting with their six children for the bus home to Elad. Many buses to other destinations stopped to pick up passengers, and in all of the activity nobody noticed when little Nosson Goldstein, all of 3 years old, mistook another lady for his mother and followed her onto a bus headed for Netivot! Nosson took a seat in the back of the bus and settled in for the trip. It was only 15 minutes later that he noticed that his family was not on the bus. By that time, the bus was already zooming down an intercity highway, and Nosson felt very alone. He started to wail in such a way that the entire bus was shaken. No one on the bus knew who the child was, or to whom he could be returned. Needless to say, they could not calm him down, either.

One *bachur* had an idea. His parents lived next to the bus stop in Bnei Brak, so he called them to ask if they could run down to check there if anyone had lost a small child. Sure enough, the *bachur's* phone rang after a minute and his father reported that pandemonium reigned at the bus stop, as they were desperately looking for a missing 3-year-old.

Both problems were solved at once! Now the Goldsteins knew where their child was, and the passengers on the bus knew where the child had to be returned. Now the question became whether the parents had to chase down the bus to recover their son, or if the bus should turn around and retrace its route, in order to return the child to his parents. In addition, if the bus does have to return to its point of departure, do the Goldsteins have to compensate the bus company and the passengers for any losses they incurred by being delayed in the process of returning their lost child?

The Chazon Ish[68] told Rabbi Dov Yaffe that when one finds a lost item, it is sufficient to inform the owner that his property is in the possession of the one who found it, and one does not have to deliver the item to the owner's home. However, that may only apply when it is equally difficult for either of them to travel to each other. If only the finder has a car, his mitzvah would include delivering the item as well, but he may stipulate that he wants to be paid for his travel expenses.

In this case, it would certainly be easier for the bus to turn around than for the parents to give chase in a taxi. This is especially true when the child is panicked; it might even develop into a

---

68. *Sefer Pe'er Ha'dor* 4, p. 217.

case of *piku'ach nefesh*. One may even do *melachah* on Shabbos to save a child in panic, lest the child die of fear.[69] All the passengers are obligated to assist the driver in this mitzvah of saving/returning the child, and therefore the bus should turn around and bring Nosson back to his parents.

As far as paying for the trip, the Goldsteins would have to pay only for the actual cost of the trip, but would not have to pay anything more than expenses. They do not have to reimburse the passengers, because one does not have to pay someone for having done the mitzvah of *hashavas aveidah*, and all the passengers have that status. Even if they suffered monetary losses in addition to or due to the delay, that is merely *grama*. The parents would not have to pay them unless they can be considered negligent for not having watched their child with more attention, in which case they would have an obligation to pay, *b'dinei Shamayim*.

However, one could debate whether the child is really considered a "lost item." A child is not his parents' property. Perhaps returning the child is just an act of kindness, for which one would be allowed to charge for his time.

The truth is that even if the child is not considered "lost property," the mitzvah of *hashavas aveidah* remains. The Gemara in *Bava Kamma*[70] states that if someone sees his friend lost in a vineyard, he may enter the vineyard and break twigs along the way in order to mark a path for his safe return, in order to help his friend find his way back out. The Gemara learns from the wording of the *pasuk* commanding the mitzvah of *hashavas aveidah* that one has a mitzvah to return his friend to himself, by putting him in the right place if he is lost. Accordingly, even if there is no mitzvah of *hashavas aveidah* in giving the child back to the parents, there is a mitzvah of *hashavas aveidah* in helping Nosson return to his proper place. That, of course, would be to his parents' open arms.

---

69. *Orach Chaim* 328:13; *Mishnah Berurah* §38.
70. 81b.

In summary, since it is easier for the bus driver to return to Bnei Brak rather than for Nosson's parents to come after the bus, and since all the passengers on the bus are equally responsible for returning the lost child, that is how they should proceed. Nosson's parents would at most have to reimburse the driver for the expenses involved in the extra journey, but perhaps the mitzvah is not to return the parents' child, but the child to his home, in which case the parents would not have to pay.

So Close

מוֹצָא שְׂפָתֶיךָ תִּשְׁמֹר
You shall observe what emerges from your lips
(23:24)

Q Chaim was walking to shul after *Shalosh Seudos*, in order to *daven* Maariv with the early minyan, when he spotted a $100 bill on the side of the street. He figured that he could not afford to pass up this find, so he covered the bill with his shoe, and waited for Shabbos to be over. He decided to *daven* Maariv at the later minyan, which began after Shabbos was over. As he stood there, he was approached by a poor man. The man informed him that he knew why Chaim was standing there. He had seen the bill earlier in the day, and had planned on taking it for himself after Shabbos was over.

Chaim believed him, but according to halachah the poor man did not have a right to the money, because merely seeing a lost object cannot acquire it for the finder.[71] However, Chaim felt that he did not want to deprive the man completely, so he promised that he would give him $20.

After Shabbos was over, Chaim bent down to retrieve his find, only to discover that although on one side it looked like a $100 bill, on the other side it was an advertisement for a printing shop. Chaim was disappointed that he had wasted his time, waiting for nothing.

The next day the poor man approached Chaim to collect the $20 that Chaim had promised that he would give him. Chaim said that he would give him the entire windfall, and showed him that it was just an advertisement. The poor man was unimpressed and insisted that he still wanted the $20 that he had been promised. Chaim maintained that had he known that the bill was not real, he never would have promised anything to the poor man. The man asserted that Chaim never stipulated that his promise was conditional, and now Chaim's promise is like a *neder* to *tzedakah*. Does Chaim have to pay him the $20?

The *Shulchan Aruch*[72] states that *tzedakah* is included in the halachos of vows, and if one says that he will give *tzedakah,* he creates a *neder* that he must fulfill.

Nevertheless, Chaim does not have to pay, because this is a case of *tzedakah* that was pledged by mistake. He never would have promised the poor man such a generous gift unless he had thought he had found so much money. The conditions of his gift were obvious to everyone, and he was not required to declare them verbally.

The *Rema*[73] rules that if someone mistakenly pledged to *tzedakah*, it is not binding. Similarly, the *Rema*[74] writes that one who

---
71. See *Bava Metzia* 2a.
72. *Yoreh De'ah* 257 §3.
73. Ibid., 258:2.
74. Ibid., 232:6.

says, "If Ploni was there, I will give 1,000 zuz to *tzedakah*," because he was certain that Ploni was not there, and he then discovers that Ploni was there, does not have to pay. It is considered a mistaken *neder*.

The *Shach*[75] quotes the *Mizrachi*[76] that in all laws of *nedarim* or sanctifications we rely on *umdena* (presumptions) to determine the person's intent at the time that he obligated himself. The same is true regarding gifts to the poor. Therefore, Chaim is exempt from paying.

Paying on Time

בְּיוֹמוֹ תִתֵּן שְׂכָרוֹ
On that day shall you pay his hire
(24:15)

Q Ari dedicated his life to the education of his sons and daughters, following in the ways of Avraham Avinu, of whom Hashem said: *For I have loved him, because he commands his children and his household after him.*[77] Hashem's love for Avraham stemmed from the fact that Avraham was transmitting his legacy to future generations. Indeed, Ari was very successful, and when his eldest daughter reached marriageable age, she truly personified all that a Jewish daughter should be.

The matchmakers, realizing what a "catch" she was, set straight to work, and before long, one of them

---

75. Ibid., 251§9.
76. Responsa *Siman* 53.
77. *Bereishis* 18:19.

succeeded in finding the girl's match, from the best of the *yeshivah bachurim*.

The families celebrated the engagement in a catering hall near their homes, and at the end of the evening the caterer came to request payment for his services. At the same time, the *shadchan* was standing nearby, eagerly awaiting his fee, but was too embarrassed to ask for it. Ari knows that the *shadchan* would really like to be paid now as well, but Ari had a problem. He only had $1,000 in his pocket. To whom should he give it; to the caterer or to the *shadchan*?

There is a mitzvah in the Torah to pay a worker's wages on time.[78] There are two types of *shadchanim*. One is a *shadchan* who was approached and contracted to find an appropriate match. That *shadchan* is like a hired worker, and should be paid on the day that the services were completed.[79] There is, however, a different kind of *shadchan*, one who, with Divine inspiration, had an idea, and offered the suggestion on his own initiative. The *Vilna Gaon*[80] writes that this *shadchan* is not a hired worker, but likened to one who planted a field that needed to be planted, without permission from its owner.[81] Such a person is to be paid in accordance with the owner's benefit, but is not considered a hired worker.

Responsa *Halichos Yisrael*[82] elaborates that a *shadchan* who initiates a match has no claim to be paid on the day the services were rendered. Rav Elyashiv proves this from a Gemara[83] that is also brought in *Shulchan Aruch*.[84] When one hires workers via an agent, and the agent stipulates that the one who sent him will

---

78. See *Bava Metzia* 113a.
79. Ibid. 63b.
80. *Choshen Mishpat* 87 §117.
81. *Bava Metzia* 101a.
82. *Siman* 1.
83. *Bava Metzia* 110-111.
84. *Choshen Mishpat* 339: 7.

pay the workers, there is no prohibition of delaying payment if one does not currently have the means to pay. Certainly in a case where the worker initiates his own job, there would likewise be no prohibition to delay the payment if the funds were not currently available.

Rav Elyashiv added that even if the *shadchan* was approached, as long as it was not stipulated that he would be paid upon the engagement, and if there is no such prevailing custom, one would not have to pay the *shadchan* until the wedding takes place! This is apparent from the *Terumas HaDeshen*[85] and the *Rema*[86] who write that the obligation to pay is after the wedding, and they do not differentiate between the types of *shadchanim*. Even if a *shadchan* was a hired worker, unless the prevailing custom is different, he would not have to be paid before the couple was married.

Accordingly, Ari should pay the caterer, since according to some *poskim* one must pay for rented property on the day that payment is due to avoid the prohibition of not paying on time (*bal talin*).[87] The *Ketzos HaChoshen*[88] writes that since *bal talin* is a Biblical prohibition, one should be stringent even on rentals. The *shadchan,* in contrast, will have to wait.

---

85. 25.
86. At the end of *Choshen Mishpat* 185.
87. See *Devarim* 24:15.
88. 339:1.

Each Person Is Punished for His Own Sin

אִישׁ בְּחֶטְאוֹ יוּמָתוּ
A man should be put to death for his own sin
(24:16)

Q Chatzkel was a distributor for an electronics company, and he traveled in the company's car from city to city, and from store to store, to accept orders. One day he was on the highway and realized that it was very close to sunset. He pulled over to the side of the road to *daven* Minchah. When he returned to his car to continue driving, he pulled away from the shoulder without fastening his seatbelt, intending to buckle up shortly. However, he was spotted by a police officer who pulled him over to write him a ticket. Driving without a seatbelt commands an exorbitant fine and taints the driver's record. Chatzkel pleaded for mercy, and he begged the policeman to issue a ticket for a less-serious offense. The officer understood that Chatzkel had gotten the message and decided to look for a less-serious offense. He began to inspect the car and he noticed that one rear light was not working. The ticket for that violation was less costly, and it would not appear on Chatzkel's driving record.

Because he does so much driving on their behalf, Chatzkel has an agreement with his employer that any tickets that are issued because of the condition of the company car are covered by the company. Tickets issued due to faulty driving are paid for by the driver. Can Chatzkel pass the ticket on to the company to pay, since the ticket was issued for the vehicle's broken light, or is it his own responsibility since he was stopped for driving without a seatbelt?

The *Rambam*[89] writes that if thieves accost a person entrusted with the safekeeping of valuable items, and the victim offers them the items in order to save himself, his liability depends on the following: If the victim is known to be wealthy, the thieves probably came to rob him, and he has to pay for the items that he used to appease them. If, however, he is not known to be wealthy, the thieves probably came to steal the items, and he would not have to reimburse the owner for having given them away.

In our case, the police stopped Chatzkel for his own infraction. The rear light would have gone unnoticed, and it was Chatzkel's infraction that caused the policeman to notice it. It would therefore seem that Chatzkel should have to pay the ticket.

However, the comparison is not exact. In the case of the thieves, the *shomer* handed the items to them. In our case, Chatzkel merely pleaded to be assigned a ticket with a lesser fine. The policeman noticed the broken rear light on his own.

Another reason to excuse Chatzkel is that when the company gave him a car without a working rear light, they obligated themselves to pay that fine. This is because they assigned him a car that did not satisfy traffic regulations. Thus, Chatzkel did not sacrifice the company's money to save his own; the company caused the damage to themselves.

Practically, Rav Nissim Karelitz ruled that Chatzkel does have to pay the ticket since it was his negligence that caused the policeman to pull him over.

---

89. *Hilchos She'eilah U'Pikadon* 5:3.

פרשת כי תבוא / Parashas Ki Savo

An Accessory to the Crime

וְאֶת לַחֲצֵנוּ
And our oppression
(26:7)

Q The Cohens lived very comfortably in their small apartment for several years, but after Hashem blessed them with many children, they began to feel cramped in their limited space. They wanted desperately to expand their apartment and saved a large sum of money to that end. Although they were required to have their neighbors sign an approval to allow them to build, their neighbors had committed themselves to willingly sign the papers when necessary. One day, Mrs. Cohen needed her vacuum cleaner, which she had lent to her neighbor, Mrs. Levy. Mrs. Levy was at work, and none of her family members would be home at this hour, but Mrs. Cohen had the key to the Levys' apartment, as well as permission to enter if the need arose. Mrs. Cohen let herself in and discovered Mrs. Sacker, who worked for the Levys cleaning their home. She was also a neighbor in the building. She was in the midst of robbing the Levy home! Mrs. Sacker was holding a large wad of bills that she had found hidden under the carpeting. The thief did not lose her cool, and she delivered an ultimatum to Mrs. Cohen. She threatened that if Mrs. Cohen would dare to breathe a word about what she had seen to anyone, Mrs. Cohen could forget about Mrs. Sacker agreeing to the desperately needed expansion of the Cohens' apartment. Mrs. Cohen now wants to ascertain if she has to warn Mrs. Levy about her cleaning lady's activities, even though by doing so she will be relinquishing any hope she had to enlarge her apartment. Is she allowed to keep quiet to avoid confrontation and the great loss that it will cause her?

The Gemara tells us that one's own[90] belongings take precedence to those of others. In other words, if a person finds a lost item, and the effort and expense involved in returning it to its owner will cause a loss to the one who found it, he is exempt from fulfilling the mitzvah of *hashavas aveidah*, because one is not required to impoverish himself to perform it. This ruling is cited in *Shulchan Aruch*[91] as well.

In light of this halachah, the point could be argued that although one would have to report a robbery to one's friend in accordance with the mitzvah of *hashavas aveidah*, if such an act would cause him a loss, he would not have to do so. In this case, Mrs. Cohen's report will cause her to lose her chance to expand her apartment, as well as depreciating the value of her property,

---

90. *Bava Metzia* 30a.
91. *Choshen Mishpat* 264:1.

as the Sackers will never agree to let her build. Thus, it might seem that Mrs. Cohen could remain silent.

The truth is that Mrs. Cohen must inform Mrs. Levy of what she witnessed. This is not only an issue of *hashavas aveidah*, but of being an accessory to the crime. By remaining silent, Mrs. Cohen is becoming a partner in Mrs. Sacker's robbery. By keeping the crime a secret, Mrs. Cohen is covering up for the thief in order to expand her own apartment!

Tosafos[92] states explicitly that when one knows that an *aveirah* will be committed and does nothing to prevent it, it is considered as if he himself perpetrated that *aveirah*. In such an instance, his silence is not merely a passive act, but it is as if he himself took an active role in the transgression! This teaches us the severity of allowing an *aveirah* to be committed without attempting to stop it.

However, *Tosafos* is discussing someone who knows that his friend wishes to commit a forbidden act, e.g., enter into a forbidden relationship. This ruling would not necessarily apply to a case involving money. For example: Akiva's friend lost his dog and Akiva, a respected judge, knows where the dog can be found, but it would be disgraceful for Akiva to return the dog himself, Akiva is not obligated to return the dog to the owner. Likewise, if Akiva sees someone preparing to steal his friend's lost dog, he is not obligated to demean himself in order to prevent the thief from taking it.

One could infer from *Tosafos* that if one was in the process of recovering his own lost object, and suddenly saw someone trying to steal his friend's lost object, there would also be no obligation to try to prevent him from doing so at his own expense. In such a case, a person's own property takes precedence. The exemption from *hashavas aveidah* would extend to not having to prevent the robbery as well.

In our case, however, the situation is different. In the case in *Tosafos*, there was an exemption from the mitzvah of saving his friend's property, whereas in our case Mrs. Cohen is abetting the

---

92. *Shevuos* 30b, d"h Aval.

thief by yielding to her threat. Consider the following case: A man was desperate for money and he caught a thief in the act of stealing. If the thief would offer him a large sum of money to keep quiet, his own desperate need would not justify his silence regarding the crime. Similarly, Mrs. Cohen will have to inform her neighbor as to her discovery even it means that she forgoes permission to enlarge her apartment.

Loyal Support

אֲשֶׁר ... יָקִים אֶת דִּבְרֵי הַתּוֹרָה הַזֹּאת
Who will ... uphold the words of this Torah
(27:26)

Q Kollel Chazon Moshe opened its doors in the year 5764. The *rosh kollel* was a charismatic and energetic *marbitz Torah* who attracted very fine *avreichim*. Menachem Presser devotedly sent a check every month to help cover the *kollel's* budget. One day, 10 years after the *kollel* had opened, the *rosh kollel* regretfully announced that he would be closing the *kollel* for reasons beyond his control. Menachem selected another *kollel* to continue sending his monthly contribution for *hachzakas haTorah*.

One and a half years later, the original *kollel* was able to reopen, and the *rosh kollel* sought out his original supporters to help the *kollel* get back on its feet. Menachem does not have the financial ability to support both *kollelim*, and is unsure if he should renew his support for Kollel Chazon Moshe, or if he should continue to support the *kollel* to which he has been contributing for the past year and a half. Where should he send his monthly check?

The *Shulchan Aruch*[93] discusses the case of a person who assumed the role of performing a particular mitzvah in the community, e.g. *gelilah*, and was forced to stop due to infirmity, or due to poverty such that he could not afford to continue paying for the mitzvah. Consequently, the mitzvah was transferred to someone else. The first person eventually recovered and desired to have the mitzvah restored to him. If at the time that he stopped he had the ability to continue and simply did not wish to do so, then he has lost his claim to the mitzvah. If, however, he was truly unable to maintain his standing, and now he can, then the mitzvah should be returned to him.

The *Mishnah Berurah* records a similar case of a *chazzan* who fell ill. The community may appoint a new *chazzan*, but when the first *chazzan* recuperates, his position should be returned to him.

Perhaps the same principle would apply in this case, as well. If the original *kollel* closed for reasons beyond its control but held out hope that it would reopen at a future date, that is similar to someone who fell ill and whose original status deserves to be reinstated upon his recovery. If the *kollel* had closed indefinitely, then it has lost its standing, similar to a *chazzan* who moved out of the community, or someone who willingly gave up his custom to perform a communal mitzvah.[94]

In truth, there is a difference between the two cases. A *chazzan*, or anyone who has tenure to perform a communal mitzvah, already holds the position and has the right to maintain it, as well. In contrast, the *kollel* has no claim on its benefactors' money. Had Menachem wished to transfer his monthly donations to another

---

93. *Orach Chaim* 153:22.
94. See *Mishnah Berurah* §115.

institution, even while the *kollel* was still open, he certainly could have done so. He has no financial obligation to any specific *kollel*; each donation is a new act of generosity. Therefore, if the original *kollel* closed, and Menachem has already transferred his *tzedakah* elsewhere, perhaps he should not withdraw his support from them.

This case might be compared to the Gemara in *Yoma*[95] which discusses someone who set aside a sheep for his *korban pesach*, and the animal was subsequently lost. After the man set aside a replacement *korban*, the original animal was found. The halachah is that the owner may choose which of the two sheep he wants to offer as his *korban pesach*.[96] One could extrapolate to this case that Menachem could donate to whichever *kollel* he chooses.

However, these two situations are not identical, either. In the case of a *korban*, each animal has already been sanctified as a *korban*. Thus, the owner has the right to choose between them. In this case, neither *kollel* has attained any special status vis-à-vis its supporters. The question is an ethical one. Hence it is logical to compare it to the case of someone who maintained a communal position, as the second *kollel* would never have received Menachem's support had the first *kollel* not closed. Since the first *kollel* closed only because it was forced to do so, it is proper that Menachem reinstate his support once it reopens.

---

95. 62a. See *Panim Me'iros* Vol. II, 125.
96. The remaining animal is left to pasture until it is blemished; it is then sold, with its proceeds to be used to buy an animal that will be brought as a *korban shelamim* (*Pesachim* 9:6).

Miss Judged

בָּנֶיךָ וּבְנֹתֶיךָ נְתֻנִים לְעַם אַחֵר
Your sons and daughters will be given to another people
(28:32)

Q Avi was celebrating the week of his *sheva berachos* and was enjoying lunch with his *kallah* in his mother-in-law's kitchen. While they were eating, his mother-in-law asked if he had $50 to lend her until the evening. Avi answered that he did and drew a crisp bill from his wallet. He turned to his *kallah* and whispered, "Let's see when I get this one back." His *kallah* smiled and did not say anything.

His mother-in-law was shocked. How could Avi suspect that she would not pay him back? What had she done to deserve such suspicion? And in addition, how could her own daughter, who knew how carefully their family behaved regarding any financial dealings, have remained silent in response to her husband's comment? How could she not defend them from such a vicious accusation? The mother-in-law did not say anything at the time, but her blood began to simmer.

After two days of stewing, she could not contain herself any longer, and she approached her daughter to discuss Avi's horrible insult. At first the *kallah* could not remember the comment. She asked her mother if she was sure that her *chassan* had insulted her. This just increased her mother's already volatile temper. She thought that her daughter was trying to protect her new husband and had no regard for her own mother's pain. The mother repeated the *chassan's* insult to her daughter to remind her how he had cast aspersions on her trustworthiness.

The daughter apologized immediately for the pain that had been caused, but explained that her mother had not understood her new son-in-law's words. As it happened, Avi had a habit of marking any bill that passed through his hands. He liked to see if the money that passed from person to person would eventually come back to him. The very morning that he loaned his mother-in-law the money, he had a $20 bill returned to him! He had marked the bill that he loaned to his mother-in-law as well, and that was what he meant when he said, "Let's see when I get this one back." His comment was completely innocuous when understood in the proper context.

Avi's mother-in-law wants to know if she violated the mitzvah of judging her son-in-law favorably.[97] Does the mitzvah still apply, in a case where her daughter's explanation was something she never could have imagined? Second, does she have to ask Avi for *mechilah* for not having judged him favorably? Is the obligation to judge someone favorably a mitzvah between man and his fellow man, in which case it would be appropriate to ask for *mechilah*, or is it a mitzvah between man and Hashem, and *teshuvah* is sufficient?

A Rabbeinu Yonah writes in *Sha'arei Teshuvah*[98]:

If someone is present when his friend says something or does something, and his words or actions could be assessed in a positive way, if the friend is a God-fearing individual there is a mitzvah to judge him favorably, even if it seems more likely

---

97. *Vayikra* 19:15.
98. *Sha'ar* 3:218.

that his words or actions were inappropriate. If the person is average, and is usually careful not to sin but sometimes fails, one should still decide that his words or actions were not inappropriate, as *Chazal* teach us,[99] "One who judges others favorably, will be judged favorably (by Heaven)," and this is the Torah's obligation to judge others favorably.[100] Even if it is more likely that his words or deeds were inappropriate, it is still proper to leave it in doubt, and not decide that it was inappropriate.

In this case, the positive way of assessing Avi's words was very unlikely, and therefore it would seem that the mother-in-law did not have a mitzvah to judge him favorably. However, the Chofetz Chaim[101] writes that it is a good character trait to judge others favorably, even if it is more likely that the negative explanation is true. The Gemara in *Shabbos*[102] cites several stories that support this point.

It appears that judging favorably is a mitzvah between man and his fellow man, as *Rashi*[103] classifies it under the heading of bringing peace between man and his fellow. When one does not attribute ill intent to his friend's actions and assumes that he was forced to act that way or that he intended to do something good, that promotes peace between people.

In addition, we find that when Eli the Kohen Gadol falsely suspected Chanah of being drunk, he blessed her that Hashem should grant her request.[104] The Gemara[105] learns from this episode that whoever suspects someone else falsely must bless that person. That would certainly imply that the sin of suspecting someone

---

99. *Shabbos* 127b.
100. *Vayikra* 19:15.
101. *Hilchos Lashon Hara, Klal* 3, *Be'er Mayim Chaim* §10.
102. 127b.
103. *Be'er Mayim Chaim* §10.
104. *Shmuel I* 1:17.
105. *Berachos* 31b.

is between man and his fellow man. Although one could argue that Eli had actually accused Chanah of being drunk, and therefore he had certainly slighted her and had to appease her, the Gemara still implies that the suspicion alone is sufficient to require appeasement.

In short, Avi's mother-in-law cannot be faulted for her conclusion, but she would have done better had she indeed given him the benefit of the doubt.

פרשת נצבים
Parashas Nitzavim

Mighty Fine Wine

הַנִּסְתָּרֹת לַה' אֱלֹקֵינוּ
The hidden [sins] are for Hashem
(29:28)

Q When Aryeh came home from shul on Shabbos night, he was met by the heartwarming sight of a beautifully set table. In the center of the table there was a special bottle of wine. Aryeh read the label of the bottle aloud: "The Wine of Salvation." There was a picture of a *tzaddik* on the label, and underneath, a description of the contents. This wine contained within it some of the actual wine that the *tzaddik* had used for *Kiddush* and *Havdalah*!

Aryeh wondered where his wife had gotten such a unique bottle of wine. She replied that she had participated in a fund-raising event sponsored by a certain *tzedakah* organization. She added that she heard that one who drinks from this special wine can merit special Divine Providence. Perhaps the wine would be a *segulah* to help them find *shidduchim* for their two daughters, who had been waiting for so long to meet their true *zivuggim*.

Aryeh's eyes lit up, and he made *Kiddush* on the wine with great emotion. When he finished reciting the *Kiddush*, he drank the entire cup of wine. During the *seudah*, Aryeh drank another two small cups, and with each cup he *davened* to Hashem that he should be *zocheh* to marry off his daughters.[106] This scene repeated itself at the day *seudah* as well, and finally, at *Havdalah*, Aryeh finished the bottle.

After *Havdalah*, Aryeh asked his wife why the organization had given her the bottle. She responded that they had announced that they were giving out only 20 bottles, and whoever donated at least $1,000 would receive a free bottle.

Aryeh jumped out of his seat. He could not believe that his wife had donated so much money without his consent. He already gave generously to other *tzedakos*, and the additional thousand dollars was way beyond their budget. When he asked his wife why she had not told him how much the bottle cost before he opened it, she responded that she did not want to talk about money on Shabbos, and innocently thought that Aryeh would have agreed that it was well worth the money.

His wife was sorely mistaken. Aryeh phoned the head of the organization that night. He insisted that they return his wife's check, and he would pay them for the bottle of wine. The halachah explicitly states in the *Shulchan Aruch*[107] that one who collects *tzedakah* may not accept a large donation from a woman without her husband's permission, and doing so is tantamount to stealing.

---

106. See *Halichos Shlomo, Tefillah* 14:11.
107. *Yoreh De'ah* 248:4.

The fund-raiser readily agreed to return the check, as soon as Aryeh would return the bottle of special wine! Aryeh admitted that he had drunk the wine, but defended himself by explaining that he never would have done so if he would have known how much it cost!

The fund-raiser apologized, but explained that each bottle was worth at least $1,000 to them, as they had sold the other 19 bottles for that amount or more. If Aryeh could not produce the bottle, he had no right to ask for his money back. Who is right?

If, in fact, the wine has a market value of $1,000, as people who believe in its *segulos* would be willing to pay that amount for the unique wine, then Aryeh cannot ask for his money to be returned, because he received full value for his money, i.e., a bottle of wine that has a market value equivalent to the value of his wife's check.[108]

However, if there is no market for such wine, as people would not be willing to pay 100 times the actual price of such a bottle, and one could receive such a bottle only by donating to the *tzedakah* organization, then Aryeh could request that his money be returned. In this case, the wine is not being sold, but being given as a gift in return for a large donation, the size of which Aryeh does not authorize his wife to give. Then Aryeh would have to pay only the actual price of the wine, and the *tzedakah* organization would have to return the remainder of his donation.

---

108. Editor's Note: This case is not similar to the question of the man who unknowingly borrowed a very expensive bottle from his friend (see "Valuable Wine," p. 149), because in that case he asked for a simple wine and had no idea that he had received something radically different. In this case, the man knew exactly what he had received; he just did not know how much it cost.

Who Is Fooling Whom?

וְהַנִּגְלֹת לָנוּ וּלְבָנֵינוּ

But the revealed [sins] are for us and our children

(29:28)

Q Dan Goodman, an affluent stockbroker, wished to build a home in *Eretz Yisrael*. Since his nephew, Joey, was a successful contractor living in *Eretz Yisrael*, it was only natural that Dan should hire him to build his dream home. Dan was very specific in instructing Joey that he wanted to spare no expense. All the materials should be the very finest, and all the workers should be expert craftsmen. Dan would pay any price to ensure that his house would be constructed with top quality.

Joey understood that this was a once-in-a-lifetime opportunity to earn a fortune. He carefully followed his uncle's instructions and researched the prices of the most-expensive materials. At the same time, he also researched the least-expensive materials. Not having been raised with Torah values, he proceeded to buy the cheapest materials available, but charged his uncle the highest prices. Joey pocketed the difference.

Dan knew nothing about construction and had no inkling of his nephew's deception. Finally, the building was complete, and Joey invited his uncle to tour his dream (or nightmare, as the case was) home. Joey had affixed a fancy facade, and his uncle effusively praised the workmanship, never suspecting that he had been fooled.

Two years passed, and no unusual problems surfaced while Dan enjoyed his new home. Joey, in contrast, began to have some major problems. He suffered a few setbacks in his work, and his financial situation deteriorated daily. During this period in his life, Joey slowly began to come closer to *Yiddishkeit*, and he decided to discuss his financial difficulties with one of the *tzaddikim* of the generation. The *tzaddik* suggested that Joey engage in some soul-searching to try to pinpoint any notable wrongdoings. Perhaps Joey had cheated someone in the past, and that was causing his fortune to dwindle.

Joey did not have to look too far back. He seriously regretted his dishonesty, but had no idea how he could rectify the situation. Of course, he would have to find some way to return the extra money that he had charged his uncle for the expensive materials that he had never purchased, but did he have to return the money he had spent on the inexpensive materials as well, as his uncle had specified that he did not want to use materials of such cheap quality? Does Joey also have to refund his builder's fee? The most aggravating question is, does Joey have to confess his dishonesty to his uncle? (It should be noted that although Joey used cheap materials, the house was not made out of cardboard, and would certainly serve his uncle for many years to come.)

First of all, Joey should engage the services of an expert contractor to provide an exact evaluation of the current building's value, and the difference between that price and what Joey charged. The discrepancy should be returned to Dan.

The Gemara in *Yevamos*[109] teaches that one may alter facts for the sake of keeping peace. If Joey were to confess his wrongdo-

---
109. 65b.

ing to his uncle, it would probably destroy their relationship and cause a tremendous rift between them. Therefore, while Joey must confess the truth to his uncle and express his incredible regret for what happened, he may temper his confession by saying that he relied on others who promised him that he was receiving premium-quality materials, but he recently discovered that he had been fooled. Hence, he begs his uncle's forgiveness for his negligence. [In truth, Joey did rely on false information from his *yetzer hara* (evil inclination), which assured him that he was doing nothing wrong. Now he realized that he had been fooled, and he never should have given in to his greed.] This approach will allow Joey to repent, while preserving his relationship with his uncle.

Teshuvah Pays

וְאַתָּה תָשׁוּב
And you shall return
(30:8)

Q Dov foolishly "borrowed" Meir's CD player without permission, and subsequently lost it. He is too embarrassed to admit his misdeed, yet he has to return that which he stole. He would like to invite Meir to his house for a delicious meal, free of charge. In that way he will have paid off his debt, as the *Rema*[110] rules that when one invites his friend for a meal he is allowed to charge the guest for the food. Would that be an acceptable way of making amends?

---

110. See *Rema, Choshen Mishpat* 246:17.

A The halachah that one could charge his guest for the meal that the latter has eaten does not apply in all cases. The *Aruch HaShulchan*[111] writes that if it appears that the guest has been invited for a free meal, he may not be charged. The *Rema* is only addressing a situation where it might be assumed that the meal is in return for payment. One who has been extended a friendly invitation or is a steady guest would not have to pay.

The *Levush* also writes that one could charge his friend only if he did not invite him in the way that one invites a guest, but rather he feeds him without having invited him.[112]

The *Aruch HaShulchan* adds that even if he has to pay, it is at a discounted price. The *Machaneh Ephraim*[113] explains that one could claim that he would have eaten less had he known that he would have to pay. He only has to pay according to the standard that he usually eats, even though he enjoyed the meal fully.[114]

Therefore, the possibility of payment in this way could only be a consideration if Dov will serve Meir a meal outside the context of a free invitation, and Meir will have been spared an expense equivalent to the value of his CD player.

Even so, Dov should not repay the theft in such a manner. The Mishnah in *Demai*[115] states that a person who hosts a Kohen or Levi at his table may not feed him *ma'aser* without informing him. The *Mishnah Rishonah* explains that by not informing him, his host is tricking him, because the man thinks he is eating his host's food, when really he is eating food that is rightfully his.

In our case as well, Meir will think he is benefiting from Dov, when in truth he is eating the value of his own CD player. In

---

111. 246 §19.
112. See also *K'sav Sofer, Choshen Mishpat* 21, who quotes the *Ran*.
113. *Nizkei Mamon* 3.
114. This can be proven from the case of orphans who *shechted* and ate a cow that they found in their father's yard, thinking that it was their father's. If they discovered that the cow was really borrowed, they only have to pay two-thirds of the price of the meat to the owner, because had they known that it didn't belong to their father, they would not have eaten such expensive fare (*Bava Kamma* 112a).
115. 4:4.

addition, Dov has not really paid back his debt because he will undeservedly earn Meir's appreciation in return for the meal.

Rav Moshe Feinstein[116] wrote to someone who had stolen from a *tzedakah* organization, that if one donates anonymously to a charity from which he has stolen, it can be considered that he has returned what he has stolen. If, however, they will consider it a new donation, and honor him and show appreciation for his kindness, it cannot be considered that he has returned his theft. In our case as well, if Meir will feel gratitude toward Dov, Dov has not really given Meir that which he owes him.

If he is too embarrassed to return the cost of the CD player, Dov should do what it says in *Shulchan Aruch HaRav*[117]: Dov should slip extra money into the sum that he gives Meir in regular business transactions, or entrust the money to someone else to add to his dealings with Meir. Alternatively, he could slip the money into Meir's pocket when he is not looking, in a place that Meir will definitely find it.

---

116. *Igros Moshe, Choshen Mishpat* 1:86.
117. *Hilchos Geneivah* 8, based on *Bava Metzia* 64a.

פרשת וילך
Parashas Vayeilech

Everyone Makes Mistakes

וְעַתָּה כִּתְבוּ לָכֶם
So now, write ... for yourselves
(31:19)

Q Eytan Sofer had just finished his thirteenth *Sefer Torah*. The *Sefer Torah* was very beautiful indeed, and was sold for a very handsome sum. The *sofer* wanted the client to know how confident he was that the *Sefer Torah* was of the highest caliber. Eytan agreed to refund $100 for any mistake that was found!

The purchaser had the *Sefer Torah* checked, and sure enough a mistake was discovered in *Parashas Toldos*.[118] Instead of writing, אַתָּה עַתָּה בָּרוּךְ ה׳, the *sofer* had written, עַתָּה אַתָּה בָּרוּךְ ה׳. He had reversed two words! Is that considered as if he made two mistakes,

---
118. *Bereishis* 26:29.

and he has to return $200, or is that called one mistake, and he has to return only $100?

A The crux of the issue is that there are definitely two mistakes that have to be corrected in the *Sefer Torah*, but they are rooted in the single mistake of the *sofer*. The *sofer* made one mistake by reversing the order of the words, which caused him to write two words improperly.

The *Shulchan Aruch*[119] rules that a *Sefer Torah* that was found to have three mistakes must be edited completely before it is used, since its status has been designated as certainly containing mistakes. The *Aruch HaShulchan*[120] writes that some questioned why three mistakes in a *Sefer Torah* are enough to confer such a status on the *Sefer Torah*. When a food is found to be infested with worms, it is not halachically considered to be infested unless the food itself was the source of infestation.[121] If bugs came into the food from an external source, they would not change the food's status. The *Sefer Torah* was certainly not the source of its errors, so why should it be labeled as if it was? The *Aruch HaShulchan* writes that it is not the *Sefer Torah* that is suspect, but rather the *sofer*. He is the source of his mistakes, and the *Sefer Torah* he produced must be examined because of his status, since now his writing has been found suspect to contain mistakes!

According to the explanation that the errors in a *Sefer Torah* are a reflection of the one who wrote it, it makes sense that in our case it would only be considered one mistake, as the *Sefer Torah* reflects that the *sofer* erred just once. The *sofer* wanted the purchaser to have confidence in the *sofer's* talents, and if so, there is only one "strike" to hold against him. Therefore, perhaps it would be sufficient to return just $100.

On the other hand, since there are two corrections that need to be made, and it is possible that they would have caught only

---

119. *Yoreh De'ah* 279:3.
120. Ad loc.
121. *Yoreh De'ah* 84.

one of them, and then the *Sefer Torah* would have remained *pasul*, the additional mistake increased the chances of the *Sefer Torah* remaining unkosher. Perhaps they are considered two separate corrections, and each one of them should require the *sofer* to pay its own penalty.

However, it seems that the *sofer* never really intended to pay for his mistakes. He just wanted to show what an expert *sofer* he was. Therefore, in our case, it would seem that we should view it as only one mistake, since it was really only a single error, and it would be sufficient to pay the buyer $100.

Cover-Judging

וְעַתָּה כִּתְבוּ לָכֶם
So now, write ... for yourselves
(31:19)

Q One of the shul members donated several sets of *sefarim* on condition that they would never be sold. Recently, those *sefarim* have been reprinted with nicer letters and a layout that is more pleasing to the eye. May the *gabbai* of the shul sell the original *sefarim* to antique collectors in order to fund the purchase of newer versions of the *sefarim*?

A Yeshivah Eitz Chaim is in close proximity to the Machaneh Yehudah marketplace in Yerushalayim. After several terrorist attacks that took place in the vicinity, parents were afraid to send their children to learn there. Rav

Elyashiv ruled that it is permitted to sell the yeshivah building and use the money to build a *cheder* and yeshivah elsewhere. This is despite the fact that it was written in stone on the yeshivah's walls that the building should never be sold; this directive was only relevant as long as the building served its function as a yeshivah. Once it could no longer serve its purpose, it could be assumed that the original donor would want the building to be sold.

The same should apply to this case as well: the *sefarim* should be sold in order to perpetuate the purpose of the one who donated them.

Rabbi Akiva Eiger[122] gave specific instructions to his son regarding the printing of *Responsa Rabbi Akiva Eiger*:

> I beseech you, my beloved son, to pay close attention that the paper should be beautiful, the ink black, and the letters pleasing. In my opinion, the soul is impressed, the mind is broadened, and the concentration is enhanced when one learns from a beautiful and graceful *sefer*. These factors awaken and bring joy to the soul. The opposite is true when the conditions are reversed, and the print is smudged. It is almost along the lines of what *Chazal* teach us about one who learns without sweetness …. Proper concentration and joy are as essential to one's learning as the soul and the life force are to the body.

These words of Rabbi Akiva Eiger prove that beautiful *sefarim* are indeed superior to those that have lesser esthetic appeal.

Rav Chaim Kanievsky was asked if the old *Megillas Esther* in the Lederman shul could be replaced, as many of its letters had begun to crack. Rav Chaim answered that as long as the old *megillah* could be repaired, they should not sell it. As long as the *megillah* is kosher, it is serving its purpose in its full capacity, and should

---

122. Brought in the introduction to *Responsa Rabbi Akiva Eiger*.

not be replaced. This is not the case with *sefarim*, whose beauty is integral to their purpose: to facilitate learning with great desire, as Rabbi Akiva Eiger taught us.

A Lifesaving Sefer Torah

וְעָנְתָה הַשִּׁירָה הַזֹּאת לְפָנָיו לְעֵד כִּי לֹא תִשָּׁכַח מִפִּי זַרְעוֹ

Then this song shall speak up before it as a witness, for it shall not be forgotten from the mouth of its offspring

(31:21)

Q Mr. Horowitz is a Holocaust survivor who lost his entire family in the Nazi devastation. After the war he remarried, and he and his wife were blessed with a baby girl. Years passed and his daughter was *niftar* without having had any children. After all of his suffering, Mr. Horowitz felt very broken, and in an attempt to alleviate some of his pain he commissioned the writing of a beautiful *Sefer Torah* in memory of his children. He lent the *Sefer Torah* to the shul in which he *davened*, and they gratefully used the *Sefer Torah* every Shabbos.[123]

A few years later, Mr. Horowitz relocated to a different city, and after he was confident that he would remain there, he asked Shimon, one of the members

---

123. The *Midrash* (*Bamidbar Rabbah* 14:6) says that it is a special merit for one who does not have children to commission the writing of *sefarim* and to then lend them to others.

of his new shul, to approach the *gabbai* of the previous shul on his behalf, to request that his *Sefer Torah* be returned to him so that he could transfer it to his new shul. Mr. Horowitz stressed the urgency of his request by saying that he felt that his *Sefer Torah* is all that he has in the world to remind him of his children, and that having it in his shul was a matter of *piku'ach nefesh*.

Shimon traveled to Mr. Horowitz's previous shul and informed the *gabbai* that Mr. Horowitz would like to have his *Sefer Torah* in the shul in which he *davens*, detailing the urgency of the matter. The *gabbai* refused to discuss the issue. He insisted that the *Sefer Torah* had been lent to them, and they had the right to continue using it!

Shimon felt that if he would return home without the *Sefer Torah*, it would be too much for the elderly Mr. Horowitz to endure, and it might actually cause his demise. Considering the situation, Shimon believed that the obstinate *gabbai* left him no choice but to visit a local hardware store and return with a large pair of clippers. When the shul was empty, he clipped the lock of the *aron kodesh* in order to retrieve Mr. Horowitz's *Sefer Torah*. Suddenly, he heard people coming. He quickly closed the *paroches* to cover up his work, and intended to wait for a more opportune moment. In the meantime, a childhood friend of the *gabbai* came into the shul. Shimon asked him to try to convince the *gabbai* to return Mr. Horowitz's *Sefer Torah*. It took 40 minutes, but in the end, the *gabbai* relented and agreed to part with the *Sefer Torah*.

Shimon wants to know if he has to pay for the broken lock. After all, at the time that he broke the lock, he was engaged in a mission of *piku'ach nefesh*, and therefore he should be exempt according to the rule of "All who save are exempt."[124]

---

124. See *Bava Kamma* 117b.

There are three issues that need to be clarified:

1. Was the *gabbai* obligated to return the *Sefer Torah* when the owner requested it back?
2. If the *gabbai* is obligated, but he refuses to return it, is Shimon exempt from paying damages when he takes the law into his own hands?
3. Is Shimon exempt from paying damages because of the Rabbinic enactment that all who are involved in rescue are exempt from paying damages?

The *Rishonim* disagree as to whether when one loans an item for an unspecified length of time, the loan is for a period of at least 30 days, or whether the owner can immediately request the return of his item. The *Shulchan Aruch*[125] rules that he can. The same should apply to a *Sefer Torah*. The *Shulchan Aruch*[126] writes that one who lent his house to a shul and subsequently had a fight with one of the members cannot prevent his adversary from entering the shul in his home, unless he prohibits the entire congregation from entering. The *Sha'ar HaTziyun* explains that he may place this ban effective immediately, as an item loaned for an unspecified amount of time may be collected immediately.

However, not all cases are equal. The *Baraisa* in *Maseches Smachos*[127] teaches that one who lends his cloak to his friend who is going to pay a *shivah* call in a house of mourning may not ask for his cloak to be returned until the mourning has passed. Similarly, one who borrows a suit for Yom Tov does not have to return it until after Yom Tov. The same is true for someone who borrows a suit for his *sheva berachos*. It follows that if the shul borrowed the *Sefer Torah*, and they do not have another one to replace it, the owner could probably not ask for his *Sefer Torah* to be returned until they have a replacement. וצ"ע.

---

125. *Choshen Mishpat* 73:1.
126. *Orach Chaim* 153:16.
127. 3:12.

One could argue that Shimon is exempt from paying for damaging the lock because he was simply enforcing the law, albeit on his own. Assuming that the *gabbai* was obligated to return the *Sefer Torah* and was unwilling to do so, Shimon would even be allowed to break the lock. The *Shulchan Aruch*[128] states that a person may act on his own to enforce justice in his own affairs. If he sees that his friend has stolen his property, he is allowed to take it back. If his friend tries to prevent him from doing so, he may even strike him in order to retrieve the stolen item.

If one is even allowed to inflict bodily harm on someone who is trying to steal from him, he could certainly damage the thief's property in order to retrieve his stolen goods.

However, it is not clear whether one could enforce his own justice through an agent. The *Rema* cites the *Terumas HaDeshen*[129] that one may not employ non-Jews to that end. The *S'dei Chemed*[130] cites the *Tehillah L'Dovid,* who concurs with this conclusion, and argues with the *Kol Shmuel* and the *Tola'as Shani* who quote the *Rema* that one may never employ "others" to enforce his own justice, which would include employing Jews as well. The *Orach Mishpat*[131] quotes the *Ma'ayan Gavim*, who writes that one cannot employ Jews to enforce justice, because that task is reserved for *beis din*. (The *Rema* specified that one could not employ non-Jews only because no Jew could accept the job because of the prohibition against his becoming involved.)

Even according to the opinion that one is allowed to enforce justice for someone else, Shimon would not be allowed to break the lock for that reason, as the lock belongs to the shul, and not to the *gabbai*. Just because the *gabbai* is acting inappropriately, that does not permit damaging the shul's property. Instead, Shimon should have called the *gabbai* to a *din Torah* and let the *beis din* handle the situation.

---

128. *Choshen Mishpat* 4:1.
129. 304.
130. *Klalim, Ma'areches* ע״ין *klal* 1.
131. 4:4.

Shimon's main claim that he should not have to pay is because he was involved in a lifesaving mission. He was fearful that Mr. Horowitz's heart would not survive the stress of being separated from his *Sefer Torah* that meant so much to him. The Gemara in *Bava Kamma*[132] states that if someone is pursuing someone else to kill him, and a third party tried to save the one being chased and damaged someone else's property in the process, he does not have to pay for the damaged property. If we will obligate him to pay, people will not want to save people who are being pursued. This is the ruling of *Shulchan Aruch*,[133] as well.

It would seem that Shimon's application of this halachah is incorrect. This halachah is only applicable when someone has to act immediately, and he damages property as a result of his haste, or if there was no other avenue available to save the victim without destroying the other's property. In this case, time was not an essential factor. This can be proven by the fact that in the end, it became apparent that it was not necessary to break the lock, after all.

Moreover, who is to say that Shimon's assessment that it was actually *piku'ach nefesh* was correct? Hashem gives a person the fortitude to deal with tragedies that come his way, *Rachmaneh litzlan*. When Rabbi Shlomo Zalman Auerbach's wife was *nifteres*, his mother-in-law was still living. She was very elderly and in a weakened state. The *nifteres* had been her only daughter, and the family was fearful that if she became aware of her daughter's demise she might not survive the blow of the tragic news. Rabbi Shlomo Zalman disagreed. He insisted that she should be told and have the opportunity to attend the funeral. Otherwise, she would be inconsolable because she had not been given the chance to do so. When they told Rav Shlomo Zalman their fears of her reaction, he responded that *Rashi* writes that when Sarah was informed that Yitzchak had almost been slaughtered, her *neshamah* left her body. One can infer that had Yitzchak actually been slaughtered, Sarah

---

132. 117b.
133. *Choshen Mishpat* 380:3.

would have been able to survive, because when Hashem sends a tragedy He also sends the strength necessary to cope with it.

One might point out that in *Parashas Vayigash*, Yehudah argued with Yosef, stating that if Yaakov will see that Binyamin does not return, Yaakov will die. Why should that be so? Wouldn't Hashem give Yaakov the strength to endure this tragedy as well?

Perhaps Yehudah understood that Yaakov looked upon Binyamin not only as a son, but as one of the tribes of Hashem. Just as Eli the Kohen Gadol fell from his chair and died when he heard that the *Aron HaKodesh* had been captured, so, too, Yaakov would see Binyamin's capture as one of Hashem's *aronei hakodesh* being taken captive, and he would die from the pain of the *Shechinah*.

One could argue that not returning with the *Sefer Torah* is still a matter of *piku'ach nefesh*, because some people could react to such a tragedy in a way that may shorten their lives. Rav Elyashiv agreed that it is indeed proper to suspect that it may be *piku'ach nefesh*, and Shimon was allowed to break the lock. Nevertheless, the shul should be paid for the lock, because although *piku'ach nefesh* is sufficient reason to allow breaking the lock, one would still have to pay, as is written in the *Shulchan Aruch*.[134]

However, it is not Shimon who has to pay, but Mr. Horowitz, since the lock was broken in order to save him. It is similar to someone who had to break a window in order to attain lifesaving medicine for a person in danger. The one who broke the window does not have to pay for the window, but the person who needed the medicine does, since it was his life that was saved by having the window broken.

---

134. *Choshen Mishpat* 359:3.

פרשת הולכינו
Parashas Ha'azinu

On-the-Job Training — Without Telling the Boss

יִפְרֹשׂ כְּנָפָיו יִקָּחֵהוּ
Spreading its wings and taking them
(32:11)

Q Sara applied for a job at Mr. Feldman's factory. She submitted a resumé stating that she had experience. Mr. Feldman directed Sara to be interviewed by Mrs. Goldschmidt, one of his senior managers, to determine if she was capable of filling the required position.

Sara confided in Mrs. Goldschmidt that she actually had no experience at all. She came from a broken home and had moved from place to place. She had no money for food, and she was applying for this job as a last-ditch effort. If she was not hired, she would not be able to survive. Mrs. Goldschmidt was very moved by Sara's plight, but she could not provide her with employment without first consulting a Rav. She told the Rav that she felt that Sara was indeed capable of becoming proficient at the job within a few months, but in the meantime, the boss would be paying her a salary without receiving his money's worth, as Sara's abilities did not truly fit her job description. In addition, Mrs. Goldschmidt will also be taking time from the company in order to train Sara. Is Mrs. Goldschmidt allowed to hire her for the job?

A It is likely that under the circumstances, Mrs. Goldschmidt would be allowed to tell the boss that Sara is capable of getting the job done, as Sara has no other option, and she will certainly apply herself to learning the necessary skills. With such dedication she will certainly succeed.

The Gemara in *Kesubos*[135] tells the story of Kalba Savua, who vowed that his daughter and her husband, Akiva the shepherd, would not receive any benefit from his property. Years later, he approached Rabbi Akiva (whom he did not recognize as his son-in-law) to annul his vow. Rabbi Akiva asked if he had intended to make his vow even if he knew that Akiva would become a great *talmid chacham*. Kalba Savua answered that if his son-in-law would have learned even **one chapter** or, for that matter, even a **single halachah**, he would never have made the vow.

Rabbi Akiva then revealed that he had been Akiva the shepherd. Kalba Savua fell on his face, kissed Rabbi Akiva's feet, and gave him half of his wealth.

Tosafos questions how Rabbi Akiva could have annulled the vow based on a circumstance that only came into being after the vow had been taken.[136] *Tosafos* asserts that it is natural for someone who goes to learn to become a great scholar. Rabbi Akiva had

---

135. 63a.
136. A vow can be annulled only if it can be determined that it was made erroneously; i.e., the one who made the vow was not aware of certain factors. A circumstance that only arose after the vow was taken is not a valid reason to say that the vow was taken erroneously. See *Nedarim* 64a. Annulling vows requires a Rav who is well versed in the intricacies of the laws of *nedarim*.

already agreed to go and study before the vow was made, and therefore his rise to greatness was only a matter of time.

The commentaries point out that there have been many people who have set off to learn, and yet they did not become great people. They resolve this difficulty by explaining that if someone goes to learn with Rabbi Akiva's determination, then he will certainly become great.

It would seem that the same is true in this case, as well. If Sara is greatly motivated to succeed, as she realizes that this is her last hope, she will certainly succeed, and perhaps Mrs. Goldschmidt could already say that Sara is proficient in the job.

However, there is still an issue of stealing from her boss, as Sara and Mrs. Goldschmidt will not be rightfully earning their wages, despite the fact that Mrs. Goldschmidt is doing a great mitzvah. It is not permissible to take *tzedakah* from him against his will. Therefore, Sara and Mrs. Goldschmidt should find a way to return to the company whatever part of their salary they did not deserve, or work overtime until their debt is repaid.

A Moving Story of Two Cows

וְשֶׁן בְּהֵמֹת אֲשַׁלַּח בָּם
And the teeth of beasts shall I dispatch against them
(32:24)

Shmuel was passing Avigdor's field when he spotted two cows standing and enjoying a leisurely lunch, munching on the wheat stalks that were soon to be harvested. One cow belonged to his neighbor Levi, and the other cow was ownerless. Shmuel can manage to take away only one of the cows, preventing it from damaging Avigdor's field. Which cow should he remove? Whichever cow he chooses, he will be saving someone from a loss. If he chooses Levi's cow, he will be sparing Levi from having to pay for damages. If he removes the ownerless cow, he will be saving Avigdor, because the ownerless cow has no owner to pay for the damages the cow causes. Which cow should he chase away?

On the one hand, Levi should have to pay damages, because he is being negligent by not watching his cow. Therefore, Shmuel should take away the ownerless cow in order to save Avigdor's produce.

On the other hand, Rav Baruch Ber Leibowitz[137] writes in the name of his rebbi, Rav Chaim Brisker, that the obligation to pay for damages is not merely a financial obligation, but also indicates that it is forbidden to damage someone else's property. Thus, preventing Levi's cow from eating is saving Levi from an *aveirah*, in addition to saving him from having to pay. Therefore it would seem preferable to lead away Levi's cow.

However, it is possible that one is only in violation of having caused damage if he does not compensate the owner for the damage he caused. Once he pays for the damages, he may have absolved himself of the *aveirah* as well. Since Levi had been negligent in watching his cow, it would be better to save Avigdor from a total loss. Shmuel should therefore prevent the ownerless animal from damaging Avigdor's crop.

In addition, Levi's loss is mitigated by the fact that although he has to pay Avigdor, he has gained by the fact that his animal has been well fed.

If, however, Levi is poor, and Avigdor is wealthy, it would be better to save the poor man from loss than the wealthy man, as

---

137. *Birkas Shmuel, Bava Kamma* 2.

would be the halachah if one found the lost item of a poor man and a wealthy man at the same time. In such a case it is a mitzvah to return the poor man's item first.[138]

Fasten Your Seatbelt

וּרְאֵה אֶת אֶרֶץ כְּנָעַן
And see the Land of Canaan
(32:49)

Q Hashem has given man the ability to fly! One of the most useful applications of this ability is flying to *Eretz Yisrael*. As the flight usually lasts for many hours, it is necessary to *daven* on the airplane. Is it better to *daven* on the airplane with a minyan, which usually entails crowding into the back of the plane, or to *daven* alone while sitting in one's seat? On the one hand, it is always better to *daven* with a minyan and, in addition, to be able to answer *Borchu*, *Kaddish*, and *Kedushah*. On the other hand, it is much more comfortable to *daven* in one's seat, which lends itself to *davening* with greater *kavanah* (concentration).[139] Which is the preferred choice?

A The Gemara[140] states that passengers on a ship at sea are considered individuals, even if they have enough men to form a minyan. *Responsa Zecher Yehosef*[141] explains

---

138. See *Chashukei Chemed, Sanhedrin* 8a.
139. This question is based on the premise that forming a minyan will not disturb the other passengers or crew, and will not cause a *chillul Hashem, chas v'shalom*.
140. *Rosh Hashanah* 17b.
141. Vol. 4, 235.

that even if they have 10 men, they do not enjoy the status of a *tzibbur* because they are not settled in one place, as the ship is in constant motion.

The *Netziv*[142] cites a similar explanation from the *She'iltos*. Even if many people gather on a ship, they are considered like individuals in comparison to the rest of the world. A regular shul with 10 men carries the weight of the entire world because that is a normal situation. Voyagers, who are generally a minority, even if they happen to have 10 men, are considered negligible in comparison to the rest of the world.

Accordingly, perhaps *davening* on an airplane does not even have the same status as a conventional *davening* with a minyan, and there is greater reason to prefer *davening* in one's seat if doing so will afford one the ability to have more *kavanah*.

---

142. *Ha'amek She'eilah* 66 §9.

פרשת וזאת הברכה
Parashas V'zos HaBerachah

Be Fair to the Wealthy

יוֹרוּ מִשְׁפָּטֶיךָ לְיַעֲקֹב
They shall teach Your ordinances to Jacob
(33:10)

Q Yisrael is a serious young *avreich* who learns in Yeshivas Beis Yom Tov. His job is to learn with *bachurim* who are having difficulty understanding the Gemara. The yeshivah allowed him to choose between two *bachurim* who needed a *chavrusa*. Both were very intelligent, and only needed a little direction and encouragement. Yisrael does not know which boy to choose. When he investigated the boys' backgrounds, he discovered that one of them comes from a poor family, while the other one comes from a more well-to-do family. Should Yisrael give priority to the boy from the poor family in accordance with *Chazal's* teaching,[143] "Be careful with the children of the poor, because they are the ones who will be successful in Torah."?

---
143. *Nedarim* 81a.

When *Chazal* cautioned us to be careful with children from poor families, they did not intend to exclude children from wealthy families. They merely wanted to warn that one should never discriminate between children on the basis of financial strata. One should never underestimate a child's capability due to a lack of funds. On the contrary, children from less-comfortable homes tend to be less spoiled, which is more conducive to the demands of vigorous learning. If, however, a boy from a wealthy home will apply himself as much as his less-wealthy counterpart, and he is accomplishing in his learning, *Chazal* did not intend to say that the boy from the poorer background would be more successful.

There are Torah giants who come from wealthy homes. Kilav was the greatest Torah scholar in his generation, and he was the son of David HaMelech. Shlomo HaMelech, the wisest of all men, was also the son of David HaMelech. All the *Nesi'im* who were members of the dynasty of Rabban Gamliel were extremely wealthy, as were Rabbi Elazar ben Azaryah and Rabbi Elazar bar Charsom, and they all achieved greatness in Torah.

Therefore, if Yisrael cannot decide which boy to choose, he should not discriminate against the boy from the wealthy home, who may prove to be just as capable as his less-wealthy counterpart. Rather, Yisrael should use different criteria to decide. *Chazal* teach us[144] that there are four categories of students:

1. One who grasps quickly and forgets quickly, his gain is offset by his loss.

2. One who grasps slowly and forgets slowly, his loss is offset by his gain.

3. One who grasps quickly and forgets slowly, this is a good portion.

4. One who has grasps slowly and forgets quickly, this is a bad portion.

---

144. *Pirkei Avos* 5:15.

The commentaries explain that if there are only enough funds to support one student, priority should be given to the student who is more likely to succeed. If both of them are of equal capability, then the decision should be made by making a lottery between them.

Rav Meir Shapiro, the founder of the Daf HaYomi movement, would often tell the following story, which had affected him deeply and served as a model for him as to the importance of educating every *Yid*.

When he arrived at his first Rabbinic post in Galina, he took note of one of the students, who was gifted with sharp wit and quick understanding. The boy had a thirst for learning, but due to the fact that he was the son of a simple shoemaker, none of his teachers afforded him very much attention, and his raw talents were left unappreciated.

Rav Meir could not allow this situation to continue. At a public test of the students, which was attended by a large crowd as well as by the leaders of the community, the Rav called on this boy to recite the Mishnah in *Bava Metzia* 37a. The boy related the Mishnah, "If two people entrusted someone with their money for safekeeping, and one gave 100 coins and the other gave 200, and when they came to retrieve their money each one claimed that he had given the 200, the trustee should give each of them 100, and the remainder should stay with him until Eliyahu HaNavi comes. If two people entrusted someone with valuable vessels, and one was worth 100 coins, and the other was worth 1,000, and each one claimed that they had given the one worth 1,000 ..."

The Rav interrupted with a question for the student: Why, when the mishnah discusses money, it discusses values of 100 and 200, and when the Mishnah discussed utensils it switches to 100 and 1,000? The boy's response was brilliant! The Gemara[145] has a rule that a person prefers one measure of his own produce over nine measures of that of his neighbor. That rule does not apply to

---

145. *Bava Metzia* 38a.

money, so an extra 100 is enough of a temptation for one of the men to covet the greater amount. When it comes to utensils, an item that is merely worth double one's own item would not be significant enough for someone to desire that of his neighbor, and therefore the mishnah had to discuss an item that is worth more than nine times the man's own item!

Rav Shapiro was overwhelmed by the young boy's breathtaking analysis. He continued to ask the boy another question that had perplexed him, in front of all those assembled. He pressed for an explanation as to why the boy was learning in such a low-level class that did not befit his intelligence.

The reply was sharp and to the point. He retorted that it was because the current committee had forgotten *Chazal's* warning to be careful with the children of the poor. This prodded Rav Meir Shapiro to open a *cheder* in which the boys were taught according to their intellectual abilities, irrespective of their financial status. Eventually, this served as the impetus for him to found the great Yeshivas Chachmei Lublin.

Public Property

כִּי שָׁם חֶלְקַת מְחֹקֵק סָפוּן
For that is where the lawgiver's plot is hidden
(33:21)

Q Anshel was finally able to realize his lifelong dream of traveling to Europe to *daven* at *kivrei tzaddikim*. At a certain *beis hachayim* he discovered that there were many supplicants who would camp out in the area for several days in order to *daven* at these *kevarim*, which were far from the nearest settled town. Anshel purchased the tract of land adjacent to the *beis hachaim* and had it cleared for the benefit of those who came to *daven*.

Eliyahu visited the same *beis hachaim* approximately a year later. With his keen business sense, he realized that he could easily garner lucrative profits with a relatively small investment. Eliyahu erected a building with several floors and portioned off private sleeping quarters for those who came to *daven*. He hired someone to rent out the rooms at a very reasonable rate.

One man stayed in one of Eliyahu's rooms, but refused to pay. He claimed that the land had been donated for the visitors' benefit, and Eliyahu had no right to build on the land, let alone to charge rent!

Eliyahu asserted that an empty lot is of no use to anyone. He had invested his money to provide a facility, and for that he deserves to be paid. He is not charging anyone for the land, but for the use of the shelter and his beds.

Who is right?

A Perhaps the building does not belong to Eliyahu at all. Perhaps it is considered public property, since it was erected on the land that had been donated to the public! The *Rashba*[146] rules that if someone erected a building on his friend's empty lot, the builder has no right to live there; the owner of the property must reimburse the builder for his expenses, and then he can use the building for himself. Accordingly, the visitors may claim that the land and the building belong to them and to all of *Klal Yisrael,* and Eliyahu only has the right to collect his expenses.

In truth, the cases are not really comparable. The owner of the empty lot has no interest in someone building on his

---
146. Cited in *Beis Yosef, Choshen Mishpat* 375, and *Shulchan Aruch* ad loc. 7.

property. Therefore, he has the right to reimburse the builder for his expenses and then evict him. In this case, had Eliyahu not arrived on the scene, the land would have remained undeveloped for years.

Although those who visit the cemetery might very well be pleased that someone took the initiative and put up a building on the land that belonged to the community at large, the building would still belong to Eliyahu.

This case is comparable to the Gemara in *Megillah*[147] that states that one may not rent out a house to others in Yerushalayim, because the land does not belong to him.[148] Rav Elchonon Wasserman[149] questions why homeowners in Yerushalayim could not charge rent for the use of their houses. Even if their land is considered public, the stones and beams are certainly the property of the homeowners. Rav Elchonon cites Rashi, who explains that one could not charge someone who had come to Yerushalayim for Yom Tov, as the mitzvah of traveling to Yerushalayim for Yom Tov creates a public need, and the land was given to the homeowner only on condition that he would not charge rent for those arriving for Yom Tov.

This seems to imply that this was a special dispensation that existed only in Yerushalayim in the time of the *Beis HaMikdash*, and otherwise, one could charge for the use of his building, even if the land did not belong to him. In this case, no one stipulated that Eliyahu could not charge rent, and therefore he should be allowed to charge for the use of his structure.

Moreover, Eliyahu can certainly charge for use of the beds and any other furnishings that he provided. Although the Gemara in *Megillah* brings an opinion that one could not charge those who came to Yerushalayim for Yom Tov for their use of the beds,

---
147. 26a.
148. Yerushalayim was not distributed to the original settlers of *Eretz Yisrael*, and those who settled it did not acquire the land, as Yerushalayim belongs to the nation as a whole.
149. *Kovetz Shiurim Bava Kamma* 95.

the *Rambam* does not quote this opinion in his halachic works. Hence, just as one could even charge for the use of one's beds in Yerushalayim, so Eliyahu can certainly charge for the beds that he provided, as well.

Together Is Better

וַיִּשְׁכֹּן יִשְׂרָאֵל בֶּטַח בָּדָד
Thus Israel shall dwell securely, solitary
(33:28)

Q Zalman was interested in moving, and he identified two possible places to live. One was a private house, and the other was a three-family house. Each of them has advantages. In a private house, he could avoid friction with his neighbors, as when people live in close proximity, at times it can lead to disagreement. On the other hand, if he has close neighbors, they can help one another, and the opportunities for *chesed* abound. There are mitzvos that can be done with neighbors, such as *eiruvei chatzeros*, or arranging *shiurim*, especially for the women. Which home should he choose?

A The Gemara in *Makkos*[150] quotes Rabbi Yose, the son of Rabbi Chanina, who said that Moshe Rabbeinu decreed four things for the Jews, and the later prophets nullified his decrees. Moshe said that *Klal Yisrael* should live in isolation: *Thus Israel shall dwell secure, solitary, in the likeness of Jacob.*[151]

---
150. 24a.
151. *Devarim* 33:28.

PARASHAS V'ZOS HABERACHAH / 445

Amos negated the decree when he said, *Please refrain! How will Yaakov survive, for he is small?*[152]

The *Iyun Yaakov* explains that Moshe wanted each Jew to live in his own house to avoid the dissension that is prevalent in communal living. Perhaps this is what Haman's referred to when he said that the Jews are scattered among the nations. Moshe said that the Jews are like Yaakov, whom the *pasuk* describes as remaining by himself,[153] yet he was able to defeat the angel of Eisav. Amos negated Moshe's words, and declared that we cannot compare ourselves to Yaakov; we need each other's presence to remain strong.

According to this explanation, it would be preferable to live in a multifamily house where neighbors can help one another to serve Hashem. If there are more opportunities for *chesed* and Torah learning in communal living, it is certainly worth the effort required to keep the peace.

The Chofetz Chaim presents a similar idea[154]: It is better to learn with a *chavrusa* if that will enhance the learning, even though it also presents the possibility that they may be tempted to discuss *lashon hara*. Nevertheless, when they unite for the purpose of Torah and are careful to retain their focus, that is preferable to sacrificing the quality of their learning just to avoid the possibility of stumbling in forbidden speech.

---

152. *Amos* 7:5.
153. *Yaakov was left alone* (*Bereishis* 32:25).
154. See *What If,* Vol. 1, "It's Not Easy Being Green" (p. 401).

Glossary

Aliyah (pl. *Aliyos*) — lit., going up; the act of being called to recite a blessing at the public reading of the Torah

Amos — cubits; each a distance of 1½-2 feet

Amud — 1. lectern or podium. 2. one folio of the Talmud

Aravos — willow twigs; one of the Four Species taken in hand on Succos

Arba Minim — the Four Species taken on Succos

Aron Hakodesh — Holy Ark

Arvus — responsibility that all Jews have for each other's observance of the mitzvos

Aseres HaDibros — the Ten Commandments

Aseres Yemei Teshuvah — the Ten Days of Repentance between Rosh Hashanah and Yom Kippur

Askanim — community activists

Ashkenaz — referring to Jews of European descent or their customs

Aufruf — pre-wedding event in which the groom is called to the Torah the Shabbos before the wedding

Aveirah (pl. *Aveiros*) — sin

Avel — mourner

Avodah — lit., work; task; the service of Hashem, whether in sacrifice, prayer, or self-refinement

Avodah Zarah — idol worship; idolatry

Avreich (pl. *Avreichim*) — young married man

Ayin hara — evil eye

B'dinei Shamayim — an obligation between the person and Hashem

Baal korei (pl. *baalei keriyah*) — person who reads the weekly Torah portion aloud on behalf of the congregation

Ba'al Teshuvah — returnee to his/her heritage, i.e., religious observance

Ba'al Tokei'a — the person who blows the shofar during the prayer service

Bachur (pl. *bachurim*) — young man; an unmarried young man, often used to denote a student in a yeshivah

Bar mitzvah — 1. 13-year-old boy. 2. ceremony marking the coming of age of a Jewish boy

Baruch Hashem — lit., Blessed is Hashem; an expression of appreciation of Hashem's goodness

Bedi'avad — after the fact

Bedikas chametz — the search for *chametz* carried out on the night before Pesach

Bein adam la'chaveiro — between man and his fellow man

Bein adam la'Makom — between man and Hashem

Bein hazemanim — intersession

Beis din — Rabbinical Court

Beis hachaim — cemetery

Beis HaMikdash — Holy Temple

Beis midrash (pl. *Batei midrash*) — study hall where Torah is learned, often used as a synagogue as well

Ben Torah — lit., "son of Torah"; one who studies and observes the teachings of the Torah

Bentch — (Yiddish) 1. recite Grace after Meals. 2. to bless someone

Berachah (pl. *Berachos*) — blessing

Berachah le'vatalah — blessing recited in vain (for no purpose)

Bikur cholim — lit., visiting the sick, the Torah commandment to care for the ill

Bimah — lectern used for the Torah reading

Bircas HaMazon — Grace After Meals

Bircas Kohanim — the Kohen's blessing to the congregation, included in the repetition of *Shemoneh Esrei*

Bitachon — lit., trust; trust in Hashem

Bitul Torah — negation of Torah learning; wasting time that should be used to learn Torah

Blech — (Yiddish) a sheet of metal placed over a stove top above the flame to permit keeping the Shabbos food over the fire

Bris, Bris Milah — circumcision

Chacham (pl. *Chachamim*) — wise people, sages

Chalilah — Heaven forbid

Chalitzah — a ceremony to sever the marriage requirement between a man and his late brother's wife, when the brother died without leaving any children

Chametz — leavened foods prohibited during Pesach

Charatah — regret

Chareidim — those who are strictly religiously observant

Chas v'shalom — Heaven forbid

Chassan — groom

Chassid (pl. *chassidim*) — very pious individual

Chassidus — the study of Hassidic thought

Chasunah — wedding

Chavrusa — study partner

Chazakah — tenure; established right

Chazal — acronym for *chachameinu zichronom livrachah*, Our Sages of blessed memory

Chazarah — return; repetitive study

Chazzan — cantor

Cheder (pl. *Chadarim*) — Torah institution for children

Cherem — ban

Chesed — kindness

Chillul Hashem — desecration of Hashem's Name

Chillul Shabbos — desecration of the Sabbath

Chinuch — Jewish education; a parent's obligation to train a child to perform mitzvos

Chiyuv (pl. *chiyuvim*) — lit., obligation; refers to a mourner for a parent, who has precedence to be *chazzan*.

Chol HaMoed — intermediate days between the first and last days of Pesach and Succos.

Chumash (pl. *Chumashim*) — one of the Torah; the Five Books collectively

Chuppah — wedding canopy

Chutz la'Aretz — anywhere outside the Land of Israel

Daf — lit., page; one folio of the Gemara

Daf Yomi — daily study of one folio of Gemara

Daven, Davening — praying

Dayan (pl. *Dayanim*) — rabbinical court judge

Din Torah — case brought in a Rabbinical court

Dina d'malchusa dina — the laws of the government are to be obeyed

Divrei Torah — lessons or short speeches on Torah topics

Eidot HaMizrach — Sephardic prayer service

Erev — the eve of...

Eiruv — lit., mixture; halachic device; refers to *Eiruv chatzeros,* a string surrounding an area's perimeter to allow people to carry within that place on the Sabbath

Eretz Yisrael — Land of Israel.

Esrog (pl. *esrogim*) — a citron, one of the Four Species taken in hand on Succos

Fleishige — (Yiddish) made with meat

Frum — (Yiddish) religious; Torah observant

Gabbai (pl. *Gabbaim*) — aide to a Rebbe; man in charge of running a shul

Gadol — an outstanding Torah scholar

Gadol Ha'Dor (pl. *Gedolei Ha'Dor*) — Torah leader of the generation

Gan — kindergarten

Gaon — revered Torah scholar

Gehinnom — Hell

Gelilah — rolling closed a Sefer Torah after it has been read

Gemach — free-loan society

Gemara — the Talmud

Gemilus Chassadim — acts of loving-kindness

Geneivah — theft

Geneivas da'as — deceit

Get (pl. *Gittin*) — halachic bill of divorce

Gilgul — previous or subsequent lifetime

Grama — indirectly caused damage for which Beis Din will not obligate one to pay, although he is still liable according to the Heavenly *Beis Din*

Gut voch — (Yiddish) post-Sabbath salutation: "Have a good week"

Hachnasas kallah — sponsoring a bride with things she needs in order to marry

hachnassas orchim — inviting guests

Hachzakas HaTorah — strengthening Torah observance

Haftarah — selection from the Prophets read following the Torah reading

HaKadosh Baruch Hu — lit., the Holy One, Blessed Is He (i.e., Hashem)

Hakaras hatov — expressing gratitude

Halachah (pl. *halachos*)— Torah and Rabbinic law

Hallel — lit., *praise*; a prayer of praise

Hashavas Aveidah — returning a lost object

Hashgachah pratis — individual Divine Providence

Hashkafah — outlook; a concept of *emunah*

Hatzalah — rescue; aid

Havdalah — lit., separation; prayer recited as

the Sabbath or Festival comes to an end
Hechsher — Rabbinical approbation; kosher certification
Hefker — ownerless property
Hefsek — interruption
Heter — permission; something permitted
Hiddur mitzvah — enhancement to a mitzvah
Hy"d — acronym for *Hashem yikom damam*; May G-d avenge their blood; i.e., death
Issur — a prohibited matter or act
Kaddish — memorial prayer for the deceased
Kabbalah — Jewish mystical teachings
Kallah (pl. *kallos*) — bride
Kana'im pog'im bo — zealots are to slay him
Kares — excision: Divinely imposed premature death decreed by the Torah for certain classes of transgression
Kashrus — relating to Jewish dietary laws
Kavanah — intention, esp. when reciting a prayer or performing a mitzvah
Kedushah — sanctity; holiness
Kesubah — marriage contract
Kezayis — olive-sized piece
Kibbud Av V'Eim — honoring one's parents
Kibbud (pl. *kibbudm*) — lit., honor; the honor of being called to the *bimah* during the reading of the Torah or to be a participant at a religious ceremony
Kiddush — 1. mandatory blessing over wine expressing the sanctity of Shabbos or Festivals. 2. (l.c.) a reception after Sabbath morning prayers at which Kiddush is recited and refreshments are served
Kiddush Hashem — sanctification of Hashem's Name
Kiddushin — marriage
Kimcha de'Pischa — lit., flour for Pesach; charity given specifically to the poor to purchase food for Pesach
Kinyan (pl. *kinyanim*) — literally, an acquisition; usually a transfer of an object or a contract to make a verbal agreement a physical reality
Kiruv — outreach; outreach movement drawing people to Torah observance
Kivrei tzaddikim— gravesites of *tzaddikim*
Klal Yisrael — Jewish people in general; the Jewish nation
Kli (pl. *keilim*) — a utensil
Koach — strength; ability; energy
Kodesh HaKodashim — The Holy of Holies

Kohen (pl. *Kohanim*)— Jewish priest
Kollel (pl. *kollelim*) — academy of higher Jewish learning, whose students are mostly married men
Korban (pl. *korbanos*) — a sacrificial offering
Korban ha'omer — the barley offering brought on the second day of Pesach
Korban HaEidah — a communal offering
Korban Pesach — the Passover Offering
Kosel HaMa'aravi — Western Wall
Kriah — 1. reading 2. tearing one's clothing on hearing of the death of a close relative or at the funeral of a close relative
Krias HaTorah — the reading of the Torah in the synagogue
Krias Shema — 1. the three paragraphs of the Torah recited twice daily, beginning with the words "Shema Yisrael, Hear, O Israel." 2. the recitation of this liturgy
Lashon Hara — evil gossip
Le'chatchilah — to perform a mitzvah in the most preferable way
Lein — (Yiddish) to read; esp. used to refer to reading the Torah in shul
Levayah — funeral
Lulav (pl. *lulavim*) — palm branch, one of the Four Species taken in hand on Succos
Maariv — the evening prayer service
Ma'aser — tithes
Ma'os Chittim — funds collected to help the needy buy provisions for Passover
Mabul — the Biblical Flood
Machlokes — an argument; a dispute
Machzor (pl. *machzorim*) — holiday prayer book
Maftir — the last segment of the Torah reading
Mahn — manna
Marbitz Torah — one who disseminates Torah
masechta (pl. *masechtos*) — tractate of Talmud
Mashgiach — 1. (u.c.) dean who oversees yeshivah students' spiritual and ethical development. 2. kashrus supervisor
Mashiach — Messiah
Masmid — exceptionally diligent student
Matanos l'evyonim — gifts to the poor mandated to be given on Purim
mazel — fate; good fortune
mazel tov — congratulations
Mechallel Shabbos — one who desecrates the Sabbath
Mechilah — forgiveness; giving permission for someone to do something to harm you

GLOSSARY / 449

Mechutan (pl. *mechutanim*) — parent of one's in-law children; one's relative through marriage

Mehudar — beautiful

Mekach ta'us — a sale conducted under false pretenses or in error

Melachah — labor; any of the 39 labors forbidden to be performed on the Sabbath

Mezakei harabim — to strengthen the community's Torah observance

Mezuzah (pl. *mezuzos*) — small parchment scroll in a casing, affixed to a doorpost and containing the first two paragraphs of the *Shema* prayer

Mi'd'Oraisa — of Biblical origin

Mi'd'Rabbanan — according to the Rabbinic enactment

Mi shebeirach — prayer invoking Heavenly blessings

Middah (pl. *middos*) — character trait; attribute

Midrash — homiletical teachings of the Sages

Mikveh — ritual bath

Minchah — the afternoon prayer service

Minhag — common practice

Minyan (pl. *Minyanim*) — quorum of ten men necessary to conduct a prayer service

Mishloach Manos — gifts of food sent to friends on Purim

Mispallelim — congregants

Mitzvah — Torah commandment

Mizbei'ach — Altar

Mochel — forgive; to forgo one's right; to grant permission to expose his shortcomings

Mohel — one who performs a ritual circumcision

Morah — a woman teacher

Muktzah — an object that may not be handled on Shabbos

Mussaf — additional prayer service recited after Shacharis on Shabbos, Rosh Chodesh, and Festivals

Mussar — ethical teachings geared toward self-refinement; reproof

Na'anuim — wavings, as of the Four Species

Nasi (pl. *nesi'im*) — the leader of the Jewish people

Navi (pl. *nevi'im*) — prophet

Neder (pl. *nedarim*) — vow

Neshamah — soul

Niftar (f. *nifteres*) — deceased

nusach — 1. style of prayer service. 2. melody used during a prayer service

Olah — offering that is completely burned on the Altar.

Oleh — one who goes up to the lectern during the Torah reading

Onen — one whose close relative has died but has not yet been buried

Oness — one who was forced to do something

Parah Adumah — red heifer, used in certain ritual purification processes

Parashah — the weekly Torah portion

Parnassah — livelihood

Paroches — the curtain in front of the Aron HaKodesh

Pasken — to render a halachic ruling

Pasuk (pl. *Pesukim*) — Scriptural verse

Pasul — invalid

Patur — exempt

Perutah — a coin with minimal value

Pesichah — the honor of opening the ark that contains the Torah Scrolls

Petirah — demise

Peyos — sideburns or sidecurls, worn by Orthodox Jewish males

Pidyon Haben — redeeming a firstborn son

Pidyon Petter Chamor — redeeming a firstborn donkey

Pidyon Shevuyim — the mitzvah to ransom Jewish prisoners

Pikuach Nefesh — a case of life and death

Pirsumei nisa — to publicize the miracle

Poskim — halachic authorities

Psak — halachic ruling

Rachamim — mercy

Rachmana litzlan — Heaven save us

Rebbi — teacher

Reshus harabbim — communal domain

Ribbis — interest; halachic prohibition against charging interest

Ribbono Shel Olam — lit., Master of the World; i.e., Hashem

rosh yeshivah — the dean of a yeshivah

Ruach HaKodesh — Divine Inspiration

Sandek — the one who holds the baby during the bris

Satan — the prosecuting angel

Schach — the roof of the *succah*, generally made from leaves, branches, or bamboo

Seder — 1. study period. 2. (u.c.) Pesach-night ritual during which the Haggadah is recited. 3. set time, usually for learning.

Sefer (pl. *Sefarim*) — holy book

Sefer Torah — Torah Scroll, written on parchment
Sefiras HaOmer — the counting of the seven weeks between Passover and Shavuos
Segulah (pl. *segulos*) — spiritual remedy
sela'im — stones; rocks
semichah — Rabbinical ordination
Seudah — festive meal; esp. a meal served on Shabbos or Yom Tov
Sha'atnez — the prohibition against wearing garments containing both wool and linen
Shacharis — morning prayer service
Shadchan — matchmaker
Shalom — peace
Shalom Bayis — domestic tranquility
Shalosh Seudos — the third Shabbos meal, eaten on Shabbos afternoon
Shamash — attendant; sexton
Shas — Talmud
She'eilah — question, esp. a question asked of a rabbinical authority regarding a halachic issue
Shechinah — Presence of Hashem
Shecht — (Yiddish) to slaughter an animal according to halachah
Shehechiyanu — blessing recited on certain occasions, expressing gratitude to G-d.
Sheva Berachos — 1. the seven blessings recited under the chuppah at a wedding. 2. the festive meals, celebrated during the week after a wedding, at which the seven blessings are recited.
Shidduch (pl. *Shidduchim*) — marriage proposal
Shinui reshus – transference of possession
Shiur — Torah lecture
Shivah — seven-day mourning period for a close relative
Shofar — ram's horn blown on Rosh Hashanah
Shomer Shabbos — Sabbath observer
Shtiebel — (Yiddish) lit., room; a small synagogue, often situated in a house; small synagogue, used mainly by Chassidim
Shul — (Yiddish) synagogue
Siddur (pl. *Siddurim*) — prayer book
Simchah — rejoicing; festive event
Sofer — a scribe who writes religious materials such as a Torah Scroll, a mezuzah, tefillin, etc.
Sotah — a woman suspected of an illicit relationship, who, in Biblical times, was subject to the test of the bitter waters (see *Numbers* 5:12ff)
Succah — booth in which Jews are commanded to dwell during Succos
Succos — the festival during which one dwells in a *succah*.
Takanah — enactment
Tallis — four-cornered prayer shawl with tzitzis, worn during morning prayers
Talmid Chacham (pl. *Talmidei Chachamim*) — Torah Scholar
Tanna — a scholar of the Mishnah
Tefillah (pl. *Tefillos*) — Jewish prayer
Tefillin — phylacteries
Tehillim — the Book of *Psalms*.
Tekiyos — the sounds of the shofar blasts
Tenaim — premarital contract
Tereifah — unkosher due to bodily defects that will cause the animal to die within 12 months
Teshuvah — 1. repentance 2. response to a halachic question
Tevillas Keilim — the ritual immersion of food utensils purchased from a non-Jew
Todah — 1. "Thank you." 2. thanksgiving offering
Toivel — to ritually purify via immersion in a *mikveh*
Tzaddik (pl. *Tzaddikim*) — righteous person
Tzedakah — charity
Tzibbur — congregation
Tzitzis — fringed garment worn by Jewish men and boys; fringes at the corners of a tallis
Vasikin — the Shacharis service recited at sunrise
Yahrtzeit — (Yiddish) anniversary of a death
Yerushalayim — Jerusalem
Yeshivah — a school of Jewish studies
yetzer ha'ra — evil inclination
Yetzias Mitzrayim — the Exodus from Egypt
Yid — (Yiddish) Jew
Yiddishkeit — Judaism
Yi'ush — giving up hope of retaining ownership; usually applies to a lost object.
Yiras Shamayim — lit., fear of Heaven; connotes an all-pervasive attitude of piety
Yungerman (pl. *yungerleit*) — (Yiddish) young married men, usually referring to those studying in a yeshivah or kollel
Zechus — merit
Zivuggim — partners; fated marriage partners
Zocheh — to merit

Index of Sources

Sefer Bereishis

Parashas Bereishis
- Hidden Treasure — Yevamos 108
- Sleeping In — Yevamos 549
- Just the Fax — Yevamos 738
- Life Insurance — Yevamos 393

Parashas Noach
- Saving It From Their Hands — Bechoros 187
- One Lucky Dog — Yevamos 457
- Glass Houses — Eruvin 671

Parashas Lech Lecha
- House Arrest — Rosh Hashanah 128
- Obligations — Yevamos 486
- Ma'aser! — Yevamos 328

Parashas Vayeira
- Same Place, Same Time — Rosh Hashanah 208
- Location, Location, Location — Bechoros 492
- A Lack of Communication — Rosh Hashanah 441

Parashas Chayei Sarah
- A Bargain — Yevamos 106
- A Domestic Match — Yevamos 478
- Putting One and One Together — Yevamos 507

Parashas Toldos
- The Best Policy — Yevamos 65
- Buyer Beware — Yevamos 720
- Dealing With the Sly — Niddah 360

Parashas Vayeitzei
- Where There's a Will… — Yevamos 802
- How Much Is It Worth? — Bechoros 116

Parashas Vayishlach
- Broken Telephone — Rosh Hashanah 95
- Time Is of the Essence — Yevamos 307

Parashas Vayeishev
- Yagati U'matzasi! — Rosh Hashanah 205

Parashas Mikeitz
- A Day in the Fruit Store — Zeraim 349
- Read the Fine Print — Rosh Hashanah 438
- Magic — Yevamos 816

Parashas Vayigash
- Occupational Hazards — Niddah 469

Whose Wedding Is This, Anyway?	Avodah Zarah 197
A Likely Story	Yevamos 797

Parashas Vayechi

Looks Can Kill	Yevamos 861
Attendance Mandatory	Yevamos 120
Acidic Speech	Yevamos 249

Sefer Shemos

Parashas Shemos

A Timely Gift	Rosh Hashanah 69
The Right Name at the Right Time	Yevamos 235
Lasting Impressions	Yevamos 391

Parashas Va'eira

Keep Your Cool	Rosh Hashanah 93
Privileged Animals	Yevamos 346
A Sweet Pitch	Yevamos 476

Parashas Bo

A Potentially Dangerous Snack	Eruvin 202
What Motivated You?	Zeraim 48
The Honor of Performing a Mitzvah	Yevamos 596

Parashas Beshalach

(Not) A Time to Sing	Yevamos 599
All for the Boss	Rosh Hashanah 163
Keeping the Peace	Beitzah 285

Parashas Yisro

Out of Order	Avodah Zarah 42
Valuable Wine	Niddah 239
To Understand a Mitzvah	Bava Metzia 152

Parashas Mishpatim

Sudden Impact	Rosh Hashanah 301
Return Policy	Rosh Hashanah 410
Mis(ter) Understanding	Rosh Hashanah 271
Kosher Loopholes	Shevuos 216
Hidden Costs	Yevamos 598

Parashas Terumah

Almost the Same	Shevuos 75
Dangerously Armed	Rosh Hashanah 289
A Bad Shidduch?	Yevamos 55

Parashas Tetzaveh

Presents of Mind	Rosh Hashanah 129
Broken Heart	Yevamos 353
The Flood Is Over	Rosh Hashanah 329

Parashas Ki Sisa

Precious Time	Eruvin 485
Kiddush Hashem vs. Tznius	Eruvin 423
Publicizing Those Who Do Mitzvos	Eruvin 425

Parashas Vayakheil
Public Relations	Yevamos 284
From Rags to Riches	Rosh Hashanah 80

Parashas Pekudei
Something Went Wrong	Rosh Hashanah 56
False Representation	Rosh Hashanah 220
The Same Pocket	Bechoros 672

Sefer Vayikra

Parashas Vayikra
A Gift in the Mouth	Rosh Hashanah 131
How Does This Sound to You?	Niddah 323
Breaking Even	Eruvin 682

Parashas Tzav
Don't Sell Yourself Short	Yevamos 590
Golden Dust	Beitzah 204
A Friend Indeed	Rosh Hashanah 124

Parashas Shemini
Expensive Tastes	Yevamos 490
Half a Hechsher	Niddah 187
No Good Deed…	Zeraim 340

Parashas Tazria
Due Honors, Part I	Yevamos 317
Due Honors, Part II	Yevamos 319

Parashas Metzora
Safe Keeping	Niddah 439
Buried Treasure	Niddah 440
Cannot Part With Art	Avodah Zarah 437

Parashas Acharei Mos
An Expensive Dip	Rosh Hashanah 146
The Winning Ticket	Yevamos 648

Parashas Kedoshim
Older Parents	Zeraim 113
An Irregular Story	Yevamos 827
All That Glitters	Yevamos 492
A Waity Decision	Yevamos 129
Soon There Will Be a Beis HaMikdash	Rosh Hashanah 420

Parashas Emor
A(n) (Un)Hairy Situation	Yevamos 423
To Fix or Not to Fix	Rosh Hashanah 247
It Was an Acci-dent	Rosh Hashanah 249

Parashas Behar
Deafening Silence	Yevamos 426

Parashas Bechukosai
Fare Is Fair	Rosh Hashanah 233
Davening With Heart	Avodah Zarah 163
Wholesale or Retail	Avodah Zarah 439

Sefer Bamidbar

Parashas Bamidbar
    Name Change — Rosh Hashanah 233
    The Gift of Pidyon Haben — Bechoros 573
    Tzedakah, Tzedakah — Makkos 212

Parashas Nasso
    Shamefully Yours — Shevuos 67
    Call for Peace — Yevamos 79
    The Zechus to Give — Yevamos 173

Parashas Beha'aloscha
    A Really Nice Gift — Eruvin 383
    A Recipe for Disaster — Yevamos 167
    A Loan on Time — Yevamos 546

Parashas Shelach
    Stretching Time — Rosh Hashanah 166
    Hot Buns — Rosh Hashanah 274
    Knot So Simple — Yevamos 83

Parashas Korach
    Space Management — Rosh Hashanah 202
    Pick It Up! — Rosh Hashanah 210
    Getting Your Priorities Straight — Bechoros 581

Parashas Chukas
    Part 1: A Man's Real Station in Life — Rosh Hashanah 368
    Part 2: A Man's Real Station in Life — Rosh Hashanah 370
    L'ilui Nishmas — Yevamos 765
    Zealousness — Yevamos 689

Parashas Balak
    To Return or Not to Return — Eruvin 455
    It's Worth the Pain — Zeraim 434
    A Good Investment — Yevamos 105

Parashas Pinchas
    The Gift That Keeps on Giving — Shevuos 196
    Preserving Special Relationships — Eruvin 287

Parashas Mattos
    Who Should Pay Whom — Bechoros 545
    Best-Laid Plans — Beitzah 266

Parashas Mas'ei
    A Time to Rejoice — Yevamos 643
    An Eye in the Sky — Yevamos 834
    A Jewish Auction (Not Made in China) — Bechoros 156
    Vocational Hazard — Makkos 61

Sefer Devarim

Parashas Devarim
What Drives the Driver?	Yevamos 522
Work Site or Vacation Site?	Avodah Zarah 191
Good Things Come in Small Packages	Bechoros 502

Parashas Va'eschanan
The Lesser of Two Evils	Shevuos 231
Coming Home Late	Yevamos 90
Return Policy	Yevamos 300

Parashas Eikev
Getting Involved	Rosh Hashanah 188
Bad Answer	Yevamos 668
Is First Come Served First?	Shevuos 62

Parashas Re'ei
Free Rebate	Zeraim 52
A Matter of Heart	Bechoros 123
It's Not an Expense — It's an Investment	Rosh Hashanah 46
Multiple Answers	Yevamos 475

Parashas Shoftim
Early Bird?	Yevamos 293
One Fine Day ...	Zeraim 364
Coming Late for an Appointment	Niddah 441

Parashas Ki Seitzei
Really Lost	Rosh Hashanah 431
So Close	Avodah Zarah 137
Paying on Time	Eruvin 206
Each Person Is Punished for His Own Sin	Zeraim 365

Parashas Ki Savo
An Accessory to the Crime	Eruvin 184
Loyal Support	Rosh Hashanah 74
Miss Judged	Shevuos 172

Parashas Nitzavim
Mighty Fine Wine	Yevamos 660
Who Is Fooling Whom?	Yevamos 529
Teshuvah Pays	Zeraim 323

Parashas Vayeilech
Everyone Makes Mistakes	Makkos 667
Cover-Judging	Yevamos 414
A Lifesaving Sefer Torah	Niddah 522

Parashas Ha'azinu
On-the-Job Training — Without Telling the Boss	Shevuos 180
A Mooving Story of Two Cows	Shevuos 189
Fasten Your Seatbelt	Rosh Hashanah 209

Parashas V'zos HaBerachah
Be Fair to the Wealthy	Rosh Hashanah 83
Public Property	Rosh Hashanah 66
Together Is Better	Makkos 216